Alone on the

IAD PRESS

The life and times of Alec Kruger

Alec Kruger and Gerard Waterford

Published by IAD Press in 2007

IAD Press is the publishing arm of the
Institute for Aboriginal Development Inc.,
a not-for-profit Aboriginal community
controlled organisation.

IAD Press
PO Box 2531
Alice Springs NT 0871
Telephone: 08 8951 1334
Facsimile: 08 8952 2527
Email: sales@iad.edu.au
Website: www.iad.edu.au/press

© Alec Kruger & Gerard Waterford 2007
© Photographs: individual photographers & collections as captioned

This book is copyright. Apart from any fair dealings for the purpose of private study, research, criticism or review as permitted under the *Copyright Act 1968* and subsequent amendments, no part of this book may be reproduced, stored in a retrieval system, or transmitted in any form or by any means electronic, mechanical, photocopying, recording or otherwise, without prior permission. Please forward all enquiries to IAD Press at the address above.

National Library of Australia Cataloguing-in-Publication data:

Kruger, Alec, 1924-.
Alone on the soaks : the life and times of Alec Kruger

ISBN 978 1 86465 078 5

1. Kruger, Alec, 1924-. 2. Aboriginal Australians - Biography. 3. Stolen generations (Australia). I. Waterford, Gerard, 1957-. II. Title.

305.89915092

Book design: Darren Pfitzner
Cover photography: Roy McFadyen and Darren Pfitzner
Printing: Hyde Park Press, Australia

The Institute for Aboriginal Development Inc. is assisted by the Australian Government through the Australia Council, its arts funding and advisory body.

Dedication

This book is dedicated to my loving and beautiful wife Nita and our family. Their compassion, love, commitment, respect, patience and understanding gave me the strength to move on in my life. I learnt to accept and embrace all the changes the world has to offer – to treat others with dignity and respect and help those in need.

I also dedicate this book to all the friends and family members who have encouraged and inspired me to write my book. This has brought us even closer and maybe we have learned much more together.

To my mother Polly and father Frank and my brothers and sisters – thanks for the love we have shared throughout our lives.

Alec Kruger

Gerard Waterford is a social worker and counsellor employed by the Central Australian Aboriginal Congress in their Social and Emotional Wellbeing Program. He holds a Batchelor of Arts, majoring in History. Gerard has worked with Alec Kruger for the past five years to support the writing of Alec's life story.

Gerard wrote and edited the *Images Of Fathers* series (1999-2001) for the Newcastle Family Support Service. He has produced and co-produced many major reports and strategic planning documents. In addition to Alec's book, Gerard is supporting a number of other men to develop their stories towards publication.

Contents

Acknowledgements

Preface

My family story 1

The early days 11

Stolen away 25

Pine Creek 35

The trip to the Telegraph Station 43

The Bungalow years 51

Cowboy dreaming 67

Growing up 103

Army years 121

Travelling man 145

Pearling in the Top End 161

The drover's life 173

Seasons in the sun 187

Still moving 213

Back in Alice Springs 225

Family life 235

Changes 247

The Katherine years 267

The homecoming 275

Harry Creek 301

Family History 336

References 339

This book contains names and photographs of people who have passed away. Please use this book with care.

Acknowledgements

This book has been written with the help of a lot of people and organisations. In particular, I would like to acknowledge Lisa Watts, who as manager of the Central Australian Stolen Generations and Families Aboriginal Corporation (CASG&FAC) supported the idea of Alec and I working together to tell his autobiography and then provided the practical assistance to get it happening. She organised me as a counsellor from Central Australian Aboriginal Congress to get Alec's story down as a book. She also assisted with editorial comments, ideas and assistance with funding submissions.

Our thanks go to the members of the CASG&FAC committee for their help throughout the last five years. Also the staff – Jackie Baxter, Heather Shearer and, more recently, Craig Gallagher and Toni Arundel, who have taken over Lisa and Jackie's role in the organisation.

Alec and I would like to thank the Congress Social and Emotional Wellbeing Program, especially the former manager, Dawn Fleming, and the Congress Executive and Board for its support in the development of the project as a whole. Colleagues Franny Coughlan and Christine Palmer were a great help. We have borrowed material from Franny's earlier social history documents, but it was more their encouragement and enthusiasm that kept the book happening.

Alec and I received support from the Northern Territory Government History Grants that allowed us to visit people and places that were important to Alec's story. We went to parts of old Loves Creek Station, Wave Hill, Darwin and lots of towns in between. It helps memory if you actually get to go and visit again. It enabled me to see the places where his life story had been played out.

We thank the Northern Territory and National Archives Services for their assistance with getting access to old files and reports.

Beattie Mayo, who is married to Alec's nephew Des Mayo, provided an enormous amount of information, ideas and support. She had done a lot of family research prior to our project starting and generously provided information needed for the book. She also used her links to the Northern Territory Genealogical Society to follow up material and sort out mysteries.

We also thank the Ahmat, Kruger and Mills families for their assistance on our trips to Darwin and Katherine.

Mostly we would like to thank Alec's kids, particularly his daughters, Anita and Melly, who got everyone to read through all the drafts of the book. They did the talking with the Institute for Aboriginal Development (IAD) to get the book published. Larry and Noel Kruger also helped out with the readings and trips. Alec's grandson, Alec Kruger, came with us on the trips making it much easier for everyone. Also Aaron Davis for reading extracts of the book at the Darwin 'Wordstorm' Festival in 2006.

Thanks also go to Gerard's wife Jo Dutton, for putting up with the book taking over most of Gerard's free time. She helped with editing and setting up the book, as well as assisting on the evenings when the family came over to read parts of the book.

Thank you to Roy McFadyen for his generous permission to reproduce some of his photographs and to the Northern Territory Library for their assistance in sourcing quality reproductions from the McFadyen Collection.

Lastly we would like to thank Josie Douglas at IAD Press for persevering despite the book taking a lot longer than we had originally intended. IAD's support role was then taken over by Marg Bowman and then Jill Walsh. They have been very generous with their time and energy. It is a much better book for the extra time everyone has spent on it.

Alec Kruger and Gerard Waterford, 2007

Preface

Alec's desire to have a written record of his life grew out of his wish to provide his stories to his family and the broader community, and writing this book was designed to also be a gently healing journey for him. Like many men of his age, Alec was largely silenced by the expectations of masculinity when he was growing up. You didn't want to be seen as a whinger or a bragger. Better to swallow and pretend everything was okay. Better never to talk of being afraid or of any strong emotions.

So it has taken a long time for Alec to decide what it is safe for him to speak about and to give it an emotional framework. For over four years we have sat together while he tells what he remembers and I push him for how it might have felt. I would frame the memories against known social history events. He would recall new stories. I would attempt to place them in the narrative. He would correct the mistakes until we settled on a version of events. Then we would move the story along again. At different times family and friends contributed information, or a new document would come to our attention. We would often go back into the book to include the new stories, shaped by how Alec interpreted them.

Some spellings in this book, particularly Aboriginal names, have been rendered phonetically, to reflect how Alec says them, or have been sourced from contemporary sources, such as the T H Strehlow Diaries.

Alec has lived and continues to live a busy life. He has survived and developed as a storyteller. Perhaps as a product of growing up in a hard and racist world. From an early age he has had to rely on his wits and charm. He is good at the 'keep smiling, keep moving' approach to life. As a boy it was essential to avoid the attention of supervising staff. Later it was equally useful for dealing with the bullyboys and government men.

These days Alec still occasionally chaperones tourists around Alice Springs and the Bungalow. He tells the old stories for new staff at the Central Australian Aboriginal Congress. We are going to continue to document his stories in print and film. Alec tells a great story. He judges his audience well. He can milk a scene for pathos and humour. He is good talking with small groups. He remains a bit of a ladies' man, even in his eighties.

Alec has a reputation for having a kind heart and a generosity of spirit – for being there not just for his kids and grandkids but for others as well. Looking after other people is what gives his life meaning. He was never out of a job for long. He is a jack-of-all-trades, always putting up his hand for things if it meant the difference between working or not. He could turn his hand to most things. He was never one to have other people do things for him if he could do them himself. He needs to keep busy. It is perhaps a restlessness born out of his early experiences. It keeps the demons away. Reduces the power of the bullyboys to take over his life.

The book does have a political agenda. When you look at the circumstances of many Aboriginal people in Central Australia and you hear and see the media coverage of their plight and the circumstances, people, organisations and systems that are supposedly to blame, it is suggestibly easy to think not a lot has really moved forward. Why are Aboriginal men committing suicide at record levels? Why do Aboriginal kids go to badly structured and basically racist schools? Why do people have one house per ten adults across most of our remote communities? Why are Aboriginal people dying of diabetes, renal failure, heart disease and preventable illnesses at rates unthinkable in the rest of the Australian community?

Some politicians might blame corruption. They might blame the Aboriginal community itself. But the real reasons are found in a long history of oppressive government practices and abusive individuals. The real stories of Aboriginal history have to continue to be heard, perhaps through a Truth and Reconciliation Commission like in South Africa. A racist, apartheid system was supported in this country in the nineteenth and early twentieth centuries. It was different but perhaps just as bad as in South Africa. How much better have things really got in the early years of the twenty-first century? The neglect and silence in government should continue to shame us all. There is a lot that remains to be done. This book attempts to be part of creating a better future.

I hope you enjoy reading the book as much as we have enjoyed sorting through Alec's rich life, and getting some of his stories down in print.

My family story

My journey began on Christmas Day 1924. On that day Yrambul Nungarai gave birth to a boy. On the banks of the Katherine River at a place called Donkey Camp. I was called Bumbolili in my mother's language. My father named me Alexander, Alexa, or Alec. It was his brother's name. I was their last child.

I was the only one of us kids born at Donkey Camp, so the place has special meaning for me. Seems a funny thing to hang on to since I didn't get to know it very well. I was one of the taken-away babies, snatched from my mother's arms at three and a half. But I was nicknamed 'Donkey Camp' during my time at the Bungalow. The boss there had spent time in the Top End and knew my father well. He knew my story. Donkey Camp became a part of my dreaming. I have spent much of the last seventy-odd years pulling these stories together, making sense of what happened to me. Not just me, but thousands of other kids born in the Northern Territory when governments were able to steal away Aboriginal children and place them in institutions. It has taken me a long time to come to terms with what happened.

By Christmas the monsoonal deluge has started in the Top End. Most days, the rains come in the morning. Sometimes it can be so heavy you can't see across the road. The rain brings a coolness with it. The steam comes off the ground as the rain clears. With the heat comes the humidity. You get your work done as early as you can. Or wait till evening. By ten o'clock it's good to be back under the verandah. You can drowse your way through the midday hours of oppressive heat — often forty degrees and a hundred per cent humidity. Even breathing makes you sweat. Then you wait for a breeze. With a bit of wind you might get a storm at night. A tropical storm with dark clouds on the horizon, gusts of wind, then the first flash of lightning, thunder – and only afterwards comes the rain. The temperature might drop to the low thirties and a balmy breeze might help you get off to sleep.

I was born during such a day. Mosquitoes in clouds would have appeared at dawn and dusk. During the day they would have been replaced by sticky flies. I hope it was an easy birth. My mother was a small woman. I was her seventh child and she was only twenty-nine. You can't have a siesta during childbirth. Hopefully I was born in the evening with the coolness following rain still in the air.

Yrambul Nungarai didn't have an easy time as a mother. Kids taken away, children drowning. A husband on the road for six months and more at a time. But I survived. Most of us did. Even the ones she grew up for my father. She had dozens of grandkids, even more great-grandkids, and now lots of great-great-grandkids. We are outbreeding the white bullyboys and the bosses. Her descendants are reclaiming the Territory. That would have brought a smile to her face. But perhaps she always knew it. She always had her faith and her hope.

With the start of the rain the roads in the Top End closed down back in 1924, both the track up to Darwin and those into the interior. The railway still hadn't crossed the Katherine River. It was before the all-weather roads and high bridges. Once the rains came the train was put away. The rivers and creeks cut off the towns. For Christmas only the local families would stay.

The officials from down south and anyone who belonged somewhere else had jumped the boat from Darwin or headed their horses into the interior a month or two before. You wouldn't have been able to ford all the creeks and rivers once the Wet set in, even if you could drag a horse slipping and sliding up the hills and down the gullies. And then persuade it to step into a fast-running stream full of floating logs and animals. Then there was getting yourself across the river, holding on to the horse's tail. Near the sea there was the possibility of huge saltwater crocodiles sharing the water. And the snakes liked to share the high ground. So no one ever came or left during the Wet. You were stuck pretty much where you were for the next three or four months. If you really wanted to be somewhere else you had to walk, each step sinking knee-deep in mud and slush. And hope the rivers hadn't risen so far as to take out the flying foxes that spanned some of the worst of them. Possibly you could cover ten kilometres over a day of hard slog.

Christmas in the tropics was for the ones who stayed behind. The ones that belonged in the place and who would probably never leave. People would make a big effort to celebrate. Christmas puddings that had been prepared in November were brought out of storage. A beast was killed and specially prepared. Chooks, and even pigs, were slaughtered. People gathered for the feast.

My father, Frank, was a generous host. He had lots of good friends, and there were always people about needing a place to camp and food to eat. As well as the young and fit there were the old ringers and crazy prospectors. They might be crippled up and wheezy. Often sick with the grog. But in their youth they were champions, all of them. Only their mates remembered their heroic feats with horses, wild cattle and a few bottles of rum. My father gathered such men around him at Christmas.

I was one of those that belonged. But I was stolen away. Even so I was one of the lucky ones. A survivor. Not many of the people from the early part of my story survived. Us boys locked up in institutions desperately hung on to each other. Did it tough together. It was the friendships that pulled me through. Holding on to friendships when you were moved about by the bosses. It was easier as we grew older. It was hard times in so many ways. But there were good times. We had our dreams. We had respect in hard work and making do. I'm not sure my kids and grandkids have any real idea of how hard it really was. That is what has driven me to get this story out. They need to know. And I need to tell my story. You would never want it to happen again.

My family story

Memories of my mother

Except for when she returned to her Mudburra country Polly was what everyone called my mother. She was born near Wave Hill Station in 1895. She was named Yrambul after the root used to make love potions to woo a desirable man. Frank Kruger played that man in her life until his death in 1938. The name Nungarai describes her place in the kin relationships of her community.

Polly, Alec's mother (left) with Bobby, his sister photo courtesy Kruger family

My mother held strong opinions and knew how to be heard. She was a hard-working spiritual woman, later heavily involved with Mr Jeremy Long's Christian Mission at Rockhole. She was a good mother to her children. But most of us were taken away from her. She tried but couldn't pull us back. My father wasn't able to stop them. She grieved for us, but kept her faith, kept busy with her community.

I met up with her as a young man in the army. My brother George took me. It had been sixteen years since I had seen her. She had no time for soldiers. There had been too many bullyboys with guns and uniforms in her life, riding down on their horses and terrifying and killing her people. She didn't think they were heroic. She knew them as murderers and cowards. She didn't want her son being a soldier, and she let me know it. Her religion gave her a voice. She liked her men gentle and caring. She was wailing on

Wave Hill and Victoria River Downs cattle stations were set up in the 1880s and 1890s at a huge cost to the local Aborigines. The Wave Hill on Mum's birth records was the administrative name for a huge region. It stretched away from the Overland Telegraph Line that ran north-south and divided the Territory. It went west all the way to the Western Australian border. To the south it disappeared into the Central Australian deserts. Katherine was the next region to the north. It was all called Wave Hill because the police station was thereabouts.

By 1890 many Mudburra family groups were settled around Wave Hill homestead and its Wattie Creek outstations. They had close connections to Mudburra communities to the north on the Camfield River, and east across the Murranji scrub towards Newcastle Waters. It was all Mudburra country. I suspect Mum was born further north and east than Wave Hill Station. My family had connections to the Pigeon Hole area along the Camfield River, the eastern outpost of the huge Victoria River Downs cattle station.

My mother had an early relationship with Jimmy Gibbs. He was a young white stockman working at the station where her family lived. There is no way of saying whether she liked her men white and hard working or was just looking for survival options when white men were usually the only way forward. Jimmy was a decent fellow from all accounts. He became a friend of my father. He eventually left my mother to find work at Elsey Station and later developed a cattle station on the Roper River in East Arnhem Land. My mother became pregnant to him and had a daughter, Ada Gibbs. While Jimmy Gibbs acknowledged Ada, he followed the rules of the time and left Mum to bring up Ada within our family. It would have been difficult for a young Mudburra woman and her child to accompany her partner into other tribal lands. Whether she was given a choice is hard to say. It was an age when white men automatically made these decisions for young Aboriginal girls. Jimmy went on to new relationships with Aboriginal women local to where he was working.

Ada didn't have a lot of early choices. She was taken away by the local police as a young girl to the newly opened Kahlin Compound. She had some family contact but basically grew up with other taken-away kids in Darwin. When she left the institution she married William 'Putt' Ahmat. William's father was a pearl diver. Born in Singapore of Chinese descent, he had spent time on Thursday Island, marrying a woman whose mother was Islander and father was of German and Tongan descent. Ada and William had lots of adventures, with Ada evacuated south with her kids after the bombing of Darwin. But they were Darwin people and that is where they returned.

the other side of a fence to me. But there was no getting past the soldiers on guard there. The sergeant threatened us both. If I had stayed it would have got worse. With my brother I went back to my real life in the army.

She was a bit hard on me about becoming a soldier. I was just surviving. I never shot at anyone. The only enemy I saw was on the football fields. I was just trying to keep in with my mates. I had money in my pocket for a change. And she was a stranger to me. She wanted to reclaim me but it was too big a gap. I suppose there was a part of me, deep down, that resented her powerlessness. Resented my father dying. Even after the war I couldn't stay with her. We had no shared history or language. My life was pushing me along a different path.

I was a thousand kilometres away on the back of a horse when she died. We had never really built up much between us. Her funeral happened before I even heard. Not that I could have left my mates with our exhausted footsore cattle. You didn't leave your cattle or mates on a long droving trip unless you died yourself. Then they left you.

Today one of my kids goes by the name of Polly. My mother was a strong woman and I am proud of her. I hope she would be proud of me today. No longer a soldier, I'm an old man who has paid his dues. Like her, I have tried hard to be there for those needing me. But it hasn't always worked out. Like her, I haven't always been powerful enough to protect those I love.

My mother's family had lived across the Mudburra tribal areas hundreds of kilometres south and west of Katherine. She came from a big family. She was a full sister to Anzac, Hector, Jack Gallagher, Pigeon Hole Bob and Hobble Dunyari. They were all Jungarai to her Nungarai, in her Aboriginal kinship system. I was told one of her tribal sisters was the child of the policeman for Wave Hill. The drover Jack Althouse was said to be her tribal brother.

My grandparents were survivors of the takeover of their lands by white pastoralists. I have not been able to find out my grandparents' story. Polly was born as Australia slid into economic depression. This meant the cattle barons of the Top End couldn't sell their cattle profitably. Many abandoned their leases. Others just sat back, living off their gardens and animals. Playing the big men with their guns and horses to a captive Aboriginal workforce. Like always they had a murderous police force and a racist administration to help with the job of building up their empires at the expense of Aboriginal tribes.

This allowed you to re-brand all stray stock. Taking cleanskins from the big stations was a major industry in the Top End. In the early days small stations were a way of getting rid of the Aboriginal groups still living tribally in the back country. Stealing cattle from the big mobs allowed small stations to establish their own instant herd without spending much money or effort. But it didn't make you popular.

Once cattle prices increased before the First World War, Victoria River Downs, Wave Hill and the other big stations found it was no longer possible to put up with the loss of cattle to smaller pastoral leases. Using the police and force of numbers they closed them down. They employed extra stockmen and Aboriginal trackers to go after straying mobs. The police started prosecuting small station owners. There were threats to run them off their land. Leases were sold or surrendered. Frank sold out to assist his uncle full time with the management of Willeroo Station.

My father was a generous, kindly fellow who liked kids. He knew how to put people at their ease. He was good to his mates and always happy to help someone in trouble. He wasn't a drinker, which was unusual in the grog-soaked white community of the Top End.

Like his uncle Tom, my father had an entrepreneurial spirit and always had a big plan on the boil. He was a gardener and a breeder of Spanish donkeys. He didn't mind hard work and mixing it with the boys, but he could also play the toff. He had connections with both ends of town. The better-off white police, administrators and businessmen tended to be transient in the Top End. A few stayed and became part of the towns, but most went stir crazy in the heat and took the first opportunity to head back south. My father was a bit of an oddity in staying. His relationship with the Aboriginal community also seemed less exploitative than most. Perhaps it was the influence of a religious upbringing or commitment to some socialist values. But he also had entry to another world through his uncle Tom.

Like my mother, my father had had earlier relationships. Perhaps he liked his women black and strong. I never knew how many kids he had. His first child, George, was born at the turn of the century. His mother was from Renner Springs and died when George was little. George was too old to be taken away when they opened up the Kahlin Institution in 1913. In the early days there tended to be different rules for boys and girls anyway. The boys were kept for stockwork, while the girls were often 'saved' from a life on the Aboriginal camps. Anyway, George got to stay at home.

My father's next child was Alice. Her mother was from around Mataranka. Like most of us, Alice ended up in the Kahlin Institution. She was registered as a Kruger there. She married a Larrakia fellow, Rupert Mills, and had two children. These days her children and grandchildren are part of the Larrakia community that runs the Darwin Aboriginal organisations.

After her first husband died Alice lived with George Cummings, an Aboriginal fellow of mixed descent from Tennant Creek. George worked as a miner there. They even spent a few years in Alice Springs when George had the job as boss for the Alice Springs Council. But they spent most of their time around Tennant. As an older woman Alice used to go back and forth to Katherine. I never knew about her until she was a full-grown woman. But I got to know her better in Alice Springs and later on in Katherine.

My sister Bobby never really left Katherine. We didn't catch up much. She married Dick Brumby and they had their own life. Her granddaughters are an important part of the Jawoyn Association that was formed in the seventies to unite all the different tribal groups living in Katherine to try to deal with mining leases and royalty payments. The whole Jawoyn movement was a big struggle with family members taking up different sides in some of the early fights for control. Bobby's granddaughter, Lisa Mumbin, now works in the management of the organisation.

My older sister Gladys, the daughter of Polly and Frank born in 1921, was taken with me to Kahlin. She ended up married and settled in Darwin with a big mob of kids. She and her husband Johnny Ahmat were always good friends to me. I also had older brothers called John and Leslie. They drowned at Knott's Crossing within a kilometre of Donkey Camp, in one of the huge floods that happen when cyclones hit the Top End. Being only three and a half when I was taken away, I can't remember them at all. I heard the story later. It must have been another huge blow to my parents.

Then there was Jimmy Gibbs' son, Jack, who lived a while in Alice Springs and married one of my wife's sisters, Melba Palmer. I knew them well enough. It was hard for me and my family to catch up on all the missing years. We tried to get together a few times. But life was busy for us all and it was hard to keep up much closeness when we lived so far apart. We used to catch up on the odd visit. Now they are all gone. I'm 'the last of the Mohicans'. It has been left to me to tell the story. I hope they feel okay about my efforts. I've got a lot of respect and love for them all.

After Jimmy Gibbs left, my mother married a Mudburra fellow. He was from the Willeroo area north of Wave Hill. She had her second daughter, Bobby. As a full blood Aboriginal child Bobby did not get taken away. The policy of removing children only applied to children of mixed European and Aboriginal descent. Bobby remained with Mum, growing up by her side. Bobby's father died or was killed. Later, Mum entered a relationship with another white cattleman. This was my father, Frank Kruger.

My father's story

My father was of German and English descent and was fifteen years older than my mother. His father was called Franz (and later Frank) Kruger. I have no memories of these grandparents either. And they left no books or journals. I have found out what I know as part of doing this book. The records show that Franz Kruger arrived in Adelaide from Hamburg on the SS Papa on 26 July 1877. He was twenty-two. Hamburg was a huge port city, so perhaps my grandfather was a sailor. More likely he had travelled from Kruger heartlands in the north-east of Germany to catch the boat. Perhaps there was gold fever in the family. The Kruger name shows up in the goldrushes of the Top End in the 1870s and 1880s. And Krugers made millions mining gold in South Africa. My brother George talks of Krugers from South Africa turning up at my father's funeral. So perhaps all these people were family.

My grandmother, Frank's mother, was Mary Pearce. Her family were English and arrived in Adelaide from Sussex on the Taymouth Castle on 3 May 1854. Her father got a job managing Mt Eba, a sheep station in the deep north of South Australia. I know the country a little. It is very marginal and rainfall is scarce. It must have been an isolated life of hard work and struggle. Mary grew up in this remote part of the world. I do not know how Mary and Franz met but they married in Adelaide on 13 November 1879. My father was born there on 18 September 1880. Two brothers and a sister followed in the next four and a half years.

My grandfather, Franz, was reported as having died in the late 1880s, or rather he was declared dead for my grandmother's purposes. He reappeared on the public record when he married Annie Bishop in Sydney on the 2 April 1901. He applied for a certificate of naturalisation in Sydney in 1914, having become a railway cook and with a new life in New South Wales. He died in 1931 without meeting any of us grandkids.

My grandmother got remarried to William Welsh in 1893. They had five children and moved to Windsor just out of Sydney in New South Wales. My father was a young boy when his father disappeared. He had a brother, Alexander, some fifteen months younger than him. Alexa they called him. After my grandfather's disappearance Alexa was cared for by my grandmother's older sister, Sarah Pearce. Sarah had married Edward Swensson. Alexa was adopted and brought up with that surname. He apparently only found out he was a Kruger when he needed documents to get married. That must have been a big shock.

My uncle Alexa is mentioned in my family story where none of the others are. He helped out my sister Gladys when she was evacuated with her kids during World War II. A train guard named Swensson came around with money to help set her up in Balaclava. And perhaps he was one of the Krugers that came up for my father's funeral.

My father appears to have finished his education while living with his mother and stepfather in New South Wales. He studied agriculture, and then followed his Pearce uncles to the Top End of the Northern Territory. My father's stepbrothers and sisters, the Welsh side of my family, seem to have prospered and multiplied. I have had no contact with any of them. Perhaps as part of getting this book out we can get together and share our stories.

My father's uncle Tom Pearce was a man of substance around Katherine. He became famous as 'Mine Host' in Mrs Aeneas Gunn's novel *We of the Never-Never*. Tom had gone from stockwork at Springvale Station to managing the Sportsman Hotel, then on to owning Willeroo and Delamere Stations. It was Tom Pearce who organised for my father to open up a cattle station on a newly issued lease on the edges of Willeroo Station at a place called Spring Creek. It was on Mudburra tribal land, just north of the Murranji Track. Perhaps my father met and started a relationship with my mother while living there. The lease stretched south towards Montejinni Station. Many decades later some older Aboriginal stockmen showed me where my father's rough hut had been. My father had built himself a room of sorts and established his herd just back from the creek. Aboriginal families working as his stockmen lived in a camp just downriver. By design his hut and land were located where mobs of cattle off nearby Victoria River Downs Station (VRD) tended to head during the height of the Wet season. Unbranded cattle were considered fair game. You branded them and moved them into your own herd. If you were really clever you registered a brand that allowed for the original brand to be easily altered to appear to be your own.

The early days

The Pearce family in South Australia

My father's uncle Thomas Henry Pearce started the white side of the family's adventure into the Northern Territory. Tom was born in December 1862 in Strathalbyn but grew up with his family in the isolated world of Mt Eba Station, south-east of Coober Pedy.

South Australia had been desperately recruiting immigrants from Great Britain and Europe for the first convict-free colony in Australia. Colonel Light and the 'First Families' of Adelaide sold dreams of land and wealth to struggling Europeans searching for the possibility of living more like the landed gentry in the rich pastures of an unexplored country. The successes of America and the eastern states of Australia were used as lures. New immigrants came mainly from overcrowded areas of Great Britain, Ireland and Northern Europe, shipped in through the port of Adelaide. These were free men seeking to build pastoral and farming empires in the surrounding Aboriginal lands. But the gap between those with land and their immigrant employees remained a chasm. Wages were better and work plentiful but only a few of the newcomers succeeded in making the transition to owning their own bit of country capable of sustaining a family. And most of those that succeeded came to Australia with their own family money and connections anyway. Some of the Pearces succeeded. The vast majority of immigrants became wage slaves in a new land.

The climate in South Australia didn't support the ambitions of those who owned the land. Transplanted farming technologies didn't take into account the dry years of little rainfall that barely sustained the ragged grassland. The South Australian administration found bits of money to fund explorers to open up the countryside to the north. Men with sheep and cattle rapidly followed in their footsteps. In some areas the Aboriginal tribes organised and held up this invasion. But they were beaten back by superior weapons, a more mobile army on horseback and an enemy that could concentrate its forces to attack en masse. A police force was recruited to help deal with 'the Aboriginal problem'.

But as the explorers and colonists went further north they ran into the fierce South Australian desert country that extends up into Australia's centre. The dream of an inland sea and rich pastures in the centre of the continent proved to be a mirage. Central Australia had little enough permanent water to sustain the existing Aboriginal family groups through the area's long periods of drought.

My great-grandparents, Francis and Margaret Pearce, emigrated from England with their first child, William. They became the managers of Mt Eba Station on the southern edge of the South Australian deserts. The place was unrelenting gibber and sand country with barely a tree of any size. Without fences the sheep needed shepherding from the attacks of dingoes in lambing season. It was hard to find men to shear the sheep or affordable ways to get the wool down to the markets in the south. Droughts were more common than good rainfall years. What my great-grandparents made of it is unrecorded. But the unrelenting sunshine, red dust and open spaces must have been an enormous culture shock for them. An enormous change from the farmlands of Sussex.

The Pearce family's dreams of wealth must have evaporated quickly enough. But the family stayed on and tried to make a go of the place. My grandmother, Margaret, was born in January 1860. Then nearly three years later Tom came into the world. There was another sister Sarah, a younger brother Fred, and perhaps others that I haven't found in any records. They were on Mt Eba when gold was being dug up all over Victoria and New South Wales. Keeping workers was difficult as many men headed towards the new discoveries. The miners didn't necessarily stay long nor did goldmining make many of them rich. But the dreams of gold and the nomadic lifestyle set the mood across much of Australia for generations to come.

For the young Pearce kids, William, Margaret, Tom, Sarah and Fred, the times at Mt Eba were decades of isolation, hardship and struggle. Their father must have been a terribly self-reliant man. Their mother, a miracle worker. They were many days away from medical assistance. Illnesses must have been terrifying. Burying children is a terrible thing. Mutton and potatoes would have been the staple diet. Maintaining a garden was near impossible but an essential part of surviving. Finding enough water to keep a garden going was the eternal challenge.

Food and supply orders would have been sent to Adelaide perhaps once or twice a year. You needed to be very organised to do your shopping like that. The camel trains coming to collect the wool would have brought the supplies. Occasional travelling hawkers might have brought top-up supplies and news from the outside world. The rare swagmen and possibly other station families from even further into the interior were the only visitors. It was an entirely self-contained world. There was possibly a cook, blacksmith, stockmen and shearers in season, as well as local Aboriginal families sharing the space. The place didn't run to a governess to teach the children, for Tom is reported to have taught himself to read and write as a young man. But despite the determination and backbreaking labour it doesn't appear that the dreams of making or saving money eventuated. The family must have longed for places that were easier than the dry dusty world of Mt Eba. The kids seem to have taken the first opportunities to leave for other places. My grandmother married early and her brother Tom hit the road at fifteen, Fred joining him a year later.

The early days

Young Tom Pearce arrives in the Top End

In 1862 the explorer John McDouall Stuart and his small team succeeded in becoming the first white men to complete a south-north crossing of Australia. It was Stuart's third and last trip north. He nearly perished, being carried for the last part of the journey. He never recovered and died young. Only eight years after his extraordinary expedition, the South Australian government commenced the Overland Telegraph Line, a single line of wire stretched four metres above the countryside to link Australia with the rest of the world, completing it in 1872.

The late 1870s saw another dream being played out. Having not found the fabled inland sea and well-watered pastures in Australia's centre, the tropical north was promoted as the new land of opportunity by the South Australian government. A wealthy Adelaide-based physician, Dr Browne, had secured the lease on a vast area on the banks of the Katherine River in what South Australia had claimed in the 1860s to be 'its' Northern Territory. The explorer brothers, Alfred and Arthur Giles, were recruited to gather sheep, a few cattle and a team of men to travel overland through Central Australia and deliver the stock to the newly named Springvale Station. In 1878 they passed close by stations like Mt Eba. They had the best provisioned droving team ever seen in that part of the world.

The travels of Giles' droving team must have been a huge social event for the isolated families of northern South Australia. Alfred Giles was recruiting bushmen and stockmen with a bit of back-country experience. Many of the stations must have lost staff. When Giles stopped at Charlotte Waters in 1878 to shear the sheep, 'his shearers included…young Tom Pearce'. Tom was next reported travelling as one of Giles' bullock team drivers . My great-uncle was fifteen at the time. But he was a big strapping country boy already approaching six foot. My great-grandparents had obviously done a great job in feeding him over the years.

The droving team arrived into a community officially named Emungalan but known as 'the Katherine'. This small settlement on the side of the river consisted of not much more than an overland telegraph building and a police station. Prior to the expedition's arrival the white population was tiny – perhaps half a dozen men. The new arrivals made a huge impact. Tom Pearce stayed on and helped Arthur Giles build the new Springvale Station homestead.

The dry season in Katherine was the time to get things started. The temperature drops into the mid-twenties. Humidity is lower. In the old days, the town would come back to life as the rivers dropped back into their banks, the roads opened up and travellers started rolling in. Coming from Darwin, Katherine was the last centre of white civilisation before you hit isolated cattle station country. Coming from the interior it was the first place with a few of the comforts of town life.

Katherine was and is a beautiful place. With its river, waterholes and the Katherine Gorge nearby it is very different from the dryness of most of the Northern Territory. Children can swim throughout the year. You can grow anything. If you survive the heat, humidity, flies and mosquitoes of the Wet season, you get months of balmy tropical dry season weather.

Tom Pearce got a lot from his family. Like them he had the strength of character to be able to work hard and live apart. Apparently he usually travelled alone and overlanded in preference to travelling known routes. He was an accomplished horseman with a great passion for the animals. His bush skills must have been quite prolific for him to be comfortable in the rugged isolated world of Aboriginal Australia. He was also known for his capacity for and commitment to getting things done.

After the work at Springvale ended, Tom was contracted to re-build two hundred miles (320 kilometres) of overland telegraph line. The original wooden posts had to be replaced with iron ones because of termites. My great-uncle Tom was said to be so strong he could lift the four metre iron poles single-handed. Even so, he would have needed a small team of men. At a young age it seems Tom was able to contract for work and pull it off. Reading and writing would have been an important part of contracting for work, so it was well that Tom had learnt how to read and write.

The scourge of the Top End was tropical fevers like malaria, yellow fever, even influenza. There were few doctors and little access to any medical treatment. Fever killed many more of the white men who ventured into the North than were finished off by hostile Aborigines. In 1903 it killed Mrs Gunn's husband, 'the big Maluka', and ended their two years in charge at Elsey Station. Tom Pearce got a bad dose of fever in 1883, but was one of the lucky ones who survived. These diseases and other epidemics killed off huge numbers in the local Aboriginal communities.

Aboriginal history in the Top End

For the Northern Territory Aboriginal tribes, the invasion of their traditional lands by white pastoralists from the 1870s on must have been terrifying. The pastoralists treated Aboriginal laws and customs with contempt. Try as they might to negotiate, the Aborigines were moved off the water holes or killed. Tribesmen from other areas were made to work as native police. But they would not have left their own country unless forced to by fear of the consequences of saying no. Their 'reward' was the exploitation of other tribes. It was a very successful tactic to subdue the tribes as the white invaders rolled further and further into Aboriginal lands.

I have not heard of major conflict between the Aboriginal tribes close to Katherine and the leaseholders of Springvale Station. There was plenty of water in the Katherine River and at first the few sheep and cattle didn't interfere too much with traditional Aboriginal gathering and hunting. Most Aboriginal families kept a distance from the town and the new sheep station.

For my Aboriginal family in Mudburra country the invasion was much grimmer. The Mudburra tribal groups owned lands that began about one hundred and fifty kilometres west and south of Katherine. Their northern border was near modern-day Top Springs, extending through to what is now called Pigeon Hole Station, up the Camfield River towards Wave Hill Station lands and back east into the Murranji scrub country.

The first major incursion into Mudburra country was led by the Western Queensland boss drover Nat Buchanan and his two brothers-in-law, Hugh and Wattie Gordon. In 1878 they overlanded 1,200 Hereford cattle to establish Glencoe Station east of Pine Creek to the north of Katherine. They must have nearly passed the Giles expedition and my great-uncle Tom on the road. In 1880 Nat led seventy men working in ten teams to push 20,000 cattle up to Glencoe. He used the money from this trip to buy land. With Hugh and Wattie he established Wave Hill Station at Wattie Creek.

The Mudburra, whose country he invaded, were reportedly ferocious warriors. But they didn't appear to slow him much. His cattle spread along the rivers and permanent waterholes of the vast grasslands where they largely fended for themselves. A worried Aboriginal community must have wondered what to do. The cattle were easy pickings but proved expensive. Police, Aboriginal trackers and station staff mercilessly pursued families who speared cattle. Where they didn't catch the culprits they were likely to take revenge on any Aboriginal groups they came across, killing men, women and children.

Before the invasion, my Mudburra ancestors lived in family groups around what was renamed the Camfield River and its streams and gullies. It was well-grassed rangeland country providing good hunting. The rivers fed down onto crocodile-infested rugged lowland into the Victoria River, emptying into Joseph Bonaparte Gulf. Tribal and language groupings had fairly fixed boundaries and communities lived in family groups that moved around seasonally. They would gather together for renewal and celebration ceremonies. Rigid laws governed their society. Dances and performances transferred knowledge and initiated young people into the adult life of the tribe. Society was largely patriarchal. It respected and rewarded age and wisdom. There was active trading between different tribal areas.

From the 1870s to the 1890s there were many massacres of Aboriginal men, women and children. Many white men thought of Aboriginal people as sub-human. Missionaries and other people of goodwill didn't have the power to end the widespread genocide. Some police actively encouraged and participated in the killings. It was very rare for anyone to be charged, let alone convicted of offences against Aborigines. Many officials and missionaries even blamed Aboriginal women for leading white men astray.

Faced with being pushed off their land and starved, Mudburra family groups largely accepted what was on offer from the pastoralists. In return they got food and avoided conflict. Aboriginal men were forced to see their mothers, wives and daughters traded as sex objects. It created a lot of male anger and ended up with Aboriginal women sometimes being protected by their white bosses.

White men who lived openly with Aboriginal women were called 'combos'. Where the relationships were long-term the families were at risk of being abused by the authorities. Mixed descent relationships were made illegal. Their children faced big problems. The men were often socially ostracised. It was a very hypocritical society. There were few white women in the community and it was acknowledged in many official reports that lots of white men demanded Aboriginal women as part of their wages. Yet when they tried to be a good husband and father for their kids they were abused.

By 1900 the cattle leases were being extended into more marginal country. Wells and soaks were being expanded to allow cattle to graze away from the big permanent water sources. This took away the land of any remaining Aboriginal family groups still resisting white occupation. Without these places of sanctuary the entire Aboriginal community came under the control of the cattlemen, becoming an easily exploited workforce. The authority of the whites was based on the threat of force. Any hint of Aboriginal rebellion meant punishment. The racism of the times seems unbelievable today. When I tell my grandkids they don't believe me. You had to be very careful.

The cattle station owners were a long way from markets and government control. They were hard, suspicious men in a foreign culture. There were no short-term profits. The whites were seriously outnumbered and didn't have much knowledge of the land. They had been told of, or maybe experienced, being attacked by Aboriginal groups as they moved into the north-west. So the cattlemen worked together. They had guns and horses and recruited Aboriginal trackers from other areas. The whites were an unbeatable opponent for the small tribal groups. Traditional weapons were no match for guns. Local knowledge of the land didn't help much when men on horses could quickly ride down walking family groups. The invaders were able to isolate any organised or individual resistance. They then massacred whole families, even tribes, as payback for defiance. Whole language groups were wiped out.

But the new cattle kings needed workers to get things happening. They couldn't recruit enough white workers and they couldn't afford to pay wages anyway. So they more or less used Aboriginal people as slaves, reducing them to unpaid dependents relying on handouts.

Some resistance continued. But flour, tea, sugar, tobacco and rum were popular. Gathering bush food seemed like hard work and unnecessary when the white pastoralists could provide processed food. The cattlemen could also provide meat. Aboriginal workers were paid only starvation rations that relied on people still being able to forage additional bush food to survive. When they weren't needed during the Wet Season the rations were stopped and Aboriginal families were expected to go on walkabout to areas where enough traditional food might still be available.

My great-uncle Tom was there during this first invading wave of white cattlemen. But he comes out as a comparatively decent man. Tom had grown up at Mt Eba with its Aboriginal community. So he had some idea of Aboriginal culture and how to work within it. He seemed to have stayed apart from much of the brutality happening around him, as my father was later to do. They were not cruel and degraded misfits like many of the white men who ended up in the deep north.

The discovery of gold at Pine Creek in the 1870s had led to a big influx of miners coming from the eastern and southern states either overland or by ship through Darwin. Chinese companies shipped many more indentured Chinese workers to the gold mines. Many of these Chinese miners had previously worked the fields in North Queensland, New Zealand, New South Wales and Victoria. Some had even been to the California goldfields in the early 1850s or had worked building the American transcontinental railways. They helped construct a railway line from Darwin down to Pine Creek in 1886. Many stayed in the Top End setting up businesses, shops and market gardens. The non-Aboriginal population of the Top End rose from zero in 1870 to many thousand, mostly Chinese people.

After his work on the telegraph line, Tom returned to South Australia getting work building a road into the Musgrave Mountains. But by 1888 he had returned to 'the Katherine' and been joined by his brother, Fred. In 1886 gold had been discovered at Halls Creek, 500 kilometres west of Katherine. This led to a new wave of men overlanding through north-west Queensland. Shops in Borroloola, Roper Bar and Katherine served the travelling miners going to the new fields. Others came by ship through Darwin and again Katherine often benefited from the trade.

In 1887 Bernard Murphy opened the Sportsman Hotel and Pioneer Store at Knott's Crossing on the southern banks of the Katherine River. The place did well enough out of government men, swagmen, carters and families making their way to and from Darwin. Trade improved with the discovery of gold in 1889 just outside of Katherine at Maude Creek. Tom and Fred Pearce ran the Maude Creek grog shop as an extension of the Sportsman Hotel. They must have been tough and quick-witted to be selling grog on the goldfields. They succeeded where the miners didn't. By 1893 Tom Pearce had been appointed the licensee of the Sportsman.

Tom developed the Pioneer Store with bullock teams supplying outlying cattle stations, particularly in the Victoria River Downs and Wave Hill areas. He and Fred became respected horsemen and breeders and eventually the Secretary and Treasurer of the Katherine Racing Club. The club ran two meetings a year that were the major social events for the region. All bets were settled in the pub after the races. It must have brought in a lot of custom and satisfied their love for finely-bred racing animals. But in May 1891 my great-uncle Fred died after an accident taking a bullocky dray into Darwin. It slipped on a narrow embankment, crushing him. The funeral was huge. Fred was a much-loved man.

Tom soldiered on becoming a Justice of the Peace in the Katherine region. He regularly wrote letters to the *Northern Territory Times and Gazette* about matters of local interest and was influential in local policy making. His nature as a generous and kindly man, in addition to being six foot tall and ruggedly strong, gave him a leadership role in the community.

In 1902 Mrs Aeneas Gunn visited Katherine on her way to Elsey Station. She praised Tom, who 'greeted us with a flashing smile and laughing'. Tom gave up his cottage as a residence for the newly married visitors, who were from a different class to his usual clientele. Tom issued an order limiting the number of drinks that could be drunk at his pub while Mrs Gunn and her husband were in residence. He became good friends with Mrs Gunn and was able to provide her with some rare potatoes, later sending her seeds and clippings for her to build up her gardens at Elsey Station.

In the late 1890s on his return from one of his carting trips out to the Victoria River district, Tom is recorded as climbing to the top of a hill now called Augusta Crown. He was so impressed with the countryside that he bought up a pastoral lease of 260 square kilometres known as Willeroo Station. He also purchased Delamere Station.

Tom had a lot of ideas about how to improve the land. He imported special grasses from Asia and South Africa to improve the carrying capacity during the long dry season. He also knew the value of a good garden. He successfully grew the first pineapples in the region. He had the idea that the Top End's future might be in crops that worked in other tropical areas, like cotton, peanuts, rice and tropical fruits. He looked for crops that would survive the long transportation times of getting them to markets. But he needed capital and so turned to cattle, horses and Spanish donkeys to establish a base for his ideas.

On 27 April 1903 Tom married Mary Jennings in a large social event in Darwin. Mary was a local woman whose parents had the lease of a station down the track past Mataranka. Tom's marriage cemented his changed status in the region. At the time there were very few white women prepared to put up with the loneliness and rigours of station life. The white men of the district were mostly loners with few social skills. They lived in an all-male world of horses and grog. Tom seemed to be comfortable in most social situations in a way his peers were not. Becoming a married man continued his growth from knockabout young stockman with intelligence and talent to a man of leadership within the small community of the Top End. As he had done with his younger brother Fred, he brought some of his family with him into his new world. Around 1900 my father joined him in the Territory and took up a lease on land south of Willeroo. He worked for his uncle as a carter and drover.

Tom's wife, Mary, didn't like the isolated station life. She and Tom mostly stayed at the pub and put managers in to run the day-to-day operations at Willeroo. Tom remained the Secretary/Treasurer at the Katherine Race Club. He imported stud stallions to improve the quality of his racing horses and stockhorses. By 1905 he had 1,500 head of cattle and 420 horses and a new homestead at Willeroo. Improvements at the station included two large paddocks, three stockyards, branding yards and a dam built across the homestead creek.

In 1907 Syd Smith, Manager of Willeroo, was speared to death by Aborigines. Tom sold the licence on the Sportsman Hotel and Pioneer Store and took over the management of Willeroo. There had been a few white deaths in disputes with the Aboriginal tribe, but my great-uncle Tom was able to gain the trust of the elders. He wanted harmonious co-existence and treated the local Aboriginal families as useful and reliable. He gave them leadership roles. Aboriginal stockmen at Willeroo became known as among the best in the Northern Territory. His quest for co-existence was successful. My father followed the same 'make love, not war' path, becoming the father of children in the Aboriginal community. It was around this time that my brother George Kruger was born down the track in far-away Renner Springs.

In 1917 my great-uncle sold Willeroo to the new big player in the Top End, Lord Vestey of England. The previous cattle king, Sidney Kidman, sold out Wave Hill at the same time. Lord Vestey also purchased Ord River Station, Gordon Downs, Manbulloo (to the west of Katherine) and Springvale Station in Katherine, as well as Helen Springs and other stations further to the south. At the time of the sale Willeroo covered 6,475 square kilometres and carried 8,000 head of cattle and 300 horses including twenty imported stallions. My great-uncle, ever the entrepreneur, got a very good price and moved to Sydney.

Thomas Pearce was one of a few home-grown Territory success stories. He didn't succeed at the level of Sidney Kidman or Nat Buchanan but he had come a long way. In twenty-five years he had gone from being a labourer on a bullock team to a grog shop runner on the goldfields, then to publican and finally he'd joined the elite class of wealthy landed gentry.

My father's story is more difficult to piece together. He wasn't as prominent on the public record. He didn't have the wealth or authority of his uncle. With my mother Polly at his side, my father was considered a 'combo', a man who had 'gone native' and seen by some to lack respectability. My father continued carting from Katherine out to the Victoria River Downs district. He also did station work. My parents had two boys, John and Leslie born to them on the road. These kids joined Bobby and George. Eventually they moved their growing family closer to Katherine when my father leased land on the King River near Maranboy, just to the south.

In 1913 large deposits of tin had been discovered in Maranboy. With the expansion of these tin mines during World War I my father got the contract carting tin from the crusher to the railhead at Emungalan and back. With my brother George as his offsider, he expanded his operations and continued taking supplies into the Victoria River area. Polly and the smaller children were able to stay home at their King River base. The land was used to breed up Frank's Spanish donkeys. Those not needed for his carting business were sold to prospectors and other carters. My family expanded again when Gladys was born on the 1 August 1921 at Maranboy.

In Sydney, Tom Pearce's wife, Mary, died in the Spanish influenza epidemic of 1919. My great-uncle must have been devastated. They had been married sixteen years but didn't have any kids. As a widower of fifty-six, he said that he could not live in the city without ending up in 'the nut factory or the cemetery'. He returned to his life in the Territory. For a while he lived with my father and his old mates near Maranboy. But he later bought into Sidney Kidman's Crown Pastoral Company, which owned Central Australian stations. Tom managed the Allandale Station near Oodnadatta and later Crown Station on the Northern Territory–South Australian border.

These stations went sour when the Indian Army stopped buying horses from Australia in 1922. This loss of revenue saw them suffer. Tom left the Territory for Scott's Creek near Adelaide to tell stories and catch up with friends. He died in 1952 at the grand old age of eighty-nine. He had survived all his mates and even my father, by seventeen years. His wish was to be buried amongst his friends at the old Elsey Station cemetery and his grave stands next to other characters that populated Mrs Gunn's *We of the Never-Never*. Pearce Street in Katherine and Mount Pearce on Willeroo Station are named after him.

Donkey Camp

In the early 1920s it was Commonwealth Government policy to develop the Northern Territory through agriculture. My great-uncle and my father agitated for increased government support. A railway line through to Adelaide was proposed. Peanuts were to be grown on the Daly River just north and west of Katherine. In 1923 the government recommended a cotton industry be developed along the Katherine River. Under the proposal, rent was waived on farming land for the first twenty-one years. This was to allow the new farms to develop. Even so, there wasn't much demand for the land.

My father was one of the new farmers. He shared high hopes with Russian immigrants and some from the local Chinese community. The Kruger farm became known as Donkey Camp, after he moved his Spanish donkeys onto the place. Today it is called Kambechie after the waterhole on the property. It's a hobby farm with horses and a coffee house. At the time of my birth on Christmas Day 1924, the place was quite new, with recently built corrugated iron sheds on dirt floors.

The Katherine River cotton experiment didn't last long. Profits were low despite the crop fetching good prices. The cost of transporting the crop to England was too much. Many farmers, including my father, started growing peanuts instead. He also bought two house blocks in the newly gazetted township of Katherine that developed when the rail bridge was built across the Katherine River. The old township of Emungalan was abandoned.

You couldn't sell peanuts at a profit because of the growth of peanut farms in Queensland But I remember a big bag of my father's peanuts being sent to me at the Bungalow. To make ends meet, Frank kept selling his spare donkeys. They maintained a big garden. But Frank and George had to keep on taking paid stockwork wherever they could find it.

Later, in the mid-1930s, the farm was leased to his neighbour George Lim for market gardens. When my father died in 1938 the lease seems to have been taken back by the government. Polly and us kids, as Aborigines, didn't get any benefit from thirteen years of improvements during our family's life there. My brother, George, said some Krugers appeared for the funeral. They took my father's things that he had stored in trunks under his bed, sold what they could, gave George some money and mentioned South Africa. George never saw them again.

Poverty and struggle were nearly everyone's experience of the Top End. For the Aboriginal tribes the cattle industry had destroyed their way of life. For the swagmen and bagmen that came north for gold or stockwork, life wasn't much better. The farms and stations were too far from markets and too isolated from services. There wasn't much opportunity. Bad seasons, regular floods and poor prices eventually forced many of the new white settlers to leave Katherine and the Top End.

Stolen away

I have been to the High Court of Australia as part of a test case for us kids taken away. The court rejected our claims for compensation. Some people said that since we had 'had our day in court' we should just forget about it. Get over it and move on. That would be a hard thing for many of us to do. We feel that justice has not been done. We were fighting shadows. The biggest problem faced by our lawyers was to be heard at all. Because of the statute of limitations we couldn't claim in a lot of areas. The lawyers couldn't get much historical documentation about what had really happened all those years ago. No one seems to have written anything much down. Or the papers had got lost. We couldn't be heard because we couldn't prove anything. Without supporting records we were stuck. The courts seemed to accept that our parents might have said it was okay to lock up us kids. It was possibile that the ones in charge thought that imprisoning us would be for the best. Anyone who was there knew differently. But us kids were old people by this time. The white bosses and most of our mates were dead. We had survived. No one wanted to talk about the kids that didn't make it. They weren't claimants in the case.

I have talked to lots of people who were in the institutions. I have searched for official documents in the National Archives and other places. But it is impossible to get information on what exactly happened to me and my sister. It was not even recorded anywhere that I was in Kahlin and had been taken away from Donkey Camp. Lawyers and other people supporting me have been looking but there may be nothing to find. The paperwork, if there was any, is lost. I didn't seem to officially exist for many of the early years of my life.

We were able to confirm that the police had been active taking children of mixed descent from their parents in the Victoria River and Halls Creek regions in mid-1928. Myrtle, Maud, Maggie and Mary Campbell, who became friends with my sister, Gladys, were taken as part of this. On their way through Katherine with a group of kids these police from out-of-town came to Donkey Camp and took me and Gladys too. My sister, Bobby, was not taken. She was of full Aboriginal descent. Nor were Leslie and John taken. Perhaps they were away with my father. Perhaps they had already drowned. I have been unable to find any records of them, except my mother's death certificate that says she had me, Gladys and one dead son. I have been told that early in the morning police on horseback came down the road to Donkey Camp. They say the visiting police had heard there might be mixed descent kids staying at Donkey Camp. My father, George, and all the men were away working. The police faced a mob of Aboriginal women. We were snatched from our mother's arms before anyone could raise the alarm. My mother and the other women were taken by surprise. Us kids couldn't be hidden. They had us rounded up before anybody could organise a diversion.

I was not much more than a toddler and my sister had just turned six. We were taken and locked up at the police station, waiting with the kids from the West to be taken on the train to Darwin. They say the police were looking for older kids really. Gladys and I were an afterthought.

George said my mother followed us, hoping for a way to get us back. When the train to Darwin arrived we were locked up on it. When the train stopped for the night at Pine Creek us kids were locked up in the Pine Creek jail. My mother was on the train. She stood at Kahlin's wire fence waiting to catch sight of us. Having kids taken had happened to Polly before with her first baby, Ada. Now it was happening again. Like all the Aboriginal mothers, she didn't get to take us back. To the authorities she was just another crying Aboriginal woman at the fence who didn't understand that the institution would train up the children for a 'better' white world. She stayed with Ada. The authorities threatened her with arrest, and eventually she went away. Probably they threatened Ada as well.

My mother went back to my father in Katherine to make a life for her remaining children. Ada had a place outside Kahlin in the Aboriginal compound and could sometimes be there for us. Alice Kruger was also there, but none of us really knew of Alice. It seems she was working in the home of Dr Cook, the Chief Protector of Aborigines for the Northern Territory. The same fellow who probably signed off on us being picked up. It is hard to know what Alice could have done even if she knew what was going on. She and Ada were just teenagers. They had survived growing up at Kahlin. I suppose they knew we would have to survive too.

I've had lots of time to think about why it had to happen to us. Possibly it was personal. My father was still the carter of supplies out to the cattle stations in the north-west. So the police who picked up the Campbell girls probably knew him or knew of him. Perhaps he had tried to stop those other kids being snatched away. My father or my great-uncle may have been offside with someone who could authorise a raid at Donkey Camp. Perhaps my mother had offended someone in town. But it could also have been the act of an individual policeman or government worker. They may have been true believers in enforcing the Aboriginal Ordinances. We might have just been in the wrong place at the wrong time.

That is the trouble with such an ugly law. Its enforcement could be arbitrary. It was a way of keeping people under control. My family was not powerful enough to get the decision changed once us kids were taken into the system. Possibly it was the fear of us kids being snatched away that had kept my father and mother out of Katherine so long after Willeroo was sold in 1917. In Maranboy, we might have been protected by sympathetic friends and good police. We don't really know the story. That was the trouble at the High Court. That is why it is unfinished business for the lot of us. We still want to discover more of our side of the story and get a bit of justice happening.

The Aboriginal Ordinances

Us kids were taken under the *Northern Territory Aborigines Act 1911*. This allowed the Protector of Aborigines in the Northern Territory to remove children of mixed Aboriginal descent from the care of their mothers and fathers, and away from their Aboriginal heritage. It also allowed the government to make decisions for Aborigines about where they lived, worked or went to school, how they spent their money (if they had any), who they married, where they travelled, what they owned and whether they could drink alcohol.

The inhuman treatment of Aborigines was okay because we were deemed to be less than human. In an extension of this thinking, it was believed that Aboriginality could be bred out of people. If Aborigines bred only with white people they would become whiter too. At some point we would be white enough to live 'normal' white lives without government 'protection'.

Some religious leaders of the time held similar views. Blackness showed the stain of original sin. At the other extreme Aboriginal people were seen by some as noble savages that had existed before the Garden of Eden. They thought we were incapable of living in the modern world. In their opinion we needed to be baptised and 'protected' from the abuses of white civilisation, but not be allowed an equal status or citizenship. So, when I was born, people of Aboriginal descent couldn't grow up their own families, get work, get married or escape the authority of the Protector of Aborigines. This meant being told what to do by just about any government official, white boss or bullyboy.

It remains very real living history for many of us in the Aboriginal community. Child protection agencies still have huge numbers of our kids in care. Poor health, lack of education, bad housing and unemployment are still terrible burdens on the Aboriginal community. Prisons are full of our people. We are surviving, but it will take us a long time to recover from the terrible treatment dished out under racist laws and ideas of white supremacy.

The history of the Kahlin Institution

To put the law into practice the Commonwealth government established children's institutions. When they started it was about education. Kids were taken into a big boarding house so they could go to school. In 1913 Kahlin Compound was established at Cullen Bay in Darwin. At about the same time the Bungalow started behind the Stuart Arms Hotel in Alice Springs. By November 1913 a one-teacher school opened in Kahlin. The first teacher was Mrs Jacobs, then, in 1915, Mrs Holtze. In the same year Robert MacDonald was appointed the first supervisor. He was described by Val McGuiness, one of the residents in 1918, as 'a big man, he must have been six foot four, six foot five and he weighed about eighteen or nineteen stone …He was an absolute brute as far as I was concerned.' With his appointment his wife got the job as matron. The employment of married couples was preferred. It saved on wages and was meant to reduce the risk of the men interfering with the girls. These people were before my time but probably Ada, Alice and Jack Gibbs would have shared the space with them.

The Kahlin Compound grew rapidly. It became sixteen weatherboard houses with a storeroom, coach house, fowl run, laundry, dormitories and a kitchen. It was described by the novelist Xavier Herbert in *Capricornia* as a 'miniature city of whitewashed hovels crowded on a barren hill.' Herbert spent a lot of time in Darwin and the Top End. One of his jobs was working as fill-in supervisor at Kahlin.

Around the original Kahlin Institution grew a bigger Aboriginal community. Mothers and families moved to be close by their children. Local Aboriginal families used it as a centre of relative safety. When they got out of Kahlin, my sisters Ada, Alice and Gladys formed relationships, got married and grew up their own children around the place. Better the devils you know than the dangers of being isolated and at risk from strangers. Kahlin also became an employment agency, the place where the white community could get Aboriginal domestic staff and Aboriginal labourers were given work with businesses in town and out bush. Darwin was desperately short of workers.

By 1923 some in the government felt the compound did not create enough separation for the children from the rest of the Aboriginal community. We had to be saved from our Aboriginality. Mixing with our Aboriginal family members stopped us becoming part of the white community. If they'd had the money the government would have completely separated Kahlin children from the surrounding Aboriginal compound. But as usual funding was a problem. They made do with building a new kids' residence and putting a big wire fence between the Institution and the rest of the place. By 1924, the new Kahlin Half-Caste Children's Home had been completed in Schultz Street, just outside the existing Aboriginal compound at Myilly Point. Mr and Mrs MacDonald remained in charge.

By the time of the 1928 Bleakley Inquiry into Kahlin and other children's institutions, Kahlin had seventy-six inmates in a house large enough for one big family. There were nine adults, three teenagers and sixty-four kids from eleven down to four months. Gladys and I were among the sixty-four children sharing the floor space. The inquiry into the Bungalow in Alice Springs painted an even worse picture of overcrowding and abuse.

Borrowed memories

Daisy Ruddick, one of the residents at the time I was there, describes the scene at Kahlin as '…floggings every day. We'd get flogged by the matron. And we'd get flogged by the girls in charge of the dormitory.' It was to this place that Gladys and I were delivered in 1928. Kahlin was the only place we saw for the next four years. I can't remember my mother at the fence. I can't even remember my sister, Gladys, who must have been looking after me. Not even my older sisters, Ada and Alice, who lived in the shadows of the place. I was only six in 1931 when a government decision saw me moved on again.

Gladys stayed on much longer, only leaving when she turned eighteen. Most of my sisters and brothers were at Kahlin from when they were children. I was the youngest taken in our family. So many of my circle of friends in adult life shared the dormitories. In some ways it was the only home many of us remember.

They tried hard to force family away from the institutions. The Aboriginal mothers risked losing their rations and even going to prison if they tried to take their children back. For Aboriginal families there wasn't much employment in the late 1920s. Even if the fathers had full-time work, the wages and conditions weren't good. Many had mustering jobs where they were away for four or so months. Or they had seasonal work as contract stockmen or at the mines. Once the job was done they were laid off. It was tough times so they needed rations. You couldn't afford to lose them.

Me being so young and then separated from my family for so long, I have no clear picture of how the story unfolded within my family. But even my father, Frank Kruger, nephew to the well-known Tom Pearce, was not able to get us out. When you look at why my father didn't use the power and wealth of his uncle to make more of himself in Katherine in the early days, it was perhaps a fear of his children being taken away to the institutions. It had happened to Ada, Alice and the children of many of his friends. The few children who were able to avoid the institutions were those living out of town with a supportive landowner okay about hiding them out. Mum, my brothers and sister, Gladys, stayed out of town during the early years.

When my parents needed to go to town they camped away from the places where they risked us kids being caught. Some families built hideaways and trained their kids to bolt to them at the first hint of visitors. I have heard of Aboriginal mothers adding colour to their light-skinned children by rubbing crushed charcoal mixed with fat onto their bodies. It didn't always save them. Some police ordered kids washed as a check. Some parents were forced at gunpoint to surrender their kids. For us they probably knew where we were and waited for an opportunity.

It has been said that some babies were taken for their own protection, because they reminded mothers of their brutal white fathers and times of much sorrow. Some say that a few white fathers sent their older children away for an education. Lots of individual stories. Anyone who might have been able to tell me bits of my own story is long dead. But only a fool would believe the bullyboys. There were no free choices when the authorities controlled your life.

When he took up Donkey Camp in 1924, it must have been my father's big chance to set his family up. But it ended in great loss. It was too close to town to avoid the authorities. Too much in the faces of those who said my parents were immoral and saw us kids as the products of sin. The whole community suffered from the cruelty and stupidity of the government at the time. But it was us kids and our families that lived the pain day-to-day and bore the brunt of the abuse.

As a child I had no mother's arms to hold me. No father to lead me into the world. Us taken-away kids only had each other. All of us damaged and too young to know what to do. We had strangers standing over us. Some were nice and did the best they could. But many were just cruel nasty types. We were flogged often. We learnt to shut up and keep our eyes to the ground, for fear of being singled out and punished. We lived in dread of being sent away again where we could be even worse off. Many of us grew up hard and tough. Others were explosive and angry. A lot grew up just struggling to cope at all. They found their peace in other institutions or alcohol. Most of us learnt how to occupy a small space and avoid anything that looked like trouble. We had few ideas about relationships. No one showed us how to be lovers or parents. How to feel safe loving someone when that risked them being taken away and leaving us alone again. Everyone and everything we loved was taken away from us as kids.

The Department gives 14 July 1928 as the date of Gladys's admission to Kahlin Compound. I have not located any record of my own removal and arrival. The lack of records was because our names were often changed, or poorly noted. The files were not maintained in any useful way. People say that some parents were told that their children were dead. Some kids seem to have been adopted out with few checks or safety nets. Institutional staff seem to have been allowed to have kids taken interstate, even overseas, without anyone really knowing. Our families had no rights to any information about us.

I remember some mothers from Wave Hill and Mudburra country being around Kahlin from time to time. My sisters have told me that my mother stayed trying to make things okay for her baby boy. They say my mother couldn't get permission to come into the compound. I know other mothers were allowed to work at the house, or got permitted to visit the compound, probably because their children were considered no risk of running away. My mother was a passionate woman, and they wouldn't have liked that.

I can't remember blankets, just sheets. Darwin is a warm place but in winter when it can get a little nippy at night, all us kids had to huddle together for warmth. My sisters, particularly Gladys, talked of having to look through rubbish bins for food scraps because of hunger.

Ethel Buckle, one of the residents, describes the home as 'having three bare bedrooms which contained very few beds. The inmates slept on the floor, sharing the few mattresses. There was never enough bedding. Those not fortunate enough to have a mattress slept on the bare floorboards with a blanket over them for warmth. The small children, especially the brothers and sisters of older girls, often slept at the foot of their sisters' beds. In the morning the mattresses were removed, stools and some desks installed and what had been a dormitory was transformed into a school room.'

I would have been just three-and-a-half when I first became a resident in mid-1928. I was probably one of those younger brothers sleeping at the end of my sister's mattress. Perhaps neither of us had mattresses. It is hard to picture three rooms being bedrooms for seventy-seven people. Even if the adults slept elsewhere and there were just the sixty-four kids, it means an average of twenty-one kids per room. My sisters say it was really bad; the little kids crying all night.

According to Ethel, 'The meals consisted of a bit of porridge in the morning with no sugar, hardly any milk and cocoa for breakfast … for dinner time we had stew brought in from the compound in a kerosene bucket and then they used to just scoop it out.' Everyone was always hungry. To supplement their diet the kids resorted to bush tucker, or otherwise they experimented with what was available. According to Daisy Ruddick, anything that looked edible was food 'if it didn't cause frothing at the mouth'.

Ethel remembers having 'jam tins for our plates, jam tins for our tea and cocoa.' Nellie Cummings recalls the kids used to watch each other like hawks. The faster they ate the more they got. Some of the older girls, according to Hilda Muir, used to hide the few forks and plates, cups and spoons whenever they were lucky enough to get them, to make sure they'd have some utensils for the next meal.

Maggie Tilmouth, a resident in the late 1920s, recalls that forks were used to comb hair. Usually though, the children's heads were shaved to prevent lice, or as punishment. Maggie says, 'We didn't even know how we looked until Sally Grant got a jam tin and said, 'Here, come here you fellas!' so then we could see how we looked for the first time.' Punishment also meant the strap, the cane or whip, usually given by the superintendent. Sometimes the children were made to stand outside in the sun with their hands on their heads. Other times kids' faces were whitewashed. They were tied to the beds or made to do hard physical work. Offences covered such outrages as talking at night, running away, fighting, swearing, talking to full blood Aborigines and leaving the home without permission.

Stories I was told of back home

I am not really sure what was happening at home in Katherine at this time. My father was relieved from his carting job with what had become the Rundle's stores. He was told that he couldn't run a 'book up' system with his old mates. He had been giving tobacco and rations to unemployed men from other people's packages, on the promise of repayment when the money came in. These blokes always eventually paid it back. But they had a new bookkeeper at the shop. The old ways didn't suit the new style of management and my father was replaced.

In 1931 Katherine experienced huge floods that would have wiped out my parent's riverbank farm. When the water finally drained away they would have had to start again. Perhaps it was in this flood that my brothers, Leslie and Johnny, were drowned.

My mother probably found religion around this time. The missionaries and churches came to the Territory with the Depression. There's nothing like unemployment and dispossession to focus people on the possibility of a better world after death. She must have found some peace from all her sadness in the teachings of Father Long and she became born-again.

It was also in 1931 that I was packed off to a new place. Nobody asked me or my family whether I wanted to go. Kahlin had become too much of a disgrace with so many of us kids stopping in such a small place. We were put on the train to a new place set up at Pine Creek. I left Gladys and my older sisters behind. Gladys would have been ten. I was six. My family probably eventually found out in the usual gossipy way of the small Northern Territory community.

Pine Creek

I was taken to Pine Creek with twenty-seven other boys. More boys came later. Many were from the Daly River area. I was six years old and leaving behind what family I had. It must have been a terrible disconnection but I can't remember any of it. It was not until after the war that I saw any of my sisters again. No doubt the sadness of that time and not having my sister about has been buried away somewhere.

A lot of my lifelong friends shared my time at Pine Creek. From all accounts, it was a much better place than Kahlin. It was smaller, more relaxed and we were freer to be out and about. There were times when we could just run amok in and around town. I was no longer a baby and perhaps that was part of it too. We had some good times at Pine Creek.

There was Tom and George Kelly, Nugget Kopp, Freddy Muggleton, Harry Bennett, Nugget Blackmore, Joe Egan, Mickey and Billy Goodall, Joe Croft, Henry Peckham, Johnny Pan Quee, Jock Cassidy and lots more. Joe Croft was a close mate. I still catch up with his daughter Brenda, who is a manager at the National Galley in Canberra. Tom Kelly was a few years older than me. George must have been his much younger brother. Johnny Pan Quee's father was Jimmy Pan Quee who had a peanut farm on the Daly River. Freddy Muggleton was also from the Daly River area. Freddy ended up as a stockman working a lot down in Alice with me.

Some of the boys I can barely remember and have never seen since. The place was full of boys. Almost too many mates. You couldn't get away. Most of them came along to the Bungalow later on when we were moved again. Some ended up droving or living in Central Australia like me. I shared most of my life with Nugget Kopp – house, kids and just about everything else.

The Pine Creek Institution was run by the local policeman, Tom Turner, and his wife. She was a nurse and looked after any doctoring needed. Jock Jones and his wife were in charge of the kids' quarters. They were on friendly terms with my parents, and later turned up at the Bungalow when they got the job of supervising that place together. I had been in the Bungalow at Alice Springs for some time when they arrived. I was certainly happy to see them. Also our Aboriginal women helpers worked at Pine Creek. I was only six so they seemed grown up to me. Perhaps they were just teenagers. They must have come down with us from Kahlin. They did the cooking and washing. I suspect they had been ordered to go with us and had left family themselves back in Darwin. Their names were Marjorie Morris, Alice Bourke (or Burt) and Bet Bet (Williams) Gallagher. There were too many of us boys to be mothered much but it was these women who were there for us at the time. Bet Bet's mother was the young girl named the 'Black Princess' in Mrs Gunn's book of the same name.

I can't remember the Pine Creek Institution as a cruel place. It was not like the way Kahlin is described by my sisters. Perhaps I was protected from the worst of it, being one of the younger ones, but there was certainly never enough food. It was the Depression and the government never paid much to see us looked after. As little as they could get away with, and even less than that often enough. But it was easier to cadge food around Pine Creek. We were free to roam around during the weekend and holidays. Nor can I remember a muster system or a whole lot of punishments. Us boys hung around as a mob. There was safety in numbers. We came home for meals because we were all starving. We were locked in at night, but I suspect this was because we felt safer that way rather than to stop us taking off.

I can't remember kids running away. It was talked about a lot, particularly by the older boys. But even though Pine Creek was on the road out of Darwin we were all a long way from home. The Daly River boys were the exception. For the ones from further out running away would have involved weeks of walking and hiding out. Most were from further out west of Katherine: from Victoria River Downs, Wave Hill and stations out that way. None of us had any real bush skills. We didn't even know if we had a home to go to. We would have been too scared of the night-times anyway. Kaditja men stories and hungry spirits on the prowl kept us at home. We slept nearly on top of each other. Like all kids we were scared of things going bump in the night. Things that could sneak up on you and kill you stone dead. We were terrified of being caught away from home after dark.

I was at the 2002 premiere of *Rabbit Proof Fence* in Alice Springs. What a beautiful, powerful film. My emotions were bouncing all over the place all the way through it. It told lots of things that stirred old half-forgotten memories. I was a bit worried after the film that people might think us kids in our Northern Territory institutions were cowards for not doing the same as those girls and just taking off. I suspect this struck a bit of a chord with the whole group of us there from the our Stolen Generations group. What if we had just taken off? What if our families had stood up and fought back more? I was nervous that people around me watching the film would think less of us. That it would feed the idea that it was somehow our fault and we could have done something about it. That sort of thinking is a load of rubbish, of course. I just imagine one of my young grandkids trying to walk a couple of hundred miles across the crocodile-infested swamps of the Top End, avoiding police and anyone else who might turn you in.

Most of us were taken as quite young kids and knew no other life before the institutions. We had been kicked hard for a long time. We did what we were told. At least when we were looking right at the bosses. You would behave yourself in front of anyone who could hurt you. You could do what you liked once they were gone. But you had to be very careful not to get caught out. And they knew what to look for. They were adults and we were just kids.

Those girls in the film were something special. A tremendous courageous group. They had only just got snatched away and placed into an institution when they escaped. They were lucky to have survived their trek home. Escape wasn't the story of anyone I knew. Perhaps some kids got away or died in the attempt and I didn't know about it. The Kaditja stories did it for us. What were the alternatives? It was far too late by the time you were inside. You just hoped that by being good and keeping out of their way you would survive for another day.

Pine Creek was a largish country town. In those days it was where the train stopped between Darwin and Katherine. Everyone got off and overnighted at one of the pubs or boarding houses. The poor ones camped out in their bedrolls. The train came every Wednesday with whistles blowing and a puff of smoke. When we could, we would stop what we were doing to rush down there. It was an outing for us. We would see what we could cadge from the passengers getting off. At some stage my father used to be one of the regulars on the train as a buyer for one of the stores in Katherine. He always had a tin of boiled lollies. I was very proud of him. I can't remember other family visiting. Perhaps my mother came, but I can't remember meeting her. Travel was expensive. Possibly it was too much for her, or she thought it would be too much for me. Maybe it was kept from her where I was. In any case there was no going home for any of us that I remember. It would have been hard for those of us staying if someone had left, though we were used to people disappearing from our lives without explanation.

It was always great to see Dad at Pine Creek railway station when he appeared at the door of the train, smiling down at all us kids. One of them was me, his youngest son. I was the one that he didn't get to parent much. I think about my own kids sometimes. Especially those that I wasn't there for much. You try not to worry about what you can't change. He must have been like that. Just doing his best and playing the cards as they'd been dealt.

Pine Creek had been an active goldfield since 1871. Smaller than Darwin, but much bigger than Katherine or Alice Springs at the time. Pearl Hearney ran the church. A white lady, Mrs Shunky, had a big general store. Wing Chong had a shop too. George Stevens had the butcher shop. There was a pub run by Jim Dowling. There was a bakery run by Ei-yoo. There were lots of Chinese about and they ran the market gardens and stalls. They came around with fruit and vegetables in an old dray selling door-to-door.

There was a Chinese joss house in town. We were sometimes able to sneak food when there were funerals and other religious occasions. Food would be left at the place or on the death monuments, and we would try to sneak in to eat it. The Chinese priests would say it was the spirits coming to eat it but it was just us kids. It was a good arrangement with everyone happy enough. The place got trashed during the war when everyone was evacuated. It was so badly damaged that they didn't fix it.

There didn't seem to be many Chinese graves around Pine Creek. Where possible the Chinese still sent the bodies of their countrymen back to China. Rumour had it that gold was also taken out of the country in the coffins to avoid taxes. Some Chinese who had become wealthy in Australia had been able to send for brides from China. Others married into the Aboriginal community. We spent a fair bit of time trying to sneak into the market gardens. We would hang around the fences or in the bushes, planning how we might get in and out, taking away some mangoes or vegetables without getting caught. Usually we would get chased away fairly quickly. But they were never that mean about it. I suspect the Chinese were sorry for us. Some of them had their own kids taken away.

There was a very small Aboriginal community around Pine Creek. George Stevens' butcher shop was where many Aboriginal families were employed. His station next to town was where they lived. I didn't see other permanent camps around. I remember being told at one time, how there had been a big fight between two tribal groups out at Umbyara Gorge. This might have kept people home.

The old Aboriginal people were still protecting their sites. You sometimes ran into them if you wandered away out towards the edge of town. I remember once a mob of us was sent away by an old man, Hector Kurra, from one area we had wandered into. It was the place now called Coronation Hill. There were native plum trees all through that place and as usual we were chasing a feed. So we had been climbing for fruit when we first saw him standing there looking at us. We took off. The next time, when we were mucking around there, we came across his spear stuck in the ground. He was standing back again. But it was pretty clear that he was warning us that we were coming too close to the boundaries of sacred grounds.

After that he was always around to hunt us away from the site. One day we got up the courage to ask him why we couldn't walk in some areas. He said that walking on the land risked waking up the spirits with the noise of our footsteps. If the spirits woke up they would be angry and the land would erupt with fire and smoke. Hector Kurra was always looking after this land, walking about with his spears. As young kids we took Hector's warning seriously enough and kept away.

Some Aboriginal families worked on the stations in season and travelled through town before moving further back out to bush camps. They might stop for a few days or weeks camping with family or on the edge of town. Mr Turner, the policeman, didn't seem to worry them or chase them away. You could walk around wherever in those days. It was a nice place to grow up. There didn't seem to be a big grog problem, but we were in bed fairly early. So we mightn't have noticed anyway.

There was a big unemployment program at Pine Creek with a lot of white men from other places camping on the edge of town. They were swaggies or bagmen escaping from the south because of no work happening down there. There was a 'work for the dole' type of scheme to build an airstrip. Some of the blokes got paid rations for their work. Others might get a bit of work on the railway line. It was the Depression, so not much work was happening anywhere.

White women and children across Australia couldn't get government support unless they were deserted and their husbands not findable. So a lot of fathers hit the road looking for work. Some ended up at places like Pine Creek. They had their swags and camped where they could. To get rations or work you had to be registered with the police. For us kids, the swaggies were often good for a bit of food. Most were a long way from home and were missing their kids and loved ones. They wouldn't have known much about how their own families were surviving without them. We were happy to help them out of their loneliness if it meant a feed.

Pearl Hearney took all us kids to Sunday mass and Sunday school. The church was just across the railway line. It was Pearl who arranged for Father Davis to visit and had me and others baptised and confirmed in the Anglican Church. I enjoyed the church stuff. It was gospel style with hell and brimstone sermons. I kept up the church stuff right through the institutions. Not that we had a lot of choice in the matter.

We went to the normal white-fellow school in Pine Creek. It was all right. I don't remember any trouble. I was in the little kids' classes. The

Dowling kids were all there. I was a restless sort of kid and never showed a lot of interest in schoolwork. They let me go a lot of the time. I was always wanting to be outside running around. Looking for an opportunity.

No one had great ambitions for me as an academic and I can't remember learning much of anything in the school. I could smile, avoid being singled out by someone with too much time on his hands, and move on quickly even in those early years. Like all the kids brought up in institutions, you got pretty good at giving people what they wanted while they were directly there in your face. Then doing what you could get away with as soon as they were gone.

Certainly they never taught me to read and write. I learnt that in the stock camps later on. I don't remember feeling like I had missed out on anything then. Later on perhaps. My own kids all went to school and were made to keep at their books. But it didn't happen for me in the two years at Pine Creek, and I didn't get much out of my next schooling experience either.

The Pine Creek Half-Caste Institution for Boys was closed in 1933. Most of us were sent down to the Bungalow in Central Australia. It saved the government a bit of money to have us all squashed into a bigger place. A few were sent to Darwin and then on to one of the new missions starting up in the islands. I don't know how it was managed. There was no asking us or even warning us. A decision had been made in Canberra or Darwin and we were uprooted again. I was very sad to leave Pine Creek.

This time we were taken even further away from any family. My mates at the institution became the only family I had. I didn't see the Top End again until I joined the army and was posted back up that way. That was ten years later and I was a man. When I left Pine Creek I was eight years old.

Later on I was told that there had been a review done by the Reverend Griffiths from the Methodist Church in Alice Springs. Apparently some of the ladies of Pine Creek were worried about having so many of us institution kids running around the place. It was probably seen as lowering the tone of the neighbourhood. I suspect they didn't like the 'work for the dole' mob either.

Anyway, they got the administrator in Darwin to listen to them. Reverend Griffiths' report said the place was working pretty well, but they decided to close it down anyway. We were to be packed up and sent on our way so that the good ladies of Pine Creek didn't have to see us making the place look untidy anymore.

The trip to the Telegraph Station

Arrangements for transporting us didn't exhaust the creativity of anyone in the Aboriginal Protectorate offices. We were posted down. You wouldn't want government officials wasting taxpayer monies on the likes of us. Not long after the roads opened after the Wet season of 1933, we were loaded onto the back of the mail truck and away we went. The government probably did up a contract and the mailman, Sam Irvine, was the lowest quote. There wouldn't have been much competition. The road to Alice was a goat track. Sam was probably one of the few regular users.

There were thirty-three of us that went down. We sat in the steel cage on a big flat-back traytop with the other luggage. Sam had the usual parcels and mailbags and stopped at every settlement to pick up and drop off mail. It was slow going with the 1,400 kilometres of rough track taking a week.

When they closed Pine Creek, the Aboriginal staff were sent back to Kahlin in Darwin. We missed them a lot. We weren't allowed to take anything with us except what we were wearing. Not that we had much more than that anyway. Jam tins full of sand with wire tied through them to be dragged along were the only toys I can remember, apart from marbles and handmade bats to hit around whatever balls we could keep. They all stayed behind. We held on to each other across the ruts and bumps. Thankfully it didn't rain. But it was wintertime and the nights were colder as we got further into the desert country.

We must have gone through Katherine, the truck driving over Knott's Crossing only a kilometre from where I was born. But I can't recall Katherine making any impression on me. There was no family to greet me. No welcome home parade. We probably camped out of town, filled up with petrol out of a 44-gallon drum at one of the shops and kept going. For all of us boys it was a journey into the unknown. The dust and windy cold were terrible. When we stopped at a town or station mailbox, us kids could get down and run about a bit. But we were told not to hold up the mail delivery schedule. There were no toilet stops or anything. You had to hang your doodle out the back of the truck tray as we were driven along.

The mailman's responsibilities ended pretty much at driving and feeding us. When the truck finally stopped for the day he threw out a big calico camp mat for us to sleep on. We were given some porridge in the morning and black tea. Bread or damper with a lick of jam was lunch. He cooked up stews at night. We ate them sitting on the canvas around a campfire. Then it was turn in and go to sleep if you could. The stars in the desert were something else. You might wake up in the middle of the night looking at a million stars. The dingoes would be howling in the distance.

Eventually the truck crept into the northern edges of Alice Springs. The road through the mountains and across the creeks into Alice was as bad as anything on the whole trip. The mailman turned off to the Telegraph Station about three kilometres short of the town itself. This was to be our new home. It felt good to be off the truck. But there was a big mob of strangers waiting. Kids hanging around looking at us. We huddled together. We had arrived at the Bungalow, which was to be my home for the next two years.

The arrival

Anyone going out to see the Telegraph Station these days is not going to get much of a picture of what the place looked like when I first saw it. They've ripped down all the thrown-together tin dormitories and the other shacks and sheds that were everywhere. There are lawns where there used to be just bulldust and rubbish. As it's presented today you might think it was a really nice place. Why are all of us complaining? Well, in my time, it wasn't very nice at all. It might have worked as a telegraph station and home for a dozen people, but with 140 kids living there at its peak, it was an overcrowded prison. There was no grass then and the place had very basic kitchen areas, toilets and showers.

In the 1960s they started another Aboriginal compound further out of town at a place called Amoonguna, and closed what was left of the Bungalow, handing the site over to the National Parks. They didn't want to recall our history so they decided to tart the place up, forget about what happened to us, and remember the good old white Telegraph men from the frontier days.

We didn't get any kind-hearted Telegraph Station boss waiting for us. Mr Freedman and his wife were there. He was the supervisor and she was the matron. No one looked pleased to see us. Sam the mailman, having done his duty, got back in the truck and kept on going into Alice Springs. So we were there. Mr Freedman rang the bell and the hundred-odd residents were lined up. We didn't know anyone. We were not used to being lined up much, but we were put into line alongside them. The other residents were mostly from around Alice Springs and were family for each other. Some of the older women were mothers and aunts for the kids. But we only had each other. Us Pine Creek kids pretty much stuck together as a group all the time at the Bungalow. It was safer that way.

Winter in Central Australia was a shock for us after the tropical warmth of Pine Creek. Being born and brought up in the tropics I had never known the cold. We were put into a long tin shed that was the boys' dormitory. Thirty-three of us plus the boys that had already been around the place. More than sixty in total. The girls had another dormitory. The women and babies had another shed. There was the supervisor's house and other stone buildings including our eating area, kitchen and bakery. It was late in the afternoon when we arrived. We were told to wash under the taps and be seated at the long tables in the eating room. The food was what we were used to, a thin watery stew, but less of it to go around than at Pine Creek. We noticed that straightaway. Then it was off to our dormitory and sorting out the mattresses. There were no sheets, just thin blankets. As night fell the lights were turned off and we were locked in for the first of many restless nights.

My world in Alice Springs was much harsher than the one I had left behind. There wasn't much mothering for us around the place. We were just extra mouths to feed. No extra staff had been provided. The dormitories were much too small. You had to fight for your spot. Nobody wanted us there. This included anyone in charge. We were taking food and blankets from their own kids. And soon enough even newer kids were taken away from their homes and added to the mix.

A brief history of the Bungalow

The Bungalow had originally been set up in 1913 when an Aboriginal woman, Topsy Smith, moved from the Arltunga goldmines into Alice Springs. Arltunga had been a substantial mining town in the 1880s, but had virtually shut down when the easy-to-get gold had run out and the Government battery had been closed. The publicans moved on, miners packed up their wheelbarrows and every one headed off to the next gold rush town. The fairly big Aboriginal community, drawn to the place for casual work and food, had also moved away back to traditional camps on what were now stations, or into Alice Springs itself. Left behind were a few old-time fossickers and a small Aboriginal group dry panning in the creeks and tailings of the old mines.

Mr Smith was just about the last of the old men to leave. Topsy Smith was his wife. He traded what little gold they could find in exchange for flour, tea and whatever else they needed. But 1912 was a hard, dry summer. The water at Arltunga had always been bad but good water became even harder to find. Topsy had built up a big mob of goats that provided milk and meat for the family. But without water the goats were struggling along with everything else. It was Mrs Hayes from Undoolya Station who came to the rescue. She took out her horse and cart, helped Topsy Smith and her seven kids pack up and took the kids into the police station at Alice Springs.

Topsy followed behind, shepherding her mob of goats. Topsy needed a place to stay in Alice Springs. She also had the idea that her children should have a decent life and education. The policeman, Sergeant Robert Stott, arranged for the Government to allocate enough money to build an iron shed near the police compound. That was the start of the Bungalow. The goats were confiscated so that they could be looked after in the government pound. Rations, wages for an Aboriginal gardener and someone to look after the goats were found by Sergeant Stott in his role as the Aboriginal Protector. He was a good man in lots of ways.

After a fairly short period of time the shed provided for Mrs Smith and her children was also used to house other kids of mixed Aboriginal descent in the town. The Aboriginal families were struggling with little paid work and the loss of their traditional hunting grounds. It wasn't them that the government wanted to help out. It was the kids with white fathers. Often these fathers were well-known local men – miners, shopkeepers, stockmen, policemen, telegraph station staff, linesmen or people from the pastoral leases. Others were travelling workers. Some were still about the place and kept a bit of an eye out for their families. Others had died or moved on. The mixed descent population continued to grow with the realities of lots of comparatively powerful white men living in a community with no available white women and a powerless and exploitable Aboriginal community.

In 1914 a school was set up in Alice Springs for the few local white children and Ida Standley was appointed as the first teacher. In 1915, Ida Stanley requested to be allowed to teach the Aboriginal children living at Topsy Smith's Bungalow. She became the non-resident matron of the place. Topsy Smith helped her in the classroom and stayed on as houseparent. The half-dozen white children were educated in the morning, and then an hour and a half was provided to school the Bungalow kids in the afternoon. At the insistence of the white parents, the desks and the children had to be scrubbed daily.

By 1920 the Bungalow had expanded to a ramshackle collection of three sheds. Mrs Standley lived close by and the resident staff were Topsy Smith, two goat herders, a gardener, his wife and three Aboriginal assistants.

By 1921 there were forty-two residents. At the same time the Alice Springs white population was recorded as thirty.

The trip to the Telegraph Station

By 1926 there were twenty-four ex-Bungalow girls and boys in domestic work in Adelaide. This employment had been arranged through Sergeant Stott. He had become a one-person employment agency. In 1927 Mrs Standley reported that there were eight white children at the Alice Springs school and forty-one children of mixed descent getting the one and a half hours of schooling in the afternoons. The records show twenty-eight boys and twenty-nine girls living at the Bungalow.

There were changes afoot for Alice Springs with the extension of the rail line from Oodnadatta. White residents worried about the impact of railway construction workers on the Bungalow residents. Sergeant Stott had finally retired. Mrs Standley struggled without his active support. As much as anything else he was good at controlling the other police in town. The Stuart Arms Hotel was just a short walk from the Bungalow and some of the white residents complained that drinkers at the pub forced themselves on the young women of the Bungalow. They thought railway workers would do the same. It was decided at the end of 1928 to move the Bungalow to Jay Creek, about fifty kilometres west of town, despite that area previously having been declared unsuitable because of the lack of safe water. No one consulted the mainly Eastern and Central Arrernte residents about whether they wanted to be moved onto a patch of scrub in Western Arrarnta country, a long way away from family and protection.

An old and frail Ida Standley, some of the older girls and most of the kids were moved out to Jay Creek. Ida was given a tent under a bough shelter to live in. The few older girls and the kids lived in buildings made of the sheet iron salvaged after the old Bungalow buildings were pulled down.

Her children persuaded Topsy Smith to stay in town. She was older by this time and Jay Creek would have exhausted her. It was a long way out. There were no medical supplies, fresh fruit, vegetables, tools and no means of communicating with Alice Springs.

In early 1929 Mrs Standley became too sick to continue to teach and manage the Bungalow. A passing missionary, Ernest Kramer, and his wife took over running the place, while a longer-term replacement was sought. Mr and Mrs Thorne, who had previously worked out at the Oenpelli Mission in the Top End, were given the job. But they stayed only a couple of months, saying the conditions were too shocking for them to keep working there. It was a terrible place with blistering heat in the summer, falling down shelters and poor water. Everyone was sad to be there. It was other peoples' country. But the authorities were saving money. They provided only two hurricane lamps, six bowls and twenty towels to go around. There was one arithmetic book and no exercise books. Schooling just wasn't allowed to happen once Mrs Standley left.

In April 1930 Mr and Mrs J.K. Freedman, who had been at the Forrest River Mission in north-west Australia, were appointed to replace the Thornes. Things had not improved but, for whatever reason, the Freedmans stayed on despite the poor accommodation and lack of food, water and any of the other things that might have made the place livable. Mr Freedman was a brute of a boss. Jay Creek was out of sight and out of mind. Possibly that was the attraction for him. No one with the power to change things cared enough to do anything about the Jay Creek Bungalow, or the kids forced to live there for nearly three years. It became very difficult for families to visit. While Mrs Freedman and others perhaps did their best, the residents had no proper health care. Deaths of kids went largely unrecorded. Reviews of the Jay Creek institution by visiting missionaries and others condemned the conditions.

Hetti Perkins, a young woman then who went on to be the mother of a large family including Charles Perkins, replaced Topsy Smith as the Senior Dormitory Girl when the move was made to Jay Creek. Hetti started out in the kitchen and helped manage the food supplies. Being seen as the Aboriginal person controlling the food made her quite powerful but not always popular. She was often accused of bias. When there's not much to go around people always think they are missing out.

Meanwhile in 1929 the railway reached Alice Springs. A lot of new people moved to town, and a lot more money flowed in. No longer was it necessary to cart everything on camels across the gibber sand plains to and from Oodnadatta. Cattle and wool could be taken to the railhead in Alice Springs where they went straight to markets down south. The drought of the late 1920s finally broke and the water supply became less of a problem. People started to eat better again.

By 1930 the name of the township was formally changed from Stuart to Alice Springs. In 1932 the telegraph and postal services were moved into town and the stone buildings built in 1871 for the Alice Springs Telegraph Station became empty. The administration was finally shamed by the appalling conditions at Jay Creek to move the Bungalow to the empty Telegraph Station. Even though there were now more buildings than at Jay

Creek, the Institution could now be seen and judged by the whole town. The accommodation was found wanting. The problem was solved by building some long sheds to be the kids' dormitories. Perhaps even then they had the plan to move us boys down from Pine Creek.

By late 1932, the new dormitories were ready. The fifty-seven kids and carers at Jay Creek were told to walk the fifty kilometres into town even though November is a hot month with temperatures often in the forties. The Freedmans had a horse-drawn dray to take blankets, clothes, heavy items and the young babies. But children as young as three started out on the long walk. They started early in the morning and the older kids soon stretched well ahead. By early evening the younger ones had managed to walk or be carried twenty kilometres to near Simpson's Gap. Finally the dray returned and picked them up.

Being back in town was a great thing for the Bungalow residents. Mr Freedman had run Jay Creek as his personal kingdom. Out at Jay Creek there was nowhere to run away to and not many visitors to keep an eye on him. Mr Freedman had his dogs and his secret supply of alcohol. He could pretty much do whatever he liked. His wife couldn't save anyone. Town residents didn't have a clue or didn't want to know about what might go on. But being back in town saw things settle down. The police, the churches and the Aboriginal community could see what was happening. They could help out with food supplies and medical assistance.

I have talked a lot with the Jay Creek mob. I know a fair bit of their stories. We shared the space at the Telegraph Station Bungalow and Mr Freedman for more than a year. We have since worked together setting up the Central Australian Stolen Generations and Families Aboriginal Corporation.

Things at the Telegraph Station site were a bit better for a while. But then us mob of boys from Pine Creek arrived. And the government started to be more active in taking more children away from their families. So times became more difficult again. Overcrowding and hunger became usual once more. The Jay Creek mob were not glad to see us. You could understand that. But it wasn't our fault. We didn't want to be there either.

The Bungalow years

The first couple of weeks at the Telegraph Station were the worst. It was cold and getting colder. We only had shorts and a shirt to run about in. No shoes or anything warm. Mr Freedman was not an easy boss to work out. He wasn't like the Pine Creek bosses. He loved playing the hard man. Even ordering us out of bed late at night for some imagined crime. Most of the time he would just ignore us. But more often than not he liked to have us under his control.

Us Pine Creek boys didn't know the routine. So it was usually us that got hammered when he felt the need to make a point. He would keep us lined up on parade outside on a cold night for as long as it amused him. He had a whip and loved getting it out. Anything he didn't like he would single out a few kids and whack them. That wasn't the worst of it either. He used to lock kids in the cellar, or make us stand on fence posts with our arms stretched out in just a pair of shorts on cold winter nights for hours on end. If you fell off or dropped your hands you risked being beaten. He was at his cruellest when no one was about.

Another punishment was getting all the boys lined up in two rows armed with belts. The one being punished had to walk between the rows getting hit. If someone didn't whack you hard enough they would be next. Other times you would have to take off your pants and bend over a box to be hit in front of all the girls. I remember getting caught one day when dinner was called, having wet pants from swimming. Mr Freedman made me take them off and sit without my pants during mealtime. It was terrible with everyone looking at me, laughing and whispering. But I learnt to get on with things. You didn't want the other boys on to you. Otherwise you had no one left at all. I was eight by this time and had already survived nearly five years in the institutions. I always tried to be one of the tough kids. It meant being a bit of a loner often enough. I was really more of a talker, but keeping moving and keeping out of the line of fire was the way to be.

The reign of terror

Pretty soon after we arrived there were a whole lot more kids coming in. The place had three-tier bunkbeds and could sleep up to one hundred and forty-four kids. One huge shed was the boy's dormitory and there was a smaller one for the girls. All us boys were jammed in together with no privacy. Bottom bunks were for the younger kids and bed-wetters. There was nothing worse than waking up on the bottom bunk stinking from the piss of the boys upstairs. It was hard to breathe, especially when the doors were closed in summer. Some of the young kids, especially the new ones, would whimper a lot. You tried not to think about it or you would get a bit stirred up yourself. We shut them up if we could; toughened them up so they could survive. There were no sheets, just thin ex-army blankets. Us boys dressed in shorts with belts of sorts to keep them up. Over time we got more clothes. You had shirts and a guernsey. There were no undies. Each item of clothing had a name tag. Wednesday was washing day when the Aboriginal women would have the copper going all day. You had a couple of sets of clothes to last you the week. If they got too dirty or ripped, you were in trouble.

The food was dreadful and there wasn't a lot of it. Breakfast might be a slice of bread and a bit of porridge. On a good day lunch was a thin meat stew with another slice of bread. At dinner you sometimes had a third slice of bread with molasses. We were always on the scrounge.

There was a big mob of goats kept for milking. They were tethered out in the hills around the Bungalow. They were probably built up from Topsy Smith's old mob from when she walked in from Arltunga. We would often try to sneak a suck of the milk. We'd drain their udders if we got the chance. Usually we had someone on the lookout. We would take it in turns. You were lucky to get a slurp before someone was pulling you off for their turn. We were in big trouble if we were caught. Someone would start to notice the empty udders and set a trap. Kids dobbed. It was hard not to. But dobbers would cop it later. Anyone caught by the bosses taking food was dragged off for a flogging. Being starving hungry was always a major issue. The goats were sometimes killed for the supervisors' meals or for visitors. But we never saw much meat. We just got the smell of it.

There was a big vegetable garden. We were not allowed anywhere near it. You would be flogged if you were caught taking stuff. Even being seen lurking around could get you the look and a flogging if it was Mr Freedman. Mostly the punishments were done as public humiliation. But you also risked being hit at just about any time from any adult around the place. Nowadays teachers get sacked for touching kids. But in the Bungalow they could half kill you without anyone blinking an eye. You needed to be careful not to look the wrong way or irritate them in any way.

Most of the Aboriginal staff were young women who weren't family for us and thought we had it pretty easy. It paid for us Pine Creek kids to keep a low profile and hang in a group. Keep smiling, keep your eyes down and keep moving out of the line of sight. That way you weren't noticed.

One Sunday every month was visitors' day, but none of us Pine Creek kids ever had a visitor in all my time at the Bungalow.

It was better for the local kids. They had aunties and uncles, full traditional Aboriginal people, throwing bush tucker over the fence for them. Old aunties like Auntie Kupitj would turn up late at night. This was very much against the rules. There was a curfew around the town and the Bungalow. But they would risk throwing a stone on the roof of the dormitory to wake the boys. They might bring kangaroo and other bush food and stash it in the bushes where their relatives could find it in the morning. We sometimes got a bit extra this way.

A lot of the games we played had to do with food. Us kids learnt how to make and use slingshots. In any free time we would hunt small birds. Occasionally you got lucky and hit a bird. Usually it was just stunned so you had to be pretty quick or it would be off again. You would grab it and wring its neck as quick as you could. Then it was straight into building a small fire with the bird jammed on a stick. It was incinerated rather than cooked and pretty raw on the inside. If you were lucky and nobody saw, you might be able to eat it all yourself. More often you had to share it.

Us kids fancied ourselves as bush tucker experts. Bush tucker spots were discovered and carefully watched. The trick was to get the bush tucker fruit before someone else took it. But we needed to let it grow and ripen a bit. It was a balancing act. We would watch a spot for days waiting for the right moment. Then you would come along and the plant would be stripped. Someone had picked it raw.

It was usually a contest with the Jay Creek mob. Sometimes we stashed the food to ripen up. Other times it was eaten raw. A lot of us had sore bellies and runny shits from eating things raw. Often the young kids were used to test stuff that looked a bit dodgy. It was a bit of an initiation thing. We were pretty clueless as to what might be edible around Alice Springs. If we were unsure that a plant was food, we would look for a volunteer to try it first. If the kid didn't die or start frothing at the mouth, then you were probably okay and everyone would tuck in. The joys of eating bush tucker are exaggerated. But hunger was a good sauce.

Mostly on weekends and school holidays we could just wander around. Summertime we were always down the waterhole any chance we could get. This was the original spring-fed water that gave the town its name. It was hot as hell around the tin sheds and grounds. Forty degrees plus in the shade for much of the summer months. Fifty plus out in the sun. The water was beautiful, and we would be in and out for as long as we could. The pool was a safe place to be. You could hear the bell and keep track of what was happening.

Mealtimes were the main time when all us kids got mustered up. You were so hungry you had to be almost dead to miss a meal. We were always worrying for food. About twice a day outside of mealtimes they might do a roll call. It was random. If you were late you were in trouble. If you missed one entirely you were in big trouble. They rang a bell that could be heard from a fair way away. You had a few minutes to get back and get lined up. If you were too far away, or out of hearing, then you could expect to cop it. The random roll calls meant that the kids couldn't get too far away. The bosses tended to know when something was on and liked to catch us out if they could. You had to be pretty quiet if you planned to get away for a while.

The Freedmans didn't do much in the way of schooling. Too many of us for the classrooms. There weren't books or equipment. The exception might be if there was a visitor coming. Then you might have to hang around the compound looking suitably happy. There were a few jobs for some of the older trusted kids around the garden and animals. But this was for the privileged. In the early days us Pine Creek kids hardly ever got these jobs. Except perhaps as very heavily supervised punishment. Even later on it wasn't me that they picked. Time at the Bungalow often moved very slowly. Chasing and riding the donkeys was how a lot of time was spent or we would make up our own games with handmade hockey sticks, cricket bats and balls. The best adventures were going for a wander or spending time plotting a way to get on the goats or into the gardens or one of the storage sheds.

The storage area was fenced off. It had tinned foods and bulk food that didn't need to be kept cool. The fence around the storage area stopped you knocking off a tin, even if you had a long stick. And the punishment for trying to sneak something from the pile was always severe. Some kids were locked in the cellar with the snakes, frogs and spiders for days and nights as punishment. You could hear them cry in fear all night. The cellar was a Coolgardie cool room built underground. The floor was a couple of feet into the water table and awash with water. Shelves kept meat, vegetables and dairy foods cool by the evaporation of water from the floor. There were narrow steps down to the shelves. This area was also locked up and the food secured away from us, even when we were locked up inside.

The main water supply was the swimming hole just up the dry riverbed. It was refilled from the underground river flow. In my time it never went dry. That was why the Telegraph Station was set up there in the first place – good permanent water. Nowadays the river is dammed a bit upstream for Bond Springs Station and the water hole is much smaller than it used to be. As a kid, swimming during the hot months was very popular. But you had to be dry for mealtimes. A couple of kids were supposed to have drowned in this waterhole. It had the reputation as having a rainbow snake in it. Proper cultural way children are supposed to avoid the place. But this wasn't an option for us kids in the forty-plus heat of summer.

The Freedman's had two daughters, Judy and Joan. They had little to do with us kids. Mrs Freedman was a bit of a shadow round her husband. Sometimes he would come over to the dormitory half-charged and wake us all up. We would be ordered out of the room and sent away out of his sight for the night. This was perhaps a way for him to spend time with his girl interest of the time. Us boys would camp in little groups huddled together just up the river near the waterhole. In the morning he would sober up and get nervous about what he had done. At one time he even rang the police to help him find some of us. We were being a little bit more leery of him than usual and travelled a bit further away. Mrs Freedman must have known of his behaviour without being able to do anything about it. Perhaps she was part of getting him exposed, charged and convicted.

For in 1934 Mr Freedman was imprisoned for having 'immoral relations' with one of the girls. Basically, one pregnant girl named him as the father and they believed her enough to convict him. Nobody I knew was sad to see him go. He was a bully who enjoyed flogging us. God knows why he became a missionary. But that was the trouble. It was bad enough being snatched away from your family, but then no one cared enough to protect us from the sick sad people that often enough ended up taking these types of jobs. There were some good ones too. But now it is pretty much out in the open that you have got to watch out for the ones who say they are looking after kids.

Mrs Freedman and her girls stayed for a while after he went to jail. She kept on working at the school with Mrs Styles. She kept on looking after the girl's side, so I didn't really know her much. It must have been humiliating for her. Then she was replaced and disappeared. I don't remember shedding any tears.

The new superintendent

The replacement for Mr Freedman was Bob Hamilton. It must have been late 1934. Mr Hamilton was safe enough, but mean and fairly humourless. He was the senior policeman locally and as such was the Aboriginal Protector. He was temporarily in charge while a full-time replacement was organised. It might have also been his job to arrest and prosecute Mr Freedman. Whatever he felt about that, it didn't mean he was going to go soft on any of us. I remember Bob Hamilton as an old-style copper determined to beat the devil out of us. When he moved to the Bungalow it left only one copper, Tony Lynch, at the Alice Springs police station. This caused more than a few problems and we were made to feel it was our fault. Mr Hamilton moved in with his wife and only child, a son who was also named Bob. Bob Junior was the same age as me and he was a good bloke. He tended to mix up a lot with us boys. He ended up staying around town and later went on to work at the Alice Springs motor registry.

After some months of recruiting, Bob Hamilton was replaced by Jock Jones and his wife. Jock had been a drover before becoming a copper for a while. He was a fair bit more relaxed than the other two before him. Us Pine Creek mob knew him and his wife. She had been the nurse for a while at Pine Creek and had ended up as the matron. Jock Jones was a tall man, well over six feet in my memory. He was a happy fellow in his late forties. I liked him a lot and he looked after me a bit. His wife was a nice person too. They didn't have any children of their own. He knew my family fairly well from being around Katherine and stopping out at Donkey Camp. It was almost like having a family again. I got some news from home for the first time in a long time. He must have passed on that I was okay and in Alice Springs, because the bags of peanuts started arriving again like at Pine Creek.

Jock had worked a lot around Katherine. He nicknamed me 'Donkey Camp' from my father's place. This name stuck with me all the time I was at the Bungalow. Times were much better with Jock Jones. He was friendly with the kids. He didn't believe in the endless beatings. Life was more peaceful. He wasn't always trying to catch you out by ringing a bell or calling a roll. We could wander about a bit more freely. We were still always hungry and on the lookout for food. But the food got better too. We still spent a lot of unsupervised time scavenging for bush tucker and food scraps, but it wasn't as desperate. Jock Jones was still there when I left in 1935. He was replaced at the end of 1936. I heard about it when I came in for the races.

The Bungalow school

With our arrival from Pine Creek the population of the Bungalow increased to more than one hundred and it kept growing. Government policy had changed. They started finding some money to give us kids in the institutions a bit of an education. They also started pulling in older Aboriginal kids of mixed descent from the cattle stations with the idea of getting them into some schooling. Not long after we arrived in 1933, the teacher at the white school in town, Nancy Taylor, was instructed to supervise the teaching at the Bungalow. Then in November 1933 Eileen Styles was employed as an assistant teacher and nurse to help the Freedmans in running some classes. Then Miss Randall became the first full-time teacher at the school. By 1935 an experienced teacher, Miss Maisie Robb, was appointed for three years to concentrate on getting better education happening at the Bungalow. After she married later on I knew her as Mrs Chettle.

I had had a bit of schooling in Pine Creek. Not much of it survived the early days at the Bungalow. Mr Freedman didn't work hard in the classroom and I spent more time outside than inside doing any work. But by the end of 1933 with Mrs Styles we were all back in the classroom copying things off the blackboard. Kids started school at seven or eight years old. Those younger than that wandered about the place with the women and senior girls.

The classroom was a stone building, part of the original Telegraph Station. It wasn't very big. It was divided into three smaller spaces for kids of different ages. They tried to teach us a bit of reading, writing and arithmetic. The large numbers of kids made it really hard.

If you misbehaved you were sent out of the classroom and punished. Some kids, like me, were almost always outside. After a while we would drift away from the school and into some other activity around the place. There were a lot of kids like me. We left the Bungalow without being able to read or write anything much more than our name. After I left the Bungalow the school was closed and Hartley Street School was built. This time the Bungalow kids were mixed in more with the white kids.

The school day started with a wake-up call at around seven o'clock in the morning. This was followed by breakfast and roll call. The teacher was brought to the Bungalow school by the local police in their buckboard ute. It was part of the coppers' job to get them to work. School would commence about ten. I can remember Mrs Randall arriving. She was very strict and it was hard work. Then there was Miss Robb. She was better. Miss Robb's family had a property called Lambina Station down near Oodnadatta. Her father had been a horse exporter to the Indian Army. Later I knew them because they bought Loves Creek Station horses from the Bloomfields. I used to help break their horses into the saddle. After I left for Loves Creek in 1935 the teachers were Miss Penry and, later still, George Bohm. The school had moved to town by this time.

Classroom punishment was standing in the dunce's corner, getting kicked out of class and the cane if you were really offside with the teacher. Lunch was at midday for an hour. School finished at about three o'clock with the police ute arriving to pick up the teacher. There was a piano in the classroom and time was spent singing songs. These were all the old-time songs. I enjoyed the singing and was pretty good at it. It was these songs that I sometimes droned to the cattle on long droving trips.

After classes finished it was free time until the dinner bell rang, usually a bit before sundown. After dinner the kids had showers every night before bedtime. Then we were herded into the dormitory and the door would be shut with a padlock. I had a fairly ordinary school career. I learnt enough later on as a drover when Splinter Prendergast taught me. After that I worked on it myself. Some of the kids were good at school and the teacher usually worked with them. The rest of us were just filling in time. You didn't go up automatically each year like today. You were expected to complete certain books to get on to the next level. Most of us just did what we couldn't get out of. Education wasn't seen by us as being a big part of our future or something that might save us from a life of hard work and low pay. I forced my own kids into going to school every day. I knew it was important by then. But I had no parents pushing me. I was dreaming of life in the long paddock where men were men, and women and children were not much part of the story. I was only ten when I left school behind.

Some of the kids did really well and stood out even with the poor schooling. They got selected and pushed ahead. The churches were a part of this. An Anglican priest, Father Smith, took a number of the local boys seen as academically talented down to Adelaide so they could continue their education. My friend Joe Croft, who had been at Kahlin and Pine Creek with me, was sent to All Souls College in Charters Towers. This was because he had no family connections in Adelaide and Father Smith had a brother at All Souls. He was able to support Joe going to the school. Joe went on to start a degree in engineering. His university was interrupted by the war and Joe joined the army. After the war, he went back and completed training to become a surveyor.

Joe Croft was a taken-away child from the Victoria River Downs area. But he came back to Alice Springs in the fifties, working and playing football with Pioneers. We shared the football field on lots of occasions. Joe was a leader of men and a good captain. He was a great player. Later on he moved to Canberra and participated in a lot of the debate on Aboriginal issues through the sixties, seventies and eighties. I caught up with him occasionally and I would see him in the news. He ended up working with the Department of Native Affairs in a senior position. He died in 1996 and I went up to Wave Hill where he was buried with ceremony as a Gurindji man back home on his tribal lands. As well as a friend he was a bit of a hero for some of us. Of the rest of the Pine Creek mob I think only Henry Peckham and Nugget Kopp might have got selected out. They were both naturals at everything, especially sports. Most of us were more outside boys. More interested in chasing the donkeys than schooling.

Donkey cowboys

There were mobs of half-wild donkeys hanging around in the hills, left over from the days they were used as cart animals for the goldfields and stations. They were wonderful fun. You had status and something to do if you had a donkey. We would chase them until we had them cornered. You would jump on and steer them with a stick, tapping them on their cheek to get them to change direction. There were no bridles or ropes. They didn't like it much and spent a fair bit of effort trying to lose us. But we had numbers and a lot of time on our hands. So we stalked them and drove them back towards the Bungalow. There was an old yard out the back and out of sight where we could pen them in. You felt like a person of substance with a donkey under you.

The kids with the donkeys were the kings outside the playground. We could trade favours for rides. We used to tie rattles of old jam tins filled with stones to the donkeys to rev them up a bit. They hated the noise and tried hard to get away from it. We could play out our cowboy fantasies to an admiring audience. At least till someone pushed you off to get their turn. It was us Pine Creek kids that had the donkey thing going. I had a passion for them, being nicknamed 'Donkey Camp' and having a father who was into breeding donkeys. So it was very important to me. We had our own donkeys, gave them names and quietened them down. They were our pets as well as our little bit of freedom.

Trouble was that the bosses didn't need the donkeys. They would let them loose from the yards in the night or go around untethering them in the hills.

The next day us boys would be in hot pursuit. We would pick up their tracks and follow them. Sometimes it involved heading into the hills out Emily Gap way. Even through the Gap onto the plains beyond. In those days traditional Aboriginal people used the Gap for cultural reasons. You might get a bit of a warning about being in the wrong place at the wrong time. But this didn't slow us down much. We were on our mission to recapture our donkeys. We would usually get a flogging when we finally turned up at the Bungalow. But we would have the donkeys back tethered around the place. They would be available for our real and imagined adventures.

Donkey chasing was one of the few times we hung around with some of the white town kids. There were not many of them but a few of the railway families had kids. The Sullivans were one large family. Bill was one of the younger ones. He has now retired back in Alice Springs after decades as a drover and station worker. I remember running around with him as a kid. Murray Neck was another.

In my sixties my donkey story continued a bit. I was involved in the Tuberculosis and Brucellosis campaign to shoot out all the wild donkeys in the hills and cattle stations of Central Australia and the Pitjantjatjara homelands. The donkeys had bred like rabbits and were eating out the country. They are still a huge problem in some areas of the Top End. But they are nearly entirely gone around the Centre. They have become a note in the pages of history. My own family's connection with donkeys is also a thing of the past. Unlike the camel, donkeys were not picked up in any wave of nostalgia. There are no hippies taking tourists on donkey walks along the riverbed around Alice Springs.

Fun and games

Sport was the other thing that brought us into contact with the town kids and the wider world. We were sports mad. We spent lots of afternoons with knock-up sticks playing endless games of hockey. It was all at a furious pace with kids everywhere. Cricket was big for a while. One year Wesley College in Melbourne sent up a school cricket team to play the locals. It was some sort of cultural exchange, probably arranged by the Methodists. God knows what they made of the Bungalow. We got a sprucing up for the occasion. And got to play with proper equipment for a change. Marbles were also very popular until all the marbles were lost. There was also a bit of football when a ball could be organised. You could see the talent.

The Bungalow years

One Christmas a couple of sets of boxing gloves were given to us by Mr Jones or Bob Hamilton. We had a boxing competition in a mock-up ring. Kids paired according to age, size and ambition. I fancied myself a bit at the time, but there was always someone to give you a flogging. Boxing was big around the country towns. Visiting troupes would turn up to take on all comers. The young men with a few grogs in them would step up to impress the girls or each other. Five pounds or more if you lasted a couple of rounds. The pros would play with them a bit before putting them away. There were even talent scouts visiting the towns looking for potential boxers.

We never went on trips anywhere at the Bungalow. Not even picnics during the holidays. There was no money for that type of thing. Good times were infrequent. But on Anzac Day the old soldiers held a big town sports day that we could enter. There were prizes of five shillings for the winners of the foot races and smaller prizes for other events. We were very eager to win such a huge amount of money. Not that we could have hung on to it I suppose. That sort of money was the stuff of dreams. Unfortunately I wasn't a great sprinter or athlete. But my mates, Joe Egan and Nugget Kopp, were very competitive and won a few events. Jock Jones even arranged for Nugget to go south for athletics training. He was good enough to be professional, even running in the Stawell Gift. But he got homesick and came back to marry one of the Palmer girls. She was a sister to my own wife though he was married a long time before me.

Another event was the race meetings held twice a year in August and around Christmas at the racetrack north of town. It was a short walk west of the Bungalow on the other side of the main road. A lot of the stations would set up camp in the creekbed between the track and the Bungalow. The Aboriginal stockmen were often family for some residents. Some of the young ones had even spent time at the Bungalow. Food scraps and handouts could be cadged from them or scavenged. We spent a lot of time hanging around these camps and the racetrack during the meetings, particularly on the last day when the Aboriginal stockmen got to race. They were my heroes. Real life cowboys like in the movies. I would hang about even if it meant a flogging when we got back late for roll call.

We saw movies very occasionally at the new Capitol theatre. Cowboy movies mostly, Roy Rogers and Tom Mix. Like all kids we wanted to be the good guys, wearing the big white ten-gallon hats. In real life we were more like the Native Americans. It wasn't a time when the Indians got to tell their side of the story. They were the savages, treacherous and sly. We only learnt something of the real Indian story much later on.

1938 Children from the Bungalow visit our race-camp close to the original Alice waterhole. The lad above with the checked shirt is Alec Kruger. The lower left, also in a checked shirt, is Walter Doolan photo courtesy Roy McFadyen

Around the playgrounds I was the cowboy on the donkey saving the day. We had our country music too, full of lonesome cowboys. Strong men with hearts of gold, doing it tough for the family. They were good days when we got to go and see a show, sitting at the front so we didn't dirty the seats for the good white folk. We didn't get Jaffas to roll down the aisles either. But it was mesmerising seeing the cowboy stories on the big screen.

Church

The churches came to Alice Springs with the railway. By the time we arrived from Pine Creek they were getting busy saving souls. Their role increased once Mr Freedman was arrested. Us kids were deemed Catholic, Anglican or Methodist depending on what records had been kept. Mostly it was on names or personal choice. Sometimes we vaguely knew. I was sent to the Anglicans.

The Anglicans, Catholics, Methodists and even a few visiting ministers came out of a Sunday for religious services and Sunday School. My priest was the Rev. P. McDonald Smith who started working with the Bungalow kids in November 1933. Later there was Father Leslie. I was an altar boy at various times at the Bungalow. There was lots to do as an altar boy in those days. We were ringing the bells, responding to the priest's words and getting up and down with the priests. We were put into training with only a few of us succeeding in getting the job up at the altar. I was good at getting jobs, even in those days. I liked the religious talk. Must have got it from my mother. I suspect I would have made a good preacher man if things had worked out differently.

Other religious people visiting the Bungalow included old Stan Griffiths, the Methodist preacher and Father Maloney for the Catholics. I remember them all as good men who treated us kids well. Having people take an interest in what was happening to us kids certainly helped a lot.

Catching up with my father and brother

My father and brother George caught up with me once at the Bungalow. They had come through Alice Springs with a mob of cattle headed south in the winter of 1934. On their way back they stopped for a week at Basso's Farm to freshen the horses and get ready for the trip back. Basso's Farm was quite close to the Bungalow. With some of my mates, I was able escape and spend some time with them between roll calls. I had a family at last. This is the first time I can remember meeting George. He was a full-grown man and kindly to us all. Dad looked much the same, behind his stockman's clothes and boots. He still had his smile and found treats for us. I loved having these big men as my family. But it couldn't last long. I knew I wouldn't be heading off with them. Perhaps later when I had got an education, was what my father seemed to suggest. Running away with them might have been possible. But my father didn't mention it and nor did anyone else. He shook my hand when they left saying he would be back for me. But it would be the last time I saw my father.

Except for this time, I didn't think of running away from the Bungalow any more than at Pine Creek. Where would I go? I was even further from home than before. And even local families didn't take their own kids back. They didn't have anywhere to hide and it would get everyone into too much humbug. For the Pine Creek mob, leaving the Bungalow and hiding from police was not a choice. We talked about it and even occasionally made a bit of a start. Especially in the first months when Mr Freedman was acting so strange. But the Coniston Massacre talk scared us. If the cops didn't get us, wild blackfellows would. We stayed at home at night behind locked doors. Running away was only a dream.

The line-up

In early 1935 Tim Shaw, Harold Thomas and other older teenagers of mixed descent were brought into the Bungalow. They already had years of experience as stockmen on Brunette Downs, having spent all their lives in the Aboriginal camps. To me and the other boys they appeared full-grown men with beards. But they were only teenagers. They were part of the government's new scheme that was supposed to teach older boys some trade skills. For all of them that meant teaching them to read and write.

The Bungalow staff were worried at having older teenagers living at the place. They were concerned about the teenage girls forming relationships with them and becoming pregnant. There was a culture of Aboriginal girls getting married early and of them being exploited for sex at very young ages. Previously some girls had been placed at young ages in outside employment. But I can't recall this happening at my time in the Bungalow. The girls grew into young women working around the institution. Now they had these displaced Aboriginal men within their walls. The day-to-day routines allowed only a little time and opportunity for relationships to build between residents. But that was seen as enough. So the staff were keen to get the older boys on their way back into employment.

In 1934 new gold discoveries saw the population of Tennant Creek take off. Four of my mates were sent up to Tennant Creek. Nugget Blackmore was one of them. Harry Bennett was another. Some of the boys even went as domestics. Tennant wasn't seen as a safe place to send young women. I suspect the boys weren't very safe either, but that wasn't thought about much in those days.

The workers on contract, like Nugget and Harry, and later me, were supposed to be paid under a welfare-administered trust system until they were at least eighteen. After that you could apply to be given some of your earnings back. At any time if the bosses didn't need you any more you would be taken back to the Bungalow and reallocated to another employer. If you ran away or approached another employer for work, you would be taken by the police back to your original employer or to the Bungalow.

Potential employers were allowed to pick kids from a line-up at the Bungalow, which had become a sort of unofficial labour exchange. If they didn't like the look of you or thought you were too scrawny you would be passed over. In 1935, when I was ten, I was picked out of the line with Tim

Shaw by the Bloomfields for Loves Creek Station. I was proud at the time and wanted to be picked. At the same time Henry Thomas and Joker Pearce were picked by Ted Hayes for Undoolya Station.

The contract was between the Aboriginal Protectorate and the employer. The housing and welfare for the worker were supposed to be assessed and monitored. There were supposed to be minimum conditions for clothes, accommodation, food and the like. The reality was different. There was nobody to do any follow up and the station owners and other employers were powerful men.

They told me that money would be paid into a trust fund for me. I was to be able to collect it when I was eighteen. It never happened. No one ever found a contract. There was no money paid into any fund. No one went out to check on anything. Most slaves had it better than I got at Loves Creek. The next year, 1936, the Aboriginal Protector for the Northern Territory, Doctor Cook, put an end to placing boys under fourteen into employment. But I had already disappeared from the system and no one came to rescue me.

I was an exception all the time at Loves Creek. The Bloomfields were experts at exploiting Government systems. They even did it to their neighbours. Basically. once at Loves Creek you were treated by the Bloomfields like all the other Aboriginal workers, and given no more money than they thought they could get away with. In lots of ways you were treated worse. I was kept away as much as possible from building up any relationships with the local mob. It was only when a white bloke, Roy McFadyen, came later on that I got the idea that escaping was possible, that not everyone got treated like I did out at Loves Creek.

Cowboy dreaming

I was scared but pleased to get picked out of the line and to be heading off into an adult world. I had seen movies and played cowboys and Indians. I had this picture of myself riding around, the king of all I surveyed. On a big stallion, hat held high in the air, as I gave a little wave. The adoring crowds cheering me on my way. The 'lone ranger' of the Territory. It was a beautiful thing. In my world men on horses were the kings of the open country, and got to play the big parts. My father and brother were horsemen. I wanted my share of the cowboy dreaming. I was a champion with the donkeys. The little kids looked up to cowboys.

There was a shortage of stockmen. It had been a decade of reasonably good rains. Prices were on the way up and the stations were heavily stocked.

With the depression years at an end, people in the cities had money for meat. But on the cattle stations the supply of unemployed swagmen who had filled the jobs was drying up. Most had gone back to the cities. So the cattlemen were asking the Government and the Bungalow bosses if they had any workers wanting to head out into the world of the cattle stations.

The Bungalow was overcrowded with nowhere to house the older, often initiated and sexually active, teenage men. The schoolteachers couldn't do much with them given the huge numbers of younger kids already in the classrooms. So the bosses decided to put them on contracts and send them back out into the world. Unfortunately working for Louis Bloomfield and his son Harry was not like in the movies. Being sent out to a station worked out okay for lots of kids, but not really for me.

I still question how it could have happened. There are few answers. My group that had come down from Pine Creek were all of that age where the government was wondering what to do with us next. The older ones were already leaving for new places. I saw a lot of them go. Some went back to family. Others went directly into jobs. None of those that left came back. No one was there to say to me, 'Why not wait for a few years till you're bigger?' Watching my friends head off was very hard. They were the only family I had really known. So I wanted something to happen for me. What was I going to get out of a few extra years at the Bungalow and school?

It seems to me that they could have sent me back to the Top End to be grown up by family. My father was still alive then. But perhaps they had entirely lost me in the system. There were a lot of us kids taken into the institutions as babies. Not many of us carried any history with us. The Aboriginal Protection Board administrators lasted mostly a couple of years before heading elsewhere. The system ran on a lot of neglect and convenient thinking. Files were vague and incomplete. My lawyers and the entire High Court system didn't come up with much information on how decisions about me had been made. I only have my own childhood memories and those stories I have managed to keep alive.

I don't know how I ended up going away, but it seemed like a good idea to me at the time. I just can't see how it would have seemed like a good idea to any of the adults about the place. People must have known the Bloomfields. Had some idea about how they liked to save a few dollars. I didn't have a clue. I doubt I could have said no anyway.

Whatever was said or promised, the facts were that when Harry Bloomfield, from Loves Creek Station, and his brother-in-law, Ted Hayes, from Mt Undoolya Station, were looking for workers for the 1935 cattle muster, they came to the Bungalow. A few of us were rounded up and paraded in front of them. I was younger than they usually allowed us kids out into employment. But I was a solid fellow who could pass as older than I was. I puffed out my chest and was pleased to be picked. I was restless in the Bungalow. It was my eighth year in institutional care and I was well and truly over being bossed about.

They sent me as company for Tim Shaw. We didn't really know each other. Institutions are like that. You would think Tim's own country up in the Barkly might have been an option if it was stockwork that was going to happen. He could have linked back in to family and friends. Instead he faced being a newcomer with little language and no connections on Loves Creek.

Taking leave from the Bungalow wasn't a drawn-out affair. No tearful goodbyes with the Pine Creek mob after all those years. Just a 'see you later' as me, Joker, Tim and Harold packed our meagre belongings. A few mates were sorry to see me go. The other kids would have scrambled to take over our beds and anything we left. Harry Bloomfield and Ted Hayes wanted to be off straightaway. We left with not much more than the clothes we had on. No boots, hats, blankets or change of clothes. These were supposed to be provided by our new employers. So after a brief consultation with the management, Harry and Ted were off. They picked up their wives from their houses in town and we hit the road. Harry's wife, Mary, sat with him in the front. Tim and I crouched on the tray of his truck. We followed the tracks of Ted Hayes' vehicle. Off we went east in a puff of dust along the old Undoolya road. It was the last time I saw many of the kids from the Bungalow for a long time. Some that I had lived with for years I never saw again.

The first stop for us was about twenty kilometres east of Alice Springs at Undoolya Station. Ted was married to Jeanie Bloomfield, Harry's sister. Harry had married Ted's sister, Mary Hayes. Hillbilly stuff. But who else was there to marry after all? It was my first time at Undoolya Station or anywhere much outside Alice Springs. Undoolya Station had a large Aboriginal camp of maybe fifty people. They were mostly local families that had lived around the place forever. The Hayes were not bad bosses. Not as hard as the Bloomfields. Nor was the station as isolated.

Like me, it was Joker's first time out of the Bungalow. He was an older boy of thirteen or fourteen, with family from the Alice Springs area. A big and solid boy too. We hadn't been close at the Bungalow. Us younger Pine Creek boys stayed pretty much to ourselves. I saw little of him after I left Loves Creek. He had a better time of it at Undoolya than I had at Loves Creek. Joker never left Central Australia but continued as a stockman at Undoolya when I joined the army in 1942. Like many a Bungalow boy, Joker stayed single all his life. As an Aboriginal stockman from an institution, you were set up to struggle to build your own family. You were an outsider from the white and black communities. The stockwork kept you out of most social scenes. You never really had a place to call home. Never enough money to feel you could settle down with a wife and kids.

Harold Thomas didn't go into the army either. But he gave up stockwork in the 1950s. He ended up working with Tom Coles, Nugget Kopp and others for the Department of Works driving around with the stock route bore maintenance crew. Harold was a fellow who did marry and have a family. His wife was Joker's sister, Sportie Pearce. They had a mob of kids. Later on, Harold lost his right arm driving with his elbow resting on the window. A cattle truck took it off when he drove past it on an old corrugated country road. The truck driver probably never even knew he had been hurt. Harold is still alive and living in a Housing Commission flat in Alice Springs with his big mob of children, grandchildren, and even great-grandkids.

Loves Creek Station

We didn't stop long at Undoolya. Harold and Joker were sent off to work out their living arrangements. Harry and Mary said their hellos and goodbyes and we continued on to Loves Creek, another fifty-odd kilometres east. The old Undoolya Road travelled into the Eastern MacDonnell Ranges through Mt Undoolya Gap and then across land belonging to the Garden Station. We finally entered the Loves Creek pastoral lease. From there it was a further kilometre or so to the old homestead.

It was getting on a bit when we arrived. Tim and I were told to set up camp under a bough shelter near the homestead. The old boss, Louis Bloomfield, looked us over. Mr Wallace, his head stockman, was about and said a few words to Tim. There were a couple of girls working at the house who checked us out. But Louis Bloomfield wanted us newcomers separated from his local Aboriginal stockmen and their families who were camped further down the creekbed. Unlike Undoolya, Loves Creek had only a few Aboriginal families camped on the station. The Bloomfields liked it that way.

Our bough shelter was a rough affair. Tim had been expecting it to be ordinary but it was a real disappointment for me. The Bloomfields just headed off to the homestead leaving us to sort things out. They left some rations and pots. There was no building, just a rough roof that the wind blew through. It was never going to keep much of the rain off. There was no floor or furniture, except for two bedframes. These had been made by tying two solid gum branches together in an X-shape to form the two ends. Two planks were tied with plaited greenhide to the top of the Xs and framed them up as a rectangle of sorts. An old canvas cover was stretched over the sides to stop the frame collapsing and to keep the fragile camp bed off the ground. We had been given a couple of thin old blankets. It was the start of winter and getting cold. We worked out later that saddlecloths from the shed were good to supplement our blankets on cold nights. But you had to remember to put them back early and not get caught. Else you would get a growling or worse.

I was more than a bit nervous and distraught by this stage. It was strange new country for me. The whole day had been a test. The beds were pretty useless. We ended up sleeping huddled between two small fires that Tim made and that we kept going through the night. I was lucky to have Tim for company at the start. He could tell me what to do. But it was new country for him too. My first night outside the institutions was a tough one. I was to have many more hard nights before escaping into the army seven years later.

The next morning the cows and the galahs woke us up. It was a cold wintry dawn with dappled sunlight coming through the gum trees. It takes a while for the sun to get above the mountains that are the backdrop for N'Dhala Gorge. We hadn't slept much and I was a bit fragile. The house girls brought us some tea, sugar, damper and jam. Tim boiled a mug of hot sweet black tea from the billy. Mr Bloomfield Senior could be seen striding into the shed. The Aboriginal camp came slowly to life and Bruce Wallace turned up to introduce himself. Then Louis Bloomfield gave us a job preparing horseshoes. It was just before the cattle muster was to start. Tim was to work with the stockmen. I was an extra mouth to feed. But Louis promised to keep me busy.

The area around the sheds and yards was men's space. The Aboriginal blokes were lively enough with plenty of joking around nearly always in language, especially if the Bloomfields weren't about. Everyone else seemed to know what they were doing. I just kept moving and trying not to get in anyone's way. It was a scary day with plenty of people coming to check us over. They were friendly enough but not speaking much English. There were a few kids about as well, laughing and playing. But I wasn't going to get to play around with them much.

Loves Creek homestead had grown slowly from its early rough beginnings in the 1880s. It had a good spring providing plenty of sweet water to the house. But the station itself had been so marginal that it had been abandoned a few times when the market or season was bad. The Wallis family had originally taken the lease. They had sold it on to Louis and his wife, Lillian, in 1913. It was too far from markets and too difficult to keep stock numbers up. Even when they took to running their stock on to neighbouring stations. The hard early years at Loves Creek had taught the Bloomfields to be tight with their money.

Louis was nearing seventy by this time. He was old-fashioned and didn't believe in wasting money on improvements for staff. He had lived as a young man in the 1880s on Henbury Station, a hundred kilometres south and west of Alice Springs.

Louis had shared management responsibilities with another young fellow called Allan Braeden. They seem to have shared just about everything including the young Aboriginal house girls. Louis had at least two children while at Henbury – Baden and Susie. Baden's mother was a mixed descent woman called Jessie whose father was thought to be Walter Parke, the original owner-manager who set up Henbury Station. As well as Baden, Jessie had a son, William, and two daughters, Eileen and Elvira, from her Aboriginal husband. After that she had another son, Johnson, whose father was Allan Braeden. Louis's daughter Susie was sent south as a young girl to get an education. Another house girl called Leisha was Susie's mother. Leisha had another child, Sarah, with Allan Braeden and four other children with her Aboriginal husband. It was all happy blended families down at Henbury. A fairly relaxed station that never made a lot of money.

The domestic scene at Henbury was repeated throughout much of remote northern Australia. The white bosses got to pick sleeping partners from the often very young Aboriginal girls living and working around the place. The boys weren't always safe either. There were lots of white stockmen who saw opportunistic sex with Aboriginal people as part of their wage package. Consent wasn't required. In 'the good old days' the rape of young Aboriginal staff by some white men was blamed on the promiscuity of the whole Aboriginal community and culture. The girls might have been promised wife to a local Aboriginal bloke. But that didn't stop many of the white bosses. The Aboriginal men had to wait until the white bosses had finished. Often this included having to look after any mixed descent kids that came along as a result. If you didn't accept the rules around the rights of whites to your women and children you would get a reputation as a cheeky fellow. You could be sent away or 'disappeared'.

From all accounts, Louis was a more easygoing bloke in those Henbury days. His son Baden would have been nearing forty when I met him at Loves Creek. He was born a long time before Louis had even met his wife, Lillian Kunoth. In fact Lillian and Baden were not that different in ages. Baden, like many other sons of the better station bosses, was kept close and trained as a stockman. Like others he rose to get the job of head stockman, and even went on to own Indiana Station.

Lillian Kunoth's parents had owned Utopia Station up the Sandover Road north-east of Alice Springs. She was a teenage bride. There are lots of sayings about old men having difficulties when they marry young wives. In Louis's case, he gave a lot of ground around the house to his more determined wife. Lillian was a bit of a tartar. She thought that Aboriginal people needed to be taught to be busy and industrious. I suspect Louis occasionally longed for the easygoing friendliness of Henbury. But he must have swallowed and got on with his life. When Lillian was in her moods he left the house for his gardens, saddlery or to visit his precious racehorses.

Louis was an early pioneer in the Centre. In those days, many of the station owners, their managers and the permanent white stockmen had long-term relationships and children with their Aboriginal staff, especially if they were single men. It was widely known but not spoken about within proper society. The children of these relationships were often recognised and looked after by their fathers, especially if their father didn't go on to marry a white woman. If you married, the wife and extended family were usually more reluctant to accept your earlier mixed descent children. Inheritance and other issues came into play. But mostly it was the racism of the times.

Baden was lucky enough to have been born before the institutions were set up. So while I was dragged off from the age of three, Baden had been allowed to run free with his mother and family at Henbury, recognised by and being around his family. He grew up to become a great stockman. As a young man he had made his own way, working hard across a lot of the local stations. He prospered by selling horses and doing contract-mustering work. But because he was Aboriginal he increasingly struggled to get respect or even invites into the houses within the small racist white community of Central Australia. Despite his business success he still came across to Loves Creek when his father needed a hand. He stabled his horses in the paddocks during the off-season and did a lot of his horse-trading operations from there.

Harry was Louis and Lillian's only son and in his early thirties. He was more like his mother than old Louis in lots of ways. But he occasionally had flashes of being there and caring for people. He looked up to and got on with Baden. But he was a racist like his mother and tight with his money. Not generous with his praise or friendly with the Aboriginal staff. He thought nothing of eating well and looking after himself when his stockmen were eating maggoty meat and living hard. He was never going to share what he thought of as his inheritance as a white man. He always thought of Loves Creek as his. You would never get an invite to the meal table from any of them. He had married a young wife. That relationship was always a struggle. He was a lonely, sad man in lots of ways.

In 1935 the place remained pretty rustic. In the early days the station had been financially borderline. This was especially after the market for horses had fallen over in the early 1920s. Up till then Louis had been making most of his money breeding and selling good quality riding horses as remounts for the Indian Army. But with the spread of trucks as a means of transport, horses weren't required any more. This was followed by the drought of the mid-1920s. Things hadn't picked up until the railway came to Alice in 1929, making it much cheaper and more reliable getting cattle to southern markets. And there was good money in cattle. But the older Bloomfields weren't exactly reinvesting in the cattle side of the station. Instead they bought a place in town and enjoyed the company of the other try-hard newly rich pastoralists. Building up the cattle stock was largely Harry's idea.

Loves Creek homestead 1939. Lower left is all that remains of the original, this housed Mr and Mrs Bloomfield (senior). The next house is that of Harry and Mary Bloomfield, today, Ross River Homestead photo courtesy Roy McFadyen

Around the house there was an extensive garden worked a bit by Louis, Lillian and by the female domestic staff. Cabbages, tomatoes, watermelons, rockmelons and other vegetables were grown in season. Not that any of it hit any table anywhere except in the main house. Meat and damper were the food of the Aboriginal stockmen and their families. When not working the garden Louis was often in the saddlery making his own rough saddles. He wasn't one to waste money buying good riding saddles for his stockmen when the old ones could be dodgied up for another season.

The station lease covered some fairly rugged mountainous areas with the homestead perched at the western edge. It had some small river-flat paddocks nearby. These were kept for the Bloomfield racehorses, a few milking cows, old cattle for eating and the usual herd of goats for milk and meat.

Much of the working part of the station was serviced from two outstations. One was called Atnarpa, fifty kilometres further north-east past the goldmines of Arltunga. The other outstation was down on the Hale River in the south-east at a place called Limbla. The cattle grazed around waterholes dotting the beautiful riverbed between these two outstations. Loves Creek ran some eighty

Cowboy dreaming

kilometres from above Ruby Gorge down to where the Hale became a series of swamps on the edge of the Simpson Desert.

The start of the muster was a busy enough time. Too busy for anyone to show me what to do. So I got on with what I was vaguely told. Tim was able to help me out a bit when I was at a loose end. At nights we could talk a bit more freely. He was happy to be out of the Bungalow, but Loves Creek wasn't a very easy place. He must have missed his home and family at Brunette, even worse for seeing the local Arrernte families about the place. But there was no going home for him either.

We never did use the beds. It was warmer sleeping between two fires, as near to on top of them as you could get. I slept better after a while. But I remained emotionally and physically exhausted from getting used to the place and the work. They had me fixing up the fencing to keep me busy and out of the way. That first year I wasn't going out on the stock camp with the horsemen. Louis Bloomfield was to have me helping him out, well behind the action.

Beginning a muster, a small mob watering at Eemaritta (Amarata) waterhole on the Hale River 1938 photo courtesy Roy McFadyen

Toughening up

It was the night-times that would weaken me. The evening meal was stew served up at the kitchen, delivered by the house girls and eaten around our small fire. After washing and taking back the pannikin, I would lie back in my thin blankets and fall fast asleep. Tim must have found me poor company. The house was soon enough silent. As I drifted off I could hear the far-off noises from the Aboriginal camp – dogs fighting, small kids playing, and the occasional chanting and dancing of the community.

But I would wake up well before dawn. It might be because of the cold. Maybe Tim had been building up the fire again before slumping back to sleep wrapped up in the few blankets that made up our swags. Possibly there might have been a dingo howling, an animal noise in the distance or the movement of night birds. Once awake it was hard to get back to sleep. You would know that you had the long cold hours to get through before the dawn. Before a weak winter sun might warm your bones again. These were the loneliest times when you thought of your mates and how far away you were from anything you knew. I hated Loves Creek and struggled with the lack of warmth in everything that was happening. I would feel the tears well up behind closed eyelids. But there was never anything I could do about anything. It was my ongoing initiation into an adult world. You had to swallow your sadness, get up every morning and get on with whatever was happening. That was how I had to survive.

You couldn't imagine a bigger contrast than between Loves Creek and the Bungalow. It was so quiet. No kids in their hundreds spilling out everywhere. No games of hockey or running in a pack to find the donkeys. No hundred boys snuggling up and drifting towards sleep. It shocked me how alone we were. I was sometimes terrified. It was worse than if Mr Freedman was coming at us. It got so that I would hardly talk for days on end. It would get worse but I couldn't imagine that at the time.

If someone had asked me then whether I would like to go back to the Bungalow I suspect I would have burst into tears and been gone in a flash. But it didn't happen. I got a bit more used to keeping quiet after a while, knowing my place at the bottom of every pecking order that was in operation. The Bloomfields were so distant and dismissive, especially the women. It was like you were one of the dogs about the place. I only heard from them if they had a job or if I was in trouble. The house girls were my usual contact point. They were friendly enough. But we would get into serious trouble from Mrs Bloomfield if we so much as looked too long at each other. Let alone speak more than a few passing words.

The Eastern Arrernte language was a mystery to me, so I was left out of the Aboriginal conversations. I was just an uninitiated stranger. A boy without a relationship to any of the families. Gradually they fitted me in but only on the edges. I got given a skinname. They taught me something of their language and culture. But in the early days I could have disappeared and not many would have remembered me even being there.

Over the next few months I got to know the Loves Creek personalities a bit more. The Aboriginal camp was straight downriver about three hundred metres away. There were about twenty people living there. The senior Aboriginal family was Bruce and Eliza Wallace. Bruce was of mixed Aboriginal descent and born at Loves Creek. He must have been in his forties when I arrived in 1935. He was six foot tall and solid. Having injured himself he was not doing a lot of stockwork any more, but was put in charge of building projects and maintenance work. He looked after the yards and wells around the station. He did most of the negotiating with the Bloomfields if something was happening.

His wife, Eliza, was the daughter of 'Line Party' Bob, a leading stockman from neighbouring Undoolya. I met 'Line Party' Bob later on. He was an older Eaglehawk gentleman and still a respected stockman into his sixties and seventies. Dick Eritja was another of the older Eaglehawk men from Undoolya. Eliza was a lovely woman, light-framed, gentle and motherly. She took me a bit under her wing. But the Bloomfields kept me and Tim separate from the locals as much as they could. I was there to work, not to be mothered within the Wallace family.

The Wallaces had two daughters, Peggy and Kathy. Peggy was the older. Kathy was about my age. Peggy worked as a housemaid with Joan Jones, and had been one of the Aboriginal faces I had seen at the homestead on arrival. The house girls were restricted from going down to the Aboriginal camp. Like me, they were being taught how to live like the white fellas. Not that we were ever going to be allowed in. Peggy might visit her mother after work but had to sleep at the homestead – Lillian Bloomfield's rules.

Joan Jones was about the same age as Peggy and a few years older than me. She was originally from Tennant Creek way and had come through the Bungalow. I think it was her sister Nancy Jones who later married George Bray. George was running the well at the Harts Range Store. Another Aboriginal girl, Nelly Gardiner, arrived later at Loves Creek and worked in the Bloomfield house. There were also Cathy Kerrin, or perhaps her name was Clarke, and Topsy Tucker working as house girls at the main homestead over the years I was out there.

As well as two daughters, Bruce and Eliza Wallace had three sons. Albert was the oldest and about Tim's age. His brother Jack or 'Winch' Wallace was a bit younger, in his mid-teens. They were busy organising to go on the muster when we arrived. Donald was the baby of the family, some years younger than me. He and Kathy were still hanging around with their mother at the camp.

Jim Doolan, or 'Goggle-eyed' Jim Woritnja, as he was called, was also living in the camp. He was a slender bloke perhaps in his forties, married to a younger pretty woman called Molly. Jim Doolan had been a police tracker at Finke. They had only just arrived, having come up to Atnarpa with the last big Aboriginal men's ceremonial journey called an Urimbula, that had started earlier in the year. This ceremony was written about and recorded by the anthropologist, Ted Strehlow, in his book on the Arrernte tribes. Goggle-eyed Jim got work at the main Loves Creek homestead after the ceremony finished.

After the muster finished the Doolan family worked during the dry times pulling water from soaks down Limbla way. Jim seemed to cope with the isolation better than most. He was a quiet bloke who went his own way. Over time I found him a bit short-tempered around people, particularly where his wife was concerned. He tended to be very jealous of anyone hanging around.

Molly Doolan was perhaps ten or more years younger than Jim. She kept to herself. This wasn't so hard to do. The Loves Creek Aboriginal community was quite traditional. There was a strict observance of avoidance relationships where certain people had to keep away from people who had particular relationships to them. The couple had two sons, Walter and Paddy Doolan. Walter was a bit older than me. He was one of the younger blokes off on the muster. I spent a bit of time aspiring to be as good a rider and cattleman as Walter. It took me a good few years to be confident on a horse. I didn't end up getting much of a chance to learn. Walter stayed on at Loves Creek Station when I headed off to join the army. Paddy hardly did stockwork during the time I was at Loves Creek. He was only a young kid when I arrived.

Bill Wibblidge and his wife Louisa were other residents. They had kids too, grown up and working around the place. Bill was a good bloke in his late thirties or forties. He had been born around Loves Creek or the neighbouring place of Little Well. He was of full Aboriginal descent with two daughters, Kitty and Lena. Kitty grew into a tall, solid, good-looking woman who later married Walter Doolan.

Other residents included Drover Jim and an older bloke, Fred Alchilpa. Drover Jim, who had connections with the Harts Range mob, was a good stockman and lived around the homestead. Fred, in his fifties or sixties, was camped away from the main camp, further out from the homestead. He had two hundred or more goats that he shepherded. Of a night he mostly camped at Shannon's Well, south of Loves Creek homestead before Salt Well. Other times he lived closer in at what was called Camp Blackfellow. His goats were the staple meat for the Aboriginal stockmen. You didn't slaughter the old cattle unless you were going to salt away a lot of meat, or had a big occasion happening. Fred's goats could also be milked every day.

The older people coming in from the outstations included Tim Kolbarinja. He was mainly based at Limbla, well east of the homestead. His country included Little Well and Agulpura. Tjeria, who I knew as Jerry, was from out that way too. Jack Rara and Kauta, who were boss men for the tribe and rainmakers, were mostly out near Limbla. There was also Nelson who got his name from having one eye like Lord Nelson. He too was mainly based near Limbla.

Out at Atnarpa were Atnarpa Dick and Peter Ulyerre with his wife, Maggie. A few other individuals would come and go for a short time. But the Bloomfields wouldn't usually ration them since the changes to the government policy of subsidising Aboriginal food on the pastoral leases. Mr Bloomfield would keep an eye on who was about and move them on. People could only stay a couple of days.

Around the homestead were some short-horned Hereford milkers. The house girls milked them when the cows had a calf. You would pen the calves up at night and milk in the morning if the season was good. In bad seasons you didn't milk. Otherwise the calves would suffer too much and you wouldn't get much milk anyway. They had some milkers when me and Tim arrived. It was these calves and their mothers that had woken us the first morning. Fairly early on I got the job of penning up the calves at night and rounding up the cows in the morning getting them into the bails. The girls did the milking. The bucket would go to the creamery for separating. Mrs Bloomfield would supervise. They would take off the cream and butterfat to make butter for the homestead table. We didn't get any of it.

Louis Bloomfield was not really much of a cattleman. He preferred his racehorses first and other horses second. Cattle came a distant third. If he could have continued making money breeding horses he would have never got into cows at all. But cattle were where the solid money was.

Around the homestead Louis had stables for his many racehorses. These were kept separate from the working horses. Most of the stock horses were grazed some fifty kilometres away in the flats called Paddy's Plains, north-east of the homestead towards the Arltunga goldfields. He also had a team of Clydesdale horses in paddocks close to the homestead. These were used for pulling work-drays around to build and repair yards. They were also used to scoop out soakages and waterholes that became blocked with sand. You could make new soakages with these horses. He also had some camels trained to pull a cart that he used during the muster. It became my job to be with Louis during the muster, plodding along in his camel-drawn cart a day or so behind the main party and pushing along the cattle that had been separated off to go to market.

I was told by Louis not to speak with the Aboriginal workers at the main homestead. They had their work to be doing. I was another class of station worker. He got angry if I was seen even hanging about down towards the laughter and games of the camp. Of course Tim and I were old hands at avoiding and ignoring the white bosses and their silly rules. Where possible we mixed in, slowly getting known and being given roles in the community.

An exception to the 'no talking' rule was during the muster when you were allowed conversations incidental to the work at hand. Even little jokes were okay. This didn't help me much at the start. I was expected to hang around, often alone, in an adult world of silences. Even later on, when I might get a trip in to Alice Springs, I was not allowed to visit or associate with the Aboriginal families. Us workers couldn't even visit our own mothers. Not that I had a mother in Alice, but some of the others did. The town itself had a six o'clock curfew. If you were on the streets after this you could be arrested. You also needed an exemption to associate with non-Aboriginals. Not that the Bloomfields allowed any of us much leisure time in town. It was straight back to the station after dropping off the cattle or the horses.

I didn't stay long at Loves Creek homestead. The working camp further out at Atnarpa was to become my principal place. It was only during muster season that I ended up spending any time around the old homestead. It was when we were bringing in the fat cattle bound for Alice and the markets down south.

The cattle muster

The cattle muster meant being out in the countryside many miles away from the homestead for weeks at a time. The starting point for the muster was always Atnarpa outstation. For the cattle muster there were Albert, Johnny and Sambo Williams from neighbouring Ambalindum Station, accompanying Harry Bloomfield, Walter Doolan and Tim Shaw when they headed off to round up the work horses from Paddy's Plain. Some of the young horses had been roughly broken into the saddle at the end of the previous season. Others were seasoned stock horses that had been on previous musters. They would have been running free on Paddy's Plains for six months or so.

Five horses would be collected for each man. These had to carry a man and his gear for much of the next three months. Once they were in the yards, the horses would be handled and reacquainted with the saddle. It took a bit of effort to get them back to being ridden again. They would be shod for the rough riding ahead. Hobbles would be organised. Then the muster team would head north and east to the furtherest Loves Creek' cattle mobs at Stuart's Waterhole. After that they swung south down the river to Ruby Gap, Amarata, Atnumpa, Coulthard Waterhole, through Cleary's Creek, Dead Horse Waterhole, Bronco Bore and into the eastern outstation of Limbla. Some crews would swing further south and east into the swamps called the Nunnery. Another crew might head south and west down towards Little Well. Then the whole camp would leave the Hale River behind to swing west, going through Pulya Pulya Waterhole, Gaylad, Mulga Dam and Shannon's Well back to Loves Creek homestead and then on to the railhead at Alice Springs.

Most nights of the muster there would be a bit of a meeting to plan what would happen next. Harry Bloomfield and the senior stockmen would make the decisions. Two might be sent off to go this way, another two there, and another lot somewhere else. Then other stockmen would push the 'coaches' along to different meeting spots set up at the previous night's meeting. The 'coaches' were a mob of quieter, older cows and calves that helped settle down the rest of the herd. Small mobs from different watering spots would be pushed into the main mob by the riders sent to muster the different spots.

In hindsight I would give the Bloomfields only a bare pass as cattlemen, even though Harry was much more modern in his ideas than Louis. Because the Loves Creek mobs had not been handled much by men on horses, they were very nervous of the riders. Once the riders got near a watering hole where cattle were likely to be, each group of stockmen would circle around the scrub, pushing the cattle together until they felt they had all of them bunched up close. The coaches should then be in a position ahead of you.

The idea was that the wilder younger cattle would drift into these 'coaches' and be held in a group by them. It required a lot of patience. If you moved too fast or had the 'coaches' placed badly, the small mobs might just scatter into the scrub. You then had to spend another few hours, even days, trying to regather them. When things went well the new mob would settle down themselves. Riders would then circle the mob, turning any cranky old bulls or adventurous young ones, back into the main group. The new mob was then pushed to where they could be held for a day or so. Because the Bloomfields didn't have yards it was usually a small valley edged on three sides by cliffs. You would just need to have riders to guard the end.

The crew would then get to work on the mob. To brand calves in the open requires a lot of skill. You would travel with a gate and lengths of fence. These would be set up and you would push a group of cattle through. As it passed along the fence lines, a calf would be roped and held to the gate. A stockman would grab it in a headlock and the gate was lowered to the ground. If it was a smaller animal you might just rope and wrestle it down in the open. You would lie on the animal while tying a front and rear leg together to stop the young calf from moving about. An iron brand that had been heating in the fire was then used to burn a mark in its flank. Then if it was male, a knife would be used to cut its scrotum and hook out its balls. These would be sliced off and thrown in a pile. The wound would be splashed with a tar mixture. The stockman would then jump off, untying the leg rope and the calf would be released to go back to its frantic mother. It was a noisy dangerous place with calves bellowing and cattle milling about.

The idea with a brand was to make it as difficult to erase or brand over as possible. It was before the time when calves were also earmarked for identification. In the old days cattle that were unbranded were often mustered off one property, branded and pushed onto a neighbouring station. Once branded it became very difficult to claim ownership back, even if you could follow the trail of stolen beasts from your place to the new station. The really dodgy operators tried to register brands that allowed them to alter or re-brand cattle. But this was getting more difficult as property owners became more careful to have unique and hard-to-change brands, and most of the ways of altering or erasing brands became known to the authorities. Louis's Loves Creek brand was three boomerangs meeting at 120 degrees. Harry had recently been given his own brand as part of his having his own herd. It was LTL. I'm not sure what it stood for.

Once the calves were branded you pulled out any other cleanskins in the mob. The task of roping the bigger, wilder cleanskin cattle, often dehorning them and castrating the males, was much more difficult than catching the young calves. These were beasts that had somehow managed to miss previous musters. This was why you tried to muster thoroughly each year even if you didn't send a mob to market. You didn't want to leave the cattle too long or they would become too scrubby. Neutering the males saw them fatten up and become more placid. You didn't want a mob of older muscle-bound bulls in your paddock. They caused too much trouble and often they had to be shot out if too many were about because they damaged the cows.

It was hard work to bring down a bigger animal. You aimed to isolate the animal and get it running. Then you would work it to the side of the mob before riding in to separate it from the rest of the milling cattle. Another stockman followed in case you got into difficulties. This was skilled work and you needed a good horse.

The beast was urged into a gallop and then tripped and tied up. To trip a full-grown animal required timing and technique. While they are galloping you lean down from your horse and grab their tail. When the beast twists its head to try to butt you, you have to yank the tail in the opposite direction, pulling them off stride and on to the ground. It's a bit like tripping kids up in the playground. The stockman then had to secure their front and back legs with a rope and hold them down. If you made a mistake you risked having a hole drilled into you from their horns, or the horse getting damaged. You also risked broken bones if you came off the horse wrong or got kicked. It was heavy and dangerous work even for a fully-grown man.

After the branding you would separate the full-grown castrated males, called bullocks or steers, and some older cows that seemed beyond breeding. You would select them out into a smaller mob. These would eventually be sent south to market. The bullocks were called 'fats'. That was how Louis liked his cattle being sent to the saleyards. Fat and well treated. They would be pushed along slowly as the rest of the muster crew headed for the next waterhole. In theory you also selected out any cattle with neighbouring brands. These were supposed to be returned to the station that owned them at the end of each mustering season. But the less scrupulous were known to keep a cow that had a young unbranded calf. The Bloomfields often branded and claimed the calf. They were not above hanging on to neighbouring beasts either. You couldn't sell them but if you needed a killer you only had to get rid of the skin to conceal your theft. They also weren't worried about letting a well-bred neighbouring bull hang around during the rutting season. It could only improve the bloodlines of the herd. They were even known to encourage a few across a fence line, or to create a break in the fence if necessary.

I had to stay behind at the homestead initially that first year as the stockmen rode off to Atnarpa. Tim went with them. Our bough shelter was a lonely place for me. All the women and kids were still about, but I hated being treated as one of the kids and staying behind. During the next couple of days I got to work with Old Louis. It was our job to pack up the big old dray. This had the cooking supplies, spare horseshoes and everything else needed for the next few months.

During the mustering season the diet was pretty much corned beef, tea and damper. There were never any potatoes, onions or other vegetables for the Aboriginal staff anyway. So the food supplies were pretty easy to put together. Not that Louis needed much of a hand. He had the house girls. But he liked having extras to boss about a bit. We packed and stacked. When he was happy and the muster had had time to collect up enough fats for us to tail, we headed off at a slow walk. We took the back route south and then east through N'Dhala Gorge and Tommy's Gap, skirting the northern route through the Chabbana Waterholes into Atnarpa. From there we headed east using Cleary's Creek, then pushed onto the Hale River itself. We had a team of camels to pull the dray around. It was my first look at the place. It was striking countryside of deep gorges and beautiful waterholes reflecting the deep purples, oranges and reds of dawn and dusk. Big established white gums and ironwoods towered over us. But I was too young to really take it in, being impatient to rejoin Tim and the men at the muster camp. It took four days and they were glad to see us and the supplies.

Alec Kruger (in check shirt) and Johnny, ready to snig rails and posts from Atnarpa Creek, circa 1938 photo courtesy Roy McFadyen

Louis had organised for me to be given an old quiet horse. I was taught the basics of riding during the slow times like on the walk with the camels. I was sometimes allowed to paddle about on the old sway-backed animal following behind the fats. It had less get up and go than even the Bungalow donkeys. But it took a while to get the hang of staying on, using your feet in the stirrups, and avoiding the saddle horn while steering the horse with the reins. The hardest part was getting the horse to do anything. It knew when it had a novice on its back and just stood or would take charge. At the slightest panic it would smile and make my life a misery. Eventually I got more successful. It was the start to my life on the back of a horse.

Stopping the cattle from stampeding or wandering off, particularly during the long nights without any yards to pen them in, was done by riding around them all night. The nightriders would keep a flow of songs going to reassure and settle the mob. If the mob was disturbed by dingoes or a storm you had to get to them quickly before they got too far away. The leading cattle would need to be headed and then slowly wheeled, slowed to a walk and regathered as a mob. Riding fast to wheel stampeding cattle on a dark night was very dangerous. The horse and rider could quickly part company because of low branches, uneven ground and holes. Then you had to make sure the cattle didn't run over the top of you, pulverising your body. In the morning after a stampede you would begin the process of locating and regathering any missing groups.

Other stockmen from the muster crew helped out as the mob of fats grew in size. You didn't need to push them much. Just keep them together and move slowly downriver. The muster camp itself would move on well ahead of the tailing crew. At the next watering hole the process would be repeated. This would go on until all the waterholes had been mustered and all the cattle mobs had been largely accounted for.

The Bloomfields sent 350 head of fat cattle to market each year. Once they had that number they would head the mob of fats back to the homestead and walk them into town. So Louis's and my job was to push along behind the muster crews, holding together the fats. This was known as tailing the cattle. The idea was to just keep them happy and walking roughly in the right direction until you had the quota. The rest of the place still needed to be mustered. But then all the stockmen would come back together to push the mob back towards the homestead and into town.

It usually took two to three months between May and August, depending on which areas were due to be mustered heavily. You had to ensure that all areas were mustered over a period of time or else you risked the cattle drifting on to and being mustered by neighbouring properties. There were also the occasional itinerant cattle thieves or neighbours, working to grab a mob of cleanskins. So you needed to at least get around to branding regularly. If the animals weren't required for the market the males would be counted, castrated and left in the paddocks to fatten up.

The Bloomfields didn't believe in wasting money improving the herd by buying stud bulls. Instead, they might select a couple of the more promising types during the muster and leave their balls intact. As a strategy it had limited value, because the mob would start to get inbred. That was where the neighbouring bulls were a useful resource to add to and improve the herd's gene pool.

Cowboy dreaming

At the end of the muster everyone came back and we turned the mob to Alice Springs. We headed down Goat Camp Creek south of the homestead through the gap in the ranges at Mt Undoolya and into town through St John's Valley. There the mob was pushed along Chinamen's Creek and on to the cattle trains for Adelaide.

Dropping off the mob was a time of celebration. Often it was completed in time for the August race meeting in Alice. But the Bloomfields didn't like their workers staying in town. The contract stockmen were paid up in town after the cattle were on the train. For some it meant going to Fogarty's shop and the Afghan traders down along the river. Everyone except me was on at least £4 wages. While others could stay in town, or go home to catch up with family, the Bloomfields insisted on Tim, me and a few other full-time employees leaving town the same day. We headed back to the station to work on the racehorses.

We branded and broke in new foals from the mob in the main homestead paddock. This usually happened in September. The horses were rounded up down on the flat open area called Salt Well on the other side of the Ross River past N'Dhala Gorge. From there they would be brought back to the homestead yards. Once these good quality horses were broken in to the saddle they would be given to the station workers for a while to get them used to being handled and ridden.

Generally some twenty or thirty would be sold off to the Chettles as ready-to-be-ridden horses. The Chettles had a little station called Lambina out from Marla Bore. As old customers and family friends they would get the pick of the crop. The Chettles would sell them on. They often had arrangements with other stations. Us stockmen sometimes got to ride the leftover horses that didn't show enough promise of speed. A well-bred horse is a wonderful thing. Much easier to train up and build a relationship with. Young horses that showed a turn of foot might be trained up for the Christmas race meeting in Alice Springs.

There were always some old quiet horses kept in the homestead paddock. They could be caught fairly easily and used for any daytime job about the place. In quiet times us stockmen got on with other jobs like yard building and repairs, and making green-hide hobble straps and five-strand ropes. The only proper leather used by the Bloomfields was on their precious racehorses.

Greenhide was very inferior to the real thing. But it was free and available. When a steer was killed for meat the skin was buried in the sand or placed in a tub to soak up moisture. After a couple of weeks it was taken out and the skin stretched and pegged out. Any remaining flesh was be scraped off with a bottle or wooden paddle. Later, when it was dry, the hides would be strapped into a stretching device held down with a weight at one end. A plank attached to an auger was used to stretch it even tighter. The skin would be cut into strips and then plaited together into a rope. This rope was the greenhide. Other times strips of hide might be sewn together to make inferior hobbles or rough pieces of saddlery.

The wild horse muster

Depending on the weather, it wasn't until late in the year that the mustering of the station for the semi-wild mobs of horses happened. It also depended on Baden having a buyer for the horses, and what sort of season it had been. But lots of the years when I was at Loves Creek we would have a horse muster. Horses are more challenging to catch than cattle and you need a different game plan. Baden Bloomfield would come down after finishing his work as a contract musterer on other stations. He ran the horse muster. A lot of these wild horses were Baden's anyway. Once mustered and quietened down, Baden took the horses off to the buyers, usually in Queensland.

The wild mobs of horses were across the station, along the Hale River and elsewhere. The bloodlines of these mobs came from the horses left over from Louis's good old days as a horse breeder. Baden had added to them over the years, dropping off his droving teams between seasons. Having too many wild horses was not good for the country. So the wild horse muster was a way of making some money, keeping the numbers manageable and keeping the quality of the country and the horses up. Plus Harry was keen to expand the number of cattle that the station could handle. Taking out some of the horses was one way of doing that.

The horse muster was best done after a dry spell and before the usual summer rains. It made the horses easier to locate and catch at the permanent waterholes. The horses lose condition in dry times when they have to move around for their food and water. It was hard work capturing horses, even into well-concealed trap yards. Even if they were tired and in poor condition. So a lot of planning and cunning was required. Once Baden turned up at the station he would get us organised. We would work down the station like with the cattle muster. Once the tracks of a mob of horses were located around a watering hole, Baden would scout out a place to trap and hold them for the initial culling. Usually it would be in a gorge that could be blocked off. Other times the traps were bits of fence built as a funnel placed along both sides of a usual pathway of the mob. It was necessary to build a line without an end section to get the horses used to running along a fence line. We would come back a week or so later. Another bit of fence would be added to create a yard sealed at one end. And you could quickly seal the last piece of fence after the horses had run inside.

Tim Shaw (ex-Bungalow boy) adzing timber for the Atnarpa yard 1938-39
photo courtesy Roy McFadyen

Once a mob of horses was penned up some of the older stallions might be shot. They were often too dangerous to work with. Some of the older or injured horses might also be put down. Unbranded horses would be roped and branded. The colts and younger stallions were castrated. Those that were not going to be sold like older mares with young foals would be released for another year. The selected mob would be worked a bit by the men, quietening them enough to give us some sort of chance of getting them back to the station yards at Atnarpa.

Getting them from a remote temporary yard back to the main Atnarpa stockyard was the challenge. But Baden always had a plan. He would predict where the mob would head and have riders stationed to make sure they followed the plan. He would have experienced riders pushing them out of the yards and others turning them to where he wanted them. He would have already sent other riders via a shortcut to wait for the mob to arrive at a pre-arranged spot. Baden knew every gully and track on the place. When the horses arrived at the meeting spot, tired out and with tired stockmen pushing them along, new riders would take over and push them further along until the mob was even more exhausted. This way he got them back to the Atnarpa yards. The original Atnarpa yards were too small and fragile for working mobs of horses. Even the new yards were often stretched to handle that many horses. You couldn't yard them at night without feeding them. So once they were quietened you got them used to having green-hide hobbles around their legs. This kept them from straying too far overnight and allowed you to collect a smaller mob to work in the yards.

Sometimes the buyers wanted the horses to have been broken. If this was the case each horse was worked individually. You would select a horse in the bigger yards and, using a whip, isolate it in the smaller yard. A rope would be thrown around its neck and the horse would be pulled around by the horse breaker. 'Lunging them' it was called. Choking, pulling them towards you and forcing them to face you. First one way around and then the other, talking to them all the time, reassuring them and getting them used to a human voice. Then you would get them used to being touched. You would use a saddlecloth to brush them down. You did it both sides so that you could work either side of the horse.

We did it pretty rough and quick in the early days. These days they are much more gentle and slow with the animals. A lot more talking, eye contact and reassurance. This is the 'horse whisperer' approach. It takes a lot longer and usually the horses have a bit more contact with humans than the wild mobs found at Loves Creek. We had a lot of wild horses to break in in a short time. So it was fast and brutal. When the horse got used to a man being in charge, a bridle and bit would be placed around their neck and into their mouth. A rope was used to run them around a yard. After a while saddlecloths were tied on to get them used to having things along their flanks. Finally a saddle would be tightened on, and after a while a rider would gingerly climb aboard. The gate would be opened and the horse spurred to get going. Then the rider would be off, holding on for dear life as the horse saw the open spaces and took off. The stockman would try to ride the horse out. Another rider on a quiet horse would go with them to settle the broken in horse down a bit and in case you got in trouble.

It was dangerous work for good riders. Particularly difficult was the first riding of the horse. Some would try anything to get you off. This included rolling over, rubbing you out on a tree branch and bucking. It was important to keep the horse going forward until it was tired and beaten. With the thoroughbreds it was much the same. But you were much more careful not to hurt or injure Louis's thoroughbreds. God knows you would cop it if Louis caught you being rough with his little darlings. They were more intelligent and easier to get to do things anyway.

When all the horses had been ridden once and Baden was satisfied that they could be held as a mob, he would hit the road with them, heading east and across the plains into Queensland. He had a crew that included a few of the Loves Creek stockmen. I went on one horse droving trip with Baden, but that was towards the end of my time at Loves Creek.

The races

Louis always tried to have a couple of good horses set for the Christmas races. Much of November and December was spent getting them into top condition. Baden was the main station jockey. Louis and Baden managed to win a couple of Alice Springs Cups in their time. I became Baden's offsider. After four years or so my riding was good enough for me to be doing the track work for Baden and getting a run in the Aboriginal stockmen's races on the last day of the meeting.

Loves Creek Station kept its race camp out near Emily Soak. It had a practice racetrack. Young horses would be schooled for the races there and worked up into good chances or no-hopers. Close to race days we would move with our horses into a stable along the Charles River near the Telegraph Station. You can still see the remains of the camp there.

The horses for a day's racing were taken into town in the morning and stabled at the racecourse during the day. The other local properties had camps nearby. The Undoolya Station people were relations and camped close. Then there was the Huckitta Station mob with Roy Tilmouth, Albert McMasters and others. Garden Station had Paddy Stirling, Max Strange, Tommy Madden and George Carroll. Some of these fellows were ex-residents of the Bungalow.

The mixed descent mob from all over the place used to come in for the races. Not that I knew them that well. I knew some of their kids from the Bungalow. They were getting work in town, mining or on the stations. Mick Laughton, who I was later to serve with in the army and who had also worked at Loves Creek before my time, was one who turned up for the races with his wife, Amy, and his mob of kids out of the Bungalow. There were others from Hatches Creek, including a lot of Russians and Chinese. Locals who I later got to know well, like Dick Turner, Frank Hayes and Ben Palmer, all worked at Hatches Creek. There was Policemen's Hole near Hatches Creek where the police station had been. The Wauchope and Hatches Creek mobs would come in for the Christmas races all dressed up in suits. Before the war Mick Laughton had even managed to buy a car. These were older men and had mostly been too old to be placed at the Bungalow. But their kids spent time there and it was a chance to catch up with them.

The race meetings were a social event designed for the isolated white families on the stations. There were dances and partying until late at night. It was a time for telling stories and catching up. Most of the horses were proper thoroughbreds with great pedigrees and even a fair bit of racing experience. Others might come with less experience and perhaps a dodgy past. They may be drovers' horses or maybe some of the miners had brought them in. The horses were likely to be stirred up and difficult because of the crowds. The races were strap-start events. A piece of elastic was stretched tight across the track. As a jockey you would mill around trying to keep your horse towards the front of the line. If you were too close you risked being stung by the strap on release. If you were too far back you were eating everyone's dust. When the strap was released you were off, trying to steer the animal around to the finish line.

Most races were won and lost at the start. A lot of the horses were difficult to get to line up anywhere close to the starting line, and were left well behind the field. The horses often took charge of the rider and ended up jumping a fence or two and heading off into the scrub, with or without the rider. The crowd usually enjoyed that the most. The owner or trainer would set up a search party to try to find the beast before it killed itself or someone who got in its way. I had a few rough rides like that when the horse took charge. Especially when we were schooling the young ones at Emily Soak track. Getting them to do anything you wanted was a struggle. At the track, the noise and excitement added a real unpredictable element to a race.

The race procedures were fairly formal. You were weighed in before and after the race. Jockeys sat a bit more upright, with slightly longer stirrups than they have today. But it was semi-professional and treated that way by the local stewards. The bookmakers, stables and jockeys took it seriously too. The experienced jockeys got away with a lot. Particularly with working over a young or inexperienced rider. Crowding them or giving them a bit of a touch-up – more often verbally but sometimes physically as well. If you were unlucky enough to be caught out by the stewards you could have the race taken off you and suspended for the entire meeting. But that was unusual.

The betting was very keen and the bookmakers careful about being caught out by a ring-in or rort. It was hard to get a fair price or much money on if they were suspicious. There were no photo finishes, so it paid to be well ahead on the line. The fastest horse was not always the winner. And there were plenty of people to let you know if you had got caught out and lost a race you should have won. The Bloomfields didn't like to lose.

The last day of the races was for stockhorses and Aboriginal stockriders. This is where I got my only race starts. They were very competitive races. There was always a bit of money put up for the winner. But bragging rights was the main prize. After the three days of racing it was back to Emily Soak and then back home. You got maybe ten bob spending money for the time you were at the races.

But this was much later on in my time at Loves Creek. My first race day was spent holding the horses for the others. It was exciting to be in town after the quiet of the paddock. I didn't see much of the Bungalow mob or even the other young fellows that had escaped to other stations. It was over all too quickly and I was back at the homestead. There was a dry spell that summer and there was work to be done.

Alone on the soaks

Throughout the year there were stockmen going out on patrol to check on the waterholes, soaks and bores. Not that there were many bores on Loves Creek Station, except for a windmill at the homestead. There were only three across the whole property then. Bores cost a lot of money that the Bloomfields didn't want to spend. There was a well out near Tommy's Gap. All the rest of the waterholes were along the Hale River. Looking after the water supply was the responsibility of us permanent Aboriginal staff.

Sometimes after a dry spell, a soak would stop working or the waterholes would go dry. It fell to individual stockmen or families to maintain particular soaks and watering holes for the cattle. Otherwise the cattle would all head for the places where water might still be. Then they would eat all the grass out there and start to lose condition. Cattle will only feed within a day's walk of water. So having soaks and wells going increased the area of grassland that the cattle could eat from.

The inland rivers of Central Australia are mostly dry. But there is still water moving down the rivers in the sand. A soak was a place in the river where underground water was close to the surface. It might seep, become a damp area and even a pool. Limbla was like that. It was never dry in my time. A big pool of water was always there. Most times at other places you had to dig. You had then to keep the seepage area free of sand. This involved having planks of wood available and cut to the right lengths. The process was a bit like digging a vertical mineshaft in reverse. You placed the planks into a square in a wetter sandy part of the river. Then you dug the sand out from the middle. As you dug the square bits of wood would drop. When the square dropped to ground level you placed another layer of planks down. In this way you lowered the level down into the river so that the hole filled up. Our job was to keep these soaks clear of sand, and to get the water out of the hole into the troughs so the cows could drink. Otherwise they would trample the walls of the soakage and you would spend hours digging out the sand again to keep it working.

If it was a shallow soak then lifting the water out of the hole and into the troughs involved two or three bits of wood forming a simple Y-frame used as a fulcrum. A strong stick was placed through the Y and used as a lever. At one end of the stick was a counterweight. At the other end a hook for the bucket. The bucket was lowered down into the water and filled. The counterweight helped to lift the full bucket. Then the bucket was swivelled around and the water poured into the wooden troughs.

If it was a deeper soak, almost a well, then a pulley system was used similar to the ones used for lifting dirt from vertical mineshafts. You had a windlass frame covering the mouth of the shaft. This could be turned around and locked with a peg to prevent slipping. There was a bucket and a counterweight at opposite ends of a chain. The bucket was winched down and filled as the counterweight was raised. Then the bucket was wound up as the counterweight was lowered. At the top of the shaft the bucket was emptied into the rough wooden cattle troughs.

This was usually a job for the hot months or if there had been a sustained dry period. For much of the time that I was at Loves Creek and later at Atnarpa they had quite good rain years. After a bit of rain the Hale River became a series of waterholes. It was not necessary to have the soaks working. But in dry times they were essential.

A couple of stockmen would head out to do the top part or the bottom of the Hale. They would get a message back to the station if someone was needed for a particular soak. For much of the summer stockmen would be out in solo camps keeping the water happening for the stock. Over time I had responsibility for the Arekeya, Aluwere and Bronco Wells. This meant keeping the soaks flowing and the troughs full. There were about three to four hundred cattle using these soaks during the dry times.

I could be out on my own as long as three months at a time. It depended on when or if the rains came. To do this we were given some rations of tea and flour and a group of us might head out together. You'd go with whoever had the adjacent waterholes. We didn't get any meat or even matches. You were expected to know how to keep a fire going and how to supplement your rations. But I didn't and had a terrible time of it.

It was a little after Christmas in 1935 the first time I was taken out and shown my soaks and wells. I was just eleven and trying hard to play the big man. The other fellows with me helped with getting a fire going and then I was left on my own. I was expected to stay camped there until good rain came. Today I still dread being left alone. I get terrible panic attacks where I can scarcely breathe. I blame it on the isolation of much of my work at Loves Creek.

I had no idea what to expect. My previous time on the country was as part of the muster. I had no experience of being on my own. Let alone being left in the bush next to a soak with a few rations. I didn't have a rifle or a horse. They said they would come back and get me, when it was time. I wasn't even told how to keep a fire going. It was just me and the cattle and dingos for company. No meat or real food. I was expected, as an Aborigine, to just know how to live off the land. But I had been in institutions all my life and didn't have any idea what to do. Dingoes in packs are capable of taking out a young cow. You need to give them a bit of respect. There are plenty of stories of them attacking people, particularly a person alone in the bush.

The first night, when the dingoes started howling and coming closer, I upturned a water trough and burrowed underneath. The troughs were heavy, but terror gives you surprising strength. It was a close fit. I thought of the Kaditja men creeping up to finish me off. There was no moon about and it was pitch black. I tried to sleep as best I could. And I must have dozed off at some time because when I woke the fire had gone out. I had slipped up and the fire was dead. Everybody had said, whatever you do, don't let the fire go out. Nobody had told me what to do if it did.

I was clueless about how to get a fire started again beyond trying to stick bits of grass around the warmest spot and blowing. Rubbing sticks together looks good in the movies, but I couldn't get it happening. I was taught how to do this later on. When nothing worked I had to think about living without a fire. I was in an absolute panic. But there was nowhere to go. I didn't have a clue really about how to walk back to the homestead. And I would get a hiding if I did manage to get back. The humiliation and laughter would have been worse.

Without fire I had no food. I could make a paste with the flour but not much more. I tried to catch lizards and other bush tucker but it wasn't working out too well and I was starving. My time roaming the countryside at the Bungalow helped, but there really isn't much food on offer in the bush. Not that I could find anyway. I've got better over the years, but mostly if someone's been carrying a rifle. I thought about tackling one of the cows but they wouldn't let me get close enough. They were big too and God knows what I would have killed it with. I had to hope that someone would come back to check up on me before I passed away from starving.

After a few days I was getting very sad and hungry. I worried myself out of going hunting for fear that someone would turn up and I wouldn't see them. You start to panic like that. All sorts of weird thoughts start going through your head. The cattle had to fend for themselves. I wasn't bucketing out any water from the soak. Then, I looked up and they were there. Wild people standing and signalling to me through the trees. Naked as the day they were born. None of the trappings of civilisation as I knew it. For a moment I couldn't move. Then I leapt straight up and dived into my burrow, hiding myself away as far into the hollow as I could get. Starving was one thing. Being captured by wild Aborigines was something else. I knew what a mouse felt like with a snake following him down a hole. I could hear them talking away as they got closer. I knew I was done for.

They must have seen my tracks as I had roamed about looking for goannas, rabbits and plants. They could read the country so they must have been surprised at my stupidity. They were three old traditional men and one had his wife with him. Of course they walked straight up to me under my log. They were polite about my hideaway. Smiled and built up a fire. Then started cooking. All the time talking to me, still under the trough. They had a smattering of English and I knew a bit of Arrernte. I could smell cooking damper and hot tea. What could I do? I crawled out bum first. They laughed quietly, pretending they couldn't see me. Giving me what little dignity I had left under the circumstances.

Then it all got too much and the old men started chuckling. I ended up laughing a bit too. The old woman made a fuss of me, sitting me down and peeling off a bit of the goanna roasting on the fire. She was telling off the men in language. After I had swallowed a bite, one of the men squatted down then, bum in the air, made out like he was crawling out of a hole. They all started howling with laughter again. Even the woman couldn't stop chuckling as she was telling him to stop. After a bit even I joined in. It was a great joke. This was a very funny man. A great mimic. I nearly pissed myself I was so shaken up. Scared and laughing, almost hysterical. The old woman was patting my back and eventually I stopped laughing and calmed down enough to eat a bit more. I was starving and they had a fair bit of food. Tom and Jerry were skinnamed 'brother' to me. Tim was 'brother-in-law'. These old people pretty much saved my life.

We had little language between us, but they were lovely gentle people, happy to stick around and help me out. They taught me how to set up a fire so it didn't go out quickly. How to walk around and keep a firestick alight. How to start another fire with a notched bit of wood filled with rabbit shit or grass. Then get a stick to twirl in the notch to build up heat. How to track native animals and gather bush tucker to add to my rations. The three men were 'Big Foot' Tom, Tjeria or Jerry and Tim Kolbarinja. With them was Tom's wife, Rosie. They travelled the country in traditional patterns looking after the sacred sites in the time-honoured way.

These were ceremony men and rainmakers for the area. Old Louis Bloomfield was a big believer in the rainmakers. In a dry spell he would send us out with rations to look for them. The rainmaking ceremony always worked in my time at Loves Creek.

Later, the rain came and the waterholes had a bit of water in them. I knew someone would be out quick enough to pick me up. I was very sad to see the old people go. But the stockmen appeared on horseback. And I was back at the homestead the next day.

The old people were well known around Loves Creek, but I didn't know them at the time. Perhaps old Mr Bloomfield, or more likely Bruce or Eliza Wallace had sent a message for them to check up on me? For them I must have presented as a pretty pitiful sight. A young boy alone in the bush without even a fire and obviously no idea about how to survive. Hiding under a log. Couple more days and the dingoes would have had me. These old men and women were the last caretakers and song men for that part of country and out into the Simpson Desert. Ted Strehlow, the anthropologist, interviewed them in the early 1930s. He asked them who would look after the land when they were gone. They answered there was no one living the lifestyle left. Their close relatives were on the stations.

For the rest of the time I was at Loves Creek we caught up from time to time and they taught me more bush skills, how to care for the land, the dreaming songs and all the sacred sites in the area. I became an initiated man during this time and was adopted into the tribe.

The next time I had to go out to care for the wells and soaks I at least knew what to expect. I could keep a fire going and a firestick alight when moving between soaks and camps. I could track and hunt enough to supplement my rations with goanna, rabbit or anything else that might turn up. I knew more of the local bush tucker and where to find it. I had some ability to survive alone in the bush. And I always tried to travel with matches, but if my fire went out, I knew how to get a new one started.

I was a very happy fellow to be back at Loves Creek after the rain came. No one seemed interested in how it had been for me. There was no one to talk to about how lucky I felt to be alive. About the old people who had saved me. I had survived and it was another lesson in coping with my new world. It was a silent world of men. You didn't want to appear as a talkative girl, someone not tough enough in a crisis. Real men got gored by bulls, chucked off horses, had terrible injuries and just got up, brushed themselves down and kept on going. It was just another potential or real tragedy in a busy life. You had a bit of a laugh if you could and pretended you weren't hurt. You could never admit to being afraid. Not even to your close mates. Luckily I had the institutional training to fit right into it. The bullyboys had never entirely got on top of me.

But it made me miss my mates. Someone to share stuff with. I was terribly lonely. Tim was older and moving away from me. He had his own friendships within the community. He had his own language and had got his head more around Eastern Arrernte. He would spend time down in the Aboriginal camp.

I made more of an effort to pick up the language and understand it. I had been banned by the Bloomfields from hanging around the camp. But after my time at the soak, I started to find myself down there at night, looking in. It helped me cope with feeling so alone. Mrs Wallace and Eileen Engulpulpul both looked out for me and seemed pleased to see me hanging around more. Even if it was on the edges. Over time I was invited closer to the fire and life of the community. I got to know the routines of the Bloomfield bosses so it was often safe enough to spend time away during the nights. I gave up trying to be the Bloomfields' best boy. I developed my sense of humour from this time. You needed to be able to make people laugh a bit. Be able to play the clown. It made you acceptable and someone people wanted to be around. Everyone felt safer if you could make a joke of what was going down. Then you would hide together as a group if you were a bit scared. It was a jokey sort of culture. You exaggerated things, pulled faces, played practical jokes, fell off horses or walked into things. It was a way of keeping emotions hidden away so they couldn't get stolen.

As I got older, tougher and hung around more with the Aboriginal mob, I learnt to copy the 'yes boss, no boss, how high did you want me to jump' approach to dealing with the Bloomfields. Kept out of the way when they were looking for a slave. It was the institution all over again, but in a much bigger paddock.

I suppose it was a bit of a turning point being alone on the soaks and meeting the old people. I felt better about being black and spending time in the bush. But I still longed for a friend that was mine. I still felt very alone and often scared out there, particularly at night. I can't understand how I got treated so badly. I look at my young grandkids and think I was their age when I was left alone at the soaks. It is unbelievable. It just wouldn't happen today.

The visit from welfare

Just as life at Loves Creek was getting a bit better, I found out I would be heading off again, this time to Atnarpa outstation with Harry Bloomfield. There had been a visit from someone from Aboriginal welfare. Like at the Bungalow when some official was visiting, you would be given new clothes and tarted up a bit for the occasion. The bough shelter got fixed up and we got some new blankets. I think the welfare fellow had come to check out how Tim was going. Maybe it was to look out for me too. It was when they were bringing in the new law about the Bungalow kids not being sent out to the stations before they were fourteen. I would have been still eleven or twelve at the time. Perhaps I could have gone back to the Bungalow if that had been decided. But it didn't happen and I never saw them again. We got to keep our clothes and blankets. But the supply of them dried up again afterwards.

How Loves Creek Station could pass even a hurried inspection makes you wonder what you would need to be like to fail. I got nothing except poor rations and a bit of pocket money if we were in town. About twice a year when we hit Alice Springs dropping off cattle or horses for the races, Louis or Harry would give me a couple of bob. Sometimes they might even buy me a new shirt or trousers. I never got any boots or a hat to wear. They were very tight. Still had the first pound they ever made. There was no medical treatment. If we got thrown off a horse and busted up, the only treatment was by local nungkaris. These traditional Aboriginal healers would rub your body with goanna fat mixed with ashes from the bark of medicinal plants. This kept us going. We were ridiculously tough. Perhaps the Bloomfields would have driven us into town to see a doctor if it was life or death. But I can't recall it ever happening. Much later I needed an operation on a wonky knee to correct some old cartilage damage I got from my days riding at Loves Creek Station. The knee had to be scraped and the knee joint reset. I was told to rest up for months. It gave me plenty of time to think about the 'good old days' at Loves Creek. As I said earlier, under the Aboriginal Protectorate contract, my wages were supposed to be placed into a trust fund. As a much older teenager I got up the courage to ask the Bloomfields directly for some money. I was told to apply in town from the trust fund. When I finally did this I was told there was no record of me anywhere and no money. I was so furious that I followed others and joined the army. I still haven't got any money as compensation. No one can explain how I disappeared from the system. But nobody seems to want to own up how it might have happened either. I think the Bloomfields did a deal somewhere and made everything go away. They had a lot of Aboriginal workers that came through the Bungalow at one time or another. I don't know of anyone getting money from the trust account. But all the generation I knew in those early days have well and truly died by now. I managed to outlive them all.

Alec Kruger in the Atnarpa Creek near the goat soak 1939
photo courtesy Roy McFadyen

Growing up

By the mid-1930s Louis was an old man. I was only eleven. Even Harry Bloomfield and Mary Hayes seemed old, even though they must have been only in their early twenties. Harry had plans to build up the cattle side of the lease. Harry's wife, Mary, was inclined to get a bit romantic and sad. But it must have been hard to get romantic about being married to Harry and living out at Loves Creek

Harry wanted a place of their own away from the temptations of town. He tried hard to be there for his young wife and kids in his stubborn mean-spirited way. And he must have known that his mother would be very demanding for Mary. The outstation at Atnarpa was to be built up to

Growing up

become their new home, more in the centre of where the cattle station was being run.

Atnarpa was closer to the Hale River where the permanent water and cattle were located. But the old outstation was just a tumbledown tin shed and the yards only good enough for mustering up the horses from season to season.

It was no surprise who got the job of fixing up the place to be fit for the expanding Bloomfield dynasty. Tim and I were going to be based at the new place. Bruce Wallace was our boss, working directly with young Harry. They started making their plans and ordering in the materials. Or at least anything that they couldn't get us to dodgy up from local stuff. A young white fellow turned up from town riding in on a banged-up Indian motorbike around this time. His name was Roy McFadyen and he was perhaps eighteen. He applied for work and was given the job of helping to build Atnarpa. He was white so he was pretty much in charge. And he got closer to award wages of perhaps a pound a week, making him comparatively rich.

Roy was a stockman, who had worked a lot in the Mallee. He was also an adventurer. A nice fellow, not without a sense of humour. He was entirely different from the mean-spirited Bloomfields. He often shared his food, sometimes buying extra for us from his wages. He was a keen photographer and would get us to pose for his shots of life in the bush. He was supposed to be travelling around Australia, but ended up sticking around for a few years. He seemed to enjoy spending time with us and treated us as people capable of having an opinion. Eventually he quit because of 'the harsh conditions and the treatment of the Aboriginal workers'. He went on to join the Air Force, still taking his pictures. My only photos of my time at Loves Creek come from Roy. He came back to visit Alice Springs over the years and often caught up with us. He has recently put out his own book *At a Cost* that includes stories of his time at Loves Creek.

When the sheets of roofing tin, nails and everything else arrived on the train into Alice I went into town with Bruce and Roy. We had a team of four plough horses from the station that we used to drag the materials out to Atnarpa. Roy was an old hand at working a team of horses. We got to push the overloaded two-wheel dray up and down the goat track that was the road. It had originally been a path for goldminers heading off to Arltunga. Today it is a smooth enough two-lane gravel road passing through Trephina

Gorge out to Paddy's Plain and Arltunga. In 1937, the seventy-odd kilometres from Loves Creek took us the best part of a week. Three days travelling and a couple either side for the packing and unpacking. We had to push the dray up the hills and chain the wheels together to stop it building up speed down the slopes. If the load got away it could seriously injure the horses and the whole load might end up at the bottom of an escarpment. It was heavy dangerous work. But we got it safely to Atnarpa eventually. We did six trips for the building materials.

Roy McFadyen 1939 photo courtesy Roy McFadyen

On the positive side, once we were at Atnarpa, we didn't have to put up with Lillian and Louis. Harry, Mary and the babies roughed it in the shed while the house slowly grew. Perhaps they were glad to get away from the older Bloomfields themselves. Lillian was not without an opinion on most subjects. She liked to be the boss. I suspect Mary had no more interest in being told what to do all the time than the rest of us. We were camped out

Growing up

on the flat. The stockwork continued. So when Harry, Roy, Tim and the stockmen were out doing the stock camp, it was often enough just me and Bruce at Atnarpa with Mary and the young kids at the building site. Albert and Sambo Williams helped out from time to time, particularly when the heavy work required extra people. Harry left the ute with us.

Sometimes Mary might get really lonely and head off in the truck to the main homestead and even into town. Sometimes I got to go on the stock camp during a muster as the cook. At other times in the year, Mary and Harry might occasionally stay at the main homestead. Atnarpa was a lonely, hidden-away place. Very few visitors got that far out.

The Atnarpa house and yards under construction 1938. The wing of the yard will be relocated, away from the house photo courtesy Roy McFadyen

A house is built

Harry and Mary were to grow up their three children, Strat, Peter and Angie at Atnarpa. But not before Bruce, Roy, Tim, Albert and Sambo Williams and myself had cut down mobs of trees, shifted tons of rock and completed a rock and mortar homestead. It was rough stone dug up locally. A limestone mortar, also local, was used to fill in the gaps. Us blokes shaped the stones into a wall using a sapling framework. The mortar was applied and allowed to set. Planks for windows and doorways were positioned into the walls and slowly the rooms grew. Wooden beams and rafters were milled from the river gums and dragged close with the two-wheeled dray. They were heavy to lift and everyone was involved when the beams and roof rafters were bolted into position. The ceiling was a solid plaster render. Last the sheets of tin went on as a roof.

It was functional rather than pretty. Roy, who was in charge, was a practical builder. It didn't help that Harry sometimes had his own ideas about how to build the place and turned up wanting things changed, but the house was well positioned and not without style. From the front verandah you looked out over the purple bluffs that make up the Atnarpa range. A spur of the hill hid the house from the occasional travellers using the Ruby Gorge road.

Johnny and Alec snigging rails for the Atnarpa stockyard, in the Atnarpa Creek near Chabbana Gorge, 1938 photo courtesy Roy McFadyen

Building the house was long and heavy work that occupied us for many months. When I wasn't working on the house, they had me helping to build a new and much more substantial set of yards.

The old yards had become barely serviceable. People had to constantly patch them up. It had been hard to work horses in them without risking the fence posts disintegrating. The new yards were designed to last forever. They were still there in 2004 when I visited nearly sixty years later, looking as solid as ever. We cut down a lot of the big river gums for the yards. On Harry's instructions, we dug them in deeper than any fence post needs to be.

Growing up

We milled the planks and built a set of yards that no horse could knock down or get through. I learnt to ride and break in horses in those yards. But the work that went into them was unbelievable. The ground was like rock. It really was rock in a lot of places. Thankfully I've never had to build yards like them since.

Atnarpa was such a different world for me. At least at Loves Creek there were other kids about the place. A bit of laughter and play going on. Atnarpa was a largely silent place. I liked some things much better at Atnarpa. But there were times I was so lonely I would think I was going mad.

Over the years when Harry and Mary grew up their babies. I had the job of watching over them sometimes. Taught the older ones to ride on the quiet horses. But there were times in my isolation when I was quite the dictator with them kids. Setting them up a bit, I suppose. Enjoying my power. Crazy times. I was often a bit angry at the world.

An old Aboriginal couple, Peter Ulyerre and Maggie, looked after me a fair bit at Atnarpa. They became like guardians for me. They were funny people who liked a good story. I was told of the missionaries making one of the first visits out to Arltunga and Claraville Station. This was well before my time. The missionaries often spoke a bit of the language and had cultural interpreters with them. One time the missionaries introduced themselves as men coming to talk about the Lord Jesus.

"You mob know about Jesus?" they asked.

They didn't know, but there was an old Aboriginal man called Jesus who lived and looked after a soak at a place called Paradise. "Jesus, we know Jesus," they agreed. "He is sitting down out at Paradise."

Paradise Waterhole was east of Claraville along the Hale on the way to Harts Range. There was another soakage at a place called Jerusalem. The visiting missionaries were most impressed with the religious knowledge of the old people around Atnarpa.

Peter and Maggie had a mob of goats providing milk and meat for Harry Bloomfield in exchange for rations and being largely left alone. It is very easy to exaggerate the generosity of the Bloomfields. They gave Peter and Maggie practically nothing that they themselves might have had a use for.

A bullock killed. Peter (Ulyerre) and his wife collect the bits and pieces to take back to camp circa 1938
photo courtesy Roy McFadyen

Peter and Maggie's camp was down the slope from the house towards the flat scrubby country. They had a soak and the goats would wander about the place. Peter and Maggie rarely left Atnarpa. They were lovely people. Today their graves are close by at the Arltunga Mission. They were pushed off when the mission was based there during the war years. It must have killed them to have to move away from their sacred sites.

Ceremony

By the time I got to Atnarpa there were only the old people living along the Hale and in the desert areas east of the station. There were no longer any young families around Loves Creek living tribal lives. Everyone was living and working on the cattle stations or had drifted into town.

But I was at Loves Creek when the big Urimbula was held at Atnarpa. As a young boy new to the place, I saw Ted Strehlow and Letchuna, his camel man, come from Hermannsburg. Strehlow was there to record the event. Urimbula was the name for the big gathering of the clans. Men's business had moved from the Pitjantjatjara country up through Finke (Aputula), Maryvale (Titjikala) through to Atnarpa, eventually moving on out to Bond Springs, Harts Range and Napperby Station way to the west. Some two hundred people are said to have come to Atnarpa from all over the Arrernte homelands. For the Urimbula or the big gathering, the men all came on foot. It was the last ceremony of that size to be held in Eastern Arrernte country. The old men gathered in smaller circles after this. The demands of station work, rations and the establishment of missions challenged the old lawmen. There were big cultural events in the Pit Lands in the 1950s and perhaps out in the desert country after the Atnarpa ceremony. But the culture was badly bleeding and couldn't recover.

Perhaps it was like how I feel about Aboriginal culture today. There is little left that would stand up to much of a look. I am one of the few people who know many of the old Eastern Arrernte songs that gave meaning to that landscape. The kids need an education in white fellow ways to make it in the modern world. There is little time for months of ceremony and years of dancing and learning the country through the old stories and songs. I played my part in letting it go. Government policy encouraged us initiated men to let it fade away. And now it is hard for the young ones to have much of a feel for the old ways. Even in the 1930s life was getting much faster. In Aboriginal culture growing up into responsible adulthood should take a lot of time. Nowadays kids in their early teens think they know more than the old people. Perhaps they do, at least about technology and change. But it won't save them.

When I was a teenager at Atnarpa the old men talked about caretaking the country. But I was young and left as an angry man to join the army. By the time I came back everything had changed again. The old people were all buried at Arltunga. Perhaps it was always a bit too late for their dreams. No one knows these people and their stories much today. I'm one of the few custodians of their stories and I don't really know how to pass them on. At the Land Council meeting for Loves Creek I was mocked and humiliated. Some even said I was a weyii or uninitiated man. I got angry and that didn't help a lot. There is a lot of greed these days, but I couldn't pull off a stunt like Jesus throwing the moneychangers out of the Temple. They just turned their faces from me and the Land Council looked after their own. The stories and songs will die out. Perhaps it won't matter so much except to sad old men like Peter Ulyerre, Tom, Tim and Jerry in their day. Now it is my turn to grieve. I'm the old warrior refusing to lie down and accept my powerlessness in old age.

Some people these days get angry about me, a boy from the institutions adopted into the tribe, now carrying a lot of their stories. They accuse me of making up my stories. I felt I had already proved that I was an initiated man for the Loves Creek country. But it wasn't enough in the land claim meeting. Afterwards some apologised. Some, like Norman Wiltshire, made a point of seeking me out to say sorry. He was very sad about how I had been treated at the meeting. Aboriginal Land Rights legislation gave local Aboriginal groups the power to leave us mixed descent mob out of discussions. Ignore those that got taken away to the institutions. Even if we had grown up and been initiated when working the cattle stations on other people's lands, it wasn't enough for the new Aboriginal leaders wanting to boost up their own connectedness and access to land.

There is a lot of bullshit with some land claims. Lawyers and anthropologists are not always good at getting things right. It is a humiliating and weakening process for the whole community almost everywhere it happens. People get to lie and cheat and everything is so secretive you don't get to challenge anything. Everything gets hidden away in land council files. No one was happy with the Loves Creek results. And today there is really no one living out there full-time any more. They visit their three-bedroom homes as the places rot away with neglect. The generators get stolen and the houses get trashed. It is too lonely and scary for them out there when the sun goes down and night closes in. There is no school for children, no community life because there is no community. Even if us old people did move back, where would you sing the songs these days?

No one at the land claim meeting except Agnes was at Loves Creek back in the mid-thirties. Most hadn't been born or even thought of. At Atnarpa there was just Peter and Maggie. The old people would come out of the Simpson Desert at ceremony time and if they wanted extra money for food and things. They knew about the dingo bounty and used to kill one occasionally for its scalp and sell on the puppies. The old people were of the local Aboriginal community but lived very much apart. They got respect because of their cultural knowledge. Even Louis Bloomfield respected their

Growing up

knowledge and power. They knew all the songs and the dreaming stories. They could do magic. They saw things that we were unable to see.

It was a much quieter and more respectful Aboriginal world than is seen today. Law and culture were strong. People from different tribal and language groups hadn't been mixed up into missions and started to lose the traditional ways. Problems were sorted out in the community then. The old people knew the proper way of doing things. Even when they weren't about we knew the rules. We young fellows learnt and obeyed, scared of doing the wrong thing. Men and women often had different meetings. And people would listen. There wasn't much punishment or violence.

There was no grog madness or interfering with kids in those days. You might tease the kids and be hard on them. But they were in a different space from the men. Women were their caretakers and were treated with respect. People knew what was the right way of doing things and followed the rules around sex and marriage according to skinnames. Everyone knew their land and place. If they did something outside of the normal way they expected to be punished. They all believed in the cultural laws and the magic of the old people.

Nowadays there are many confused, angry and greedy Aboriginal people. Many don't really know their land or where they belong. These people fight among themselves and change the real story to suit their needs. The wrong people are often rewarded or punished. People are killing each other, abusing the kids and running amok with grog and violence. There is little respect for the old people, the old ways and magic any more. And it is a sadder and badder place for the loss of culture. Some of the younger ones are trying to get back the good things. They are trying to build respect for Aboriginal ways back into the community. But it seems a fairly desperate struggle.

In my own young days, you knew your position in the community by skinname and ceremony. I was given the skinname of Parultja. Trouble was, it made me the wrong skin for just about every young girl in the place. Even after initiation I had few promised wife possibilities at Loves Creek. I was family but with no marriage prospects, still a bit of an outsider in the community. I had never had a girlfriend or even been kissed when I left Loves Creek for the army at seventeen.

A lot of this skin business changed for the Eastern Arrernte mob after the war. Young men challenged the kinship system especially when they were in town. A bit of alcohol and love sickness went a long way to ending respect for kinship barriers. For me after the war, it was possible to play it both ways as a person living on the edge of the white man's world, but also as a properly initiated Aboriginal man. My wife, Nita, was right skin for me. This was important. I was also right skin for some of the women from Santa Teresa way. Those that Nita was sister cousin for, like the Ronson and Gorey girls. It was seen as borderline okay to play up with women of the right skin. Not that the wife (or the husband) quite saw it that way. But in the ways of traditional law it didn't lead to a lot of trouble. You just had to pay your dues for the privilege.

Nowadays kids take even less notice of traditional kinship obligations and have sex across wrong skins. Many don't even know their skinnames and relationships. For my own kids it didn't seem to matter. Obviously I didn't make it important enough. But losing the old ways is causing a lot of problems. Some of the young men go to bush camp just to get opportunities to go with girls who will be straight for them. For in the bush camp, the initiated man taking responsibility for you was supposed to assist your marriage prospects by getting you married up to one of his daughters and their cousins. It was an obligation on them that is now sometimes abused.

A lot of the older ones running men's culture business today don't even know much of their own stories. So they don't have much to pass on. Their own lives might be violent and abusive. And they don't want to be told anything either. Many have lost their respect. It seems sometimes they see culture as about putting out your hand for royalty money. There is little understanding about the responsibilities of being an initiated person. Many don't spend time caretaking the country or going to sites to keep them in shape and renew their power. Culture is really struggling. Perhaps it is finished and people need to move on.

For me the men's business happened over many seasons. Atnarpa was the traditional ceremony site for much of the Eastern Arrernte land. Men's business and corroborees were travelling through the place. Harry Bloomfield had a different attitude to his father and mother. You could get on with culture business at Atnarpa as long as the work was done. I was able to mix freely with Peter, Maggie and other Aboriginal mob visiting at Atnarpa. I only used our stockmen's camp for sleeping sometimes. For the rest of the time, after my jobs were finished, I could wander about wherever I liked.

Albert preparing for the corroboree to be held tonight at Atnarpa photo courtesy Roy McFadyen

At Atnarpa I was trained up and prepared. Between the mustering and other duties the old men would gather us young fellows for the different stages of the rituals. You would know they were coming by watching the fires at night. Runners going ahead clearing the way for the men's camps and fires being lit along the way. Any women or kids in the wrong place would be in big trouble. Atnarpa Station was positioned so you could look across to the east and keep an eye out for people coming through. Peter and Maggie knew the seasons and watched out for the passages. In those days it was expected that you let people know when you were travelling about the place. Fires were the proper way of doing this. Different types of fires for different types of travelling. People would respond to say if it was okay or not. You weren't allowed into other people's country without some form of permission. The fires were like the telephone lines later on. It is another thing people have forgotten how to do properly.

With the old men we were often camped at different important sites for weeks at a time. The nights would be spent in dancing, songs and ceremony. This went on over seven years as I developed into a full-grown man. I walked every waterhole and sacred site with the old men, not once, but many times. It was strict. No fighting or people running amok. You would have got the biggest hiding for even looking the wrong way at a lawman. We were all being prepared for a caretaker role for the country.

The seven years after the big Urimbula saw smaller, more local men's business happening. They were still big events in the social calendar at Atnarpa. This was when the old men brought all the Eastern Arrernte young men from Undoolya Station, Bond Springs and stations all the way out to Hart Range together. I don't remember men's business mixing over into the West, nor down towards Maryvale in the time I was out there. Business happened every year in wintertime after the cattle muster, when the work at the station was slow. The whole family was involved. The men's business done today is supposed to be the same as these rituals. But preparing the young men is essential. Today the young boys are not always ready. They don't get as much out of it as we did. They don't know the culture the way we had to. They don't have to live the life and travel the country on foot or camels, in the way we did out at Atnarpa.

Selected young boys would be approached in the weeks before the camp. It was an honour. Us boys were about twelve or thirteen years old when we were first told to come to business camp.

All the men went to the camp at the business time. A women's camp would cook tucker for the men's camp. Us boys would travel about with senior men. There would be tasks to complete and stories to learn. Resilience and respect were the main things expected. It was a feat of endurance. In my day a couple of camels were used to cart things around. You would travel all day and sing all night, learning the dances for different places and stories. These were songs for initiated men.

Food was all bush tucker, plain flour and tea. I remember the old men using the water and sugar bag as ways of disciplining us boys. You would have men in the camp who were Ambulni, or brother for you. Others who were Engulli, or not brothers. The Engulli men would set up the testing for the other group, set up the games for you to prove yourself. These were to teach boys the right way to act. It was very subtle. There was no violence or standing over people. Mockery and denial of things were used to train us. With the brothers you were expected to behave properly and respectfully. With Engulli men you could be more jokey. You keep the brotherhood forever. They were the men who went through initiation with you.

At the end of three or four weeks travelling and in bush camp there was the testing ceremony. You would have to face your family of men. People would throw boomerangs at you or other things. You would have to show you knew how to fend things off and behave like a man. There were other more painful rituals of magic and dance. Later there was coming back into the main camp. The women would cry and treat you with respect. There was a big corroboree with different old-time dances for the different groups of people.

After initiation the young men stayed in the single men's camp. There were some older single men there as well. You could go hunting with the men and walk the country. You were treated as a more equal member of the group. You could sleep with women who were the right skin for you. Not that I could ever find one. If you slept with someone of the wrong skin then it was like adultery. I was safe there too. All the women would punish the sister who had done the wrong thing. They would ritually hit her. The man had to look on. The woman was expected to take her hiding. Afterwards people would laugh and joke like nothing had happened. There might be presents to give as well. But it was finished business. It was very serious at the time of the hiding. The law was strict.

Looking back over sixty years, I think even the old men were saying the culture was dying for them. Times were changing for us all. As a generation we failed the old people and our kids. It was too hard to fight for the old ways in a wide-open new world. We were not persuaded to stay at home and honour traditional life. Often we were not even given a choice. So how could we expect much from our kids? If we did try to take them out to bush camps we would have the teachers and welfare on our backs. Perhaps we could have tried harder, but we were trying to get our kids into what we saw as the real world of education and work in the towns. It was very confusing and difficult to please anyone much.

As an initiated man you had more status within community meetings. It also meant you could claim a wife. For a young fellow it involved giving presents to the prospective in-laws and keeping them happy. This was difficult for all us taken-away ones. I was an 'orphan' boy stuck out at Atnarpa, away from my own family's country. I didn't have uncles and a father to take care of me and to lead me through the songs and ceremonies. The old men did this, but it was a fairly distant sort of fathering role they had in my life while I was growing up.

When I told the old men – Tom, Jerry, Tim and Peter Ulyerre – that I had decided to leave Atnarpa and Loves Creek to join the army, they told me I would come back. When I said I might be killed they took me to a sacred cave down the Hale towards Limbla. Old Tom placed a spear in the cave. He told me that it would protect me and give me back to the country.

I went back to the place after the war. I referred to it as part of the Loves Creek Station land claim. I took the anthropologists employed by the Land Council to check the story. The spear was still there. It draws me back to that part of the country to take over a guardian role. I would have liked my kids and grandkids to have an ongoing role by building a place out there. But this depended on the land claim for the Loves Creek area. We were left out. But no one really knows the stories for that country except me. Everyone else is dead. The missions got the younger ones. Us older ones with responsibilities faded away instead of training up people. We were off our country looking after other people's cattle.

I didn't really get back to Alice for a long while after the war. I went back looking for the old men. But they had passed away. I went out to the Arltunga mission cemetery and saw their graves. It was a shock – an ending for me. Some part of me thought they would live forever. But they were dead and I let go of my promise. There was little that I wanted from my old life at Loves Creek that hadn't died with the old people. I went back north to my new life.

A trip to Queensland with Baden

In about 1940 Baden had me on his team when they were taking the wild horses off Loves Creek and Tieyon Station to be sold as usual across the border in Queensland. They already had a buyer lined up. Some fellow living near Julia Creek past Mt Isa. Tieyon Station was run by Bob Smith and is over the South Australian border and down near Dalhousie Springs, about eighty kilometres south-east of Kulgera and one hundred kilometres south of Finke. Tieyon was another station like Loves Creek that had done well in the early days by raising horses and selling them to the Indian Army. Unfortunately like the rest of the world, the Indian Army started investing in trucks and stopped needing our horses. Louis Bloomfield and the Smith's of Tieyon Station had reluctantly made the switch over to cattle.

These horses had been allowed to breed up in the back country. But the stations were now being freed up to run more cattle, so these beautiful three-part thoroughbred stockhorses had to be cleared out. In particular, on Loves Creek they wanted to hunt up the older colts and free-running stallions that might worry Louis's great stallion, Hertum. It was Hertum that was used to improve the bloodlines of the local stockhorses. The deal was that Baden could clear out the horses and keep them. A lot of the horses belonged to him anyway and he wanted the money to buy into land.

The Tieyon Station horses had been mustered already and met us at Loves Creek. We mustered into the big yards at Atnarpa. From there we went north and east, basically following the Hale through to Harts Range. On the trip Baden was in charge of Albert Williams and me from Loves Creek, Bob Smith and another fellow from Tieyon. There must have been over two hundred horses. At night we would try to yard them or else take turns riding around them, keeping watch all night. We had five or six packhorses, carrying everything we would need for the trip. There were swags, canteen packs, meat, flour and spare horse gear. We had four riding horses each. It was a proper droving plant. We would be away for a month.

It was my first big trip away. I was delegated as the cook. Albert and the other fellow from Tieyon were the horse tailers. Everyone else made up the droving team. The horse tailers would be up before dawn and got the riding horses saddled and ready for the day's work. The camp horses would be hobbled at night. It took a couple of days to settle into a bit of a routine. We travelled in easy stages to Harts Range. From there we followed the beautiful Mitchell grass country through Tobermory, Urandanji and through to Dajarra.

My job involved cooking the dampers and corning the beef. Most nights I would make a stew with potatoes and onions. Every night you had to take the meat out of its hessian bags and hang it out to dry off in a tree. This made it last. In the morning you would cut slices of the corned beef for the lunchtime sandwiches. Then bag up the meat again and pack everything away on the packhorses. The horse tailers helped out. Then we would travel up to and past the riders to get ahead of the mob and set up the next night's camp. Along the way we might get some bush tucker, wild fruits and perhaps chase down a goanna if we could catch one. Tie it to the saddle as you went along. It was a relaxed enough crew under Baden. We had a good time all around.

The horses soon settled down and we made steady progress doing ten or twelve easy miles a day. Everyone was pretty happy to be on the road away from the station. It was my first taste of droving and I liked everything about it. The teamwork, the skills of keeping a mob moving in the direction you wanted, the fires at night, the singing and the stories. Most of all I liked the sense of arriving and dropping off the horses at Dajarra. We hadn't lost a single horse. So we had the celebratory rum or two afterwards. And the bit of a long picnic ride on the way back to the station. Perhaps it was being with Baden. Perhaps it was seeing so many new places. But I got my itch to be a drover and a travelling man from this trip. I reckon too that was when Baden decided to find a way of buying Indiana Downs. It was very pretty country and Baden was full of plans about what he might do there.

It was after the Queensland adventure that I was allowed to go up north with Baden and a few racehorses. There was nothing much happening at the station for a month or so. It was walking the racehorses in those days. There were no horse floats. What with the droving trip and the trip up north I was coming of age in a way. But I ended up back at Atnarpa; back out minding the soaks during the dry spells. They had a way, the Bloomfields, of putting me back in my box if I showed any signs of getting above what they saw as my allotted station in life. That was when they noticed me at all. After the taste of freedom and being treated as a man, I was twitching to get away and out into a bigger world.

I still think of Baden as a good friend. He was a bit of a father to me. He tried to help me out, but he couldn't save himself, let alone me, from the impact of Lillian and the Loves Creek culture. Lillian didn't want to recognise Baden, and she excluded him from the family wherever she could. Later on he often 'borrowed' me to work with him. He could just be his natural generous self away from the homestead. Over the years he spent time to teach me many of his riding and stockwork skills. He taught me how to out-think and break in horses. Baden had a deep knowledge of horses and the local countryside. He took me off with some racehorses to the picnic meetings up north at Tennant Creek, Rankine Springs, Brunette Downs and across to Camooweal. The trip was a great adventure for me. It helped me grow away from my isolated Loves Creek life.

After Louis died in 1944, Baden bought a place east of Loves Creek. It had been called Indian Well but he renamed it Indiana Downs Station after a favourite cowboy film. It was east of the Jervois Range, heading for Queensland. He later had plans for me to marry his daughter, Agnes, and work the place with him. But she was wrong way for me. Much younger and a sister in the skin relationships of the place. People would have been angry. Plus I was older and making my own way then. Perhaps if he had stayed around to talk me into it I would have gone. Baden died in 1950 and Indiana Downs went to his sister, Maggie. She moved the stock and sold the place. Agnes never got much of a look-in. She married Arnold Abbott from out Hermannsburg way.

Army years

It was after Pearl Harbor and the Japanese coming into the islands north of Australia that I remember us stockmen talking of leaving station work and giving the army a go. We had seen a lot of the white miners, white stockmen and even the town workers recruited into the army as early as 1939. Roy McFadyen had long since left and had joined up. We knew that the army was taking a lot of people and paying good money. We would be fighting for our country. People who had left to join the services were looked up to in Alice Springs. Even full descent Aboriginal people were getting paid real money and being employed to do army jobs. The army found recruiting amongst us mixed descent mob pretty easy. The idea of getting equal pay was a shock for us all. The local station owners and bosses were not happy about it.

The stations had already lost a lot of their staff since the war started. Now they were losing us. The bosses talked of it being the ruin of us, without having them as bosses telling us what to do and protecting us from our lazy and evil inclinations. What they really meant was that they might have to start paying us properly and looking after us better if they needed us to stay. I was ripe for a bit of real money and ruination. And so were a lot of my mates hanging around in Rainbow Town. That was what they called the area where I visited on my rare trips into Alice Springs. The mixed descent Aboriginal community had grown up Rainbow Town as a camping ground, just south of the town grid along the river near where the Central Australian Aboriginal Media Association (CAAMA) is today. People lived in shacks and humpies. There were about three hundred living there, nearly all Central Arrernte people. A lot of them had lived as kids in the Bungalow, either in town, at Jay Creek or at the Telegraph Station.

Living close to Rainbow Town, but separately, were the Afghan cameleers trading whatever they could. They had goats and gardens. The Chinese were there too. Ah Hong had market gardens and Syke Ahchee had his bakery. So town was a busy enough place with Aboriginal people having more work options and power than they had ever experienced before.

It was Rainbow Town that I visited on the few occasions I was allowed to spend any time in town, catching up with friends and finding out the gossip. Many of the men had spent time on Loves Creek or had worked at Arltunga. They knew what you were up against and had a strong bond of having been oppressed by the same group of bastards. You would always get a welcome. As an older teenager I had more time and ability to slip away from the overwhelming presence of Harry Bloomfield and get to know people a little.

Many had already joined up from Rainbow Town and were living in the city of army tents. We didn't feel a lot of loyalty to the old station bosses. But it was still hard to leave family and community behind.

I had mentioned to Harry Bloomfield that I was thinking of joining the army. He told me I was too young and that anyway, they were putting money away for me. It got a bit heated when I asked to go on wages. I was tired of having nothing and being treated like a slave. He said he would block me even trying to leave Loves Creek. But I was needed for picking up supplies for the muster. Once in town I was able to sneak off for a little while. I went to see the police, who operated as the agents for the Aboriginal Protectorate. They said there was no trust account and no money. I went around to Mr Sweeney at the Native Affairs office to find out where my trust account money was. He was a nice gentle fellow, well respected by the blokes that did get money there. He checked and told me straight up that there was no trust fund set up and that the Bloomfields had never paid any money into an account for me.

I was really angry. I suppose part of me had always expected that they were just ripping me off blind. They had never given me good boots, a hat or even new clothes. The blankets were always crappy and skinny. So why would they be paying money into an account for me? It was after finding out about there being no money that I became determined to get away. But there was no chance on that trip. Harry found me and I was back in the truck and back to the homestead. But I knew I just needed a bit of a head start. I decided to play it quietly and wait for a chance next time we were in town.

Three months later, after we had taken the cattle into town following the 1942 muster, I got my chance. We loaded the cattle on to the train and I knew Harry would be busy with the paperwork and gossip. Usually after muster we had a bit of the day in town. But he was still checking up on all of us workers, so I knew I had to be careful. It was a small town and he could find me quick enough. He had an edge of mobility with his ute to drive about in. After us stockmen had loaded all the cattle away we returned to our camp. This was where we always stayed after the muster. I had to tell the other blokes that I was off. They could be trusted to give me a bit of a start. So I slipped away and walked quickly through town to the recruitment office at Anzac Oval.

It was a long way and I arrived at the gate a bit flustered. Johnny Underdown was the recruitment officer and he saw me coming. I knew him a bit. He was Ly Underdown's brother and they were no friends of the Bloomfields. He knew the story of me working for nothing much at Loves Creek. With a nod to the soldiers on guard, we went through the gate and behind the fence. He took me straight into the recruitment office and started filling in my forms. Where I couldn't answer he made something up. He even told me what age to say I was. So I became twenty years old and not needing any consent papers done. I was signed up straightaway and in the army.

Harry Bloomfield turned up in his ute while I was still in the office. He had called in down at the stockmen's camp and seen I wasn't there. When he asked and was finally told that I was off to join up, he had jumped straight back into the ute and sped down, parking at the army gates. Johnny Underdown went down to meet him. Harry was carrying on that the army had one of his stock 'boys' in their office and that I was only seventeen and he would be taking me back to Loves Creek Station with him. The soldiers at the gate were happy for a bit of action but weren't going to let him in. When Johnny got to the gate he told Harry that it was too late. I was already signed up. That I was 'army property' now. Johnny would have been happy enough to play the role. The soldiers stood around backing Johnny up.

Eventually Harry gave up and they saw him off the place. Most of the army blokes were pretty happy about being one-up on any type of boss. They were pretty democratic that way. Harry threatened to go to Native Affairs and the army bosses, but nothing came of it. He went back to St John's Valley and dragged the rest of the stockmen and the plant back to Loves Creek the same day.

Getting into the army was the biggest thing I had managed to pull off in my life up to then. I couldn't quite believe that I had done it. The positive side of me joining up for the other blokes working out at Loves Creek was that they started to get paid proper wages. Harry had already been told by Roy McFadyen and others that they had no choice or they would lose men. He must have got nervous that he wouldn't have anyone left to do the work. I heard that Tim Shaw got a big pay increase and the other blokes started to be looked after much better. They knew they had other options, having seen me escape. But the pay increases seemed to work. Tim Shaw and the others saw out the war working on Loves Creek Station.

My fellow soldiers

They put me in the Aboriginal unit and I was told that I would be sharing a two-man tent. My partner in the tent turned out to be a local bloke and ex-Bungalow boy. He was another Alec – Alec McDonald. There was a mob of us mixed descent Aborigines all grouped together, mostly people I knew from Rainbow Town. I was one of the last ones in and far and away the youngest. There was yet another Alec in Alec Turner, plus Harry Bray, Jack Hughes, Don Stokes, Mick Laughton, Milton Liddle, Jimmy Smith, Mort Conway and others.

We were all pretty happy to be in the army and getting paid. The blokes with family got paid more than us single fellows and the army looked after their families a bit. We were a placid mob most of the time. Some of the white soldiers were tougher and more openly defiant to the sergeants and officers. I remained a bit terrified that they would realise they had made a mistake and hand me back to Harry Bloomfield. Don't get me wrong, it was no paradise in the tents. We copped a bit in the first weeks of the army camp. But by and large we gave as good as we got, and the other blokes came to give us a lot more respect. Life in the institutions and on the cattle camps had toughened us up.

The racism of the day still saw us separated from the main army units. But even with that it was an exciting world compared to station life. We found ourselves mixing with more strangers than we had ever had to deal with before. It took a lot of getting used to. Some were friendly and showed us how to get away with things. Others were ugly and complained about having to share the same space as us. There were bullies like everywhere else. A few of us were pretty handy with our fists. By and large this kept the bullyboys away. We hung together and mostly held our own when it became physical.

Life in the army camp was pretty comfortable compared to what we were used to. You had proper clothes and equipment. You had a coupons book that let you get six bottles of beer a week from the wet canteen. Tins of tobacco were provided. It was an entirely new world of sugar, matches, rifles and sweet things. For the first time I had money coming in and money in my pocket. More money than I had ever seen. Every fortnight you would line up with everybody else and be given your pay. It felt terrific. I was able to buy things of my own choice. The army had taken over the telling me what to do, but it didn't care what I did with my own money. Just as long as I turned up when I was told, ready for duty.

My unit was part of the Sixth Division. The old hands of the division had come back from fighting in the Mediterranean and Middle East. They had lost a lot of blokes and had been pulled out after the Japanese attacked Pearl Harbor. With us new recruits we were to be part of the defence of northern Australia and the Pacific.

Brigadier Noel Loutit was in charge of the army and in charge of the town. You would see him leading the parades and taking the salutes. He had a staff car with a flag on it and a driver. We had a fair bit of time on our hands to gossip. Officers were always the subject of a lot of scrutiny. Rumour had it that Brigadier Loutit was sweet on Mona Minahan who ran the Riverside pub. He spent plenty of time there.

All the officers and important officials had servants called batmen. They would wash the officers' clothes, iron them and lay them out each morning. They would bring them cups of tea and food, and generally do anything they wanted. One of the older of the ex-Bungalow boys, Milton Liddle, was one of these batmen. He was always one of the blokes pumped for gossip. Sometimes we would see Milton dressed up, driving around with some high-flier in his car. I knew Milton a bit. He was a lot older than me, perhaps in his thirties, and a real kind fellow, always happy to help someone out. He had spent time in the early Bungalow near the police station before they moved it out to Jay Creek. Milton's father was Angus Liddle, the builder. Angus had married a Southern Arrernte woman and had a mob of kids before eventually buying Angus Downs Station south of town near Kings Canyon.

Milton was a bit of a self-taught mechanic and I suspect he got the job because of his experience with cars. After the war Milton settled down in the Gap. Later on, a fair while after the war, I ended up working for Milton and his offsider, Donny Lynch, when they ran a firewood business. This was before I got married and before a better paying job with the railways came up. Milton was a good boss and a generous man. He would always be giving the old people, especially the widows and deserted wives, credit for their wood. He would ask what they had done with their money, but he knew how hard it was for many of them and gave them a handout if necessary. He also ran one of the first taxis in town.

In the Aboriginal unit with me was Mick Laughton. Mick had been born out at Arltunga and had worked on Loves Creek Station before my time. He was married to a local Arrernte woman, Amy Colley. They had a mob of kids taken away and ending up in the Bungalow at Jay Creek. I knew some of them from the Telegraph Station. Mick liked to play it flash if he could. I had seen him at a few of the Alice Springs race meetings. He was often hanging around with his mate, Frank Hayes.

Mick was a very genuine fellow and a good mate to me. He was a lot older and used to lead the group a bit. He had knocked about a lot down the mines and getting whatever work he could to feed his big mob of kids. He had spent time at Wauchope mines and Hatches Creek working in the government battery. He had strong ideas about what was fair and just. He didn't mind letting people know that they were taking a liberty if they needed to be told. As a result he was handy with his fists.

Jimmy Smith was quieter. He was a child of Topsy Smith who had come in with her mob of kids from the Arltunga mines as the original residents of the Bungalow. Jimmy had lived at the Bungalow until he was old enough to leave. He was related to most of the mob in Rainbow Town. His sisters included Maureen (Maudie Pope), Jean (Shaw) and Ada (Wade). His brothers included Willie and Walter Smith and he was also related to Old Jack Shaw, Frankie Shaw's father who later worked down at Arrernte Council.

Jimmy had been working as a stockman and fencer before joining up. After the war he went back to fencing. He never married but, with his sisters Ada and Maureen, had a boarding house for old ringers and prospectors down on South Terrace. The sisters used to mother the old blokes through their town drinking periods. They always got them to bed, washed their blankets and got their tuckerboxes ready for when they headed off again. The sisters were very well liked and respected. They never had any trouble with any of the fellows. If anyone acted out of line the others would quickly put him in his place.

Alec Turner was a light-framed fellow. His mother was Hetti Perkins, who had been the main Aboriginal worker in charge of services in the Bungalow. His father was Jim Turner from Garden Station. He was related to a lot of the townsfolk. Hetti had a big mob of other kids. His brothers included Alf and Jimmy Turner. I knew Alec fairly well from before the war at the Bungalow and from around the stations. After the war, Alec bought into a truck and, with another soldier Jack Neal working for him, ran his own business as a bore contractor. He made a success of it and married locally.

Harry Bray had always been in and out of town working on the stations out Harts Range way. His father was Billy Bray and his mother, Mary. Harry was a solidly built fellow who didn't mind a bit of a scrap. He got married after the war and continued working as a stockman off and on. The Memorial to the Stolen Generations that was opened in Canberra in 2004 included a letter from Harry. He was writing in the 1950s to stop the

Welfare Department taking his kids away. He also got involved in the lawsuit with me for compensation from the government for them removing us as children.

My tent-mate, Alec McDonald, was in his late twenties and after Mick Laughton, was one of the oldest of us. He had a strong sense of being treated right and felt we should be talking things up if we got treated badly. He was a big solid fellow with a big local family that included a sister, Myrtle McDonald, who I knew well. His father was Sandy McDonald, the publican out at Arltunga when it was a big goldmining centre. After the war Alec went out towards the Queensland border around Lake Nash. He ended up working with the Aboriginal Legal Aid and land council running out of Mt Isa. This was in the 1970s. He married fairly late in life to a woman from Lake Nash and had a mob of kids out that way.

Army days at Morphett's Creek. Back row: Alec McDonald, Bob Cook, Mick Laughton, Harry Bray, Alec Turner. Front row: Alec Kruger, Alec Jackamos, Jimmy Smith photo courtesy Kruger family

Jack Hughes was with us in the Alice Springs army camp, but he didn't come up with us when the unit was split up. He ended up serving out the war in Alice. He was of mixed Afghan and Aboriginal descent and was originally from down Marree way. He lived in Rainbow Town with Julia Colley. So he was a brother-in-law to Mick Laughton through Mick's wife Amy. Jack was a bit of a boxer and dangerous in a street fight. He didn't have a lot of restraint and he sometimes struggled with the authorities. He later went on to become a local fight promoter. I renewed acquaintances with him when we were both living down the Gap Cottages in the 1950s. He enjoyed a drink, especially later on in life. It saw him do a bit of jail time after the war. He had a big mob of kids, including Doreen, Reggie, Robert and Billy. He died fairly young and Julia went on later to live with Dick Smith, the drover.

Don Stokes became the corporal for the unit. He was another Bungalow boy in his mid-twenties. He was tall, kept to himself a bit and was a real gentleman. He could turn his hand to anything mechanical. Like Jack Hughes he stayed in Alice when I headed up north after the war. He ended up joining the Department of Works as a driver in the transport area, moving heavy equipment up and down the track. He became a mechanic. I saw a bit of him when I was living down the Gap Flats. He had one of the places there. By that time he was married to Clara Stokes and they had a fair few kids. On payday he would often be found down at Ly Underdown's pub. He was a lovely fellow, loyal to his mates and a good worker.

Albert Shadforth I didn't get to know so well. He had joined up with Alec McDonald when they had both been working up on one of the Top End stations. Albert got split up from us early on, staying in Alice for a while. After the war the lot of us went our separate ways and we didn't always keep in touch. None of us were big on the RSL and that sort of thing, even if they hadn't been pretty racist places as often as not. We had to earn a living and it took us along different routes.

Other blokes that joined the army included Jack Neal and Jack Ansell. Jack Neal also spent his young years at the Bungalow. He worked with Percy Lake and later Alec Turner on the bore contracts. He got a place down the Gap Cottages, married and had a few kids. Jack Ansell was a big solid fellow who had also spent time in the Bungalow. He stayed mostly around the Centre after the war and had a few kids.

Our sergeant was a local fellow, Bill Dempsey. He was a good bloke who looked after people. I got on well with him. He was a topnotch talent in the boxing ring, becoming the local army boxing champ. We would go down and watch him at the stadium, which was situated near the old racecourse. Bill even went down south for a few fights. I don't think he lost any. He was from Hatches Creek where his father was a white miner. He had done a fair bit of fencing before the war and was handy at most things. He had a sister, Lily Dempsey, and they had both been at the Bungalow. He also stayed in Alice during the war. I never heard much of him after the war. I think he became a truck driver.

Other blokes that I spent time with during the war years were Alec Jackamos and Bob Cook. These blokes were with the unit formed when I was picked to go up the track to Morphett's Creek. Alec Jackamos was an Aboriginal-Greek fellow with a big family in South Melbourne. He was a professional wrestler and later had his own business. One of his kids ended up marrying into the Simpsons, a local Aboriginal family. Bob Cook was a quieter white fellow from rural Victoria. A real gentleman and a good bloke. I never really heard from him after the war.

They were older and a more worldly group of men than me. I was the young one hanging a bit to the sides. But the work was easy enough. I was good at the training. Institutions and the stock camps had taught me how to handle the army bosses and my mates. At the start the white blokes often used to call us 'Jacky Jacky'. It was not always meant as a slur, but some of us objected to it. There were a few fights about that. We all stuck together strongly and the big blokes amongst us saw us give a good account of ourselves. The name-calling stopped pretty soon after a few blues. We even became good friends with a lot of the other army blokes.

It was around this time that some Aborigines were becoming more political, wanting better housing, better schooling for their kids and equal pay for work done. Others like me just clustered together for safety.

Despite being in the army we were still looked down on and treated with suspicion by most in the white civilian population. You had to be careful not to be seen outsmarting even the dumbest of them, or else you risked a hiding. You had to be careful not to beat them in a fight or else they might seek you out later on. So you kept your eyes low, said 'yes boss' to even the most unlikely crap, and tried to keep moving in a group wherever possible.

It can be hard to tell anyone today what it was really like in those days. After the war the world had thankfully moved on. We were able to become a more political force. We had new white supporters across the community. The new migrants knew a bit of where we were coming from. The unions that had hounded us for taking jobs from their white members became our allies and tried to recruit us. Even the Church started to treat us as intelligent and normal human beings.

You could exaggerate it, but by the 1970s we were all much more able to be black and proud. Today my young grandkids are angry, even arrogant at any vaguely racist treatment. They learn it is a bit more complicated if they end up in the courts, jails or detention centres. But they ride on the back of our survival tactics that we used in the past, and our hardworking, careful ethos. It took a long time and a lot of struggle to get to where we are now.

There were lots of brave people who didn't survive standing out from the crowd and talking up our rights. The army was the first escape that many of us men had experienced. Our women and kids had five years down south in a different world and learnt that it didn't have to be the way things were in the Northern Territory. But there were still too many decades after the war of abuse and humiliation, policies of removing our kids and racism that kept us out of schools, hospitals, swimming pools and lots more. The real changes took a long time coming.

Army life in Alice Springs

Enlistment meant that I was exempted from Aboriginal Protectorate laws. All of us were. With money and a uniform I could go wherever other soldiers could go. I had entry to the army wet canteen. I was part of a gang again. It felt great to be accepted. Our group spent many months in Alice Springs being marched around, mostly down along the banks of the Todd River. We were trained in guns, using a firing range near where the casino is today. Firing into the hills.

The army was a bit like the old Bungalow in some ways. You had to be careful with the officers. They could target you for punishment if they wanted to. Mostly this was peeling the potatoes for the army cooks. But if you really got into trouble, you would be locked up in the army prison near Mt John. Like the Bungalow the army often did things just to keep you busy and on your toes. They would call parades anytime. Wherever you were you would have a couple of minutes to get spruced up, polish your boots, grab your rifle and line up with the rest of your unit. It was a spit and polish place. Your uniform and gear had to be perfectly kept. Your rifle had to gleam. The first few days were spent just making sure that we knew who was in charge. It wasn't that hard for me. I knew the rules.

During the days and occasionally at nights they would take us on route-marches. We would be in full gear, stepping out behind the bosses for miles on end. Other times we would be unloading trains on to trucks. The trucks would then roar off along the north road in convoys. Most days we were also marched down to the river. They would have wheat bags filled with sand. We would have to charge the bags and stick in our bayonets with a bloodcurdling yell, then twist and withdraw. Another enemy bites the dust. We would be rostered onto picket, marching up and down the fences carrying just a bayonet. The roster also included guard duty at the front gates holding a rifle with fixed bayonet. The shifts would change every hour and a half during the day and night. Everyone needed a pass to come in and out. Town was out of bounds without a pass. We would have to check the passes and stop the vehicles. If you slackened off or messed up you would be in for punishment.

Food was always a priority. When you enlisted they gave you a set of two aluminium dishes called dixies that folded in and packed up into each other. One was a dish for the main meal. The other was for sweets or anything else on offer. I've still got a set today. They were also great for droving and camping. The soldiers' mess was a big Sydney Williams hut. Everyone would line up at mealtimes. There were tables of servers and you would shuffle along with your two dixies while the cooks and their helpers ladled out the food into them. The cooking was all done in the mess tent, so there was a production line happening behind to replace huge pots as they were emptied. With your meal you sat down with your mates. There were huge pots of tea stewing on hotplates. We had an enamel cup for tea. We washed up our dixies in big 44-gallon drums split lengthways that were full of soapy water. They were lined up outside on metal trestles with a fire underneath.

Breakfast was almost always ham and eggs with all the toast you could eat. Dinner was meat sandwiches. Tea was a big meat and potato stew with tinned fruit and custard for dessert. We all rubbished the food, but secretly, I thought it was pretty good. After Loves Creek it was paradise. It took a long while for me to stop eating everything I could see. I suppose that comes from never having had enough food. I used to take away food as if there mightn't be a meal the next time. It was hard to stop doing it even after being there for a while. All us institution blokes were a bit like that. If you were off duty after tea, you could go to the canteen. It sold chocolate, biscuits, lollies and soft drink. For a while my money never went far enough. I spent it on whatever sweets I could get. Then sometimes trade my alcohol and cigarette coupons for more sweets.

The wet canteen was in another huge Sydney Williams tent. The coupons allowed you to buy six longneck bottles a week. It was the first time I had seen so much beer. Out bush we never had refrigeration and hot beer is not much of a drink. Everyone drank rum. But there were no bottles of rum or other spirits sold in the canteen. Before the army I didn't drink much at all. But my preferred beer in the army became Anchor beer. They sold Westend beer as well. You were an Anchor man or a Westender. Classy people like me who knew a lot about their beer drank Anchor. The paymaster gave you a book of coupons each payday. Without the coupons you couldn't get things. You had to sit on a beer for a long time to make the coupons last.

Cigarettes were cheap at the army canteen. So civilians were always asking you to buy them and pass them on. The canteen had Red Capstan packets or you could get tins of tobacco. I don't remember seeing a lot of cigarettes before the war. It was all tobacco. For us out on the stations it had been the rough-as-guts chewing tobacco called 'nick-nick'. You would get a few slivers cut off a solid chunk of tobacco, stick it into your mouth and chew it. The traditional Aboriginal mob would mix the tobacco with ashes from local medicinal trees. Some mixes were pretty toxic and hallucinogenic. You would be feeling no pain for a while. They kept wads of it in their mouths for hours, just tasting it and occasionally refreshing it with more ash.

In the early days there was no such thing as ready-rolled cigarettes. These came with the war. Even ready-rubbed tobacco was unusual. Smoking tobacco involved shaving off enough shreds and stuffing them into a pipe. When tobacco papers came in, you vigorously rubbed the shreds together to soften them up before wrapping them in the paper. Ready-rolled Red Capstans were a luxury, even with no filters in them. But some of the American cigarettes already had filters. According to the old smokers they were something else, things of sophistication and beauty. I didn't smoke and sold on my cigarette coupons.

We could play housie-housie most evenings. This is much the same as bingo. It filled in a lot of time and basically moved the money about. You felt pretty good if you were lucky enough to win.

There was an old record player and a bit of music in the wet canteen. It was the first time I had much exposure to a lot of the popular songs. Later I would be able to sing them on the stock route and in the pubs. Occasionally they would stick up a screen and put on a movie for us. But the wet canteen didn't have any outsiders. There were never any loose women or a big drinking scene. You just didn't get to drink much even if you saved up your coupons. They were quiet drinking holes compared to the pubs of today. To get drunk you had to buy one of the black market bottles of rotgut rum. You drank them well away from the canteen.

One of the things I liked about the army was the big baths with hot water laid on. I can't remember actually having one before this time. It was such a luxury. I would sit in them as long as I could. I also loved the new uniform after the rags I had been dressed in all my life. We never bothered with any civilian clothes during the army years. There was nowhere to wear them. And nearly all the girls and families had gone down south.

A civilian Aboriginal workforce had been recruited to work for the army. They had the sanitation and clean-up jobs. Each day the army would send down a truck to pick them up. Maybe there were half a dozen or so blokes in each team. At night they slept confined in the old Bungalow dormitories of my childhood, in what was now called the Aboriginal Compound at the old Telegraph Station. Their families might be hanging around town, at Jay Creek or at the Arltunga Missions. Later on, wives were allowed. It was pretty miserable work really and not so well paid. We were the lucky ones in the army and out of the control of the Native Affairs bosses.

By the time I joined the army, the taken-away kids in the institutions had been evacuated down south. Even before that they had been relocated depending on what the Native Affairs decided was their religion. In 1939 it was off to Garden Point Catholic Mission on Melville Island, Retta Dixon Reserve in Darwin for the Anglicans or to the Methodist mission on Croker Island.

But with the bombing of Darwin the Top End missions were evacuated. The women and children were sent straight to Alice Springs on army trucks, then on to the railway heading down to Hamley Bridge in South Australia. A lot of women and children in town had gone the same way. Evacuated through South Australia and often assisted to find work down there. Billy McCoy, the supervisor from the Bungalow after I left the place and now with Native Affairs, was a big part of organising the evacuations and resettlements for the mixed descent families in Alice Springs. The whole of the Northern Territory had become a huge military region. So there were not a lot of children or young people around the place. It was strange. Mind you, Rainbow Town didn't shut down. Lots of people had work and decided to stay.

I knew a lot of the Aboriginal civilian workers from the stations. They often had a bit of money but what they didn't have was our coupons for alcohol or tobacco. There was an active trade going on between the army blokes and the civilian workers. The cigarettes and alcohol often found their way into the homes around Alice. Mostly they on-sold into the white houses where the wives of the Aboriginal civilians worked.

Australian Rules Football became a part of my life at this time. Football had been played a bit in the Northern Territory, especially in Darwin. But it was the war, the road crews from Victoria and the transport units that really took the game to a new level. There were a lot of gun footballers in the army. Two ovals were roughed out – one behind Hoppy's shop, near where Braitling School is today, and the other in Eastside, past the swamps near Centralian College. Army boots were the footwear. Everyone got to play. I got a start as a rover near the centre bounce, following the ball around. Football was one of the social events that brought people together on Saturdays. The teams played as units. Afterwards you had a few beers and got to know people a bit. It was how friendships were made. It broke down some of the racism.

Sundays saw me attending religious services. I opted back to being an Anglican and the army insisted on all us soldiers turning up. The army chaplains did the gospel readings. This happened even in more remote army camps like Morphett's Creek. Every Sunday you headed off for services with the other Anglicans. Afterwards you might get a pass-out and some time off.

From time to time parcels would come for us. These were from the Red Cross and were part of what was called the Soldiers' Comfort Fund. They were put together by families from down south. At Christmas you would get extra things. The handouts included clothes, cakes, even cigarettes and toothbrushes. The people sending them would leave a name and address on the parcel. Often there was a letter. You were expected to do the right thing and write back thanking people. I suspect some of the people sending the parcels were doing it harder than we were. But I was very grateful for the parcels. They were great.

After six months or so, the word came around that some of us would be moving north with other units. Most of my mob stayed behind, but I was one who was put on the back of a truck to head up the north road. It must have been ten years since I had come down from the Pine Creek Institution as an eight-year-old kid. It seemed like a long time ago. The trip back had some similarities, but the food was so much better.

Up the track

We crawled up through the ranges north of town as part of a convoy of trucks. The old north road was like a roller-coaster. It was chopped up fairly badly from all the army traffic. It was a skinny one-lane road the worse for wear in lots of patches where the truck tyres had gone through. And you had to pull over each time a vehicle came down the other way.

We spent the trip sardined in a mob of about twenty men to a truck, seated on wooden benches lengthways along the sides. The dust was often pretty bad, even with the canvas awning drawn shut. It was slow going up the eighty miles to Aileron. There we had a short pit stop and a cup of tea, before driving another fifty miles to Ti Tree. This was our dinner camp. Mobile kitchens doled out sandwiches and big kettles of sweetened tea were on the boil for us. After an hour or so we were back in the truck crashing through the gears the ninety miles to Barrow Creek. This was our overnight camp.

In the morning we loaded up our swags and kitbags again. We were driven through Warrabri, Wauchope, the trucking yard just out of Tennant Creek and along to a smaller camp at Morphett's Creek. It was ten miles or so from the big army camp located on Banka Banka Station. We stayed there for some time before being allocated to different units.

My unit was attached to the Seventh Australian Engineers as the 28th Engineers Unit. We worked with the road-building crews. They were mostly civilians and were called the Civil Construction Corps or the CCC. Their nickname was 'Curtin's Cunning Cunts'. The crews had dozers that pushed patches of the right type of soil up into mounds. They didn't have big crushing machines like after the war, so the soil was put through sieves called 'chinamen hats'. The soil was used to raise up the roads from the rest of the countryside so that the water would run off. It also flattened out some of the smaller bumps and dips. The sieved-off pebbles were gathered up and rolled into the bitumen to form the hard crust of the road surface. The original road, built to supply the Top End forces once the Japanese threat became apparent, was put down in about ninety days of sustained work. There were no bridges or anything. So when it rained the road had sections that remained fairly impassable. We had the job of repairing and improving the original road. They laid down a track from Tennant Creek to Mt Isa as well, to allow a supply route from North Queensland. The Americans had originally done a lot of this.

Most of our time when we weren't building up and repairing the road was spent in army drills. We had a regular route-march the five miles up to the top of Churchill's Head and down again. Other times we had the usual parades and small arms training. A lot of life in the army was like that. Keeping us busy seemed part of the drill.

Morphett's Creek was mainly a big fuel depot, so we also spent a lot of time unloading fuel trucks and filling up transport vehicles heading north. It was my new unit, the 28th Engineers, that went on to do all the government bores that I was later to use on the Barkly stock route out to the Queensland border. We stayed in Morphett's Creek for months before my particular unit was trucked up to the next supply base at the railhead of Larrimah.

Larrimah was a different sort of place on the very edge of the Japanese bombing raids. It was a huge army camp and there was a real feeling early on that the Japanese would land somewhere close by and cut off the forces in the Top End. Katherine got bombed a lot, and Larrimah occasionally saw a Japanese plane overhead. It was a scarier and more war-focused place. There was a big airstrip, Gorey, that was used for the bombing fleet. The town had a hospital. The main job we did there was again unloading trucks and loading the trains.

The big army bases in the Top End were supplied through Larrimah. So it was never ending work. In between times they had us doing parades and practising our air raid drills. Larrimah and even Morphett's Creek were active war zones. There was no football or much organised recreational stuff happening. But I can remember the huge games of two-up that used to take place. At Banka Banka and Larrimah there were often big crowds and huge amounts of money being wagered on the toss of a few coins. The army also used to run housie games in the canteen. Housie was a much slower way of losing money and much more my style.

At one time a group of us were sent north to help with building Truscott airstrip. This was entering into the war zone proper with air raids and bombs. We were in easy reach of the Japanese. We went up through Katherine and Adelaide River before heading off to the West Arm of Darwin harbour. The airstrip was named after Bluey Truscott who had been legendary in the Royal Flying Doctor Service before the war. With the fall of Singapore he became a Spitfire pilot. He was shot down and killed during the first Japanese bombing raid on Darwin on 14 February 1942. Truscott was to be a secret airstrip for flying bombing raids against the Japanese forces in East Timor and Indonesia. If the Japanese knew where it was, it would be targeted for a bombing raid of its own.

Our job was to maintain the rough strip cut out of the mangroves of West Arm. As well we had to collect 44-gallon drums of fuel dropped off from flat barges on an incoming tide. We had to manhandle the drums through the surf and on to the beach before the tide turned. The drums were then loaded on to trucks and taken to the landing strip. The Japanese were still bombing Darwin so it was a dangerous place to be. After some months there we were relieved and moved back to Larrimah.

Rediscovering family

It was while I was at Larrimah that my brother, George, found me. George had last seen me on the trip down south with our father in 1934. I had been a skinny nine-year-old kid. Then they were moving a mob of cattle and horses for Ted Lowe. It was the last time I saw my father. With the war starting and people enlisting, George had got permanent work as a fettler with the railways. After the bombing of Darwin his railway work had become part of the war effort. He was a civilian but under army control. This is what he was doing when he found me.

My brother had been told that there was an Aboriginal fellow called Alec Kruger from Alice Springs posted to Larrimah. He had managed to get a trip out there during one of his days off. I had given up much hope of having a family outside of my mates. I was surprised when he showed up, not knowing how to react. I barely remembered anything about him. But we met and talked. I liked him. He was some twenty years older than me, married and with a family. He had bought a block of land in Katherine with his wages. It didn't have a proper house yet but he had great plans.

George told of my father's death. George had been at Donkey Camp with Lily. It was Wet season and Frank was just moving things about, as you always had to do. His horse had died underneath him. No one knew why. Just one of those things. It had collapsed, crushing his leg as it went down. The horse had to be dragged off him. There was no doctor in Katherine at the time. The flying doctor service hadn't started up then. The closest nursing station was at Maranboy. The train wasn't running. So they had just cleaned the wound and set the leg in the old-fashioned way. My father wasn't one for a whole lot of fuss.

But an infection set in and they couldn't heal the wound. Penicillin hadn't been invented then. It was just sulphur bandages and traditional healing ointments. Despite these treatments and a doctor at the end of the telegraph line, the wound got worse. Gangrene set in. But no one wanted to cut off his leg. So they organised to take him up to Darwin and the hospital. The doctor there amputated the leg, but it was too late. His body had collapsed and he died six weeks after the accident. George was at the funeral along with a lot of his old mates. But they wouldn't let Gladys or Alice attend, even though both were in town working. The rest of us weren't even notified. The peanuts stopped arriving at the Bungalow. My Mum wasn't allowed to go to the funeral either, she was stuck at Donkey Camp. Frank Kruger was buried in Darwin. They bury you quick in the tropics. His other family couldn't get up for it either.

After the funeral George went back to Katherine. It was a terrible time. Without Frank to hold things together, the government took the family farm. Everyone stopping there became homeless. My Mum and Bobby had to go to the Rockhole Mission. George and Lily stayed at Donkey Camp for as long as they could. He kept things going and looked after some of my father's trucks and stuff.

Some Kruger men arrived after the Wet season in 1938. They were there to settle my father's legal affairs. They took everything that Frank owned – his trunks, books and stuff, selling off what they could. The farm was leased to George Lim next door. George was given some money and became basically homeless. The Kruger men headed back to Darwin. They said they were off to South Africa. That was the end of that.

George spoke of how my sister, Gladys, had been working at Darwin Hospital with Emma Campbell and Daisy Ruddick when the first bombs fell. Gladys, my sister Ada, and all the other women residents of Darwin and the Top End were soon evacuated down to South Australia. But the full blood Aboriginal communities were not evacuated so my mother, Polly, was living in the Aboriginal Compound that had been built at my father's place, Donkey Camp. I learnt lots of the family stories for the first time. From having no family I was being given the biggest mob of sisters and brothers, nephews and nieces. It was totally overwhelming. And then George had to get back on the train and back to work.

I visited him in Katherine as soon as I had some time off. His wife and kids were still down south. I told him a bit about Loves Creek. We avoided anything too hard. But George wanted me to see Donkey Camp and my mother. I took a bit of convincing but then we were on our way in George's car. My Mum was an older woman by this time. She was fifty, an Aboriginal woman who had done it tough.

The Aboriginal Compound operated a bit like those at the Bungalow or Jay Creek Reserve. It wasn't far east along the river towards the gorge and what was then the main Darwin road. We came to a fence on the left towards the river. It was my first look that I can remember at my father's old place, where I was born and lived my early years. The compound was gated. It had a supervisor's house back a bit from the gate. There was a big sign saying "Out of Bounds to All Troops". I stood in uniform near the car as George asked one of the residents to get Mum because her long lost son was visiting.

At the start of the war the army had taken over my father's Donkey Camp site. Like in Alice, the army needed a big workforce so Aboriginal men were recruited from all the local stations and fringes of towns. Old Springvale Station on the western side of Katherine was given new life as the Aboriginal workers' compound. The families of some of these Aboriginal workers were moved to the Donkey Camp site. The settlement had a fairly big population that included Aboriginal women in domestic employment in town.

There was much wailing and crying from down in the camp when the message was passed along. My Mum wasn't the only one with taken-away kids that had disappeared into Central Australia. My mother and some other old women started walking up to the fence. After all this time we were all a bit overwhelmed at the meeting. It had been more than fifteen years since I had been snatched and taken away by the police. For my mother to have me back standing in front of her must have been a tremendous shock.

Now I was a man dressed in uniform standing on the other side of the fence. I didn't have a lot of experience dealing with strong emotions. Institutions, stockwork and then the army had toughened me up to shut down anything too hard. It had been such a long time since I had felt my mother's hug or any family affection, not since I was too young to remember.

All the wailing and crying attracted the attention of Police Sergeant Mannion, the compound supervisor. That was the end of the visit for us. He stormed over and we were told to move on. When we said I was there to visit my mother he refused to listen. He threatened to lock us up and have us charged with cohabitation if we hung around. We were told bluntly that the compound was off limits to soldiers, even if they were family. No exceptions were going to be made. Polly couldn't leave and come with us. She was a prisoner behind the fence. So we were forced to retreat back to the car and George's place. I was really angry but I also had to leave the next day.

George's life was different to any life I knew. He had close connections across town. Perhaps it was due to the war, but the separation between the mixed descent and full descent Aboriginal mob was a lot less than in Alice Springs. Relationships and sex across the different groups seemed much freer and easier under the tropical sun. Perhaps Aboriginal culture had changed a lot with the Aboriginal community living close to town over longer periods of time. The old men had lost a lot of authority already and the young people were escaping into a broader world. It was very different from Alice Springs, let alone Loves Creek or Atnarpa.

Getting to know my mother

Eventually I was able to spend a bit of time with my Mum. She could get into town to George's place when I was on leave. But it had been a long grieving process for both of us. After my father's death in 1938, my mother and my sister Bobby had been forced off Donkey Camp. They had moved to Mr Long's mission at Rockhole, just out of Katherine. My mother had become part of the Gospel Church. In 1939, she married a Jawoyn man called Lightning. He was a traditional owner for the local Katherine area.

My mother told me of her concerns about me being a soldier. She worried that I might have to kill people. She wasn't entirely pacified when I said my work was loading and unloading trucks and trains. I hadn't had to fire a rifle in anger or been involved in any fighting. She thought killing was a very great evil. Her religious views in many areas were a bit difficult for me. I was a young man making the best of things. It was very hard to get around the cultural divide. I had lost all my local language and cultural connections. Her English was a struggle. So it was difficult for me to do much with her. I suspect it might have been difficult to find a way of spending a whole lot of time in her company, even if that was allowed.

It was much easier for me to spend time in the company of my brother, George, talking army, stockwork and men's stuff. I suppose it suited my need to be seen as a man living in a man's world. I was much too old to be mothered. Plus there was all that stuff of being left alone to fend for myself for all those years. Seeing my mother was hard for me.

After the war my mother became an ordained minister. With other Aboriginal preachers she worked alongside Mr Long, as he set up missions in the new settlements the government created to get Aboriginal people out of Katherine – into places like the Beswick Mission. Later Mr Long went back to Alice Springs and I got to know him there.

The challenges of my time in the army

I went from being a good stockman and an initiated man, well respected around Loves Creek, to being a kid in the army. I was the fellow who had never been kissed. I was naive and easily impressed by the older blokey stories. It felt good to be accepted in the company of much older men. They were married and had lived the hard life of family men around the fringes of towns and mining camps. But I struggled to be my own person. They could get drunk and find their way home. They could fight like threshing machines at the drop of a hat, and give you a hard time if you didn't jump straight in next to them. In the end I found myself giving away my knowledge of being a person of magic in the world of Eastern Arrernte culture to become a regular army bloke.

Some of the other fellows were initiated men too. Some had a history in the saddle and as good men in the stock camps. But at times in the army we were all too rough and tough. We hit the grog from time to time, forgetting what was right and wrong. We were thrown together as a group and needed to stand together or be overwhelmed by the racism of our new institutional life in a white man's army. We had some good times. There were lots of good people. But in the end I did some things that I wouldn't have done if I had been older. I certainly wouldn't have done them by myself. You get drawn into the company of older men, your mates and only companions. And sometimes other people end up making decisions that you can't stand up against. You go along with things being too weak and out of practice of how to stand alone. There were times in the army like that.

In the early days I was just pleased to be accepted by this new and older group. I was a bit of a mascot, teased about spending all my money on sweets. I was allowed to follow along into a big man's world of Friday night fights and alcohol. And I liked the confidence and warmth that it grew up in me. There was a lot of me that was terrified of failing in this strange new world. So I tried desperately to do the expected things and to stick close to my mates.

But after the months and years rolled by, there were lots of things I missed as well. I wasn't all that sure about the person I was becoming. I was often enough messy with the grog and angry at the world. There were still no girlfriends or women in my life. I learnt how to brag with the best of them. You needed to skite to not be targeted. But I still hadn't been kissed or had someone love me. This was part of my anger. The army was a womanless world. I managed to get into more than my fair share of trouble, without doing much or changing the world at all.

I was glad enough to be finished with the army when peace finally came. The money and the food had been good. Much better than on any stock camps I have ever had to survive. But food is only one hunger. I was more hungry to be away from big groups of men. I wanted more control of my life. I missed doing things I was good at. I missed the horses and the individualism of working out bush. I missed the more naive fun of being with a bunch of hopeless romantics still thinking it was important to get up in the morning and do your share of looking after the people you work with and the world you are living in.

I'm not sure how the old Aboriginal men of Loves Creek would judge my time in the army. How the women who had mothered me would have seen my life. They would have been saddened that I didn't come back to Loves Creek. That the boy they had saved and then adopted into their magic world was going to keep running away from looking after their bit of the landscape. But I would have got some respect for escaping the Bloomfields and surviving through my army days. Tom, Tim, Jerry and the others had been trapped at the Arltunga Mission, watching the men of God change their world forever. They probably would have made a sad but funny story of it, and kept on doing what they thought was the right and proper thing as the seasons rolled past and their people lost their homes. They would have worried for the country, the law and the stories. I felt these things but I took a long time to give them shape. At first I just took off. I knew I wanted to be somewhere else and to find out about myself. This was about looking for and getting to know my family. Getting on with growing up in a bigger world and becoming a stronger man within it. It was to take me a long time yet to get over all the powerlessness and betrayal of my childhood and teenage years.

Travelling man

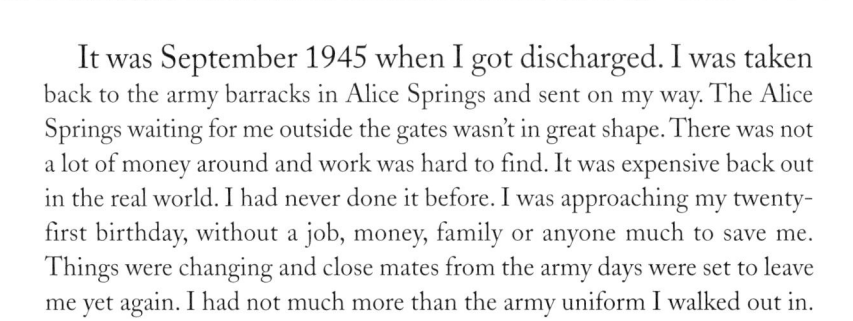

It was September 1945 when I got discharged. I was taken back to the army barracks in Alice Springs and sent on my way. The Alice Springs waiting for me outside the gates wasn't in great shape. There was not a lot of money around and work was hard to find. It was expensive back out in the real world. I had never done it before. I was approaching my twenty-first birthday, without a job, money, family or anyone much to save me. Things were changing and close mates from the army days were set to leave me yet again. I had not much more than the army uniform I walked out in.

I left the army with a lot of sadness and confusion. There was no girlfriend waiting for me. I was losing everything: friendships, the regular money and the lifestyle. The ones catching the train heading down south were waved off, mostly never to be seen again. The family blokes split off pretty quickly. They had wives they hadn't seen for years and kids that had grown up. The pressure went straight on for them to get a job and some money coming in. None of us had saved anything much during the war. Soon it was just us single blokes with no girlfriends, no money and no prospects of making any.

Alice wasn't a big drinking community. You couldn't drown yourself in alcohol even if you tried. Not like today. We had little money for booze and there wasn't much rum floating about anyway. So the celebration on leaving the army was more of a tea party. It didn't involve putting a cheque over the bar and drinking until you fell over. We would have struggled to be allowed into the front door of the hotels anyway. So what we did on leaving was catch up with people in the shacks of Rainbow Town. There were a few homemade cakes and the occasional bottle of rum to be shared around. Less often someone had a guitar and a bit of music. We might have a slab of meat if someone came in from the stations, or had knocked over a kangaroo.

The football season was well and truly over for the year. Once in a while there was a Saturday night dance. The churches put on a slide night or two and even the occasional movie. Visiting boxing troupes turned up to provide a bit of excitement. Occasionally there was a local fight night. The rest of the time you had to make your own fun. That was all the social life on offer in Alice Springs after the war.

In the few weeks I stayed in Alice on leaving the army, I caught up with some of the old Bungalow boys who were in town. They had stayed at home working on the stations. They were mostly younger. They quickly enough had to head off back to their real life. New work in the town itself was drying up with the army pulling out. Housing was a nightmare.

Us Aboriginal soldiers had hoped to return to a place where we could live on an equal footing with the white population. We weren't happy to be forced back into the overcrowded shacks and humpies of Rainbow Town. Most of us had been politicised by our time in the army. Bill Ludgate and a lot of other returned Aboriginal soldiers started talking up for proper Aboriginal housing in town. But there was to be no proper houses for some years yet. It was a fight with the old guard who didn't want Aboriginal people living anywhere near them. They wanted the social gap that comes from seeing Aboriginal people living apart in makeshift camps. They wanted a pool of workers grateful for any old handout rather than a socially active Aboriginal community asking for proper wages and conditions.

I knew that if I didn't escape I would end up back on one of the stations doing stockwork. This wasn't my dream. I had seen a bit of the world where I was treated with a bit of respect, and I wanted to recapture it. Not far below the surface smiles, I was angry enough and had a strong sense of what was right. Not much in Alice Springs seemed right for me at that time.

I decided to live by the bushman's code. Look after your mates and avoid the bosses. I had no steady girlfriend and nothing but a promise to some old men out at Atnarpa. There was little to hold me to the Alice. But what to do next was the problem. It was okay to talk about a life of mateship and freedom. But a man had to eat. The married blokes didn't really want us single blokes hanging around their women or teenage daughters. Their wives didn't want to feed us. Nor did they need us dragging their blokes away from home. It quickly became time for me to get a job or move on.

While the war lasted it had brought a new excitement and energy to the town. It had broken down a few of the old racist divisions and for Aboriginal workers wages were better than before. But this didn't survive the war. The whites in town and the station owners wanted the old days back. The full blood Aboriginal people that had been living around Charles Creek, along the Todd or over near the casino area, had already been shifted out of town to the new Catholic mission at Arltunga. Now the push was on to get the mixed descent mob back on to the settlements and cattle stations.

This was truer in Alice Springs than places in the Top End. The stations had struggled during the war to keep their staff. Now they were back in charge. The government had started a permit system designed to keep Aboriginal families from living in town. As an Aborigine you could be required to produce a permit to come past the town boundaries. To get a permit you needed a job. If you didn't have work you were forced back onto the missions or pastoral stations.

The war had been won, but we were going to pay for the victory for the next few years. The government had the whole country on rations. We got given a few coupons that told us what we could buy. On top of having a coupon you needed to have money as well. There was a bit of under-the-table stuff happening. Like always if you had money you had power. You

Travelling man

could make things happen. Like always, it wasn't us with the money. We were the ones that could have things done to us. Truth or justice was never a big part of it. You had to be careful and keep an eye out.

On discharge we lost our status as soldiers. Even though I was eligible, I never applied for a soldier's exemption to the Aboriginal Ordinances. These exemptions were the 'dog tags'. 'Only dogs get registered' was a saying of a lot of us blokes. If we had the exemption we couldn't associate with or marry into the Aboriginal community. Who needed that in a world where no white people were ever going to let you in?

We became the old Bungalow boys again. The ones without a place in the landscape. We soon found ourselves being bossed about by the police and any cheeky white idiot who thought he was better than us. There were a few fights. We made some enemies. The police were telling us to look out. Again my choices were limited. But I was older, smarter and the restrictions had become easier to avoid.

There was less enforcement of some of the rules than before the war. I would have been paid wages back on the stations. But the idea of going back to the minimal pay and exploitation out at Loves Creek or another station had no appeal. Louis Bloomfield was dead but Harry was not a forgiving sort of fellow. He didn't like looking foolish. Lillian was even more of a force to be reckoned with. Baden had left and was trying to buy some cattle land out east. Baden would have employed me. But I was restless and wanted to see a bit more of the world.

So I headed back to find my family in Katherine. While some of my mates had reasons to be in Alice Springs, I was a freer man who could look about a bit. It was time to hit the road. I decided to become a travelling man. I still had my army clothes that I had walked out with. People treated you different if you'd been in the army. I got a few blankets with the last of my money, made them up into a rough swag, threw in a few changes of clothes and talked a truck driver into giving me a lift up to Katherine.

Back in the Top End

It took a few days on the road then I got dropped off at George's place. Katherine was a much smaller place in those days with hardly any houses. There was a big mob of people stopping around George's shack. George was there to do the introductions. There was his wife, Lily, and their mob of kids. My sister, Gladys, and her kids had arrived back from South Australia. Ada, too, and her kids were there. So it was a big mob of family of all ages running about the place. Both Ada and Gladys were stuck in Katherine until the restrictions on going to Darwin were lifted. It was another twelve months until Darwin residents were allowed back. Quite a lot of Darwin family groups were staying in Katherine.

Ada had been joined by her husband, Putt Ahmat, down from Darwin. Putt was with his brother Johnny. I actually knew Johnny Ahmat a little. He had joined the army and served in the same unit as me in Alice Springs. So that was a bit strange, knowing him better than my family. Not that we were close. Johnny and I hadn't known of any family connection in the army. Johnny had stayed in Alice Springs when I had headed up the track to Larrimah.

Seeing my sisters felt very weird. I was tired from the trip. My oldest sister, Ada, who was good with a crowd, put on the kettle and the kids were named and displayed. They were a good-looking bunch. But family things made me nervous and stand-offish. I was a bit frozen in my smile, trying hard to be liked. I suppose I had a bit of a 'wait-and-see' attitude while I found out where I might fit into this new family of mine. It was the first sight of my sisters since Kahlin days nearly fifteen years before. I had been six or so when I was packed up for Pine Creek, leaving Gladys behind. Now I was a twenty-one year old initiated man, and a stranger. Luckily there were lots of kids about to keep things moving. Not that I was much good with kids. But they were a diversion and kept everyone busy enough. You knew where you stood with kids.

I had heard a few of the stories from George of Gladys at the hospital when the bombs dropped, but not a lot more of her life. I knew less about Ada. Now I heard of their war, working for a family in Peterborough in South Australia. It had been cold and fairly miserable. They were 'Top Enders' who liked a bit of warmth in their sun. They were all glad to be back, even if it was sleeping out with the mosquitoes in a half-built shack, not really knowing what was going to happen next. They had a home and it was in Darwin.

Gladys told the story of meeting a fellow on the train when she was first going down to South Australia. He was a train guard called Mr Swensson. He had sought her out to give her a hand and some money. Said he was related to our father. Gladys hadn't seen him since. But the money had been real handy. They had gone down south with nothing much more than what they could carry. The government didn't have much of a plan or anywhere for them to stay. It was getting colder down there too. So Gladys had been able to get the kids some warmer clothes and a bit of extra food. She had ended up working for a family down there, cleaning up and cooking. The wages had been just enough to keep them all. She had come back at the first opportunity. She didn't even wait for approval from the authorities. Just caught the first train she could to Alice then got a ride up in a truck with the kids.

I heard lots of stories, too many to take in. I had some brothers, Leslie and Johnny, who had drowned at Knott's Crossing. They were buried there, just down from Donkey Camp. Ada was Jimmy Gibbs's daughter and I was family with the Gibbs mob. My mother had Wave Hill family. Lots of stories. But they were all strangers to me really. How was I supposed to react? It was all a bit edgy. Everyone was swagging on the verandah of George's old place. George was in the early stages of building two bigger places on his block and you could see the activity. But with the post-war rationing still going on, it was hard to come by proper building materials. Putt and Johnny were helping him organise the building. So I was given a tour of the place and what was to happen. The more I got to know George, the more I liked him. He was a lot like me and always liked having a few plans on the go.

Then Johnny was off down into town to catch up with some mates and I took the opportunity to go with him. Sisters took a bit of getting used to. I was as nervous as a kitten around them for a good time. Nearly as badly as I struggled to keep a conversation going with my mother when she called in to visit. I had been a long time away. Nothing I had done and no one I knew had much meaning in their lives. Later on when Johnny and I came back and it got a bit darker, a spot was found for me to throw out my swag. I had a lot to think about. What with the mosquitoes I didn't get a lot of sleep that night.

Once George was able to beg, borrow or steal enough building materials, he started building his proper houses on Block 63 in Kirby Street. He had bought the land after my father died with the money he was given by the Krugers. One house was for him, his wife, Lily, and the kids. The other was for my sister, Ada, and Putt. George's new house was a corrugated iron structure with a concrete floor. There wasn't really enough work happening for me to be needed to help out. And I wasn't much of a carpenter. My fencing experience at Atnarpa, with a huge saw and an axe, wasn't going to be much use. But I hopped in where I could.

My mother and Bobby came around looking shyly at me. It was hard for them to get much time in town because of Aboriginal compound restrictions. It was an emotional time. Everyone was really friendly but it was still often overwhelming for me. Part of me wanted to stay, but mostly I longed to escape. I didn't know how to play the younger brother or son and needed space to deal with things.

Some of my army mates and others from my Bungalow years had ended up in Katherine. Over a few weeks I caught up with most of them. Katherine was that sort of place. Billy Goodall found me. He was a couple of years younger. We had shared the Pine Creek Institution and later the Bungalow. Billy had a brother Mick and a sister, Kitty. They were still down in Alice Springs. Like me the whole family were really from the Top End and had been sent down to the Bungalow. Billy had come up from Alice to catch up with me. He had spent the war working at Ambalindum Station. Now he had the travel bug. We both hung around looking for work together. He too stopped at George's. It was that type of place and George was that type of bloke. Real friendly and always helping people out.

Working for the railways

Me and Billy were starting to look a bit disreputable hanging around together. Then we got a break. George told us we might get a start on one of the railway fettler gangs. Billy and me lined up and were both signed on to work on a gang operating on the line north of Katherine at a place called Hawley. I suspect being George's brother eased the way for me to get the job. There were a few blokes looking for work at the time.

It was a relief to be getting out of Katherine. Sorting out family was too hard for all of us. So I suspect everyone was a bit relieved to see me go. I hated not being able to pay my way. I liked having things to do and was getting sick of having too much time on my hands. It was good to be moving again. A travelling man needs a bob in his pocket as well as a plan.

Billy and I rolled our swags and caught the train north. Hawley was a small siding past Pine Creek, with the line continuing to Adelaide River then Darwin. Our fettling gang covered the rail line between Brocks Creek

Travelling man

and Fountainhead. Hawley had a couple of railway houses that were shared by the crew. There was even a cook, a fellow called Ted McNamara. He was a great cook and spoiled us. But he was in demand and often got called to replace other cooks along the line. When that happened we fended for ourselves. Ted was an older bloke of mixed Aboriginal descent, originally from Darwin. He had a long history with the railway. The food and other supplies would come on the rail from Katherine or Darwin. You could order in.

Ted Lucy was our boss. He was a young white fellow whose parents owned the Fountainhead Hotel. It was a happy enough camp. We were living well. The boss usually disappeared up to his parents' place for the weekends, and the rest of us had the place to ourselves.

My job as a fettler involved checking the line for washouts and making sure there wasn't too much buckling of the line. The track had been laid on packed earth, raised up above the surrounding country to stop it going underwater in the Wet. This packed earth would often subside a bit, taking the sleepers and the railway line with it. Us fettlers needed to pack underneath the sleepers to keep the line securely in place. Otherwise the train might derail. Changes in temperature also caused problems. Hot weather would make the steel expand. This sometimes led to some spreading out of the gap between the two lines as sections twisted. Cold weather could see the lines contract and separate at the joins. Us fettlers needed to check, flatten out and re-secure any lines that had drifted too far out of alignment. It was constant heavy work.

Much of the time you were stuck at the camp. But sometimes you could catch the train and take a couple of days in Katherine or Darwin. I was able to spend a weekend or two keeping in touch with George and the others. Rail travel was free. I was able to get to know a bit more about the family and even met some of the broader family around Katherine. One time I met my uncle Larry Althouse, who was a brother of Polly and a boss drover. Jack was a lanky fellow and had been a good mate of my father. They had done a lot of work together over the years.

Hawley was about half a mile from a cattle station. This station had a few Aboriginal families living there. On Wednesdays when the train came in, a few of the Aboriginal women would come down to collect the mail from us. Sometimes they would come down in the balmy evenings and stay the night. Some of the older blokes had partners from the station. It was a bit like

Katherine all over again. Beautiful and sometimes available young women to spend time with. Billy was very impressed.

But I didn't stay that long, only six months or so. It was a restless time for me. I left Hawley for a job with the Main Roads department. Billy left at much the same time. I caught up with him from time to time over the years. He ended up doing some droving. He worked with a fellow called Jack Davis, mostly taking mobs from Top End stations down the stock route south to Katherine and then Newcastle Waters and across the Barkly Tablelands into Queensland.

Working on the roads

My new job was working on a road gang patrolling the highway from a base on the Ferguson River near Pine Creek. The boss was a fellow called Bob Marcum. He was a white fellow who owned a local pastoral lease called Wondi Station. The lease pushed back from the Ferguson up towards Edith Creek. The station was just a bit of scrub country much too small to make a living from. Bob worked it when he could and since he didn't make much from the place, he had a day job working with Main Roads. He was like a lot of the battling bush cockies. My father no doubt had similar stories.

Bob Marcum was a good boss. He was friends with George and some of the Katherine mob. The other blokes on the road gang included Lee Debrey, an older white bloke from down south, and Les Turley, another white bloke. It was a good camp with two or three caravans set up as quarters, kitchen and mess. We didn't have the luxury of a cook. Not that cooking for ourselves was that challenging. I had been a bit of a bush cook when I did the trip to Queensland with Baden.

Unlike the fettling job, the work was not very strenuous. You had to put the signs up on the road during the Wet if the river had come up and there was water over the road. The rest of the time was spent hanging on shovels repairing the odd pothole. I was mainly recruited for my horsemanship and ability to work cattle.

For Bob had a second business going. All of us at the camp were stockmen at heart. If a few cattle strayed on to the road we would get our horses and push the mob along some back route on to Bob's place. The money from selling them on was later split. It was going so well for a while that Bob arranged for Lee and me to take up a lease on unoccupied land near his place.

I didn't end up keeping the lease for long. We put a few cattle on this new place. The idea was to stock up with cleanskins. But like my father's story, in the end there was not a lot of money to be made from having a few scrub cattle, even if you hadn't paid for them. The police start taking too much interest if you have a lot more cattle than you should. Especially if one of the old station bosses starts complaining of being short on their count. After twelve months or so it was getting a bit hot to stick around. I decided to try my luck at a bigger game and ended up leaving Bob Marcum and the road gang.

Working for the 'Whispering Baritone'

I left the road works after catching up with a mate, Bill Riley, who I knew from the Bungalow. Bill had been at Pine Creek and was contract mustering with a fellow called Fred Martin. They needed an extra hand. Fred was an old fellow by this time. He had a bit of a colourful history as a poddy dodger and horse rustler, only just avoiding being locked up on a number of occasions.

Fred was once arrested for having a mob of horses that clearly weren't his. He had been bringing them back from Queensland when someone had seen his tracks and notified the police. This was back in the 1930s. He had been caught red-handed around Timber Creek. But on seeing the police, he had managed to set up a diversion and escaped. He laid low for a while before getting caught when he popped up for a drink in Katherine. The police took him back to Timber Creek for the trial. But somehow the stolen horses managed to disappear from a police holding yard late at night before the case went to court, and it had to be dropped for lack of evidence.

Fred Martin was known as the 'Whispering Baritone'. Even when you were sitting in a huge paddock with no one around for miles, he would lean over to talk so that no one could overhear. He always had a plan or two on the go. These plans often involved a bit of cattle duffing of cleanskins as a sideline to any legitimate work he might have on the go. By this time Fred was a battling pastoralist himself with a place called Florina Station down near the junction of the Ferguson and Katherine Rivers. It was pretty much due west of Katherine. With Billy and me, Fred got himself a job contract mustering on Vestey's land in the scrub country on the edges of Delamere Station. It was crocodile country, wild and beautiful.

Delamere had been let go during the war and wild mobs of cattle had spread out into the rougher parts of the station. Fred's arrangement with Vestey's was that he would get paid so much money for every cow we mustered, branded and delivered down south to Tom Pearce's old station of Willeroo. Catching the wild beasts in the swamps and gullies of Delamere was hard work. They were mostly full-grown beasts that hadn't seen a man. None of the males had been castrated so there were a lot of angry young bulls about the place. They had horns and a savage desire to avoid capture.

As usual Fred had a sideline that involved stocking up his place at Florina with some of the cleanskins. He kept a couple of branding irons and it was one for Vestey and a couple for Fred, and so on. Bill and me had the job of taking the small mobs the hundred-odd miles north past Willeroo Station, dodging west along an obscure back route that Fred showed us, and on to his place at Florina. The rest of the mob that we caught were then taken down to the main yards of Willeroo.

Fred then got the job of droving the cattle from Willeroo down to Vestey's holding station of Helen Springs, south of Elliott. Fred was probably lucky to get these jobs as usually Vestey's was pretty careful about who it employed. And Fred was known to have helped himself to more than his share of Vestey's animals over the years. But there was a lack of drovers and the jobs were offered to Fred because he was there.

Bill and I took Fred's droving plant of forty-odd horses up to Willeroo to start the droving trip. Fred rounded up a few extra stockmen. Vestey's soon had mustered and selected the store cattle they wanted taken. The manager counted them off to us and we pushed them slowly along the stock route south. It was towards the end of the Dry season and there was not a whole lot of feed about. Other droving teams before us along the route had taken whatever feed there had been. But Fred was an experienced hand at pushing cattle along poor stretches of country. Bill did the horse tailing. I filled in as cook. Fred had managed to get four experienced Aboriginal stockmen from Willeroo to make up the team.

It wasn't legal, but on these trips us drovers replaced sick or injured beasts by taking cleanskin cattle off some of the larger stations. Killers were also likely to be from someone else's mob. Drovers were paid by the number you arrived with. It was good to get there with pretty much the same as you left with, minus a few beasts that you were allowed to kill for meat along the way. If you lost too many there were penalties.

As a result of letting the cattle spread a bit when the feed was bad, and taking the odd beast along the way, droving crews were rarely popular with the owners and managers of the places you travelled through. Plus you only had a limited time before you were required to move on. You had to cover so many miles each day. If you didn't the stock inspectors would be on to you. But if the cattle got amongst a station herd and you had to stop to separate the two, what could you do? It might take a day to sort them apart.

If you mustered up an isolated herd in the gullies, branded them quickly and moved on with them in your mob, you were usually not caught. But you had to be pretty vigilant because the head stockmen and station managers kept an eye out and could track you if you seemed to divert on to their land. Then the police would be on to you. As I was saying, Fred was an old hand and despite the terrible mob and not much feed we arrived with nearly as many as we started out with. A masterful bit of droving. Later on, the same team of Fred, Bill Riley, and me mustered sections of Willeroo Station for wild cattle and cleanskins.

Then it was November and the build-up to the Wet made working cattle too difficult. We took the horse plant back to Florina Station. Fred had decided to go quietly for a time. He saw me right with some money, so I had more in my pocket than I'd ever seen before. He dropped us off at George's in Katherine. We had slaughtered a beast so there was plenty of tucker. George and Lily were pleased to see me.

The leprosarium

Once at George's, me and Billy split up. After a few drinks he decided to catch up with his family and caught the bus down to Alice. I was sad to see him go. We'd had a great time of it. We had built up a solid friendship in the months chasing cattle across the scrub. We had shared some exciting times and a few bottles of rum. He was a real close mate. Fred headed back to Florina. As he got older he had less time for the towns, preferring the rugged isolation of his station. After hitting the shops, paying a few bills and getting loaded up with supplies, he was off.

George had his house built by this time. It was a rambling affair made from bits and pieces of material that he had been able to buy or scavenge. His big tribe of kids had spread out to fill the verandahs and sleep-outs. Lily kept the place going. They had a lovely garden that kept food on the table. It felt like the sort of place you could comfortably grow old in. A bit of an old homestead come to town. There was a shed and camping area for people stopping in. A few of the old-timers stopped in now that the season was over.

My sisters had headed back to Darwin. Gladys and Johnny had got homesick for the sea breezes. They had packed up and headed north as soon as the army allowed families back. Ada and Putt's plan to stick around Katherine hadn't really worked out either. They had headed back to Darwin too. Katherine was dying again.

When the government had started pushing people out of the town back to the stations and the new missions, a lot of the life had gone. The army had packed up. The work went with them. The abattoir was pretty well shut down. The parties had gone with the money and the jobs. My mother had gone out east past Maranboy into Arnhem Land to work on the mission there.

George was still getting up early and working at the railways. The trains hadn't shut down for the Wet season yet. But I could see he was struggling. He was in his mid-forties and had lived hard. But it wasn't age catching up with him. His eyes were playing up and he was feeling off-colour all the time. He had skin ulcers that didn't want to heal. George didn't like doctors much. And I suspect he had an idea he might be in trouble.

Perhaps I could have stayed on and helped him out a bit more. But George wasn't one to ask for anything. He still remembered what it was like to be young and restless. Darwin was where people said I should go. So he wasn't surprised when I said I was not staying for Christmas but was heading off north. I played the rich uncle for the kids, buying them presents and treating them at the shops. I had a few drinks with George and his mates, said goodbye to Lily, left the meat and caught the bus north.

Things were happening in Darwin as the place came alive again after its desertion and plundering during the war. It was where the wine, women and song had moved to. The weather was disgustingly hot and humid. You expected that in the days before air-conditioning and fans. You just got on with things. At least in Darwin you got the sea breezes some nights when you could sit outside and feel a bit cooler. I couldn't remember Darwin from my childhood. So it was a new adventure. I was only sorry Billy wasn't there with me.

George got worse. In the months after Christmas 1947, the welfare got after him to go and see a doctor. He had taken to wearing dark glasses during the day. When they finally dragged him to the doctor he got the news he was expecting. He had the dreaded leprosy. Poor old George was packed up and taken by boat to the Channel Island Leprosarium. From there they moved him over to East Arm.

George must have hated being locked up. He had fought all his life to stand on his own two feet and to be left alone by the government. Now they had him locked away where he couldn't escape. His family didn't have his wages coming in. Lily was forced back into domestic work with a baby and four school-aged kids. Things looked fairly bleak. But eventually the railways paid him out and his pension came through. Lily at least was able to get some regular wife's money to keep her going. Things settled down in a different pattern without George around the place keeping things going for everyone.

It was a shock to the rest of us when we heard. You start getting a bit paranoid about whether you might have caught it from him, hanging around sharing cups of tea and the odd glass of rum. Leprosy made everyone real nervous. He got a hard time from some who said he should have done something about it earlier. They checked out Lily and the kids. They were okay. The family was fine.

Not long after this George was joined by our stepbrother, Jack Gibbs. Him and Ada shared a father, Jimmy Gibbs. Jimmy was an old-timer like our own father who had always battled the administration and racism of the Territory. He had worked as a stockman and drover before starting a battler's station out on the Roper River. The government had sold him out to the big money stations. His mixed descent kids had ended up in the institutions. Jimmy had often called in at Donkey Camp on his few trips into Katherine. So Jack and George went back a long way. George was about fifteen years older.

Jack had ended up working down in Central Australia after getting out of Kahlin. He had been living with Melba, one of Dick Palmer's daughters, after splitting up with his wife. He had worked as a stockman out at Bond Springs Station with Dick as the head stockman. But now the doctors had sent him up to the East Arm leprosarium too. In an act of great love, Melba Palmer went with Jack to East Arm and stayed with him. They didn't have any kids.

But this wasn't an option for Lily with her mob, even if she wanted it and George would allow it. She just had to struggle back in Katherine with hardly any money and no father for the kids. At least she had the house. But welfare was always watching for her to fail. The kids copped a terrible time at school with their father being in the leprosarium. They grew up tough and capable of defending themselves. George Junior ended up being sent down south to St Francis's Home in South Australia when he was deemed out of control.

God knows how people got leprosy. It was just one of those things that seemed to float around the Top End in the early days. People reckoned the Chinese miners brought it with them in the gold rush of the 1880s. The Chinese got blamed for most things in those days.

East Arm wasn't such a bad spot. But it was a prison. You weren't allowed out. The houses were okay and the religious sisters that ran the place treated people pretty well. There were jobs to do, art and craft things, and it was a pretty sort of place. But having a disease like leprosy is very depressing. Some of the older residents of the place were in a bad way. You could see your future in their pain and suffering.

Leprosy or Hansen's disease, as they started calling it, has been around for a long time. The Bible talks of lepers all the time. You had to wear special clothes and have a bell to ring in the old days. People thought it really infectious and were terrified of you being anywhere near them. You were excluded from the community. The disease causes the nerves in your fingers and toes to die. You lose the ability to feel things. You get ulcers and skin discolouration. Gangrene often causes fingers and toes and later whole limbs to die and fall off. It is an appalling illness that makes people look terrible.

George and Jack were lucky. They had discovered some treatments using the new penicillin drugs by the time they got to East Arm. Over the next decade they pretty much sorted out a treatment that meant people didn't have to stay isolated from the world. By the early 1960s people were being sent home from East Arm and other leprosariums. George and Jack were able to go back home.

It wasn't easy going home though, after being away so long. The splotches on your face and body and other scars of the disease stayed with you. People were still nervous around you and treated you differently. A lot of the residents at East Arm decided to stay there. It was just too hard to leave. They felt too marked up and vulnerable. The place became a sanctuary for them. But George went home. Lily had formed a new relationship after the more than fifteen years he was away. She had another child. They seemed to have sorted it out a bit. George was an undemanding fellow.

His kids were a bit more of a challenge. He hardly knew them in some ways. The older three had been away down south during the war years. Only Freddy was born after the war. Then George was away working a lot when they came back, only to disappear into East Arm after a couple of years. Now he was back, marked up and scary, wanting to reclaim his house and his life. They were all grown up. It must have been tough for everyone.

Pearling in the Top End

When I first hit Darwin I got dropped off by the bus on the Stuart Highway on the edge of the main town. It didn't take long to find Gladys's place down at the nearby Parap Camp. It was basically a collection of army surplus tents that housed a lot of the mixed descent Aboriginal families returning to Darwin after having spent the war down south. I ended up stopping with Gladys, Johnny and the kids. I still had money in my pocket. It was approaching Christmas and I was able to treat the kids to a few presents.

I was a bit of a loner and didn't really like taking up space in the family house, so often I stayed with some of the other single blokes. But it was handy to have somewhere to throw gear, especially when the storms came.

The whole camp was rough and ready. A roof over our heads, toilets, water tanks and not much more. Lots of big families. The place was overrun with mobs of kids playing their games of footie and moving as a group between houses. Occasionally welfare or the police might turn up. They would check up on who was about. Sometimes you saw young blokes sneaking out the back when the cars were coming through the front. It was a multicultural group – mixed Aboriginal descent mob, Torres Strait Islanders like my brothers-in-law that had come to Darwin with the pearl boats, people with Chinese, Japanese, Filipino, Malay, Greek and Russian backgrounds in addition to the usual English, Irish and Scottish heritage. There were the German-English Aborigines, like us Krugers, and many other ethnic mixtures. Our families had come from all over the world. Our Aboriginal heritage covered most of the Territory. Most of us had been through the institutions. Our loyalty those days was to our families, our brothers and sisters from the dormitories, and the Darwin Buffaloes football team. It was a pretty knockabout existence.

Parap Camp hadn't existed before the war. Kahlin, with its children's institution, had been the main place. But the houses had been knocked down and the government had arranged for the Anglican Church to build the Retta Dixon Home on Bagot Reserve to replace the Kahlin Compound. But us mob didn't want to live out there. It was a mosquito-pit mangrove swamp out towards Nightcliff, about five miles along the coastline. It was too far from work and the town itself.

Ada and Putt Ahmat had got one of the newer government houses closer in to Darwin itself. They had made the move about the same time I was settling in at Parap Camp. That gave me another place to go. Putt had his own business running a cordial factory. He had contracts selling to the army. I got lucky looking for work. Johnny was working mainly on the wharves and with the municipal council. He got me a start. My first job in Darwin was with their mosquito gangs. A team of us were employed by the council to go to the swamps on the edges of town. From boats and on foot we would hold hoses blowing out clouds of insecticide in an attempt to kill the larvae before they hatched. It was poisonous work. Today people know the dangers and have protective clothing and face masks. We went in our shorts. The money was average. But it was a job. Later on I got bits of work on the hygiene crews. Darwin was all outside toilets in those days.

I built a reputation for being a good worker and got starts at the wharf when it was going, mainly unloading food and goods for the new shops being built in Darwin. Occasionally the ships had to be reloaded but not much was heading out of Darwin.

A group of us young mixed descent boys lived a fairly transient life around town, doing the same type of work. It was a long party of sorts. I played football with the Buffs. It was the Ahmat team. We played hard, partied hard and tried to impress the few young women about the place with our charm and style. The lucky ones got a girlfriend and something approaching a permanent job with the council or the Department of Works. The rest of us had roll-up starts where you turned up hoping that there would be work that day. It was a bit the same with girlfriends.

Getting a start

Bits and pieces of work were okay but I wanted a solid start. It got to March. I was spending a lot of time hunting up whatever local work was on offer. That was how I became an accidental seaman. The only job going seemed to be with the pearl boats. But I was no saltwater man. The idea of going to sea didn't do much for me. The Ahmats had originally come to town as pearlers. Through them I got to know some of the people on the boats. So when they said there was work going, I headed down to the Paspaley office. I had been told by Johnny and Putt to say I wanted to be a diver. To my surprise it worked and they gave me a start.

The main ports were Broome and Thursday Island in the Torres Straits, but Darwin had a small fleet that did okay. Most of the money was in making buttons from pearl shell, rather than finding wild pearls. The war had quietened things down a bit and put the Japanese, the big players in the industry, out of the picture.

At the end of the war the Japanese industry struggled to build up its crews and get its fleets of luggers operating. The Paspaleys, a big Greek family who'd arrived in the frontier days, bought boats owned previously by the Japanese and were expanding quickly. They wanted to be like the Vesteys in the cattle game. There were still some smaller family boats operating but Paspaley was becoming the benchmark and main player. They were opening up new pearling areas up north in places like Port Essington and the Cox Peninsula.

The pearling season swings into action in March as the big equinox tides help the boats get out to good pearling areas. It could be tricky at that time of year if a late cyclone hit the Top End. Boats and crews could be lost. That is why blokes like my brothers-in-law had got out of the game. The season ran all the way through into December. Then there were a couple of months when the boats were cleaned up and refitted for another season.

I ended up signed on a lugger called the *Vivian*. An ex-Bungalow boy, Mick Heenan, was the captain. Over the next few years I worked the boats, but I never really got ahead much. It was a bit the same as droving. You were a virtual prisoner, working the season away from towns and family. Then you got a cheque at the end. A little bit as a sign on fee, the rest as a percentage of the catch. It was the bosses who made the money. You never had enough to give you a start somewhere or to see you through till the next season started. It made me sad at the time. But I made a go of it for a few years for want of something else big coming along. The cattle industry was struggling with a drought and not many cattle were being moved about. I enjoyed having a steady Darwin base during the off-season.

Mick Heenan was a bit younger than me. His father had owned Heenan's store in Alice Springs. His mother was a Warlpiri woman. He was no native-born saltwater bloke either. We were both a long way from home. He had been taken into the Bungalow at the Telegraph Station when he was five or six. It must have been between 1933 and 1935 when I was there because I can remember him as a skinny kid crying for his mother.

I had lost track of him when I went out to Loves Creek but I had heard he was sent up north with the Catholics to the Garden Point Mission on Melville Island before the war. He would have been a teenager then. As a young man Mick got work with the Catholic Brothers helping to run the boats for the mission, and with their help had largely taught himself ship's mechanics. Later he got his captain's ticket. He was a clever man. When Paspaley was desperate for new crew after the war Mick got his start as a pearling lugger captain.

Mick had a gift for practical things and could cobble together parts to keep an old diesel engine going. This was essential for the luggers around the Top End. The engines were old and likely to conk out when you really needed them. But Mick could strip them down and stick them back together again. It saved a lot of grief and he was respected for his skills.

Mick told me how he had gone back to Alice Springs once after the war and had a bit of a look around. But he was a married man by this time and a Bathurst Islander by inclination. He had a house at the mission on Garden Point and he had been adopted into the community. There was little work and nothing much to hold him in Alice Springs. I don't know if he found much of his family, so he had gone back to the sea and the mission life.

By 1948, when he got me for his boat, he was already settled down. He never hung around with the drinking crowd. In the off-season Mick would head back to Bathurst Island. I liked Mick a lot and we developed a close friendship over time. He certainly helped me out on the boat that first season.

Pearling was a dangerous business. You were working close to the coastline and if the engine failed you, or a late season storm surprised you, there could be big trouble. Not a lot of Top End pearlers grew old. Before the war the pearling companies had recruited divers and crew from Japan, Timor and the Malacca and Ambon islands of what is now Indonesia. They tended to call all South East Asian blokes 'Malays' in those days. Labour and life was seen as cheaper in that part of the world. You could exploit them more anyway. Many of them were from the same families that had been trading with the Aboriginal communities of the Gulf and diving for trepang for centuries. Some of the pearl divers had settled in Darwin. They had places down near the old police block. Many more went home if they could. But the ones in town hung around a bit with the Aboriginal and Thursday Islander communities.

The pearling life

I looked the part of a diver. You had to be tough and wiry and small like the 'Malays', so you could fit into the diving gear. It was exhausting work, but I was fit and strong from years of holding on to half-wild stockhorses. But my first time at sea was a miserable experience. I was sick as a dog. It felt like I had thrown up everything I had ever eaten. I just wanted to crawl into a hole and die. Anything to get away from the rolling of the deck. It took a long time to get anything like sea legs. The old hands just left you to it. Threw a bucket of water over you from time to time and moved you out of the sun if it got too hot.

The *Vivian* had been refitted during the off-season. It was a small lugger with not much space on deck and no room for passengers. The first night of the trip we went to anchor up near Cape Fourcroy. One of the crew threw out the anchor. Down it sank into the depths, making the noisy clatter that anchor chains do. Then there was nothing. The chain hadn't been secured to the end of the reel and the boat. So it just ran itself out and disappeared into the water.

When Mick and the others realised what had happened they were horrified. But it was gathering dark and the boat had already moved on. We turned around and the main diver had a go at trying to find the anchor. But it was too deep and dark. Hard for the boat to be kept on the spot. They threw down a mooring and we drifted around till morning. But the anchor still couldn't be located. Since you can't dive for pearls without an anchor, we had to head back to Darwin for another. It took time and we got a bit of a serve from the bosses and other people hanging around the wharf. And no doubt it came out of our pay eventually. Even though it was the fault of the mob who had refitted the boat.

The *Vivian's* crew was a mixed lot. All pearling luggers had at least two divers. The bigger luggers might have five or six. The divers relied on a rope and air pipe to communicate and breathe underwater. Responsibility for this job fell to the tender boss. Each diver had his own person holding on to their rope. Then there were general crew who pulled up the bags of pearl shell and packed them away. The captain needed to be good with an engine. Deck crew doubled up as cooks.

We only ever had one or two divers down. Ali Abdul was the diving crew supervisor, or tender boss. He held on to the lifeline when a diver was underwater. There was a system of signals that allowed the diver and tender to communicate. These were a series of short or long yanks on the rope. The tender carried a lot of responsibility, with the diver relying on him to respond quickly if his life was at risk.

The tender and crew also kept an eye out for sharks, stingrays and gropers, how long the person had been down, and anything that might be going wrong. The blokes on the boat had an idea of what was happening from the trail of bubbles hitting the surface. The diver signalled when the bag was full and needed to be pulled up, if he had run into trouble or become caught up or for any other reason.

Sharks were about but attacks were rare. The huge groper fish caused more problems. Gropers are blind blundering things that you needed to get out of the way of. Stingrays were a problem and the occasional sea snakes and smaller poisonous spiked animals. You had to be careful of sudden falls in the sea floor and coral outcrops or rocks that might cut you.

But it was being underwater that was the real killer. Depending on the depth, the diver had to come up through a number of stages to avoid the bends. The lugger had a 44-gallon drum standing upright on deck over a frame that allowed you to light a fire underneath. It was full of water in case the diver needed to come up quickly. The diver would hop into the drum, and then it would be heated up to as hot as they could stand it. It worked by slowing the release of nitrogen that had built up in the blood stream.

It didn't matter what you did, the first thing that a diver would lose was his eardrums. You couldn't work at any depth without your eardrums ripping. Until they ripped, the pain was too much to work at depth. But you would be hard of hearing for the rest of your life unless they later somehow repaired themselves.

Divers got the good money. That was why I was keen. But the possibility of a fatal mistake or being in the wrong place at the wrong time was very real. I thought it couldn't be that hard, but I was wrong. I had learnt a lot of new things in my time but it quickly became clear that diving wasn't going to be one of them. Being underwater terrified me. My imagination couldn't be shut off. I would be seeing sharks and stingrays before I even had my head strapped into the helmet. Once in the water I would be thrashing about like a dingo in a trap. I could barely control myself. A minute would feel like an hour. I would be signalling like crazy to come up.

So they quickly decided to train me up to do the labouring work on the deck instead. It was that or being fed to the sharks. There were no passengers on a pearling boat. The deck work paid a lot less money, but I survived.

Even the good divers didn't last long. After a while it just became too much. If they were lucky they might have earned enough to set themselves up in another business. Or they'd get a captain's ticket. The unlucky ones dropped back to being a deckhand like me. If you became too crazy or frail for that, then you had to retreat to a land job.

The diving gear wasn't like the cute little scuba outfits that people have these days. In the 1950s we had what was called a 'half-corselet and helmet'. A really heavy ball-shaped steel helmet with shoulder and chest extensions was placed over the diver's head. It was belted onto your body. They were like the ones you see on astronauts in the old outer space movies. You had two big circular windows for looking out. The air was pumped down a pipe connected to an air compressor. It would come in at the bottom of the helmet and escape out of a breathing mouthpiece that connected to a valve at the side. If you tipped over or got too much off the vertical, water rushed into the helmet. You had to get upright again real quick. If the compressor stopped you were in big trouble. Most shells are gathered at about twenty fathoms. That's 120 feet deep. Some divers went as deep as forty fathoms. If you're down that far you need a fair bit of time to come up.

Once you were down, the boat gently dragged you just above the sea floor. When you spotted an oyster bed you signalled the tender and the boat stopped. It then needed to stay pretty much straight above you. That was where the anchor was crucial. If the anchor started to drag or the motor took the boat somewhere else, you couldn't do the work and risked being tipped over. You might get dragged along the seabed behind the boat. I couldn't think of a worse form of torture.

You had heavy woollen pants that kept you a little bit warm. It was very cold once you had been down for a while, even in the tropics. The deeper you went the colder it got. You had thick socks and sandshoes with lead weights attached to them to keep you down. You looked and felt like an alien. You took down a chisel-type knife and a huge bag. You were lowered backwards into the water in a likely spot. This was when I really knew that I couldn't handle the job. It was hard enough trying to breathe and feel alright when you have a huge clumsy helmet over your head. From then on you relied on other people to get things right. But the slow falling backwards took more trust than I could ever easily muster. Trusting other people has always been a tough one for me. I would start twitching. Give me some wild unbroken stallion any day.

Once the diver was in the water the good ones quickly lowered themselves down the rope using the weights attached to their feet. The rope was tied to your body and had an offshoot that you held in your hand. It was the one thing that allowed you to contact the person on the boat. The other end of the rope was held loosely by the tender man and tied to the deck. They would have to play out the rope and the hose as you descended to the sea floor.

Then the motor would be slowly engaged, lifting you along until you signalled it to stop. You would drop on to the oyster bed. They could rip you apart if you weren't very careful. From there you had to stoop down, chisel in hand, to loosen the shells from their beds. You had to be very careful with the razor-sharp chisel. If it slipped you could cut into the rope, the intake pipe or wound yourself. It was not a good idea to be bleeding down on the bottom with sharks about the place. Sharks tended to follow boats about. As shells detached you picked them off and put them in the basket you were carrying.

It was difficult work. Oyster beds didn't give up their shells easily. And all the time you needed to keep vertical or water would start rising inside your helmet. The basket was attached to another rope. Once you finished a particular section you repeated the process with the boat dragging you along until you found another spot. Once a basket was full you signalled to the tender man and the crew had the job of lifting it. It took half an hour to fill a basket. It took three or four strong men to lift it to the surface and then into the boat. When it was emptied it was dropped back, using your rope as the guide. You started the job again.

Joseph Sambona was the head diver. It was his responsibility to train me up. One of the few things he didn't succeed at. He was a great diver and a careful man. We got on fairly well once he got over the problem of me not being up to diving. It put a lot of extra work on to him and the other divers.

With me on the deck was a fellow called Tender Gee. With Ali Abdul, he was in charge of the Malay crew and took a leading role in looking after the tender rope. Tender Gee was an older bloke who had spent a long time in Darwin on the pearling boats. With Mick Heenan he usually picked the spots to go diving in. Another of the crew was Mickey Smith. He was of mixed Aboriginal descent with family in Darwin. We were the peasants of the crew doing the dogsbody jobs.

The Malay blokes were hardworking and knew what they were doing from the start. Some of them shared a fair bit of the diving. We got on okay, but they tended to keep to themselves and speak their own language. It was a bit like at the stock camp sometimes when you had a few blokes from the same station and language group. They were pretty self-contained, laughing and joking amongst themselves.

On the boats

Life on a pearling lugger during season started before dawn. We all slept in hammocks strung up on deck. These would be tidied away and after a quick breakfast of last night's dinner, we'd be away, heading from our night's anchor spot to the edge of the oyster beds. The weather at that time of year was pretty much guaranteed to be soft and balmy, getting up into the high

Pearling in the Top End

twenties and thirties for weeks at a time. At night it might drop to glorious low twenties. After breakfast the equipment was got ready and the day would get started just as the sun was coming up. Sometimes there might be a couple of boats working the same bay. But usually the Top End was big enough that you didn't see another boat for long periods.

It was during the neap tide that the best pearl diving took place. The water was calmer at this time, making it easier to hold the boat in position. The diver would drop down and start his work. We would slowly head in towards shore. If you weren't working so hard it would have made a beautiful picture.

Once a basket had been hauled on deck, the oyster shells would have the meat cut out of them. Then the shells were stowed away in the hull to be sorted back in Darwin. These were called gold-lip oysters, some with small blister pearl growths. You had to be careful opening the shells and removing the meat. A slip of the knife could take off a finger. You were working close on a gently rocking boat so it was easy to make a mistake. You didn't have a lot of time so it was important that everyone kept up the pace.

The shellfish meat was laid on racks to be sun-dried. Then it was packed up and sold back in Darwin to the Chinese shops for their soups.

So from morning to nightfall the boat was on the move. It was a hard slog. By nightfall you were exhausted. There was no cook and not much chance of cooking up anything very flash. So the food was plain and mostly out of a can. Tins of bully beef, onions and rice all boiled up together with lots of curry powder. This was the standard feed morning, noon and night. The boat was too busy to worry about varying the diet. You would think that being in the middle of the ocean, we might have thrown in a line and caught some fresh fish. But the money was in keeping going while the weather held. When the hull was full we headed back to the depot in Darwin. It might take a month or longer to fill the boat. The crew got a flat rate plus a percentage of the take. It wasn't bad money but the season wasn't that long. Once the storms and cyclones started blowing up you could forget the diving. It was dangerous enough on a flat, still day.

There was the possibility of extra money for the crew in some of the other shells. Sometimes the divers would find them when they were working the seabed and include them in the basket. There was always a bit of cash for the baleen shells. These were sometimes made into lampshades and were popular household decorations. With the big beautiful ones, some of the better painters would do pictures in them and sell them to tourists and travellers. The money was split up according to a prearranged formula.

It's a changed world these days. There is a lot of money in fresh oysters. Pearling is almost an aside. The pearl shells we collected were mostly turned into buttons. Now they mass-produce plastic buttons. These days growing oysters is all done on floating tidal platforms in the rivers and estuaries. By injecting a bit of plastic into the oysters the pearl farmers are able to get a much higher rate of oysters making pearls than in the old days when we had to rely on nature doing the job.

Another season, another boat

We had a good time of it that first year. Once I had got over my seasickness and the crew had gotten over losing the anchor we had a good run with the weather, working up towards Cape Fourcroy on Bathurst Island. We drifted east along the coastline all the way across towards Croker Island and its mission. It was a good season and we had to make a few runs into Darwin to offload the shells, replenish supplies and then head back up north. It was my first real look at the country north of Darwin. And I had never been to sea before. So I have a lot of memories of beautiful wild country, especially on the trips back and forth when there was not much to do. The boat had a radio, so we knew if a cyclone was about the place. We had a few lazy days with storms threatening, making it too dangerous to put a diver down. It was on those days that you would anchor close to the creeks. I had a good time with the blokes.

Close to Christmas, with the Cyclone season coming, we packed up and hit Darwin for the lay-off. I got paid off. Not as much as I had hoped but enough for a while. I was as fit as I had ever been, even after a few drinks to celebrate being back on land. I had a run with the Darwin Buffs football team that year, playing as a rover. My brothers-in-law, Putt and Johnny Ahmat, had been champions for Buffs before the war. The Ahmats were still a big part of the club. Leo Ponds, a part Thursday Islander fellow, Ronnie Chinn, 'the flying Chinaman' and Les and George Liveres, two Darwin Greek fellows, were other players. A lot of the mixed descent Darwin mob played for the Buffs. It was good fun and I started to feel like I belonged a little in the Top End family. Darwin was really a series of ethnic communities that kept a bit to themselves. The football clubs tended to represent the various communities. So it got very tribal and competitive at times.

By the late 1940s, early 1950s us mixed descent mob were finally starting to get improved housing. Building materials were starting to hit the shops again and rationing had ended. Some of the mob got involved in local politics. We had a bit of a voice, starting to be heard in the local Workers Union. Things generally were on the up and up.

The next season saw me signed up to work on a pearling boat called the Fran. It was more of a supply boat and it even took a trip to Thursday Island. I saw where the Ahmats hailed from and met family.

The Torres Strait Islands were lovely places full of coconut trees and sandy beaches. The people were real friendly. There were a lot of musicians and there was always music and parties. We ate fish, dugongs and turtles caught off the beaches. It was a tropical paradise. It was tempting to just jump ship and stay for a while, as lots of other sailors had over the years. But it was a pretty closed community too in its way. I would have been a stranger there. You didn't always know how to take the locals. They could be a bit of a challenge. So after stopping there for a while getting resupplied, we headed back west.

Back in Darwin I got a job on the *Irene Castle* going down to Broome. We took some divers there for the boats. We were out at sea so I didn't get to see a lot of this coastline. It was work, work, work. They always wanted you earning your money. It wasn't good money but jobs around Darwin were still hard to get.

Back in town I was still staying with my sister, Gladys, and Johnny Ahmat and their mob of kids at the Parap Camp. The social life with the Buffs football mob was good on the long balmy Darwin evenings. The boys would often go fishing and crabbing together and bring home beautiful seafood for everyone. Gladys's kids were growing up and going to school.

I had another season in Darwin playing as much football as my work on the wharves and for the municipal council would allow. But I didn't go back to the boats the next year. I had a job lined up as a drover, taking me back into the world of the stock camps. There was no big reason for leaving Darwin, except perhaps that I didn't want to sign up for another trip on the pearling boats, and I missed the stock camps.

The drover's life

The good rain years of the late 1930s and early 1940s had ended. After the war there was drought along the stock routes so it was difficult to get cattle from the north-west and Top End to markets in the south. Prices were low. Sometimes station owners made a loss instead of an income after sending cattle to the abattoirs. They soon enough stopped sending them.

There had also been a wages dispute between Vestey's and the drovers in the 1946 season. Vestey's pretty much set the price across northern Australia. Before the start of the season they sent communications to their regular boss drovers to tell them how many cattle a station was sending on the road, whether they had a mob for them, what day they needed to turn up to take

The drover's life

delivery and what price was to be paid for the trip. The drover had to respond or Vestey's would offer the work to someone else. But the boss drovers knew that the pre-war payment rates weren't enough to cover their higher costs, including the new expectations of stockmen after the war. The Workers' Union got involved. The drovers argued the point as a group with Vestey's management. A benchmark new price was discussed. Some smaller stations started paying at the new price. Vestey's held out. But it appeared they would fall in line. With the new season starting they sent out letters and telegrams as usual, leaving out details as to what rate would be paid.

It costs money to set up a droving team. You have the cost of supplies for the crew, equipment for the horses and wages to pay at the end of the trip. Vestey's management waited until they had the droving teams gathered at Wave Hill and other stations to tell the boss drovers that their contracts for the year's droving were to be at the old rate. Those who didn't accept the rate could head off home. Vestey's even threatened not to send any cattle on the road that year. The dispute rolled on for weeks. The union tried to step in. They were ordered off the stations. Some drovers were told to leave.

But as Vestey's knew, a lot of the blokes couldn't afford to pay their bills without a droving contract. They had no money in the bank and had already gone to a lot of expense in setting up their teams. It was much too late to look around for work at other stations. With the season rolling on and droving teams hanging around without work these blokes would eventually be forced to cave in. Vestey's was able to persuade some of the smaller operators to accept the jobs below the new price that the drovers were trying to establish. This broke solidarity. A few walked away but many caved in. Vestey's had won.

But it was a short-term victory. Vestey's had lost a lot of goodwill. Many experienced boss drovers were so angry that they sold their horses and by next season they had left the industry. Vestey's still needed to move their cattle. It was okay the next year with drought seeing not much droving anywhere, but in the end Vestey's got stuck without enough droving teams. What teams they did have weren't nearly as good as the ones that had left. They were overstocked and needed to clear out some of the scrubby wild cattle that had built up on the edges of the big stations. It was a time of a fair bit of poddy-dodging. So Vestey's ended up seeking out some of their old boss drovers and offering them a few new incentives.

The other big player in the Northern Territory cattle industry was the Vobell's Pastoral Company that owned Victoria River Downs and other stations. Vobell's wanted to get rid of the old Hereford cattle stock and introduce the newer bigger cattle breeds that were better suited to the tropical north. To help with this, and because cheaper fencing wire was now available, they decided to split up Victoria River Downs and some of their other large holdings in the western part of the Territory. Victoria River Downs was broken into smaller stations including Pigeon Hole, Camfield and Montejinni.

Vestey's, who had Wave Hill, Mistake Creek, Willeroo and Delamere Stations, were also slowly moving to smaller stations with better fences and improved breeding programs. They used holding stations in Queensland to fatten up the old Hereford mobs being cleared off the north-western stations. In good years mobs would be pushed all the way across into Queensland. By the late 1940s cattle prices picked up as rationing ended and the drought eased. The Top End cattle industry was on the move again. They needed us old ringers to come back to work.

The Mistake Creek trip

Jack Sagagiel was one ex-droving boss contacted by John Quirk, the Vestey's manager. He'd been working on the wharves when Mr Quirk personally telegraphed him to ask him to head up a team. It was like royalty dropping in for tea. Jack was flattered and accepted the job. Vestey's organised with Norm Stacey from Beetaloo to take a droving plant out for Jack. Jack's crew would be flown out and find the plant waiting for them. It was getting on in the season and Vestey's wanted the cattle away while there was enough grass on the Barkly to get them through to Queensland.

Jack was in his fifties. He was an Aboriginal man of mixed descent who had grown up around Pine Creek. He'd had a few good years at the wharves, but like many old drovers his heart was in working the bush. With a promise of good money and horses waiting for him he started to look about and recruit a new team.

It was a small community. He knew my background as a transplanted stockman like himself. So he approached me. I was pleased to be asked and found it hard to say no. It was a big job going all the way from Mistake Creek on the Western Australian border to Queensland, four months work. The pay was good. The crew was ordinary but I was up for a challenge and a change. I accepted. It meant being off the boats and back on a horse. I was never going to get a lot of respect as a sailor. Plus it meant that I didn't have to look about for work.

I occasionally think about what would have happened if I had said no. The blokes in Darwin did pretty well over the years. But I'm not sure I could have stuck to a town life. I was too restless. So I found myself back on horseback following the backsides of the cattle again. Eating the dust of the mob.

Droving was the hardest money I ever earned. But it had a strange appeal to be working where only the toughest stockmen could survive. The money was good because you got to save it all. The boss drover looked after all your food. Plus one beast was provided from the mob for each ten days of the trip. You only had to pay for your own extras if you booked up along the route. Wages were paid at the end when the cattle were dropped off. So you got a very tidy sum. Especially when it was a long trip. We were able to play the cashed-up kings of town until the money ran out.

Old Norman Stacey was a boss drover. His sister was married into the Batherns who owned Beetaloo Station, and he was able to rest up his horses there off-season and have his pick of the mob. As Jack knew well, the 'ZTZ' brand of Beetaloo horses was much prized. Drovers would come from all over to buy Beetaloo bloodstock. Norman delivered our plant to Mistake Creek and had already set off with his own mob by the time we arrived.

There was a real shortage of experienced stockmen to make up the numbers that year. So we had a few cleanskins on the team. The second most important fellow on the team, the cook, was already organised. Charlie Windley had come up with Norman's horses. Charlie was a white fellow in his late forties who had lots of family around Tennant Creek. He had lost an arm in an accident, so was reduced to one arm and a stump. But he was a good cook. Crabby in temperament, like every other droving cook, but capable of getting a good feed together. Cooking was a big part of surviving as a team. If you had bad food dished up for fifteen weeks, you tended to lose patience and men.

Jack recruited Sandy Harris as the horse tailer. Sandy was a good stockman sitting around in Darwin like the rest of us. He was in his mid-forties and a veteran of a lot of trips. He was a mixed descent Aborigine from around Halls Creek way and a very capable horseman. Then there was Kelly Dempsey, also from Halls Creek. Kelly was twenty-five or so and like me, he had grown up on a horse.

To make up the team, Jack employed Jim Marshall. He was a white bloke in his early thirties. Jim could ride and had some stock experience on the sheep stations of western Victoria. You needed at least seven to make up a droving team. Vestey's wouldn't employ you with less. So we also had two younger first-timers. There was Richard Jan, a twenty-year-old Chinese Aboriginal from Darwin and Paulie Calma, a Filipino, also born and raised around Darwin.

We were all flown out by light plane on the mail run. It was my first time in a plane. We landed at every homestead and township on the way west, flying low following the fence lines and roads. I was a very happy fellow when we finally arrived and I had my feet firmly back on the ground. Everyone was. It is hard to get much of a taste for flying unless you have nerves of steel. On those small planes you felt every bump and air pocket. You could see the pilot struggling and hear the engine straining. You knew if the plane gave out you would be lucky to survive. The plane is quick and more scenic but give me a horse any day.

On the road with cattle

Once we arrived at Mistake Creek we set up camp. It was a few weeks wait while the station mob mustered up enough beasts for the trip. Finally Jack and the head stockman counted out the 1,500 scrubbers. At first they tried giving him some animals that were too crazy or that wouldn't have lasted the trip. But Jack was an old hand and rejected a lot. They ended up having to re-muster to get the numbers. But despite their bitching Jack held out. He had the power. You got penalised for cattle that didn't make it. Even with rejecting a lot, the mob we took were an unpromising lot. But finally we were on our way east.

It was real back country around Mistake Creek. Where other drovers working around the main highway could bring in drays and even trucks to move the equipment about, the wild gully country of Mistake Creek didn't lend itself to anything wider than a horse. Pushing 1,500 cattle through it was really hard work. It was hard enough just to get the packhorses through the scrub.

So our plant was of the old-fashioned style used at the turn of the century. Everything we needed was stored in horse-packs and saddlebags. It was loading and unloading packhorses every day, and just enough tucker to last till the next store. We needed lots of spare horseshoes and other riding equipment and about fifty packhorses in total. It was rugged country and the horseshoes were essential. I didn't know this country. But Jack and the older hands did. It was crocodile-infested and swampy near the coast, so we headed a bit south through the gullies and scrub.

Each day we were given a day-horse, then a night-horse for the night shifts. The horses had been broken in the previous year and let loose at Beetaloo Station at the end of the season. With the rest-up at the station, they were a frisky lot at the start and we had some inexperienced riders too. The new recruits had little schooling in the stockman's art. They were matched up with those of us with more experience. But it was a fairly brutal learning curve for them. Soon enough the horses settled in as the hard riding and routine overwhelmed any surplus enthusiasm they might have started with. Like the cattle the horses lost condition and energy. It was a bit the same with us. The night-horses were special animals. They needed to be sure on their feet at a full gallop in the dark. They were picked out by the horse tailer for their night vision. When a mob of cattle got a fright and took off in the middle of the night, you relied on your night-horse to follow and turn the mob and to keep you alive. You also picked them for their ability to stay awake. You didn't want horses falling asleep and walking straight into the mob, causing them all to take off.

Mobs from this part of the country were a wild lot. The only human contact they would have had was if they had been mustered and branded over the years. A lot of this mob had been hidden away in the back country. They were like the ones we had mustered off Delamere with Freddy Martin. Over-muscled, scared and stupid. Plus cattle knew when they were leaving their home. They didn't like change. Now they were being taken away from the freedom of the rangelands for a thousand mile walk across the Northern Territory into north-west Queensland. They weren't happy.

For the first few days Jack had us organised onto double night watches. We had to be constantly circling around the mob in opposite directions to keep them settled, singing the old songs or making any sort of regular noise to drown out the bush noises that might spook them. Once the cattle were nervous we were in trouble. If a few stirred and got up we needed to be there quickly before they panicked. A dropped pannikin, a loud voice or any sharp movement would be enough. Dingoes and other night animal noises could frighten them. If this mob wasn't immediately reassured the whole lot of them could take off in a mad, lumbering gallop that could see them finish up anywhere. Rounding them up could take days and you could hurt or lose cattle.

The night watches were about one-and-a-half hours long. On the double shifts riders passed each other every half hour or so. You had also to keep an eye on the campfire to make sure it didn't go out. When it was time, one of us went in to wake up the next bloke. When he was up and circling, the second fellow went in and repeated the process. The riders continued the circling and singing until it was time for the next blokes to have a spell. It was long hours with little sleep. Us riders were usually so tired that we would fall asleep as soon as our bodies hit the swag.

A few blokes sang like professionals. I wasn't that good, but I could belt out a few of the old ballads and knew a few verses, so could keep a song going for a while. When exhausted I fell back on the old church songs that had been drummed into me at the institutions. The shorter trips that I had taken with Baden Bloomfield and later with Freddy and Billy stood me in good stead for droving. But even so, on this trip I was often so exhausted that the songs came out like dirges, repeating the same couple of lines over and over again.

Some of the blokes were just terrible singers. They knew a snatch of one song that they repeated endlessly, often badly out of tune. But the cattle weren't a fussy audience. Continuous and repetitive was all that was required. Like the cook not needing to pass a personality test, us stockmen weren't auditioned as singers.

After a few droving trips we got to know the blokes you wouldn't work with again if you could help it. They might be lazy or vicious or just plain pains in the arse. We did try to work with people we liked. And often we would work for the same boss with pretty much the same team for a few seasons if we could. This first trip from Mistake Creek was a tough introduction to Queensland droving.

Routines of the road

The cook and horse tailer were woken up when the last night shift started. Usually it was the boss drover who took this shift and it was that way on this trip. Jack Sagagiel was the man to do the hard yards when staying awake was toughest. Charlie Windley, the cook, would build up the fire and prepare breakfast. Sandy Harris, the horse tailer, would be rounding up and saddling our horses for the day. Jack and whoever was on with him for the last shift came in as the sun rose. The mob would be much less likely to take off once they could see around them in the daylight. We would all be up with the sun, rolling up our swags for Charlie to stick on one of the packhorses.

In the early droving days at the turn of the 20th century, drovers would often have a couple of days between waterholes. The days of the trip were split between wet and dry camps. A wet camp was after the cattle had been watered. The next day they would be without water. Cattle actually travel faster on the dry stretches. But they also lose condition pretty quickly. In 1905 Jack Dick Skulthorpe is said to have forced his cattle for six days over 102 miles when he came across a series of dry waterholes. Even when he found some water the cattle only got half a drink before he had to push them on another fifty miles before finding good water. The record is said to belong to the Farquarson brothers of Inverway Station who, in a week, travelled 125 miles along the Murranji Track in 1909 before hitting water, losing only five beasts.

But by the late 1940s there were bores sunk every ten miles or so. The government provided a good bore maintenance team that made sure the cattle troughs and tanks were filled, so you didn't have dry days. The night camps were spaced between the bores. Each morning you aimed to walk the mob into the bore and have them all watered before lunch. We called it the 'dinner' camp in those days. It was usually around midday that you arrived.

The bores had troughs that watered up to fifty cattle at a time. One of us had to ride ahead to turn on the taps at the tanks before the mob arrived. If the whole mob rushed the water some of the cattle might be trampled and injured. The bore would be damaged. So we had to separate out fifty or so cattle and take them down in batches. The other riders would hold the rest of the mob back. Watering cattle after they haven't drunk for a day is not easy. They smell the water. It's hard work to pull them up. When one group had watered you pushed them off the bore to the other side. This continued until the whole mob had gone through. With a mob of 1,500 cattle it took a while, up to four hours in bad country. That was why the droving bosses had fought to keep the maximum number of beasts in a mob down to pre-war levels of 1,100 rough cattle and perhaps 1,300 if they had been already worked a bit. But the station owners had argued that they couldn't afford to pay more per beast to send them to market, so it had to be bigger mobs if drovers wanted to increase their own pay rate. The bosses won that battle and we had to work like slaves at every bore to get the mob watered.

It was only after the watering was finished and the cattle spread out and settled on whatever feed was about, that the horses and riders could have a drink. We would rest up, have our sandwich or whatever we had packed in the morning and try to get in a nap. If there were trees about you could get away from the heat of the day, but in lots of places, particularly on the Barkly stock route, the only shade you found was your horse and hat. The mob was given a spell until about three or four o'clock. This was a quiet time. Some of the stockmen would have a scrub and wash their clothes. If some of the cattle got too footsore on the trip you might leave them at the bore. They could rest up and recover. When the next droving team came through, the drover would bring them along in their mob if they were alright to travel.

By three or four it was back on your horse and back behind the cattle, pushing them along another five miles or so to the night camp. Cattle are not fond of moving away from water so they often tried to duck back. But once you had moved off a few miles the mob would be fairly easy and you kept going until you got to the camping spot where the cook and horse tailer had set up. It was often early evening by then.

At the start of the day the cook and horse tailer were left behind to put the supplies back into pack-saddles and get them on to the packhorses. Everything came off the animals each night and had to be packed up again the next morning. That is why the trucks and trailers became so popular. It saved the cook a lot of work. If meat was needed then a killer was selected out and held back from the mob. It would be slaughtered as we disappeared with the rest of the mob in the morning. It was roughly butchered and except for meat that would be used that day, the rest was salted away in the meat packs. Most days Charlie and Sandy would take till about mid-morning to pass us with the packhorses and gear.

The cook was usually responsible for picking the exact spot for the camp after the boss drover had told them roughly where he expected them to be. Sometimes he might even ride ahead and select spots himself. It was part of the boss drover's job to know the country ahead and plan the trip. The evening camp needed to have reasonable feed if possible. A bit of shade and protection from the wind was nice. Once the cook had found a spot then the packhorses were unloaded and camp set up. Damper for the next day and food for the evening meal was prepared. Wood, if possible, or anything else that might burn was collected for the night fire. Meat would get unpacked and hung from trees in cloth bags. And Sandy would get the spare stockhorses hobbled so they didn't wander too far away. Eventually the night-horses would be saddled and organised.

The drover's life

About ten to fourteen miles a day was expected by the stock inspectors. This was for what they called 'store' cattle straight out of the paddock. How far you went depended a bit on the nature of the country and the skill of the crew. Store cattle were pushed harder. You didn't worry too much about them losing condition. It was the fat cattle that had been looked after on good country that you moved along slower at about ten miles a day. These trips were usually only a short distance to get the cattle to markets or a railhead. The bosses wanted them to look good so they would fetch a reasonable price at the sales.

The Mistake Creek cattle were stores. They were in pretty fair condition after feeding on the Wet season grasses. But we were late in the season and the good feed was starting to disappear from the stock route, eaten out by earlier mobs. Plus because of the huge distances we were travelling, Jack was under pressure to get the miles each day or risk the cattle starting to fade away. So we were pushing them along at a fair rate. Through the early part of the season there might be as many as a dozen droving teams walking cattle from the west of the Northern Territory to Queensland. Mostly they were Vestey or Vobell teams. The smaller family-owned stations did their own droving, usually with smaller mobs at different times.

About sunset or even later, Charlie and Sandy would see the dust of the mob coming in. There would be a rider or two at the front, someone on the sides and a few blokes chewing dust at the rear. The mob might be stretched over a mile or so. We would wheel them in and settle them as best we could. The horse tailer, Sandy, would always take the first shift. On double shifts Jack would join him. The other four of us would head in for a feed. Then after an hour or so Jack would come in and be replaced by one of us on the second night-horse.

There were six night-horses saddled but mostly only two were used. They would be swapped over as one rider came in at the end of the shift and another took his place. The other night-horses were needed only in case of a stampede or if one of the horses went lame. Only the cook stayed in camp when a cattle rush happened. Everyone else was expected to be off after them.

The evening meal was important. A good cook like Charlie could make old tough maggoty meat come out okay. It was nearly always a stew, often curried. There was never a shortage of salt. After a killer had been slaughtered you might get steak, a roast or even gravied meat on the menu. You could usually have all the damper you wanted to mop up the food. Dessert was expected. It might be a roly-poly pudding. More likely it was dried fruit and custard. When all us ringers had been fed the cook would get the last of the damper mixes placed under the coals and cook it for the next day.

It was an exhausting schedule. Especially during the early days when the cattle would rush all night and double shifts saw everyone working harder. The horses were fresh too and under-prepared. New recruits could be dangerous and you had to keep an eye on them or you could spend hours fixing up the damage. If a team lost men it was a disaster. The workload was bad enough with a full crew of seven. With Vestey's another worker could be organised if you got word back. The day's work often lasted eighteen hours or more and went on for the whole fifteen weeks of the trip.

You occasionally saw the bore maintenance teams that made sure that the bore pumps worked and that the tanks were full. These teams were usually local white blokes. But there was one mixed descent Aboriginal fellow called Beetaloo Bill on the teams. They were good blokes and often helped out if they could, bringing things from town and passing on messages.

Stampede

On one of the first nights out of Mistake Creek I was rostered on a double shift with the young new recruit, Paulie Calma. It was dark and we had been circling the mob for a while. It was my turn to grab a cup of tea and check the campfire, so I left Paulie to circle the mob on his own for a few minutes. I had just ridden in and got off my horse when I heard the mob move. The cattle were up and galloping straight for me and our camp.

Fear had me back in the saddle and moving in seconds. The other stockmen, including Sandy and Jack, followed. We split up, riding cross ways and trying to come alongside the mob to wheel the leaders before they got to the camp. It didn't work and they were past me before I could get to the front. They went straight through the camp where a few minutes before people had been asleep in their swags. Charlie Windley was an old hand and had found a tree to hide behind. He would have had it marked out when selecting the camp spot. I followed one mob and kept trying to turn them slowly back around. It took a good while and it was daylight before I got back near camp and was able to put my mob into the main group.

It had been a terrible and frightening stampede straight across the packs, stores and camping equipment and only luck saw no one killed or injured.

When we did a quick count we found we had lost only a few cattle. But during the day we managed to find their tracks and get them all back. Charlie vowed to sleep a bit further away from the main camp under a tree after that.

When Jack asked Paulie what had happened, it turned out that he had seen a beast breaking from the mob and had pursued it. When he caught and turned it he hadn't slowed the animal down much and it had hit the mob at a full gallop. That was enough to disturb the whole lot.

The rush taught Paulie to do things slowly and carefully with a mob at night. Everyone was very cautious after that first rush. Just about anything would set them off. The mob didn't really settle for a long time during the early part of the walk. It was double shifts all the way into Newcastle Waters. It seemed a hard way to earn your money after the Darwin wharves. But we had in mind the big payout at the end of the trip. What else could you do?

So the first weeks through the heavily wooded escarpment country of the west of the Northern Territory passed. It was easier work in the sweet-grassed, flatter land closer to Victoria River Downs and Wave Hill. Then we got to Top Springs and the Armstrong River. From there we entered the deep bulwaddy scrub, up the rugged escarpment country and on to the rough pathway known as the Murranji Track. This was the traditional Mudburra hunting land of my ancestors.

The Murranji Track

The Murranji Track took many hundreds of miles off the earlier route up towards Katherine. But it was still 140 dangerous miles through deep scrub country. The track had originally been opened up, east to west, by Nat Buchanan when he formed Wave Hill in 1883. The crossing from west to east was first travelled in 1904 by Blake Miller, head drover for Sidney Kidman. From then on it was used by Kidman's drovers and others in good seasons. There were only two semi-permanent waterholes on the track. If these were dry or you had difficulties then you risked the death of the cattle and the droving team itself.

But in 1949 when we went through bores had been sunk at ten-mile intervals. The Mudburra warriors, who had worried the early pioneers, had been well and truly slaughtered and subdued. The remnants of the tribe were scattered, making up most of the station labour force at Montejinni, Pigeon

Hole and other outstations of Victoria River Downs, and even down on to Wave Hill Station. There would have been a dozen or more droving crews before us that season, mostly from Wave Hill and Victoria River Downs. The track was narrow with virtually impenetrable scrub on either side. The ground had a hollowness to it that made the cattle nervous and skittish. If the cattle rushed on the Murranji you had serious problems. Cattle would be ripped open, sometimes even impaled, on the lancewood and hedgewood trees that lined the route. The droving team would have days trying to track and bring back small mobs through the endless scrub. It was all hard work, double shifts and high pressure.

Once out the other side it was twenty miles south-east across grasslands and open coolabah country into Lake Woods and Newcastle Waters. We had the usual rest-up day in this well-watered area. We were given the chance to have a good scrub up and go into town to get supplies of clothes, toiletries, tobacco, sweets and whatever else we had missed on the weeks coming across. Charlie and Jack went in to replenish supplies. There was a pub and a bakery, so us stockmen got a rest from weeks of salted beef and damper. We were about half-way along on our trip.

The Barkly Stock Route

After a day at Newcastle Waters we were off with the cattle down to No. 7 Bore outside of Elliott. This was the first of the compulsory dips to get rid of any ticks the cattle might be carrying. You had to dip twice more on this trip into Queensland. If you didn't dip, the cattle couldn't go through. There were plenty of stock inspectors to ensure you complied and the boss drover had to have the papers proving the beasts had been dipped before dropping off his mob. There was a great fear in Queensland of the cattle ticks of northern Australia getting into the Queensland herds. After the first dip you turned in an easterly direction on to the breakers country that marked the start of the Barkly Tableland and its stock route. The next stop was Anthony's Lagoon and its store. Sid Biondi, who claimed to be a French count, ran the store. We stocked up again on bread and supplies and kept going.

After Anthony's Lagoon you hit the main section of the Barkly Stock Route. It was flat and treeless. Some spots you had to carry firewood or else rely on dried cow dung fires. Our cattle were in poor condition by this time. It had been a hard trip. We were in pretty shabby condition too. The cattle made poor killers being only skin and bones. Occasionally a much better

The drover's life

fed station steer was 'mistakenly' substituted by Charlie for the weekly killer. Eventually we made it to Rankin Springs store and the last cattle dip before the border. From there it was down to Moorestone. The cattle were turned off into holding yards to be fattened up for a season before a final train trip to the abattoirs of Townsville and Rockhampton.

The stock inspector was there when the mob was counted through a drafting gate into the yards. Ear marks and brands were checked for any cattle that may have merged with our mob. On this trip everything was in order. The ones left sore-footed had been balanced with the ones we picked up from earlier Vestey mobs. It helped that Jack was an old hand and always carried his own ear marking and branding equipment. We were signed off as having a full number of cattle at the end of the trip.

With the rest of the crew, I was paid off in full at Moorestone Station. But Jack gave me the job of offsiding with him, taking Norm Stacey's horses back across the Barkly to rest up during the off-season at Beetaloo Station. There was not much grass about but loose horses with light packs were easy enough work. It took a couple of weeks strolling across in easy stages. When we got to Beetaloo, Norm was there to greet us. We turned the horses into the homestead paddock and headed into Newcastle Waters.

Jack had a few drinks with us at the pub, waiting to catch Len Tuit's bus north. I decided to stick around. Freddy Martin was about the place. I threw my swag out with him and a few of his mates. I ended up getting friendly with a fellow called Cammy Cleary. It was late in the year and a lot of the drinking mob was settling in for a bit of a party. All us single blokes hung åabout down at the drovers' camping grounds between the pub and the Aboriginal camp.

That was the end of that first big droving trip for me. I didn't see a lot of the other blokes from the trip again. I heard much later that Jack Sagagiel died from a fall off his truck. He was a good boss and it must have been tough on his family. Jim Marshall ended up buying a few packhorses and heading to Borroloola. Over the next decade or two he worked on one of the stations up there and ended up buying a place. He later sold it to Ted Smith from around Alice Springs. Ted was known as 'Caravan Ted'. He was a white bloke who had worked as a brickmaker after the war. Georgie Peckham had worked for him for many years. Ted was later killed in a light plane crash. The other fellows headed back to city life and the wharves of Darwin.

Seasons in the sun

The droving community was now becoming a bigger part of who I was and what I did. It wasn't a big family. Us drovers were the modern-day gypsies working on horseback pushing cattle down an endless stock route – the long paddock, as the stock routes were called. They are all but abandoned now. Claimed by the local Aboriginal communities to set up their homelands. But in the 1940s and 1950s they were busy places. In 1949 sixteen droving teams followed the Murranji Track eastward with 22,000 head of cattle bound for Dajarra. There were cattle being pushed south through Alice Springs, west to Wyndham and between different stations. But even at its peak, you were talking no more than a couple of hundred men spread across the Top End.

Drovers operated in small groups according to a strict code of behaviour. We were away from the real world for months at a time, relying on the boss and our companions. You looked after your mates, then the cattle, and only then yourself. You were a filthy, wretched group of men on horseback doing dangerous, badly paid work, with sometimes shocking food, little water and not a lot of fun. When the wind was blowing it was bitterly cold. A bit of rain made life even more miserable. When it was hot you slowly fried. You could get three seasons in a day, and a twenty-degree change in the temperature happened most days. Swags were not the luxury items of today. There were no mattresses, pillows or doonas. You couldn't have fitted them on the horses. Swags needed to be flat against the horse to avoid rubbing it and causing sores. They were a couple of blankets rolled in canvas. Your change of clothes was your pillow. You had to be a little mad. The long trips might set you up for a while but, after hitting the pub and spending your cheque, you had to go looking for any work going.

No one I worked with got rich from droving. Even the life of the white drovers was fairly tough. Many were failed station boys. Their parents often had been battlers on unprofitable stations. But by and large, the white men were the bosses. As Aboriginal drovers we were a different proposition. The whites ran the show. They were the station owners and managers, the head stockmen, the stock inspectors, the publicans, shopkeepers and coppers. The blokes in charge preferred to deal with other whites. They could mostly read and write better than us and could get money from the banks. When the season was over they could get cleaned up and join a different, more powerful society. They got to sit up at the big table. Many were lovely fellows but we all knew the story at the end of the day. Like in the army, they were the officer class. We were always going to be the privates.

The boss drovers were pretty much white, with only a few blokes of mixed descent climbing up the ladder. Those who made it often had white fathers who had set them up by taking over a droving plant. They, like Baden, often had a bit of history on their father's land and got their first jobs working for their old man or his mates. It might have happened for me, but I was taken away like most of the others I worked with.

The more lowly white blokes on the stock routes often had a bit of a sad history. It might be a mental problem after returning home a bit shell-shocked from the war. They might be hopeless romantics with too much of a taste for the bottle and black women. It might be a wife and kids left behind in some distant part of the country. Sometimes it was running from the police. They usually had a bit of a drinking story and might end up married into the mixed descent community. They often never left the Top End.

Then there were the tribal stockmen. They were mainly employed on their home stations, especially during the muster times. These blokes were subject to the Aboriginal Protectorate rules. They couldn't be employed by the drovers without a permit. These had to be applied for through Native Affairs. Usually the local police were their agents. The droving boss employing them had to return them to their homelands at the end of the job. This might be on a bus or truck if the job had taken them a long way away and the employer wasn't heading back for a while. The idea was that they weren't left stranded at the end of the season. There were hardly any tribal Aboriginal stockmen employed in the teams that I worked for. It was too hard to follow the rule that they had to be returned to their country. It meant they couldn't apply for work as it came up like the rest of us.

The tribal Aboriginal workers didn't get straight wages. There was no award system that applied to them. Their money had to be paid into a trust fund. Usually the ones that got droving work stuck with the same boss drover and crew each season. They would be picked up at designated spots as the season started. The relationship was built up over years. This was also true for a lot of us mixed descent drovers. Under changes to the Aboriginal Ordinances, everyone except full blood traditional people over eighteen had exemptions from most of the welfare laws and could pick and choose jobs by and large. Still, if we had a good boss we tried to stick with him if possible.

When the season was on the social life of a drover was pretty non-existent. You just worked and slept. When you hit a place like Newcastle Waters and spelled the cattle, one or two stockmen might be able to go in for a change of clothes and a drink. But boss drovers always worried about losing crew to a few bottles of rum, so you didn't stay long.

At the end of season there would be the payout. This was party time with big drinking sessions. Occasionally the white and mixed descent mob drank together. But soon afterwards you would split up with people heading off to family or friends. You tended to drink until the money ran low. Then we would all be hunting around the pubs for a bit of work. Pubs were the labour market.

Pubs were very different in those days. They were men's space. Women stayed away. The drinking was mostly heavy stuff – rum and spirits. You would sit around talking up the droving stories. Sometimes there might be a singalong with all of us drunks groaning and bellowing together. Then the publican would kick us out and we would stagger to our camps. It wasn't such a bad life if you didn't sober up too often.

On the road you'd come across strict tribal communities, where the men wouldn't allow the women to drink or associate with passing droving crews. The men were very jealous. But this didn't always suit the young girls and women. Times were often tough and people wanted a life. At some places we would know that the women from the Aboriginal settlements were available. Basically you paid for female company with food and alcohol. Sometimes money was involved. But droving teams had to respect traditional cultural values. Sleeping with a woman from a wrong skin group was still punishable for the Aboriginal drovers and their female companions. The women especially could still get into a lot of trouble from the lawmen. The government had rules about alcohol and cohabitation. Basically you could get arrested for supplying alcohol or sleeping with an Aboriginal woman. You could be forced by the police to leave a community if you were suspected of these things. You were not allowed in the Aboriginal compounds or tribal areas. But ways were found around the rules.

Sleeping around a bit was okay in the droving community. It was also okay with the Aboriginal community on the fringes of towns. On lots of the cattle stations it was common enough for the visiting stockmen to share themselves with as many women as they could afford. Often the boss drover would ride ahead to give a list of the skinnames of his droving team to the community they were approaching. The Alice Springs drover Dick Smith was a great one for doing this. This was a proper way for Aboriginal people to meet suitable partners. So often you would be the right one for someone and end up with a partner for the short time you were there. Some of the blokes even came back and hitched up later. It was uncomplicated in its way. But it was before contraception. Often jealous husbands or old men who had claims to a promised wife created big dramas, especially after you moved on. Women would get flogged. Unwanted pregnancies would lead to bitterness and people seeking revenge. Some of the kids might get sent away. It was a difficult and tough life for the Aboriginal women.

In the cattle station world of the Top End there were stockmen and there were the others. If you didn't chase cattle on horseback you didn't have much standing amongst the men that I spent most of my time with. Stockmen were hard-living men who knew how to get up again every time they took a tumble. We didn't complain. We looked after our mates – the men we worked with. The ones who knew our stories and secrets. The people we relied on. The married blokes might have the 'little woman' waiting at home with the kids. They might still be there for you at the end of your real life out on the stock route. But women weren't always seen as friends and partners the way a fellow drover often was.

We were pretty clueless about women. Some of the blokes were cruel and ugly. They were often the ones who were angry about everything. You needed to be very careful around them, especially the white ones. They were bullies. They could as easily turn on you next. They were often racist too, so the Aboriginal women were specially vulnerable. I was never one of the bullies and I worked hard not to hang around with them. Perhaps it was because of knowing enough of my mother's and sisters' stories. But it was probably as much because of working hard to keep in with the blokes that were genuinely generous and okay about everything. I was taught to be respectful of the women. And I could get a bit of a patter going that kept me okay around them. Especially the older white women who had the power to put you in your place if you weren't careful and nice.

Drovers were a bit like long-distance sailors: away for months, even years, at a time. It might be decades before you would get back to a place. Most were young, single blokes with a bit of travelling blood in their makeup – an elite band of wanderers who worked closely together for months following the cattle. At the end of the trip you might only see each other in passing. But you were still connected. It was like being an initiated man. You were part of the brotherhood.

That was why a lot of us were offended when the Newcastle Waters Drover's Memorial was opened. The organisers weren't drovers. A lot of the names were a mystery to us. Some had never been overlanders following mobs of cattle along the Murranji Track and the Barkly into Queensland. There were a lot of good men that had been forgotten. Sandy Harris, Paulie Calma and Jack Dempsey weren't there. A lot of the Aboriginal drovers had been missed out. They said they would fix up the list but it never really happened.

Even when I hung up my saddle, got married and took up a town job, I was still part of the tribe. My old drover mates would see me in town and we would have a chat. Maybe have a drink for old time's sake. Find out how so-and-so was doing, who was working where and what old mates were up to. If the bloke you were talking to was struggling, you'd loan him a few bob till he was back on his feet, or invite him to camp at home. For a lot of drovers things went pretty rough once the cattle trucks took over. You couldn't say no to someone you had shared a trip with, even if the wife was angry about there not being enough room or food, and the kids had to be shifted about to fit in a smelly old drover sick with the grog and down on his luck. For most, us blokes were the only family they had left, the only ones who knew them when they were young and full of life.

A proper bush hotel

From the late 1920s and throughout the 1930s Newcastle Waters became the main meeting ground for the Northern Territory and Queensland droving teams. There were always some old swaggies holding up the bar, drinking as slowly as they could to make their pension money last. Drovers camped around to drink their cheques out after the season finished. Norm Stacey and other boss drovers rested up their horses at Beetaloo or one of the other stations close by. If you wanted a droving job at the start of the season Newcastle Waters was the place to go.

Max Schaber was the publican of the Old Ridge Hotel and the boss man of Newcastle Waters. He also had the main shop. The pub was the nerve centre of town, cashing cheques, booking up food and provisions for the regulars and acting as the main employment agency. Max was a big gruff German getting on in years when I got to know him. He relied a lot on his position. As he often said, 'When you have money you call me the German bastard, but when you're wanting to book up then you call me Mr Schaber.' He always gave book up to the droving crews between seasons. He was rarely left with a bad debt. People had to come through Newcastle Waters.

Max had run the place since well before the war. During the building of the railway around Katherine in the late 1920s, he had been a hawker with a liquor licence. At that time he had a big truck that he would fill up with kegs in Darwin or Katherine. He made his money selling grog to the railway crews and locals. Rum was the preferred tipple for the thirsty hard-drinking mob. Beenleigh Rum when things were good. Rougher stuff when times were tough. His truck would do the rounds of the work crews. When the railway construction work slowed down and stopped at Larrimah, Max had set up his truck at Newcastle Waters. This was about the time that the government started putting in bores along the Murranji Track, making Newcastle Waters a big stop-off point for the western drovers. He made enough money to build himself a proper bush hotel.

It certainly wasn't a flash place, just an iron and bush-timber shed with four or five rooms. No glass windows to be smashed. No carpet on the floor. It was a basic concrete slab that could be washed out easily when the blood flowed after a fight or the drunks threw up. The bar was just a place to hand over the bottle and a few glasses.

The other main place in town was the bakery, run by Jock Jones and his wife. This was a different fellow from my old supervisor at the Bungalow. Mr Jones was a real good old bloke. They baked a great loaf and ran a café. They had a mob of goats and sold milk and meat as well. Their daughter is June Satour who lived in Alice Springs with a family of her own. Each droving team picked up a dozen or more loaves going through. So the bakery did reasonable business in season. You could always get a bit of credit. Jock had done it tough himself and didn't like to see a man go hungry.

Newcastle Waters largely died when Max moved his pub down the track to Elliott. He could serve what was left of the droving mob from there and Noel Buntine and Peter Sherwin with their transport companies were setting up Elliott as a base. The road and bore maintenance crews built quarters at Elliott to be close to the fuel. The Junction Hotel drinking crowd and all the droving business moved to Elliott. After a while even the buses stopped calling in at Newcastle Waters. Later the highway was diverted to miss the town. If it wasn't for the local Mudburra Aboriginal community getting an excision of the old stock route and setting up there again, and Kerry Packer buying and running the old Newcastle Waters homestead, the place would have disappeared entirely.

By the 1980s, the old Junction Hotel was a ruin. They tarted it up a bit for the 1988 Bicentenary celebrations when the old pub became the Drover's Memorial. But the place never had any staff. Not even a shop or tourist agency to tell people of the good old days. Just a few plaques and displays on the wall to entertain the occasional caravanner that could be bothered to turn off the road. So it became a bit of a ruin again. I suspect the tourists are unimpressed and don't make plans to return. If I didn't have old mates and family at Newcastle Waters I'd never revisit the place either.

Alec at the Newcastle Waters Drover's Memorial Park
photo courtesy Gerard Waterford

On Wave Hill

When the money got low at the end-of-season party, people started dropping out, trying to get Wet season work or going home to family. I hitched up with Cammy Cleary. He had a contract doing fencing at Wave Hill Station.

Cammy was a mixed descent fellow from out Lake Nash way. Later on he took the job as head stockman at Alexander Downs. Cammy was a very quiet sort of bloke. He was never one to skite or brag. But he could pull off some astonishing riding feats. A renowned horse breaker, he never believed in riding in rodeos or fancy riding tricks. He liked to dress plainly, never wearing flash hats or flash boots. But he was known as one of the best horsemen around and certainly the best I ever saw. He never wore spurs, preferring to ride hands and heels. He was very careful not to be caught unawares by a horse or the cattle he was working. I never saw him thrown.

I had worked with him and Freddy Martin doing a short trip into Helen Springs one time and we struck up a close friendship. He became like my brother, a lovely easygoing sort of fellow who enjoyed a drink and a laugh. He liked a night on the piss but was always the first up in the morning. We had a good time camped out at Newcastle Waters. But then Buck Buchester, one of the Wave Hill bosses, turned up and it was time to get back to work. We rode off with him along the Murranji and down to Wave Hill Station.

Wave Hill was a place of beautiful rolling woodlands with plenty of permanent creeks and waterholes. It made great cattle country. It was also the administrative hub for the whole north-west of the Territory. The police and government set up around the station. That is why everyone was said to be born at Wave Hill. The name covered the whole of the Northern Territory west of the telegraph line, all the way to the Western Australian border.

As contract fence post cutters, Cammy and me didn't see much of the homestead once we arrived. We were given a dray loaded up with two-person saws, axes and some rations. We threw on our swags and packs. There was enough rum in the packs to keep the mosquitoes at bay. Some locals took us out to where we were to pick up the work and we were told to get on with it.

It was the start of big changes on the old free rangeland places. They were moving to smaller paddocks. The fences were needed to keep the scrub bulls out, in order to control the breeding lines of the herd. The longhorn Herefords were getting mustered up and shipped out. Vesteys was experimenting with Poll Hereford breeds and some bigger framed Angus and even Asian cattle. The cattle industry was becoming more scientific.

The local timber was bloodwood, a deep red colour inside. It was good for fences because it was hardwood and a bit resistant to termites. We were to be paid by the fence post. We'd been given a bit of a shed for our gear. We unloaded, rolled out our swags and settled in. The rain hadn't started in earnest, but there were early storms about.

A small Aboriginal community was just up the road. The old stockmen came down to check us out. They sat around drinking our tea and getting a bit of our tobacco. We didn't let on about the rum. The scene was played out slowly. They had only a bit of English and our Mudburra was very thin. It was the usual stuff of where were we from, who were our family, what were our skinnames and who did we know. They seemed like a nice lot. They knew my family and Polly. It was a beautiful evening sitting on the rough verandah with the sun setting. We were to have a good time of it at that place.

Other nights the old men spoke of when my father had a place near Cattle Creek up above the Murranji towards Willeroo Station. Some of them knew him well enough from then, from when he managed Willeroo for his Uncle Tom and later on in his carting days. He would come through Wave Hill. But the talks were difficult across the language barrier and would fall over. I was hungry for stories but the old men always talked in circles. You couldn't rush them or direct what they were going to say. That would be rude and they might shut up altogether. They thought I should stick around and learn the language. But that wasn't going to happen. I was too much of a white fella, used to the sweet things in life and the money.

Wave Hill was well timbered and we didn't have to travel far to get into the stands of bloodwood. We cut the trees down and loaded the drays. We dropped off stray timber down at the Aboriginal camp. We soon got used to the noises of the place – the cattle and horses coming in to the waterhole at night and the galahs and parrots swirling around us in the early mornings and evenings. The work was steady rather than hard. The station mob dropped off meat and rations. There'd be a glass of rum as a nightcap and the odd storm building up from the west, usually passing us by but occasionally dumping a load on our tin roof.

You knew you had made it with the Aboriginal mob and had the approval of the old men when the girls from the community started coming down to visit. They made cups of tea and kept the place looking good.

Soon enough the local copper called around. We knew the rules so we were safe enough. You pretty much had to get caught red-handed giving it to the Aboriginal community. Cohabitation took a fair bit of catching too. We were being warned though, and he took to turning up from time to time.

It became a bit of a game. Bush telegraph and smoke signals would give the warning. We would usually have the kettle on the boil by the time he turned up. The men and women would be back at the camp. Any evidence of rum had been dealt with. He was keen and suspicious but had to get going eventually.

The station mob got us to do some horse breaking after the fencing was finished. It was well into the Wet by this time. Christmas had come and gone. For the horse breaking we had what was known as a 'bagman's camp', a couple of barrel horses and a couple of packhorses. We knew the waterholes that the wild mobs of horses used and set up mobile yards to trap them. Then we broke them into the saddle. To get paid by the station we had to ride each horse before handing them over. It was tough and dangerous work, but Cammy was a champion in the saddle and I wasn't too bad myself by this time.

Working for Mick Byrnes

Billy Hayes and Cammy Cleary and I got a lift back to Top Springs after being paid up. I ended up taking a job with Mick Byrnes. Mick was a good drover and always held his team together. He was never one to growl or bully. He had high standards and if you didn't match up, you were told quietly to pack your stuff and head off. When not droving Mick had a reputation for drinking like a fish. He had been droving through the 1930s, and often teamed up with a fellow called Harry Webb, another white fellow about the same age as him. Mick was a West Australian and perhaps ten years older than me. His droving plant was an all-packhorse team with no trucks or carts. Two horses carried the water. He had other horses for meat, dry supplies, spare hobbles, swags, wood, cookware, spare horseshoes and everything else. Harry Webb was from Queensland and he too was a big solid fellow. He didn't like to talk much.

Charlie Windley, the one-armed cook from my Mistake Creek trip, was working for Mick on this trip. Charlie made Newcastle Waters, then later Elliott, his home base. It was an easy place to pick up work each season. Charlie later married in Elliott and had one son.

We were a good team of blokes taking a mob from Victoria River Downs to Wolgarra near Dajarra in Queensland. We picked up at Pigeon Hole and it took about thirteen weeks. The season wasn't too bad. We were one of the first mobs on the road so the grass was good and the cattle okay. We had a fairly good trip along the Murranji through Newcastle Waters, Brunette Downs, Alexandra Downs, Rankin Springs and Camooweal. No need for weeks of double shifts on this trip. Will Riley also worked on the team. Will said he would stop at Wolgarra to look after the cattle. One of the young women there had her eye on him. He ended up married to her and moved later into Mt Isa.

Some of us ended up jumping on the mail truck and heading for Newcastle Waters at the end of the season. From there Cammy got us all jobs helping cut more posts for cattle yards and fences at Inverway Station, near the Western Australian border. Halls Creek was the closest town and when we had some time off we went in for a drink and to party on a bit.

There were lots of Aboriginal people of mixed descent living around Halls Creek. Many had come from Moolabulla Station just out of town. It was run as a government mission. As well as having its own Aboriginal community, it was the home for a lot of the taken-away kids of local white fathers and their Aboriginal wives. As an active cattle station it taught the boys stockwork and the girls domestic duties. Some of the stockmen I was mixing with in Halls Creek had spent their youth there, like Mick Byrnes and Charlie McAdam. Later on, the Western Australian government closed the mission and shifted a whole lot of the people to the Catholic Mission in Beagle Bay, on the coast north of Broome. Over the years I got to know a fair few people in Halls Creek and stayed with them at times. My family in Katherine are married into the Halls Creek families.

The next season I took another mob with Mick. He was running two teams that year and had a contract with Victoria River Downs again. I worked with the second team. Harry Webb was boss drover. We moved 1,500 head from Pigeon Hole to Wolgarra. I stuck around Queensland a spell this time. We got a short job to deliver a mob from Wernadinga Station through Sudan Dip then on to Julia Creek and south to a place called McKinlay.

There was an initiation ritual for new drovers coming into McKinlay. The place was very small, not much more than a pub really. It is the first stop after Cloncurry and before Kynuna on the way to Winton. The local drovers would gee up newcomers with stories of the sweet, willing white ladies of McKinlay. The young fellows would get a bit hot and bothered with the excitement. The pub at McKinlay kept a mob of beautiful white nanny goats. These were the 'sweet white ladies' of the place.

Charlie Ah Li worked with me on this trip. After that he got us a bit of contract work mustering down on Brighton Downs. After that I stayed in Winton, stopping with another drover, Dave Fogarty. I picked up whatever work was around. It was a good time but once the money started to run out, so did the fun. There was not much work in the country towns. It was usually already taken by the local families anyway. The only jobs were bits and pieces of maintenance stuff on the local stations that were too small, badly paid or uninteresting for the locals to bother doing themselves.

Splinter

I met Norman Prendergast at the Australian Hotel on the Winton to Boulia road. He was a tall, light-framed white fellow with a nice attitude. He was perhaps a dozen years older than me. I had called in at the Australian after my bit of work for the Richards family who owned Wernadinga Station. Splinter, as Norman was called, was looking around for someone interested in helping him take his droving plant back to the Territory. I had let it be known I was looking for something. Good timing. I wanted a change and was a bit homesick. A trip up to Darwin and Christmas with the family sounded good. It had been a couple of years. I took the job.

I had heard of the Prendergast brothers but hadn't run into them before. They had worked the Territory route for a few seasons, mostly doing Victoria River Downs' contracts. There were three of them – Norman, Claude and Harold. They worked together and had established a name as capable drovers, taking mobs from the north-west of the Territory across the Barkly into Queensland. They all had a reputation as good company and decent blokes.

Their contract that year was with Victoria River Downs. They had another one lined up for the following year. Victoria River Downs had said they could rest up their horses back there until the next season. It was a way of ensuring they kept their drovers. So after dropping off the cattle at Wolgarra, they spelled the horses at Carandotta Station. Claude had headed back to his married life in Brisbane. He drove trams in the off-season. Splinter and Slippery, as Harold was known, had caught up with mates. Now Splinter had the job of taking the horses back.

The wages weren't much better than rations but Splinter promised me a job the next year if I wanted it. We got a lift into Winton and took the train down to Dajarra to pick up the horses from Carandotta. From there it was just the two of us and about a hundred loose horses. We roughly followed the Barkly Stock Route across to Newcastle Waters and the spelling paddocks at Pigeon Hole.

Pushing well-trained loose horses back over the Barkly was not hard work. Splinter and I shared the work and got on well. He was a reserved fellow but good company. He was shocked that I could hardly read or write. So, in the quieter times, we sat down and he taught me a bit. I had forgotten just about everything they had tried to flog into me at the institutions. Now I was older and keener. I got a fair way further along to being comfortable around words. Splinter was keen that I got ahead and it inspired me a lot. Just having someone who encouraged me. I was a bit disappointed when we hit Pigeon Hole and dropped off the horses. He was heading down south. I sat around Newcastle Waters for a couple of weeks. Then I caught the bus up north.

I had four months of that Wet season in Darwin. I got work again at the municipal council. The family was going well. Gladys had the biggest mob of children, with new ones coming along regularly. I was the sometimes cashed-up uncle treating them to new toys and adventures. At other times I was more the bagman camped on the verandah taking up space. It all depended on getting enough work.

I had a group of friends that I worked and played football with. Gladys and Johnny had a house now on Bremer Road in Ludmilla, just up from the Fanny Bay racecourse. Ada was doing well, with Putt's cordial factory making good money. I did a bit of running around with the Buffs. There were lots of good times celebrating wins and drowning sorrows after losses. But by April the cold weather twitch had started. I was talking up getting back down to Newcastle Waters to catch up with Splinter. People said I should settle down and get a job in town. But I loved the feel of sitting high on a good horse with a sense of freedom and movement.

Drought

That year it was a really poor Wet season across the north-west and Barkly. I was able to get a lift over with some blokes driving a truck to Mt Isa. Arriving at Max Schaber's new pub at Elliott was like coming home. A fair few of the mob were gathering. Elliott had a big common area around a huge bauhinia tree. Different groups of people would camp about the place. It was a great time to catch up with the gossip. Who had given the game away and gone down south, got married, died or been locked up? The skiting was something else, especially once the rum started flowing. But you found out what jobs had been lined up for the next season, who was looking for an extra man for a trip over the Barkly. You could start to plan your next year.

Having come across with Splinter at the end of the last season, I had been promised work with the Prendergast team. But because of the lack of rain the Barkly route was hardly carrying any grass. It began to look like none of the big companies would be sending mobs across. The camp was building up steadily. I knew I had made it when Mr Schaber put my drinks on the tab. I rolled out my swag with my mates and settled in, waiting for news.

The Prendergast brothers turned up. It was good to see them and to know I was on their team. But like everyone else, they couldn't guarantee that Victoria River Downs would honour the contract to take a mob across the Barkly. In the meantime we got a short job taking some cattle back to Newcastle Waters and down to Helen Springs. Once there, Vobell's management would decide whether to keep on going or hold their cattle back for the year. We rode out to Pigeon Hole and mustered the horses on the strength of this work. There was nothing else happening. At Helen Springs it was finally confirmed that the cattle would stay.

There was very little droving happening anywhere that year. Just a few small jobs, not enough to keep you in pocket money. Camping down around the waterholes close by Max's new Ridge Hotel was good fun for a while. But once the money was gone and with credit getting a bit more stretched, I put up my hand for a bit of station work. Because I had a reputation for being able to turn my hand to most things, I managed to jag a position at Creswell Downs on the other side of Brunette Downs. But it meant leaving the others to take their chances. The older fragile blokes and the ones grown a bit useless with grog sickness were left behind.

At Creswell there was some horse breaking to be done. Troy Dann's father was the head stockman. His wife, Troy's mother, was the cook. The bosses liked married couples. They stayed longer. The Danns were careful with their money and much later had enough saved to buy into a station outside Alice Springs. They were good people and that year I got through a fair bit of the season with them, breaking in horses the old-fashioned way, moving stock to where there was still some feed. When the work ran out, I ended up heading down to Alcoota, close to Alice Springs, where there was a bit of work coming up on the muster.

Sadly, I never ended up doing another trip with Splinter. A year or so later I heard he was one of the early polio casualties in the epidemic of 1951. He died and was buried in Alice Springs cemetery. He had been like a father to me. I lost a bit of my feeling of being bulletproof.

Alcoota Station

The Leahy brothers were from Adelaide where, among other things, they ran pubs. They had bought Alcoota Station and also the neighbouring station of Bushy Park not long after buying Inverway Station from the Farquarsons. While Alcoota was cattle, Bushy Park was one of the last places in the Centre still running sheep. My work extended to Bushy Park from time to time. But I was a cattleman and I mainly kept busy with the cattle work. I left the sheep to other blokes less fussy about what they did.

Alcoota Station was a big operation. The Leahy brothers had in mind to use it as a fattening station for cattle coming down from Inverway. The cattle could have a spell at Alcoota then hit the Adelaide market with a bit of condition. Ted Maurn had the job as manager. He was an older white bloke with ten years or more on me. He was originally from Queensland way, well-respected and with a reputation as a good manager. He was tall and his personality was a bit the same as John Wayne in those western movies. A hard man, but kindly, and a strong silent leader of men. He had been at Alcoota for a couple of years with his wife before I arrived.

I got the job through my mate, Bill Turner, who was an old Bungalow boy. He was the head stockman. Bill had been a bit of an uncle for a lot of the Bungalow kids. He was also a cricketer of some local fame and I had seen him play in some of the Bungalow versus Wesley College cricket games when we were at the Institution. By this time he was getting a bit past his best at cricket. But he liked to get out the stumps on long summer evenings. Us blokes would have an impromptu match. We were fodder really to Bill's cricketing skills. We would bowl and we would field. He'd hit us all about the place. Bill was a good bloke, a hard worker who led by example.

The crew at Alcoota included Tom Williams. He was an older mixed descent man, wise in the ways of horses. He was originally from Mataranka Station. He knew my father and my brother George. He had come down on the same droving trip as my father in 1934 when Ted Lowe had sold Mataranka Station and was moving all his stock to his new place at Dalhousie Springs. Tom was a small man and at times he could appear a bit frail. But he had been a champion stockman and was still working the long hard hours.

I was also working with Tommy Madden, an Alice Springs man of mixed descent in his early thirties. It was a very good crew. There were three young white jackeroos also working the place. We socialised a fair bit with the Bushy Park crew that included Sammy Langford. I got to know Sammy fairly well over the years. He later left to live near my old Loves Creek stomping ground out at Bronco Wells on the Hale River near Limbla.

At Alcoota we shared a proper bunkhouse. Wages and conditions were a bit more reasonable since the war. These changes had even flowed through to places like Loves Creek. But of course all the Aboriginal families had been moved on to the missions by this stage. So they didn't get much of a share of the improvements.

For me it was a bit of a homecoming; I enjoyed the semi-permanent work after seasons of always being on the hunt for the next job. It was a bit like being back at Loves Creek as an older fully-fledged stockman. In winter we mustered the fattened steers. The scrubby Hereford cattle of my youth had been cleared from the station to make way for the Inverway stock brought down the year before. So there weren't a lot of calves to be branded or young bulls to be turned into steers. We walked the fats into town through Yambah Station and Sixteen Mile. The trip was an easy three days on the road. They were destined for a one-way ticket to Adelaide.

Work at Alcoota followed the yearly pattern from my teenage days out at Loves Creek – the usual fencing work, making replacement hobbles, breaking in horses and general stockwork tasks like moving mobs between waterholes. The soakages had been replaced by bores and windmills by this time. In the 1950s Alcoota Station even had a mechanic employed to drive around in a truck and maintain the water across the dry months. No need any more to exploit the old men and us young boys from the institutions. No more long lonely months waiting for rain in remote camps on dry creeks, digging out the sand to get enough water to fill a trough or two for the thirsty mob. Lots of the Aboriginal families had been forced off, living on rations around missions, in government reserves or on the fringes of town.

Unfortunately, Central Australian horseracing wasn't much happening any more. Nobody seemed to bother about it at Alcoota. Not like in the Loves Creek days when it was at the centre of the social calendar. Now cars and trucks made going to town a much more frequent event. The management of places had changed with a lot of bookkeepers and bean counters running the show. The days of rum-soaked bagmen as owners and managers of the stations were changing. People drank cold beer from refrigerators now.

Temptation

About this time I ran into my old friend Baden Bloomfield. I was walking behind a mob of cattle when he turned up out of the blue. He had a mob of good-looking horses and was off to muster and move cattle off his place at Indiana Downs. We were both a lot older, but the friendship and closeness was still there.

'Just the man I've been looking for,' he said.

It had been a good few years since we'd caught up. But it could have been yesterday the way he talked. He had come good on a lot of his plans. I felt like the lonely skinny boy waiting desperately for him to turn up and save me, like in the old days at Atnarpa. We pulled up and I put the billy on to boil. Baden talked. He was off to help his sister Maggie Bloomfield take her stock to her new station. Maggie was married to Jock Nelson who went on to be a federal parliamentarian. They were moving the stock onto Mt Skinner Station that they had bought. Over tea and a sandwich he tried to persuade me to head out with him and become part of his team. "It would be like the old days, except better." Baden had enough money and dreams for both of us.

His plan was that I would become his offsider. He even suggested that I marry his daughter, Agnes, and take over as head stockman. I would be like his adopted son and heir. But throwing Agnes into the mix was a bad move. She was wrong skin for me. Sister along the kinship lines. Her mother, Eileen, had been mother for me in the old days. And I knew Baden and knew that he could be messy. If things didn't work out he wouldn't be there to save me. But despite it all, it was an intoxicating vision of what might be. One of the bosses. Perhaps even a landowner and a man who had power.

Despite the warmth of being around Baden again, I wasn't the type of bloke to just leave a mob of cattle. Baden told me that Bill Turner would figure out I had moved on soon enough and would send someone out to pick up the cattle. He would even arrange to get a message to him. It was very tempting. But I liked the Alcoota Station crew and felt obligations to them. It was against my nature to just up and leave without explanation.

Talking things up and saying that anything was possible was very much Baden's style. He was exciting to be around. He didn't mind taking a few risks and upsetting people. We could have been on our way into a bright and different future. And if I had had the time to make it alright with the Alcoota mob, I probably would have gone. But Baden said he didn't have the time. It was almost a test for me. I resisted the Baden charm and said no. Said I might try to catch him up later on. If I had just left my reputation would have been affected. I had been paying my dues proper way for some time. It was against the bushman's code to just leave the others shorthanded.

I had relied for a long time on my reputation as someone who did the right thing to get work. Baden was a part of my Loves Creek past. And I wasn't a teenager any more. The Bloomfields were not all powerful in my life. So it didn't happen. But Baden remained a hero for me.

Baden died not long after, in 1951. His racehorses were sold to Charlie Chickundi. Later one was sold on to Roy Schaber and went on to win the Harts Range Cup three times. Perhaps I could have been part of the split-up of his things after he died. But I suspect that I would have been pushed to one side, regardless of what Baden might have said. He had a white family first and second. The Aboriginal Protectorate would have been unhelpful in safeguarding any interest I might have had. After all, Agnes ended up getting nothing.

A near-death experience

I was badly hurt when working at Alcoota Station. Stockwork always carries a risk. People these days don't spend any time on horses so they don't know what big living and breathing animals they are. Unpredictable, even when you know them backwards and forwards. Every horse is an adventure. They have personalities, sometimes bad ones. You can just be unlucky. A hole in the ground or an animal coming out of nowhere and you can be thrown. A snake rearing up out of the grass. Whatever it is, a horse can panic, shift its weight suddenly, start bucking or just take off. I had seen enough deaths and accidents to know to be careful. As Cammy Cleary said, 'You should never let a horse catch you unawares.' But it happens.

It was early morning. I was alone, pushing a mob of cattle along to better water and grass. I had taken a cut lunch because it would take me all day. I was out in scrubby country, with the sun not long up, heading to a waterhole where a mob was waiting. My horse was a fresh young mare that kept trying to take charge. The usual thing was to show it, once and for all, that you were boss. I decided to stir her up a little. Take the sting out of her. The horse was twisting and bucking along, with me holding her easily, when she veered suddenly sideways. Perhaps she lost her footing. Anyway, I was caught on the hop and the mare careered under a tree. I ended up being smashed straight into a branch. I must have hit it really hard because it ripped me open from above my temple down to below my eye. I was knocked out cold and didn't wake up. Because I was working alone, it took until the afternoon before the other blokes realised I was not about. When I didn't turn up for tea they got worried.

They came for a look and found my mare wandering about. The country around Alcoota is beautiful grass and woodlands, so it is hard to track through. But they were experienced bushmen and finally chased me down. They came across me just before dark. I had been out in the sun all day.

It must have been a pretty grim picture. My face was a mess. Where my head lay there was a pool of congealed blood. Lines of blood had come out my ears and mouth. Ants and flies had settled over my face. At first they thought I was dead. But one of them rolled me over a bit and found I was shallow breathing. They wiped me clean as much as they could, wrapped me in a blanket and a shirt was borrowed to stop the bleed. I had already lost a lot of blood. They couldn't wake me. Some stayed while others went back for the station's truck to carry me in. I was gently placed in the tray on a mattress of sorts.

The flying doctor had been radioed, but it was too dark for the plane to take off and landing in the dark would have been even more of a problem. The doctors told them to drive me to the hospital. My wound was roughly bandaged to stem the blood loss. Then they headed for town. The roads in those days were fairly shocking. I would have been bumped across the corrugations, creekbeds and dips for the 200-odd miles into the Alice. People didn't think I would survive. In Alice Springs they bedded me down, connected me up to a drip and, to everyone's surprise, I survived the night.

It was three weeks before I regained consciousness. I woke up as weak as a kitten. They were worried that I might have some brain injury. I couldn't remember the accident or anything else. But gradually things started to come back and I was on my feet again. It was nice having nurses to look after me, but I was keen to be on my way. So eventually I was free to go and I got a lift back to Alcoota and the male world of my mates. I was soon back on a horse again.

I have a big scar running from my temple down to my ear from that accident. If I hadn't been found that night I probably would have died. As it was, it was a close-run thing. Despite being weeks off work, there was no workers' compensation then, or none that I was told about. So I never got any support after the accident.

My near-death experience was a shock. Like most of us stockmen, I had seen enough tragedy to know life is fragile. I had seen the old swaggies, too sick and frail to work any more, go off into the bush to shoot themselves, or head into town to drink themselves to death. But I was still young and, despite Splinter, had felt pretty bulletproof. The accident changed that. I found myself restless and irritable. I don't know if it was the blow to the head or not.

Loving Eva

After that year's muster we had some time off. Nothing much was happening at the station, so Tom Williams and I stayed in Alice for a couple of weeks. I caught up with some of the old Bungalow gang and droving mates, stopping out at Dick Palmer's camp. My old Bungalow mate, Nugget Kopp, was getting married to one of Dick and Mary's daughters. Dick always had a place for a stockman to throw out his swag and I joined them.

Dick Palmer was born at the end of the nineteenth century. His father was a white linesman and his mother was an Arrernte woman called Rowdy from the Yambah area. Later Rowdy married Wagon Jack Mpetyane. Dick and his brothers were grown up by Wagon Jack. Rowdy's country was between Harry Creek and Bond Springs.

As a young teenager Dick had started working at Bond Springs when Sidney Kidman owned the place. When Kidman sold out, Dick moved back to his family who were stopping at a place called Basso's Farm. He then got work as a stockman for the Gorey family at Yambah Station. He was promised land out there for his work, but this didn't happen. Later he got married and, with his wife and young kids, he went prospecting near Garden Station. They didn't have much luck. In the 1930s he moved back to Alice Springs. He was given a 99-year lease on a place next to Basso's Farm. He was droving locally and needed a spot for his family and horses. The place became known as Palmer's Camp. Just north of town, it became a drop-off point for Aboriginal stockmen coming in from bush and was often overcrowded.

Palmer's Camp was where my father and George spelled their horses after the droving trip to Dalhousie Springs. Nearby was Mt Nancy that was used as a holding paddock for horses owned by the livestock agent, Dalgetys. By the 1940s Dick Palmer, Mort Conway, Teddy Carter and Tom Williams all had their horses in the area. In 1981 Dick Palmer passed away. He had eleven children as well as adopting and looking after several other kids. He was kind to everybody. There was no grog at all at Dick's place.

Geoff Shaw, who went on to manage the Central Australian Aboriginal Congress and set up Tangentyere Council, was grown up there. His family camped near Palmer's Camp, relying on Dick's water supply. After the war the Shaw family moved on to Mt Nancy, building a humpy on a concrete slab left by the army. In the late 1940s Matt Savage had another droving camp around the hills at the Head Street end of Priest Street.

When I stopped with the Palmers back in 1950, it was a chance to catch up. I hadn't been around Alice much since the war. I caught up with Cammy Cleary and Billy Hayes again. Cammy was going well, running with one of Dick's droving teams. He was just stopping in the Alice for a spell. After that he worked a bit out at Harts Range and across the Sandover, at one time working on Baden's old station, Indiana Downs. Cammy's son Tommy is now living on Indiana Downs. The place was sold back to the Aboriginal community.

My other great mate, Billy Hayes, ended up getting old stock route land next to Huckitta Station. It was what they called an excision under land rights legislation. He married Harold Thomas's sister from Brunette Downs and had a family. I see one of his daughters, Paula Perkins, living around Alice now. His land claim came through in the 1980s when all us old stockmen had dreams of becoming station managers. I myself was busy trying to get up a claim on the old stock route at Harry Creek.

The droving season had ended for that year with Cammy, Billy and the other drovers dropping off some mobs from Inverway. Now they needed some people to take Dick Smith's horses back up to Inverway where there was plenty of grass and the horses could rest up for the Wet season. It was Billy Hayes, me and another Aboriginal fellow called Monkey that pushed three droving plants of nearly 200 horses back north.

The horses were in real poor condition. They'd had a long season on the road and there wasn't the usual feed about. The grasslands around Central Australia and north of Alcoota were so drought-stricken that Dick Smith arranged with the police for the horses to rest up for the maximum three-week spell at the Government Well just north of Tennant Creek.

The police used these places for their horses. The Government Well was a big permanent waterhole north of town on the west side of the highway. It was a holding paddock too for animals taken as part of police inquiries. It was near the then new Phillip Creek Mission for Aboriginal children. The mission is gone today, but remnants of the old concrete slab can still be seen there if you turn off the highway past the Threeways Roadhouse.

The Phillip Creek Mission was run through the evangelical arm of the Anglican Church. They were also associated with Mr Long's missions east of Katherine, that my mother was involved with, and the Retta Dixon Institution in Darwin. We had a hard trip north to the Government Well with little feed and poor water, but managed to get all the horses through.

I was camping at the Well when I met and fell in love with Eva Yarra, a beautiful young Aboriginal missionary working at Phillip Creek. She had been born and brought up in another church mission over on Palm Island, off Townsville. Eva was working at Phillip Creek with another young woman called Holly. There was an old white supervisor, Mr Thomas, who was on crutches when I visited. He had persuaded the Church to send Eva and Holly to help run the place while he was out of action.

Eva and Holly were in charge of the mission kids when they came down to the waterhole for a daily swim. Us blokes had settled the horses and didn't have a lot to do. So we were happy to help the young women out. Eva was educated in a way that I had missed out on at the Bungalow. She was a non-smoking, non-drinking sort of girl who talked of her commitment to the Church. But she wasn't without a sense of fun.

I supposed my accident had made me ready to look for God in my life. Especially if this new life was to include Eva. Religion had been interesting to me when I was a kid. And a bit of it still hadn't been scrubbed off. A pretty girl like Eva brought back to me a lot of the things that made me like religion. We were keen on each other, and she was interested in saving me. I was happy to be saved. Being with me was an opportunity for her to escape the earnestness, tedium and racism of the true believers at the mission, but I suspect she didn't tell the bosses that I was her special new project.

Once our three weeks were up, the police made sure we were on our way north. I was lovesick and would have probably chucked it in to stay close by if Eva had said the word. But there was nothing doing. So despite being a shocking writer, hardly able to stick a sentence together, I left with a promise between us to write. I was desperate to get back to Eva as soon as possible.

Despite having lots of tired horses and not enough men, we made reasonable time. But we had big early rain that year. The rains brought fresh feed and the horses didn't want to be moved on. They became more of a handful to keep together. So it slowed us down. The rain also saw some of the rivers rise. We got stuck at Mucka Creek near Wave Hill when it came up very quickly after a big storm. We had to wait for the water to go down enough for us to swim the horses across. It wasn't until Christmas Day that we struggled into Inverway Station. Instead of being paid off and heading to Tennant Creek I was stuck at the homestead. The roads were cut.

The station management arranged work for us, fencing, horse breaking and some stockwork. It wasn't until a month or two later that I got an old letter in the first mail to get through. Eva was back in Darwin. I was able to get paid out and catch a flight up on the mail plane to try and see her.

Back to Queensland

After we left Phillip Creek, the Church had arranged for six of the children to be taken up to the Retta Dixon Institution in Darwin. Eva and

Holly had gone as supervisors. Unfortunately, by the time I flew into Darwin and found my way to Retta Dixon, Eva had gone back to Palm Island. I had to write and wait. I went to live at Gladys's. I picked up some work with the mosquito gang spraying the waterways and breeding grounds. In our letters Eva and me decided to get married. But to do this we needed approval, not just from the Northern Territory but also from the Queensland Aboriginal Protectorate. They had to give me permits, first to go to Palm Island and second, to get married. So I knew it would take a while. But getting the Queensland side of things approved didn't happen. They knocked me back. I had to reapply and reapply. It still didn't happen.

The permit hadn't come through when the droving season started again. I made my way back to Inverway where I had work lined up, droving a mob to Wolgarra in Queensland, with Mick Byrnes as the boss drover. I was on my way to catch up with Eva one way or another. But the droving took the usual time. It was perhaps August and nearly four months before we dropped off the cattle.

I still had no approval to visit Eva at the Palm Island Mission. I was told by Queensland friends that the mission was a virtual prison. In Queensland there seemed even more rules than in the Northern Territory for Aboriginal people. I stopped around Mt Isa and Cloncurry but permission was never granted.

Eva and I stayed writing for a time. In the end we drifted apart. I gave up hope. It was hard work maintaining a long-distance relationship when you are twenty-seven, lonely and hopeless at letters. Later I heard that Eva had married a Townsville fellow called Geyer. They got a house in Hermit Park and went on to have a mob of children. I often wonder what would have happened if they had let us get married. My life could have been very different. I could have ended up living around Townsville.

I have met one of Eva's sons. He is a really good musician who did a tour of the Centre. He played a number of concerts at Basso's Farm in the 1980s and at the Yipirinya Festival in September 2001. So I got a lot of the gossip from her boy. I never got to Townsville.

And at this stage of my life I might never get there. As far as I know Eva never made it back to Central Australia either. Travelling around is much easier these days than when we were young and in love. Her boy tells me that she sends her regards and still talks of our romance. I heard that Holly married an American and went to live in the States.

Still moving

Western Queensland was a different world. The towns were bigger, your money went further and it was more relaxed in some ways than the Territory. It was still a racist place and you still needed to watch out for the bullyboys. But you could have a life a bit freer from the fear of Native Affairs and the government men. There was often a choice of work and they mostly paid award wages. I was also older and wanting something more. I had spent the last three or so years mostly on the back of a horse pushing along cattle. A big part of me was really lonely. I can now see that I wanted a family and people that loved me. I wanted Eva.

My recent life in the Northern Territory had been much, much better than the dark old days of Loves Creek. But I had little to show for all my hard work. No home to call my own. No money in the bank. No team of horses. No cattle station or even a donkey farm. No family waiting for me. No real prospects in the Northern Territory of anything happening, except going back and doing it all over again. Now two different governments weren't even going to let me see my girlfriend. It all seemed too sad. My mates told me to get over it, have another rum and climb back into the saddle. But I was keen to do something new. I decided to give Queensland a go. My mate Billy Hayes was travelling with me at this time.

The previous few years had made me feel like time was passing me by. I was in my late twenties and some of the younger blokes were marrying up and going ahead. The accident at Alcoota had shocked me. Also my mother had died. I hadn't seen her for a while and her death came out of the blue. I had been freezing in a stock camp on the Barkly at the time of her passing. Many months later I caught up with Gladys and she told me of our mother's death. By the time I got the news, the funeral had well and truly happened. I suppose Bobby and her kids were there, some other family and members of her religious community. It was the end of any vague idea I might have had of building up something between us. I had always been too late, and getting a childhood back was just too hard.

You tend to think people will wait for you. But she died and was buried at what they called the Aboriginal low-level cemetery just out of Katherine. It was not much more than a paddock off to the side of the reserve that was old Springvale Station. Today there is a motel called Mt Balloo near her gravesite. There is no headstone. Mum was fifty-five years old when she died, having led an eventful and hard-working life. There was to be no graceful and relaxed old age for my mother.

It felt time to grow up and create a family of my own. I was jealous of my mates with wives and kids waiting for them. We joked about the freedom of being single and carefree, but you can have too much freedom and nothing much you want to do with it. I was past that stage. I wanted someone to need me more.

The claypan boogie

So, on hitting Queensland, I had a plan to stay around for a while. My mate Bill Riley was married up to Ruby King and stopping with her family in Mt Isa. The Kings and their relations, the Wings, were droving families from

Camooweal. They had Chinese and Aboriginal heritage, with a grandfather who had been a market gardener and station cook. Ruby's family had moved into Mt Isa some time before. They were lovely people. They became family later on with one of my brother George's kids marrying into them.

I had a great time with the Kings. And there was a lot to do in Mt Isa. There were girls and people who were friends of friends. After a couple of weeks a group of us kept going down the road, on to Cloncurry.

Cloncurry, known as 'the Curry', was another big town. There were nine pubs there then. It was growing quickly with mining companies using it as a base. It had a lot of energy and seemed full of good, kindly people. There was a lively social life happening.

Nancy Brown, one of the Cloncurry Aboriginal matriarchs, organised and ran dances every Friday night. She had a big shed on the claypans, just out of town. Whole families turned up. The kids ran around everywhere, eventually falling asleep and being put into swags. The older people sat around playing cards and chatting. They were the chaperones, making sure there was no trouble. Us younger blokes danced the night away, getting into as much mischief with the young women as they and the chaperones would let us.

A fellow called Pat Purcell and his son played the fiddle. It was the claypan boogie around a big bonfire. Pat was a mixed descent fellow from around Winton. He had a sunny disposition, never getting the blues. He worked as a jack-of-all-trades and liked a song and dance. Sometimes there were a few other travellers with fiddles or accordions who would belt out a song or two.

There were dance games to get things moving. My favourite was 'Drop the Broom'. It was like musical chairs, except when the broom was dropped, you had to find a girl to partner you. I was a good dancer in those days and usually managed to have a mob of young women, especially the sisters of my mates, hanging around.

One of these mates was Billy Fortune. The Fortunes were a family from Kajabbi, just up north of 'the Curry'. Billy's sister, Elma, was a beautiful girl with a sweet nature, and I got very fond of her. It was easier, what with being mates with her brothers. I often stayed at their place. At the dances I always had Elma hanging close and looking to me. It was a lot of fun, having a girlfriend and being popular. It was a community in itself, the mixed descent mob in Cloncurry, and I was treated like an equal within it. But I got a bit ambitious with my social success. Elma eventually moved on to someone a bit more loyal and settled. I even had a bit of a girlfriend happening later in Mt Isa. She was the daughter of the fellow who ran the store at Anthony's Lagoon. But I was too poor to settle down. The work saw me always on the move somewhere.

The Elma Fortune romance was the real end of my dreams of getting together and settling down with Eva. I followed the rules I first learnt in the institutions. You keep moving, keep smiling, and don't let the bastards know when they have got you down.

After spending most of my money drowning my sorrows, I took off-season work up north at Wernadinga Station. The job was with a fencing contractor, re-sinking fence posts. The thick black soil of that part of Queensland saw the posts pushed upwards in the spongy soil after a bit of rain. Every few years they needed to be pushed back into the ground.

Billy Hayes was still with me and on the same crew. It was my first Christmas out of the Northern Territory. We had a quiet time out bush with the monsoon rains settling in. It was just me and Billy, the fencing mob and a few of the regular stockmen eating roast beef and washing it down with a few glasses of rum. Later the fencing job moved to Kormilaroy Station and down towards Julia Creek. It tided me over for a fair bit of the hot season.

Then I got offered better paying work cutting corkwood. It was used for firing up the steam turbine generator at the Quiradella mine. I joined up with two cousins, Teddy and Burri Ah Sam. The Ah Sams were related to the Kings and from out Camooweal way. They, too, were from a Chinese market garden background. Teddy and Burri were happy-go-lucky fellows and good workers, a bit younger than me. Later we had work pulling up and replacing sleepers on the Mt Isa to Townsville railway line. Another time I worked for a while as a fettler on the railway in Quiradella siding, out of Dajarra. That was lonely work and I gave it away.

A military reject

After the railway work a group of us decided to join the army to fight in Korea. The war had been going on for a while. The army was recruiting around the country towns having run out of volunteers in easier-to-get-to places. They had a tent at the Cloncurry Showgrounds. Despite a bit of reluctance on my part, I was persuaded to put up my hand. It was only the drink talking really, because I was having a good time of it. I didn't like the army stuff and being told what to do. But they had us signed up and on a train south before we could sober up.

About five days later we pulled into Roma Street Station in Brisbane. It was the biggest place I'd ever seen. Took ages just to get into town. Not that we had much time to look around. They had us in an army truck and out to a place called Lone Pine west up the river in no time.

The next month went pretty slowly for me. The others were taken off and into their units. But I was told to sit still while they sorted out my age and the details from my time in the army during World War II. The army is a huge bureaucracy. It was one of the things I had hated about it before. You get lost in their systems and forgotten. They didn't like that I had put up my age at my earlier enlistment. In the end I couldn't provide any proof of age or anything else. They just couldn't be bothered sorting through it. I ended up being given a ticket back to Cloncurry. The others ended up in the army.

It was humiliating getting knocked back. I was told to hand in my uniform and caught the train as directed. There were lots of surprised faces in Cloncurry and I had a bit of explaining to do. People look at you a bit funny if they think you should be somewhere else. Luckily there was a bit of work out of town, what with a lot of the blokes enlisted.

The Korean War soldiers had a very tough time of it overseas. I ended up back in the Northern Territory riding my horse behind cattle. I never really got back to 'the Curry' much after that. I suspect I would have had a much better time of being in the army the second time around. I would have been one of the older blokes in the unit so it would have been an entirely different war for me. But part of me is still pleased about not having gone.

The Elliott mob

By 1953 I was back in the Territory looking for droving work. Newcastle Waters had died and now it was Elliott, same manager but with a much flashier pub. We were all a few years older. Elliott had really gone ahead fast. The Ridge left the old Junction Hotel for dead. There must have been a couple of hundred of us camped on the creek at Elliott, waiting for the droving bosses that year. It was a grand gathering of us travelling men.

We were camped in the scrub, not far from the old bauhinia tree known as the 'Tree of Knowledge'. You chucked your swag in a fork of the tree during the day, and went off looking for ways of passing the time.

The old blokes at Loves Creek would have started a corroboree, teaching the old dances and renewing the old songs. We were telling different stories of great riding feats and heroic fights against the odds. Where the tjilpis would have been opening up old mysteries, we were pulling the plugs on bottles of rum, singing and dancing to a different, sadder, 'men's business' tune. Like them, we couldn't pass on our skills. The technology was changing things too quickly. Our kids would leave us, trying to find a way into a world that was very different from their parents' and grandparents'.

Elliott became the big centre for busting a cheque at the end of a trip, as well as for turning up to find work at the start of a new season. It was the same set-up at the different pubs along the stock routes. There was Top Springs and Camooweal competing for our business.

Us drovers often stopped for four or five weeks at the end of the season, drinking until our money ran out. We spent the days recovering, sprawled out on the pub verandah. Then spent the night drinking and carrying on. I remember more than a few nights standing on some table or bar top belting out some song. It was like karaoke nights today. Most nights we staggered out at closing time, holding on to mates while trying to remember where our swags were. It was a bit the same at the start of each season. Those of us hanging around Elliott who were assured of work, would get credit from Max Schaber.

If a boss drover wanted to keep his team he would look after them between seasons. The boss would send a telegram through to the pub with pick-up times and jobs. They had an arrangement with Max to settle up for the team on arriving. It was deducted from our payout at the end of the trip.

Max seemed happy to see me after my years away. He had old Frank McAdam, Charlie McAdam's Dad, working there at the pub. Charlie was a linesman operating out of Elliott. There were lots of old Bungalow boys about the place.

Billy Fullerton was another of the blokes working at the pub. He had been a good drover in his time. Max kept him in work cleaning up and helping out. It could get very lively when the boys had a few drinks in them. There was often a bit of music and gambling happening, and a fair few fights broke out, particularly if someone was getting turfed out. Billy was killed in a fight. It was sad and unnecessary. He was kicked to death in a drunken brawl that no one had time to stop. Wrong place, wrong time. You could be unlucky.

Jack Cavanagh was another old man working at the Ridge Hotel. He got a bit of a ribbing from us when he married a Queensland woman while on holidays. He had played the country toff in town, telling some yarns about being a big-time boss out in the bush. Whatever he said it had worked. They walked up the aisle and caught the bus back to Elliott. To say that she was shocked and unimpressed with what he could provide her at the Ridge was an understatement. You could hear their fights all the time. Plus his wife was much younger than him, liked to dress up real pretty and was flirty into the bargain. He really struggled to keep up with her. He was mocked by us for having a 'parcel-paid' wife. She became known as the 'Lady of the Ridge'. She got plenty of better offers than old Jack and started playing up to the ringers. Jack had no peace. Eventually she took off with a young fellow and headed back to the city. I think a part of Jack was almost relieved to see her go.

There was a café in Elliott run by Mrs Sullivan and her two daughters, Pheally and Barbara. Her husband, Jack, was a train driver in Darwin. Mrs Sullivan did all the cooking at the café while the girls did the serving. It was a busy life in season. The daughters got a lot of attention from us drovers. Eventually Barbara married a German fellow and they bought the pub at Rankine Springs.

Beetaloo was the big local station. Norm Stacey, Mick Beebe and lots of the other blokes around Elliott called the place home. I was friends with the whole lot of the Bathems who owned the place – Harry, John and Duncan. Their father was a white stockman who had built the place up. They had a beautiful sister that I tried to curry favour with. She was a country girl used to living hard in the saddle like the men. You almost thought she and her sisters were men the way they worked alongside you in their old hats and riding gear. Great riders and hardworkers. I had enormous respect for them. Dressed up a bit they were good-looking women. I still see one of them around today. They call her old Mrs Bathern these days. But in her youth she was a princess. She always wore an old stockman's hat and still does today.

The one-armed cook, Charlie Windley, also settled at Beetaloo between seasons, along with Jack Crouch Jungarai, who was considered one of the best cooks on the road. There was another mad old cook called Jack 'the

Frenchman'. He was usually out Camooweal way and was a dreadful drunk. He had a reputation for 'the horrors' and drinking anything with a bit of a kick in hard times. More than once he got caught getting stuck into the lemon essence that was used to give the custard a bit of a lift. When he was in a bad way he would yell out in a bloodcurdling scream, something like 'old segarnie'. No one knew what it meant. But it kept you on edge when you were camping anywhere near him. He went droving to get away from the grog and clean himself out. But it didn't always work that way if he did the ordering. He could scare the cattle something shocking when he was in the horrors and people stopped using him. He became a bit of a bar fly like a lot of the mad old cooks.

A more cheerful cook was Nugget 'Kookaburra' Newman. He was a good cook and a happy-go-lucky sort of chap. He called us to meals with his kookaburra calls. A funny fellow who enjoyed a drop of rum.

Syd Hawk had a cart that he used to travel in, selling things to us drovers like clothes and trinkets. He made enough money out of us to end up buying the pub at Top Springs.

Another fellow around a lot was a young bloke called Ray Nissan. He was a bit slow and strange. Ray used to make signs of ringing up on the telephone when he wanted something. Max looked after him a bit and gave him a job as the goatherd at the Ridge.

Charlie Ah Li, who had been on Mick Byrne's droving team, stopped at Elliott and got work as a linesman. He was a good old mate and we spent a fair bit of time together. He had an older brother, Pharlap, who was an old Mudburra man, born and bred around Newcastle Waters. Pharlap spent decades working Montejinni Station and lots of other Vobell places, even as far out as Cunnamulla. He did a lot of droving mainly for Clarrie 'Pig-Jumping' Pankhurst's droving team, one of the first fellows picked if he was available. Pharlap was a fabulous horseman and knew cattle better than just about anyone. But he preferred working close to home and was under the Aboriginal Ordinances. He was older than me and worked cattle into his old age. Pharlap built up and ran an outstation at No. 10 bore on the Murranji Track in the 1980s and 1990s. His sons work the mob of cattle now.

Elliott also was home to the Allum family – Charlie, Gilbrie, Reggie and Wally and my close mate, Pompey. In later years when I was settled in Alice Springs, I saw a fair bit of Pompey. He had a sick child that needed a lot of hospital treatment and often stayed at my home when stuck in town. Harry Baxter was another bloke about the place. He was about twenty years older than me and a very smart fellow. He was big, tall, solid and a great singer. He was of mixed Aboriginal descent and had grown up in the Top End. He and his wife, Ada, are grandparents to Jackie Baxter, now working for the Central Australian Stolen Generations and Families Aboriginal Corporation.

Ada Ahmat photo courtesy Kruger family

There were not a lot of potential partners around the place. The women were all Aboriginal. It was still technically illegal to sleep with Aboriginal women, but many men did and had kids and steady relationships. Others like me would play the field, often paying for the company with grog, food and occasionally some money. There was only one policeman and he was okay. He wasn't one to harass honest working men. There was a cheeky copper at one time by the name of Gordon Stott. His father had been boss copper of Alice Springs in the 1910s and 20s. But Stott was soon sent on to bigger and better things and we were left in peace once again.

Other years, other trips

Throughout the years I worked for a lot of droving bosses and teams. On some of my favourite trips I worked with Ray Turner and his wife, Bessie. There was never an argument. They had a big German wagonette pulled by four

Clydesdales. They even had chooks. Ray was a fellow of mixed descent from Western Australia. His wife was known as Aunt Bessie. They had three girls and Bessie was teaching them school on the road. When things were a bit slower, my job included being cook's aide and helping with the wagon. This meant catching up on my own reading and writing. Bessie liked my singing voice and I would show off during the night rides around the cattle. Trying to sing different songs to keep her happy. The cattle seemed to like it too.

My first trip with them was from Wave Hill to Moorestone. It was a long haul and hard work. We got on well. Ray was never one to bully you or set you up. A lovely sweet-tempered man who got the best out of people by being fair and reasonable. Ray mostly picked up short trips, moving fat cattle from dry stations to those that had got the good storms and had good grass. He had a great reputation for looking after his cattle and getting them from place to place without knocking them up. I got work with him because I was known as a reliable bloke. Some others would have a fight with the boss and end up leaving. I never left a job until it was finished.

I think Ray and Bessie liked me because I didn't mind having a go. I wasn't one to say it wasn't my job to do something if I was the best person to be doing it. But the trouble with short trips was that the money wasn't good and you had to find another job as soon as the trip was over. If Ray had had more work I would have stayed with him longer. But I had to take the bigger trips when they came along. Ray and Bessie ended up settling down out west when their daughters got a bit too old for the road.

I did another trip with Mick and Bill Cousins who were twins from Queensland. They ran two teams together when the work was happening. They based themselves and their horses out of Elliott. Most of the other drovers had their horses turned out at the Camooweal Pound, at Inverway or Top Springs. If you were broke and needed a job that would come up quickly in Elliott, then the Cousins were the people to talk to. It only took them a couple of weeks to get their two-horse plants together and be at some local station ready to take delivery of a mob. So station managers used them if something unexpected came up.

I worked one job with my uncle Larry 'the Larrikin' Althouse. He was an old man by then. We had a trip taking cattle down towards Oodnadatta when they were re-stocking. It was the only time I travelled with cattle south of Alice Springs. It was a good rainfall year and a fairly easy trip across the rubbishy gibber country south of Crown Point Station.

I took work at Renner Springs Station one time. Mrs Ward was running the place. Her husband had passed away and she decided to keep the place going using local Aboriginal stockmen. She was a very kind woman. She often had families asking her to look after their kids when welfare was on their backs, or someone had got too sick or died. She was really generous like that. The kids would be trained up in domestic work or stockwork, and go on to find jobs. She had the house looking spotless and the herd well mustered and organised. I just had a short time working there and had a good time of it. Renner Springs Station was beautiful Mitchell grass country, good for fattening cattle. But it had a lot of serpentine bush that was dangerous. Just the wrong height when you were on horseback. You risked whiplash from the headhigh branches.

When Len Tuit started his bus service between Darwin and Alice Springs, Mrs Ward's place became one of the stops. Even before she turned it into a business, she always had a cup of tea ready for visitors. She was known for her hospitality on the track. So she was a natural for making a bit of a business out of looking after Len's passengers. The young girls she had in her care were able to make a living working in the tea shop.

Dunmarra was one of my last jobs. The station is about 150 miles north of Elliott. A dusty petrol and grog stop on the Stuart Highway. The station owners had made more money from the pub than the cattle since the war. The owner was a rough, tough ex-policeman called Noel Healey. His wife, Thelma, was known as 'Ma'. Noel was a fighting man. He had a reputation for his hands-on style of bouncing anyone acting up. Always with a pick handle and shotgun within easy reach, he was reputed to have hurt more than a few people. Noel ended up dying in a fight when he took on one ringer too many. The fellow came back the next morning and bashed the living daylights out of him and he died. Thelma kept the place going for a while before selling up.

My work at Dunmarra was mustering. Noel went through a fair few head stockmen because he wasn't easy to get on with. But we made a go of it over a couple of musters. Dunmarra is very rough bulwaddy scrub country where it is often impossible to see more than fifty metres in front of you. Moving cattle without losing the lot was really patient, frustrating work, needing a good steady stockman. If you pushed too hard the cattle would just disappear into the scrub. Even working slowly and cleverly we lost a fair few. But Noel got his best return for some time when I was there and he was happy.

A lot of the cattle we rounded up had escaped the musters for years. So we had a lot of unbranded bulls ready to have a go at us all the time. Dunmarra has pretty much given up on cattle these days. Too much scrub and hard work. Catching tourists in the roadhouse is a lot easier.

The end of droving

It was the dry seasons that got to you. There wouldn't be much droving and the cattle trucks were increasingly getting what work there was. In dry years it was a desperate hunt for work or starve. Sometimes a station might offer you little bits of fencing. But more usually they had enough permanent staff. So when times were tough it was camping out, living hard and doing whatever was required to put a bit of money in your pocket and meat in the pot. It could get a bit dodgy at times.

I had mates across northern Australia that usually saw me through a period of not much work. But I didn't like to use them. Everyone was living close enough to the edge. Sometimes I hung around Elliott or Top Springs, getting bits and pieces of work and I could book up supplies if things didn't turn up. But I started to feel like a bar fly. There were enough old drovers holding up the bars around the place to remind me of what I could become if I didn't get out of the game some time. An old drunk in the horrors from too much metho or boot polish just killing himself slowly wasn't a pretty sight. They often ended up committing suicide. Sad old men with their stories and constant requests for a glass and a smoke between pension cheques or increasingly unlikely paydays.

Because I had my sisters there, Darwin was one place I would escape to. The council and wharves always had a few low-paying jobs. By 1953 it was getting harder to find decent wages out bush. Everyone was doing it tough. Better fences and yards made mustering easier. The bosses needed fewer blokes. They could get away with offering lower wages. Roads allowed trucks to deliver cattle to markets quicker and cheaper than even poorly paid drovers. So the number of droving teams and the money being offered were getting less. It was becoming a mug's game. As well, I wanted a bit of a town life with wine, women and song. Football and the company was a part of it too. After scratching around for a while a few of us ex-Bungalow boys headed down to Alice Springs where there was talk of a bit of work on the roads.

Back in Alice Springs

My mate Nugget Kopp and Eva Palmer, his wife, had a house down at the Gap Cottages. It was nothing special by today's standards, with fibro walls, hard dirt floors, a tin roof and no verandahs. There was an outside bathroom. But it was a house, where before we had lived in humpies and sheds. This was where I threw my swag out when I got to Alice Springs.

After the war Bill Ludgate, some of the Laughtons and others in Alice Springs had started a campaign for better Aboriginal housing. Cottages were eventually built down near the abattoirs on the town side of Heavitree Gap. The Gap Settlement was intended to get the Aboriginal families living in the pretty squalid conditions of Rainbow Town a bit further away from the white township. The old bosses wanted the place to look tidier. So the Gap Cottages were for families who had been through welfare and the institutions.

Nugget and Eva had three kids by this time – Peter, Francis and Kathy. I was sharing a room with a young white bloke called Kevin Clarke. After the war Nugget worked as a drover with another ex-Bungalow kid called Arnold Abbott. They regularly worked with a Queensland boss drover called Wasson Byers. Wasson had two droving plants and got two mobs of 1,500 cattle from Victoria River Downs Station every year. From Victoria River Downs they would walk them across to Wolgarra in Queensland. It was pretty steady droving that paid well enough.

Nugget was famous for taking on Wasson one night at the Ridge pub in the late 1940s. Wasson was an ugly bull of a man who had seriously hurt a few people in fights. He was a pig to work for, a notorious bully and was often accused of not paying people properly at the end of a trip. Anyway, Nugget had been on Wasson's team and had been dudded on his pay. Nugget fronted him about it and Wasson told him that he would have to fight him for the money. Wasson Byers was a big heavy man with very dangerous hands. But Nugget was quicker, fitter and pretty useful too. Wasson ended up flat on the ground, unable to get up. It was the only fight anyone could remember him losing. Nugget got paid for that job and after that was the first drover that Wasson picked for the season. He even got the job of running Wasson's second droving plant. Nugget always got paid properly after that fight. It didn't hurt him having the reputation for being handy with his fists when getting other work either. I was pleased to be able to call him a mate. It often saved a bit of a hassle, having him about. Arnold Abbott was one of a big family of Abbott brothers good with their fists. They ended up establishing the community of Wallace Rockhole. He also married Baden's daughter, Agnes. He was a hardworking, straight-talking, well-respected bloke.

It had been a while since I had been in Alice Springs. Some of my friends were going ahead. They had houses and young families. A lot had recently got jobs as fettlers on the railway. Wherever I stayed, I helped out with paying the rent. If you fell behind the welfare would take you off the housing list. If you got too far behind, they evicted you out onto the street, kids and all. Some desperate family would take your place, trying hard not to notice.

Some of my other mates were struggling. Drinking too much and getting into trouble, ending up in jail. Others had come off horses one too many times and were living in pain. Their women were doing it tough, even getting hurt. Welfare was threatening or had already taken some of the kids. Many families still couldn't get housing and were living on the fringes of town.

The authorities was still taking a lot of mixed descent kids. Once in care it was the same as what had happened in my childhood. They wanted to keep the kids' families as much out of the picture as possible. They told the parents that they were putting the kids in a 'proper' environment. But that could mean being half starved, bashed for looking the wrong way and sleeping in huge dormitories that were locked up most of the time. It's true the new institution bosses were mostly better. Some were good people. But the kids still risked being looked after by the religious nutters or desperate people who'd put their hands up for anything. Clearly the white kids were missing out by staying home with their families.

The Native Affairs' welfare officers often turned out to be worse than the police from an earlier era. There were a lot more of them who had nothing better to do. They were, often as not, true believers in the removal of Aboriginal kids. At least most of the old coppers knew that they were doing the wrong thing, and most avoided being involved in the removal of kids as much as they could. But the new Welfare Department was a lot more organised. They even started adopting Aboriginal kids into white families a long way from the kid's home. Lots disappeared and were lost forever. Many were the only black face in a sea of white racists watching everything they did. For people in the Aboriginal community they again lost the practical experience of growing up their own kids. The parents, in their grief, lost hope and their ability to cope. It became another generation of stolen kids.

Back in Alice in 1953, I got lucky and landed a job with Milton Liddle down in the Gap. It was going out chopping firewood and bringing it into town. Donny Lynch was working there too. Milton's wood yard was behind Wang's store, down near where the Gap Youth Centre is today. Working for Milton was okay and he treated me well. It wasn't a lot of money. But a job is a job. They only needed me for the winter firewood rush. Once the weather started to warm up the demand for wood fell away. In summer you were only supplying wood for the slow combustion stoves that people had in those days for cooking and heating water. Anyway, I picked up enough work to tide me over for the first few months.

Football was starting up and I turned out for Pioneers. It was good fun. Pioneers were winning most of the games. Not that I was a superstar like Henry Peckham. But I made up the numbers around the ruck. After the game you could wander over to the hockey field and watch the ladies turn out for the Pioneers' hockey team. The social life was not that bad.

It was still a small town with perhaps a couple of thousand people. Not a lot of Aboriginal people were about. Most of my friends from Loves Creek days were out at the new Santa Teresa Mission. The tribal groups had been largely pushed out of town and back to the stations or new government reserves. There was a fair bit of Aboriginal anger and resentment at being kept down and paid badly. It was the start of my becoming more politically aware. Some were joining unions and pushing for a better deal. I kept quiet, at that time, but my sympathies were increasingly with the unions.

Racism in town remained a big problem. Some shopkeepers still excluded Aboriginal people. You had to be careful not to be seen as uppity or demanding of any sort of equality. The local authorities could target you and make life miserable. Welfare liked people to look grateful for any bit of old rubbish thing they might give you. And welfare really liked to poke their noses into your business.

At least in Rainbow Town welfare had been forced, because of the overcrowding, to mostly leave you alone. But in the new Gap Cottages, Native Affairs' officers thought they could come in and out as they pleased. As far as they were concerned, the houses were their property and if you didn't toe their line, the whole family could be evicted. As likely as not your kids would be taken into care on top of the eviction. So when push came to shove, people were forced to shut up and do as they were told. Or else risk pretty much everything they had. We didn't like it though.

Freddy Muggleton was one of the Pine Creek and Bungalow boys around Alice then. Me and Freddy went back a long, long way. We had shared a passion for the donkeys at the Bungalow. He was a good mate. When I arrived back in Alice, Freddy had just finished a relationship with a young woman called Daisy Hull. Daisy was stopping down at the Gap settlement. I took a big fancy to her and we ended up going out for a few months in a fairly casual sort of way.

After the wood yard work slowed down, I got a bit of work out at Alcoota Station. It was after the muster and they wanted a hand doing some fencing. Daisy didn't like an absent boyfriend and we split up. It was the sort of thing that had happened to me before. You can't really have a relationship when you're out of town for long periods. But it is equally hard to attract a girlfriend without money. There was no work in town, so I had to go out bush where I had a chance of getting a start. There were no girls out bush, so you didn't get much of a chance to start up relationships. When you got back to town your old girlfriend was likely to have moved on and you started again, usually by pinching the girlfriend of another poor bastard stuck out bush. It was the reality for all us bush workers. No wonder we were all paranoid about our wives when we were away. We had been sleeping with other people's wives and girlfriends for too long. Anyway, the fencing job didn't last long and I headed back into town.

I tried catching up with Daisy, but she was going out with someone else. It was around the time the highway north was being bituminised. A mob of mainly Aboriginal blokes from Queensland had the job. They had already done the Mt Isa to Tennant Creek part of the contract. Now they were down in Alice and were starting work laying bitumen up the track to Larrimah.

Compared to us, these Queenslanders were cashed up and ready to party. We were poor and struggling to feed ourselves. They had no family connections and wanted to steal our women. The women didn't seem to mind. It turned out Daisy was going out with one of the Queenslanders, a fellow by the name of Johnny Ah Kit.

It was a pretty tough situation for us. With only a couple of bob in our pockets, and looking like we'd never been anywhere, we looked pretty daggy beside these visitors dressed up in their new gear.

Daisy's bloke didn't last that long. He kept on going up the track without her. Maybe he found out she was pregnant. Johnny Ah Kit ended up in a relationship with Stella Tennant and had a family. One of the kids is 'Jack' Ah Kit, who was a minister in the first Northern Territory Labor government.

A few of the Queensland road crew settled in Alice. There was Freddy Trindle who married Maureen Stokes. Sammy Ah Fat was another. There were the Chongs, a lot of Thursday Island blokes and a fair few with Pacific

Islander or Malay heritage. They moved behind the local crews that compacted the roads prior to its sealing with bitumen. I got a bit of work as part of a local compacting crew. It was a big occasion when the sealing unit hit town. There were some musicians amongst the teams and big parties when they arrived.

I lost track of Daisy for a time. I heard later that she had had a baby daughter, Marilyn. Daisy and Marilyn ended up going down south to Dalhousie Springs. The girl grew up not knowing her father. Daisy didn't tell her who he was. His identity became important though as part of land claim investigations. There was a big claim going on around Dalhousie with the South Australian Land Council.

Not many people knew that Marilyn was my daughter. I didn't even really know. Ruby Ahchee suspected and told Marilyn in the 1990s. Daisy confirmed it and Marilyn met up with me around then. It was a bit of a shock for us both. For my kids as well. Me and Marilyn got on pretty well and built up a belated relationship. She often calls in and catches up with us all when she is in town.

Courting Nita

In 1954 I got a start on the railways. I took it before it disappeared. A permanent job was still hard to find. It was fettling work down the line, south from Alice to Ooriminna. I knew what to expect from my time at Hawley after the war. There were gangs all down the track, replacing rotten sleepers and rebuilding sections of the line that had become washed out after rain. It was tough physical stuff when you had some emergency job on. But the rest of the time it wasn't too hard. I was based close enough to town to be able to get in whenever I needed to, and keep up a social life.

Arthur Ahchee was the railway ganger for the town and my boss. His brother, Syke, ran the goods shed. I knew the family from the old days and was a football mate with their brother Dudley. The Ahchee boys were originally from Oodnadatta way, but came to Alice Springs when the railhead was moved in 1929. Without the railhead Oodnadatta slowly died. The boys' grandparents had been among the Chinese who had come to Oodnadatta to build the railway. They had started a store for fettler families at a place on the edges of town called Hookey's Hole. They had a big market garden. Arthur, the oldest, was married to Rosie from the Aboriginal community at Oodnadatta. Arthur and Rosie had moved to Alice Springs with the railway.

Syke Ahchee had started a bakery here. Later he took the job running the railway goods shed.

Arthur was a muscular stocky fellow in his mid-fifties. He enjoyed a joke or two. He was a fair and reasonable boss. But he was really hard on people who didn't turn up or who weren't up to doing their fair share of the work. He was always one for having a cup of tea and a friendly chat once the work was done. Arthur was well liked by the railway management. He got the hard jobs done. Arthur lived in one of the railway cottages that had been built just north of the railway station.

The other workers on my fettling team included Nugget Blackmore from the Bungalow and Martin Cadona, a twenty-something fellow from the Top End. His family was originally from Malta but had settled in Darwin and later Oodnadatta. Les Thompson was another friendly fellow in his twenties. Les was of mixed descent from Queensland way. Noel Baxter was another one of the youngsters on the team. He was a fellow of mixed descent with family in the Barrow Creek area and related to the Hayes mob that ran Neutral Junction Station. These were a different family of Hayes to those that owned Undoolya.

The railway operated men's quarters for the younger single men. But you paid for them. They had married quarters as well. It was a small suburb really. I was happy staying with the Kopps so I didn't stop at the quarters. Even so, a lot of my social life was centred around the railway houses. It had a bit more of a party atmosphere than at the Gap Cottages.

I confess I had a bit of an agenda staying with Nugget and Eva. Nita Palmer was a younger sister to Eva. She was stopping at St Mary's with her sisters, Barbara and Marie. St Mary's was just through the Gap. It was a new style of institution for mixed descent kids, build in 1946 by the Anglican Church. It became a boarding school for Aboriginal children living on stations and also a place that the new Native Affairs' welfare officers used to get children out of the riverbed camps. It could be used as punishment for families that didn't do what they were told. Eventually it grew into a series of cottages with white houseparents looking after Aboriginal children.

On the weekends Nita played hockey. She was a great player in a pretty hot little Pioneers team. After the football game finished, I was one of a crowd of single men hanging around the hockey fields at the end of the games. I got lucky and won the competition to walk Nita back home through the Gap to St Mary's. Nita was beautiful, opinionated and fiery like all of the Palmers. It was a long, slow walk that gave me a chance to impress her with my charms. I had led a pretty knockabout life. So I sold myself how I thought she wanted me – as the serious older man with ambitions. I tended to agree with everything she suggested. It was to become a pattern in our life together. On a good day I thought of it as leading from behind.

That first year I got back to Alice, Nita finished her schooling and got a job working at the Kilgariff's poultry farm. She was still at St Mary's under a welfare order until she was eighteen, but they even changed that after a while, and she moved into the Kilgariff staff quarters.

There were a few of us single men walking the young St Mary's hockey players home as slowly as we could get away with. They had to be back before dark or they'd get into trouble. Most of us were older and ex-Bungalow kids. Men didn't get married so early in those days. Some of the girls needed permission and welfare wanted the men to be set up if they were going to allow you to marry.

I remember Georgie Peckham was one of us blokes walking out with the St Mary's girls. He was with Rosie Kunoth and Doris Branson at different times. Georgie was a footballer and brother to the football legend Henry 'Twinkle Toes' Peckham. Henry had worked at Ambalindum when I was at Atnarpa and had sometimes come over for the muster. So we had a bit of shared history and friendship behind us. The Peckhams were originally Katherine boys, grandchildren of Henry Peckham, the mailman of *We of the Never-Never* fame. Henry and George had both ended up at Pine Creek Institution and down in the Bungalow with me.

Henry Peckham was a sensation on the football field, setting all sorts of goal kicking records. It was Henry that set Pioneers as the team to beat in Alice. He was so good that he broke through the race barrier, becoming the first Aborigine from the Northern Territory to be recruited for the South Australian football competition. South Australian football was nearly as big as Victorian football in those days. West Adelaide was the lucky team and Henry really made them the star team in the competition. In his first game he kicked ten goals, even with a couple of big opposition players trying to shut him out of the game.

On weekends Nita visited her sister Eva. We were quite close by this time and we planned to get married. I was a very happy fellow. You get to an age when you think maybe it will never happen. That you will become like the old drovers holding up the bar at Elliott and Camooweal. Unmarried and with no family to help you when you are too old to climb back on a horse for another season. It was a big thing going steady after my years as a travelling single man.

It turned out to be really good having a job at the railways. It meant I could apply to get married and put my name down for a house. The Native Affairs' people who ran the housing wouldn't give you a look in if you weren't in full-time work and planning to get married. I had to persuade them I was respectable enough. I kept to the straight and narrow. They said no for a fair while. Nita was said to be too young. I was a risk – a knockabout labourer and thirty years old. Then Nita became pregnant and they gave their approval. We set a date for our wedding. It was 10 October 1955.

Family life

Me and Nita having decided to get married, it wasn't easy to organise. We could have just lived in sin I suppose, but we wanted to do it properly. It was important for Nita.

The ceremony was conducted within my old religious faith. Nita had been at St Mary's and knew a lot of Anglicans. So I had connected up with them again too. My strategy was to go with those who were running the show and making the decisions.

It wasn't a wedding like you see in the movies. We had no wedding organiser or much money. Dick Palmer had a lot of kids and not a lot of spare cash. None of my family was in town. My father was long gone. My mother had died saving the world with Father Long. The two of my brothers still living were locked up in a leprosarium. My sisters, Gladys and Ada, were living the Darwin life, struggling with big mobs of kids. I didn't really know Bobby at all. I didn't even know we had a sister, Alice, then. Travel wasn't as easy as it is today. So it wasn't going to be a big family affair on my side.

The family stuff was left to my Pine Creek and Bungalow mates. All of us brothers in the institutions, a lot of them recently married themselves and getting on with a town life. In some ways they knew me a lot better than my real family. They had been there as kids when things were sad and had shared the few triumphs of our institutional childhood. They had been in the army and on the stock camps, shared the long months of the droving or out on the pearling boats, and had settled in with me for drinks between seasons at Newcastle Waters, Elliott and even over Queensland way. Different ones of them had seen me through it all. Those that were still alive, in town and still talking to me came along for what moral support they could give. A bunch of late twenties or thirty-something cowboys, looking flash and mostly sober for the big event. It was a hot day with not much of a breeze. They were sweating away towards the back. Most hadn't seen much of the inside of an Anglican church, or any other church for that matter, and had no plans for coming back any time soon.

Nita, looking beautiful, had her big family along. Her father gave her away, dressed up and looking uncomfortable in formal gear. I could sympathise. None of us had the wardrobe or the practice you needed for these occasions. Nita's older brothers, wives and kids came in from the Santa Teresa Mission and other local parts. Her sisters looked gorgeous in their best dresses. People said we made a good-looking couple. Both uncomfortable in the spotlight, but trying hard to keep it all together in front of everyone, black and white alike. It was important to both of us that we looked the part. Nita because she was young. Me because I was coming of age in a different way.

The priest was Father Rodgers. Sister Eileen was one of the witnesses. As soon as we could we headed back to the Gap, to Nugget and Eva's place, where we were still staying. It was much more comfortable back there, especially after the white guests headed off.

It wasn't a big drinking sort of wedding party. We were trying hard to not get into trouble. Besides it was too hard to get the grog and everyone was struggling on poor wages. So the cakes and the food were the big events.

Soft drink and cups of tea. No one was making big speeches or that sort of thing either. More talk of cattle, horses, the football and weather. We weren't people to feel okay talking up big plans. We left that to the women. The kids and the dogs provided the energy, running through the houses playing their usual games.

The next week we got on with being a married couple. There was no honeymoon or even much time off work. With a baby coming we were working to put aside whatever extra money we could squeeze from our wages. There wasn't much left over, that was for sure. Even with me getting up and playing the best boy at the railways, I knew I was never going to be invited to sit up at the big table, join the bosses and get the big money. I always knew that. I wasn't going to get rich. Not unless I found gold or struck it lucky at the races.

1956 saw some big rains all over the Territory. It made for a very busy year as a fettler. Floods undermined the ground and the lines moved. We were often out for long periods in miserable weather trying to replace the soil and rocks that had held the lines in position. We disconnected sections of the line and replaced or straightened them out. It was hard physical work. The bosses were grateful enough for our efforts, but it didn't show much in the pay packet. The trains were often delayed that year.

Nita kept working at Kilgariff's poultry farm through the pregnancy for as long as she could. The place was down where Oasis is today. It stunk of chicken shit and death. The pay was poor. The sheds were too hot in summer and freezing during the cold months. The Kilgariffs had a big mob of kids. They were nice enough in a strict Catholic sort of way, but treated the workers, nearly all of them young Aboriginal women, like they were naughty little kids. No one was going to get ahead down there, except the Kilgariffs themselves. But there wasn't much choice of jobs for Nita, or any of us. You just had to keep fronting up no matter how patronising or ugly things got. At least I was working close to town at the railways and could be home much of the time. My fellow workers were good blokes and the money steady if not great. The bosses largely left us to it.

I was starting to find, like Louis Bloomfield, it could be hard to keep a young wife happy. It was not always the most harmonious of relationships. We struggled often enough, even if it was mostly me that had the restlessness of youth still in me. Nita was more a stay-at-home sort of woman. She had her family close by and had no ambitions to hit the road to see what might be around the corner. Soon enough she had the house and babies to keep her even more tightly in Alice Springs.

It was expected, even taken for granted, that men made the decisions. You could be pretty bullying with your wife and kids in those days. But I was never much of a bully. I could be a bit explosive sometimes, but I was pretty good at playing happy families in the way Nita wanted me to. She knew how to get anything she wanted that it was in my power to deliver.

I was a romantic at heart. Still am. I was very much in love. Nita was the more practical thinker when it came down to things. I did what I was told, tried to keep her happy. I went to church, stayed away from my old mates if she didn't get on with them. Went to work, came home. I was doing my best to fit into her family. Respect for my age and wisdom was not a big part of my story then. Nita had an opinion or two of her own that she liked to share with me. I even gave up the grog entirely for a while.

Becoming a father

We were still at Nugget and Eva's when the baby came. It was in the days when men got out of the way when their wives were having babies. It was women's business. And the start of when Aboriginal women were allowed into the hospital to have their babies. It wasn't like today when all my daughters have their partner with them through the birth. I kept right out of the picture until Nita was cleaned up, and the baby wrapped in a sheet. The little face was poking out wide-awake and gorgeous. I fell in love again. I loved being a father. Nita was so pleased with herself. She was just eighteen.

We called the baby Lynette. She was born on 11 January 1956, in the scorching Alice summer. I got to carry her about and talk her up to my mates. It gave Nita a new status in her family and more power within our relationship. I got a bit more power myself in the broader family too. Lynette changed a lot of things pretty quickly. It was an end to a good night's sleep and a quiet life. An end of plans to get back on the road. Even more than the marriage ceremony, she was our connection and we loved her for it.

It is hard exactly to talk about how I felt. Mostly it was feeling proud. Worried too, and scared of losing things. Family was real important to me.

I had always been a bit of an outsider and loner. Now I had a wife and child who relied on me. I was terrified I might fail and everything would be taken away if they wanted to.

Alec with Nita and Lynette, 1956
photo courtesy Kruger family

A house of our own

Before Lynette was even a month old we got a house of our own. Number 10 in the older part of the Gap Settlement mightn't have been very flash, and we still had people stopping around and staying. But it was a huge stepping stone for us. When you had never been the boss of your own camp, when you had a long history of being beholden to people, it was a huge thing to be able to close the door with your wife and child and think you might be in charge.

Alec in the doorway of his new house in the Gap Cottages, 1956 photo courtesy Kruger family

I wasn't, of course. It was soon clear that Nita was the one who was going to hold onto the money. And the Native Affairs' nobs could walk in whenever the mood took them. The Palmer family could stroll in too, tell you what to do and stay whenever they liked. But at least on paper I was the captain of the ship and the big man running the show. At least Nita always let me play the part when others were about. And as long as I made the same decisions as her, it was easy to feel like I was the one in charge.

In many ways me and Nita made a good couple. She was more stubborn and always knew pretty much what she wanted. She had a beautiful intensity about her. We could both sulk, but she could do it harder and walk away easier. I had the need for a lot more affection. She could be self-contained, even with her family and friends. She had our baby to keep her busy and feel okay about the world. I was more restless. Often wanting to spend more time away from home in the world outside the family. Later on I would hang around with the men after work. Play around with a few bottles of beer and pretend I was a single man again. But I always ended up back at home, got up in the morning and headed off to work.

Having enough money was always a problem. We had to rely on my fairly miserable railway wage. But we also had people staying with us to help out with the rent. We were houseproud and had things under some sort of control, at least in all the public ways. The welfare people started saying nice things about us. Sometimes the welfare officer Mrs Ballagh would even have us looking after some kids, when another family was struggling and the kids would otherwise have be sent off to the institutions. We took in Nita's sisters, Barbara and Marie, when they were allowed out of St Mary's. We had a home I could offer to my old droving mates when they passed through town. Things were on the up and up.

Nita was happy. The baby grew into a toddler. Nita was soon enough pregnant again. On 9 February 1958 we had a new baby girl, Vanessa Anne Kruger. We'd even got flasher with the names of our children. Lynette was about two years old. We were poor but content.

The Gap settlement

The Gap area in the mid-fifties was a family place. Everyone knew each other and looked out for each other's children. The ever-growing tribe of Gap kids lived and played across all the different houses. Us men often worked and played sport together. Pioneers was the only club for us. I might have been struggling to turn out for the side, but we still dominated the competition, winning most years. Nita and the other Palmer women were still playing hockey and softball, when they weren't too pregnant. They were the stars in a team of champions, often turning out for the Territory teams.

Some men were still working the stock camps and droving. They would arrive with their swags at the end of the mustering season, and they often had big mobs of meat from the stations. As well they would be cashed up and often a bit thirsty. I kept in touch a bit with the old ringers through them. They had been away over the winter months and had a couple of months off before being required back at the station. The bosses would often turn up to collect them again around November.

There were often rodeo-style competitions and knockabout football games with the kids. Us adults, particularly on the long summer weekend evenings, often threw out our swags and sat around together with some music and a few stashed-away beers and had a bit of a quiet party. We were a part of a small mixed Aboriginal community that was going ahead.

We were becoming a more political group who wanted more opportunities for our kids, and an end to having white welfare bosses walking into our homes. Lots of us were getting tired of trying to be whiter than the whites. We were starting to think of ourselves as black and proud. We were hungry for more opportunities and better money. Alliances were starting to build with the full descent Aboriginal mob living at places like Santa Teresa, Jay Creek and in the growing camps on the fringes of Alice itself. In my time at the Gap Settlement, as well as us and the Kopps, there were the Taylors, the Furbers, Mrs Le Rossignol, the Ogdens, the Sweets, Elsie Hayes, Jessie White, the Campbells, Auntie Julia Hughes, the Swans, Henry Ford and Daisy Roman, the Mileras, Jessie Bray, the Kennys, the Stuarts, the Khans, the Causts, the Egans, the Coles, the Hamptons, the Kerrins, the Millers, and Mrs Espie with her brother Mort Conway. When the newer houses were built, the Kopps, the Cassidys, Mr Kennedy and Mrs Stokes, my mate Alec Turner and his wife, the Stuarts, the Fergusons and the Tilmouths all moved in.

The people down the Gap were all houseproud families in those days. We all wanted to be independent and not rely on welfare. Most of the families had seen enough of institutions to want to keep our children safe from them. There was also a pride in being as good as the next family. And enjoying the respect and rights denied to us as kids.

Down near our houses was a grocery shop, Tang's Store, owned by a white fellow. A woman called Edie worked there and lived in the house behind. There was also Gus Brandt's butcher's shop along the riverside road. George Glass and Snowy Kenna had a store back towards Brandt's butchery. The Moslem community also used the butcher's shop. Sado was an older Afghan who guaranteed the meat was properly bled and prepared. I can remember Sado with his walking-stick going between the butcher's and the abattoirs.

There were three houses near Tang's Store where the local Afghans lived. In one house was Sallay Mahomet and his family. Next door was Mungatoon, and in the last house was old Sado. Up the river, nearer to town, were the Afghan trading shops, selling clothes and stockmen's outfits.

Another member of the Afghan community was Charlie Sadadeen. His herd of goats still dotted the hills like when I was growing up. They were feeding where the Olive Pink Botanical Garden is today. Goat meat was still a staple food in those days. As well as the goats, Charlie had a large orchard and vegetable garden about where the council lawns are today. He sold grapes, watermelons, tomatoes, cabbages and other vegetables. Nearby was the old Ahchee's bakery.

There were a few down the Gap who played the guitar or sang a bit. Herbie Laughton was one, but then he got a house in Eastside and wasn't about all that much any more. We had singalongs and a chance for people to catch up with the gossip. There wasn't a lot of drinking. Perhaps a couple of bottles snuck in and shared around discretely by the men. This was the Gap mob.

Friends around town

Lots of families lived at the back of white people's houses. The blokes worked in town while the wives were the child carers and housekeepers. Nearly every house in town had someone else living there. Some families of railway workers had their own rented railway cottages. Other families were not far away, camped in the old Lutheran Church mission block. There were the Armstrongs, the Buttons, Jack and Fanny Miller and family, the Corrigans, the Flys, Glenn and Gladys Smith, Eli Rubuntja and Leonora, Kenny and Hilda Swan and the Coxes.

On the east side were another seventeen houses. With the camp and the Gap mob, this was just about all the Aboriginal families living in town. A few artists and other Western Arrarnta families camped at Morris Soak. More Eastern and Central Arrernte families were stopping around Middle Park and Charles Creek. There were a few south of the Gap at Ilparpa Camp. And mobs of kids everywhere. But Alice was a quiet place. Except for some big event there were fewer Aboriginal people around town than at any time I could remember.

My companion from Loves Creek days, Tim Shaw, and his family, lived out at Palmer's Camp, Nita's parents' place. So did Alec McDonald, some of the Turners, some of the Hayes, the Davids and others. It was a meeting place for many of us, as well as travelling ringers and the like. There were a few other drovers and their families. Matt Savage and Dick Smith both had settled camps on the edges of town.

Family life

The town Aboriginal families were almost entirely separate from the Western Arrarnta families, who were restricted from being in the town areas of Alice Springs. So not a lot of mixing happened. There was even a big fence on the western edge of town to control people coming in from Hermannsburg, Haasts Bluff and the Western Desert areas. It was about where Lovegrove Drive is today. It also stopped alcohol getting from town into the Aboriginal community. Fair-skinned Aborigines had to do the grog runs.

The main entrance gate through the fence was near where Trucking Yards town camp is today. The area was a stockyard and later became the abattoirs when they moved it from the Gap area in the 1960s. Often Aboriginal stockmen working in the Western MacDonnells would be dropped off at the boundary line by pastoralists after the muster season. Morris Soak was the name of this camp. The pastoralists and white stockmen would then go on to party in town.

There was another camp, later called the artists' camp, after the Hermannsburg landscape painters. Albert Namatjira was the best known of these but there were others, including the Ebitarinjas. This was a little further west in the valley behind where Lyndavale Drive is today. The valley was called Larapinta which is the Aboriginal word for 'the water left in the stew after all the meat has been eaten'. Life was a bit like that for them. Their stews were usually made with scraps of meat bought from the abattoirs. Sometime later a lot of the Morris Soak families were moved onto a camp out at Old Ilparpa, close to St Mary's cottages. Meanwhile a lot of the artist camp mob had been moved into a camp near where the parks along Memorial Drive in Gillen are today. This was before the Gillen subdivision was started. Gradually they were pushed back into the valley as the subdivision took off. In the late 1970s, Larapinta Valley became a gazetted town camp under the newly established Tangentyere Council.

Growing the family up

It wasn't easy keeping everything going on my railway wages. So I kept looking around for something else. Nita wasn't working as she stayed at home looking after the kids and the house. Housework wasn't the easy job it is these days. There were no washing machines, refrigerators or vacuum cleaners – for us anyway. Everything, particularly the washing, took hours and had to be done manually.

Vanessa quickly enough lost her flash name and became known as Melly. When she was walking about, Nita got pregnant again. Wayne Alexander James was born on 27 April 1961. I had a son. He was a lovely baby. Soon enough he was up walking and chasing his sisters around.

By the early 1960s Lynette started attending the Hartley Street School. The only other schools at the time were the Catholic convent and Griffith House, opened by the Methodists. Later Traeger Park Primary School opened in 1965 as a school for the Gap kids. Lynette would take off with the other kids, real pleased with herself and so excited. Soon enough another baby was born. Larry was born on 13 November 1963. Nita liked the babies up and walking before the next one came along.

I had changed jobs by this time. I got work unloading the copper trucks coming down from the mines in Tennant Creek. The ore was in bags and had to be put on the train for Adelaide. Victor 'Rajah' Lomas was one of the team. He was a local cricket umpire. He had a long flowing beard and an imperial way about him, hence his nickname. It didn't take long before I moved to a job with Mr Ronberg. I knew him from Atnarpa days. He was a proper Eastern Arrernte man. We worked at a quarry just out through Heavitree Gap. Rock was taken from the quarry and crushed for the town roads. I was the truck driver.

After a while doing this I was able to get a Department of Works job, mainly driving trucks for a road gang. The bosses were good but it meant living in camps out of town for weeks at a time. We mostly worked on the main roads, stock routes and dirt tracks. Luckily it was easy enough to be in town on the weekends or for special occasions. I was also allowed a week off work to look after the kids at the time of the births.

There was always a cot next to our bed. Often there was also a young one sharing the bed itself for at least part of the night. It was before airconditioners. The houses weren't built very well for the hot weather. They had no verandahs. So on hot still summer evenings, all of us families would water whatever grass areas we had. Spray the dirt around the house too. Then we would throw a big canvas down and all camp on mattresses outside. You prayed the mosquitoes weren't biting and for an evening breeze to spring up. There would be kids and hunting dogs everywhere. The dogs were very protective, particularly of the kids.

I built a really good garden over time. We also kept chooks for eggs. Everyone had gardens and chooks in those days. You grew your own vegetables, but it was a lot of work keeping the water up. It was the start of a big drought time in Central Australia. It hardly rained much till 1965.

I even planted and grew up my own 'tree of knowledge' at the Gap place. We would often have the Santa Teresa mob stopping at that time, many of them Nita's family. Once the tree grew a bit we would all be gathered underneath, skiting about the world. The talk would swing to who had been playing around with whom and whether they were right skin for each other. I learnt a lot of things under that tree. Some were even true stories. Usually it was more a version of events that you needed to be careful repeating too much. Else you would get into trouble or get other people in trouble.

The Gap Settlement was a very controlled place. We were constantly under scrutiny about the cleanliness of our places. Our first houses had dirt floors. Nita was always careful to pass any test. If you passed the inspections with dirt floors, you might be recommended for one of the houses with concrete floors. Eva and Nugget had managed to get one. Nita was keen to keep our name on the list for the next that came up. Later, if you succeeded with the concrete floor house, you might be offered one of the Housing Commission places that were being developed on the Eastside. We remained for a long time on the bottom rung despite Nita's efforts and recommendations in our favour. There was just not a lot of new housing happening. People were not moving out because they had nowhere to go. At least not if they could help it.

Changes

Finally our time to get a better house came up. We had worked hard to be recommended by the Department for a long time but houses were few and far between. In 1961 we were upgraded into one of the newer places. Wayne was just a new baby. The place was the middle of three attached fibro cottages on Gap Road. The Kopps were in the house beside us. Nita and the kids were so happy. Eva and her kids were happy. There was a lot more room and a lot less work now we had a concrete floor. I even had space behind the place to build up more of a garden.

This was our family home for the next few years. The older kids grew up there and most of their childhood stories are of this place. Later on in 1963, when Larry was only a baby, me, Nita and the kids were relocated to a new house made of concrete blocks just across the lane. My son Wayne and his family are living there now. But I still go down to sit under the trees I planted. I was a good gardener and one of the few people to get a quandong tree to grow in Central Australia. The mulberry tree became my very own tree of knowledge. It certainly heard its share of tall stories and bullshit in its time. Perhaps especially since the younger kids started sitting under it.

My job with the Department of Works saw me out of town a lot. We were widening and straightening the old highway. The team went from Newcastle Waters in the north out to the Queensland border in the east, and down to Kulgera and across to Uluru and Docker River in the west. It was a bit the same as when I was road building in the army. You would locate good soil for building up the framework of the road so that water would run off. We were using a new type of bitumen but you still needed to mix in local pebbles. I could be away for weeks at a time, living in the road camps. If I was close I might go in for the weekends. It was hard on Nita, me being away, but Eva was next door. You still had to go where the work was. There was no dole for Aboriginal people even then.

There were no social security payments of any kind for Aboriginal people either. You couldn't get old age pensions, maternity allowances or family money. You couldn't say like people can today, 'Ah, I think I might pass on that job, thanks very much. I might see what's going in town and perhaps get the dole if nothing comes up. Perhaps do a training course or two.' Then sit back watching Austar, drinking a few green cans, smoking a lot of ganja, and generally have an okay time of it. Life didn't work like that. You said 'yes boss' and not much else that they might hear. Else you might be seen as cheeky and in need of a lesson or two in the proper respect that was owed to the white men making the decisions. You had to play it really dumb to survive.

Mostly I was working the south highway and the road to Uluru. It was the start of tourists going out to the Rock. We had the Mt Ebenezer to the Rock part of the road. They were still gravel roads in those days, replacing the old goat track. We were always losing men to other jobs. It was hot dusty work and other jobs were becoming available for a lot of the white blokes.

I put my hand up when the road team was short of a cook. It was a bit better money and I wasn't going to get any office job. So it was a promotion of sorts. It involved feeding thirty or more blokes. Like a droving team the men had pretty high standards of what was a passable meal. There was not much else for the blokes to look forward to, except the food. They worked hard and expected a lot of food. Lucky it wasn't as tough as on the stock route. We had refrigerators and supply trucks. I could order in what was needed and it would turn up soon enough. So the crew were happy enough with my efforts.

It was while working the roads down towards Uluru that I became friends with Nipper and Lively. They were traditional owners for the area. Over time we built up a relationship. They always stayed with me and the family on their few trips to town. These were old Pitjantjatjara-speaking men and caretakers for this part of the country. When they ran into the work crew I used to feed them and pack them off with some rations from our supplies. It brought memories flooding back to me of growing up out at Atnarpa with Big Foot Tom, Tim, Rosie and Jerry. I was really pleased to be able to help them out. It was a way for me to make up for running away and never going back to the country. But it didn't matter what I did, there was always a part of me that thought I had failed the old men and their Eastern Arrernte dreaming stories.

The prospector

It was after moving that I finally managed to get Nita to use a bit of money we had put aside to buy our first car. I don't think she was entirely persuaded, but other people had cars and she could see it was important. I had been driving for work and other people for a fair while now. But it was a real status thing to get your own car. I turned up with this huge American gas guzzler. It really looked something. Everyone was out and giving it the once over. It was an old Studebaker with a calico roof and spoke wheels. Beautiful. An antique even in those days. I had got it off an old fellow who didn't need it any more. Nita and the kids jumped in. We squeezed in a few of Eva's kids and went for a spin around the town, waving at people we knew. I felt like the big man. If I had had a coat and tie I would have put them on. I could have exploded with happiness.

Being mobile again stirred my imagination. We could even go up and see the family in Katherine and Darwin. It had been a long time between visits. Most of them hadn't even met Nita, let alone the kids. George Kruger

Junior was one of the few who knew them. He had been working around Alice and ended up married to one of Eva's daughters.

A car was a great thing. I was able to travel around and catch up with people. Nita never got her licence so she relied a lot on me. It also gave me the job of helping people out if they needed a lift or had an emergency. I even drove everyone out on their hunting trips. Not that the Studebaker was ideal for carting dead kangaroos. It wasn't the most practical of cars in many ways, it was a heavy and lumbering vehicle. I learnt a few mechanical skills as part of owning that car. But I was no great bush mechanic and it was really hard to get parts. Luckily other people were pretty good at keeping the old beast going and were happy to help out. But as soon as I got the money saved up I traded the Studebaker in for a more reliable Holden station wagon. You could really load the kids in and it was easy to get parts.

In the mid-sixties I transferred to a job with the Department of Mines. It was better paying work and usually saw me home at nights. I was helping out with crushing and assessing ore samples brought in by various companies and individuals. It was while working there that I formed a bit of a partnership with a white bloke called Ron Ferguson, who was also at the Department. We got to see the results of a lot of the test samples. Ron was able to get mining claims for us over bits of Arltunga and Loves Creek Station. An American mining company, Western Nuclear, was interested in the area and even gave us backing to go in to collect samples for them. On most weekends I would head east to explore for the mining company and on our own claims. I had high hopes for finally getting rich. It felt real good seeing and walking over Loves Creek again. It brought back a lot of the old stories and songs, memories of walking the place with the men.

On Friday afternoons I would pack up the car for the prospecting trip. Larry, and sometimes Melly, would come along for the ride. None of the other kids were much interested. On our way we would pick up Albert Aputanungka Williams, one of my old companions from Loves Creek before the war. Then we would head out towards a camp in the Eastern MacDonnells. The next day and a half would be spent mapping out areas and taking samples. Western Nuclear even started to pay for all the food, fuel and other costs of these trips. Unfortunately it didn't come to much. The samples were promising but never quite enough for the company to buy our claims out, or go into major production themselves. They lost interest after a while because of financial difficulties back in America. They disappeared, promising to come back. But it never happened. Me and Ron held on to the lease. Then Ron died and I passed the claims in. The dream was over.

They are talking up gold, diamonds and mineral sands in the same area now. I feel a bit like I should get my cut for all the work we did. No doubt some company using satellite equipment and with money to burn will find incredible wealth. Not being recognised as a traditional owner under the land rights claim, I won't even get a royalty.

I have had a succession of cars since this time. My best vehicle was a Holden ute that I paid $8,000 for from Kittle Brothers. It had a Japanese motor in it. It was in the late 1980s and at the time, I was setting up the Palmer claim out at McGrath's Dam and Harry Creek. I needed a vehicle to carry water to our block. There was no good source of water there then. Unfortunately all that hauling of big drums did the ute in. It is still sitting out the back of my old house in Parke Crescent, looking good when the moon is full.

Lots of visitors, lots of kids

We always had people stopping with us. There was no nuclear family stuff happening in those days. When my mate Henry Peckham was away playing football in Adelaide, his boys, Robert and Henry Junior, stayed with us for a long time. They were seven or eight years older than Lynette and started living with us when Barbara and Marie were still there. It was mattresses everywhere. This was even before Melly was born. The Peckham boys went right through school living at our place. They were like older brothers to our kids. Then there were others staying shorter times. Between me and Nita, we gave a lot of kids a safe place to stay over the years. The kids always shared bedrooms and any extra space usually ended up with some kid sleeping there. Eva was just next door with her nine kids, so they all floated between the two houses.

We mostly helped out with kids that we knew from the Gap Cottages. While the Gap was very family orientated, there were occasions when people drank too much. Some of the blokes became angry and abusive. We knew who they were, and they knew we knew, but it didn't always mean you could do much about it. When they were drinking, they didn't give their wives enough money to feed the kids. Often the women and children would turn up at our home to escape the violence. We had this role thrust upon us.

But I enjoyed it in a way. It made me feel like I was doing well, was respected and that we ourselves had escaped any risk of welfare taking things away from us. We were safe and secure in our well-regarded family set-up.

I didn't believe in harsh physical discipline for my own kids. I never hit them. If they played up they would be spoken to. Nita was all bark and not much bite too. But they were taught to be clean and respectful. It was expected that they did their jobs and kept out of mischief. This was a belief system instilled by both of us. By and large the kids went along with it. At least when they were young.

After Larry was born and we were in the new house, we had a bit of a rest from babies. Perhaps we discovered contraception or something. We even managed to pack the cot away for a while and sometimes got a whole night's sleep without some little person in the middle.

Then with Larry nearly four, Nita was pregnant again. Anita was born on 17 June 1968. So the cot was resurrected and Nita went back into baby feeding mode. She was a delightful child. With Lynette then twelve and Melly ten, she had two proud big sisters to look after her like a baby doll. Even the boys spoilt her. Luckily they were at school during the day or she wouldn't have got any rest. Anita as a name didn't stick all that well. She ended up being called Polly, after my Mum.

The contraception worked even less well after this. Noel was born on Christmas Day 1969. The same day they reckon I was born, but forty-five years later. For the first time we had two kids in nappies and often as not two kids in bed. I had to abandon the marital bed for sleeping elsewhere. It was a flat-out busy time for Nita. Not much time for our relationship. There was lots happening around town and we were just about to hit the excitement of the seventies. There were no more babies. For a while there wasn't even much of a friendship happening, as me and Nita got too busy for each other.

Social life

Our new house, with Eva next door, was a busy social hub, especially on weekends when the football was on. All through the fifties and sixties there was all the Palmer family from Santa Teresa calling in and often staying. Later on some of them moved back into town and we saw a bit less of them.

Friends from my droving days regularly called in. Pompey Allum, then living around Newcastle Waters, often stayed with us. He and his wife used to come down with sick kids. I had known Pompey originally from when we worked together for Darwin municipal as part of the mosquito-spraying gang. The Allums were a Mudburra family connected on my mother's side. Not that we talked the tribal connection stuff back in those days. Charlie McAdam and Frank Byrne sometimes stopped with us at the old house. They were old mates of mine from Alcoota days. Later Charlie got married and worked out at the Mission. He ended up with his own house and a big mob of kids. We might also have some of the old Loves Creek mob, people from work, and even family from Darwin. Then with the children growing up there were always their friends calling over.

But town itself was much quieter. Most people had jobs, even if they were poorly paid. The mission mobs were working too, in the mission gardens, cattle stations or just around the place. The community people needed permits to come into town. So there weren't a lot of homeless folk from communities walking the streets in the same way you see today. And there was little enough drinking happening. The rule at night was that you has better not be caught out on the streets, or you would be in trouble. This changed after the equal wages case and later the Referendum. By the late sixties lots of families were being pushed off the cattle stations and there was an end to the alcohol restrictions. The police were still actively giving people a hard time, but it didn't seem to matter much to the homeless mob who had not much to lose anyway. Particularly if they developed a taste for the grog.

But that was later on. In the late fifties and early sixties, families around the Gap mostly made their own fun. We were the Gappies. The kids were the Gap Angels. The kids weren't really allowed into the Capitol Cinema or entertainment places in town. But they played sport and ran around as a group and had a lovely time in lots of ways.

Boxing nights were one of the social events. Out-of-town groups of boxers would arrive to take on the locals. The Del Hunty Boxing Troupe was one. Basically if you were part of the paying crowd, you could put up your hand and have a go. If you lasted two rounds you got paid good money. After a few drinks there tended to be no shortage of candidates to give it a go. The fellows used to do it mainly to impress the girls. I had a go myself a few times, but soon got smart enough to leave it to the younger guys. The old boxing pros you fought against were just playing with you and could put you away whenever they liked. Charlie McAdam was one that gave them a run for their money. He even got a job with one of the troupes at one stage and saw a bit of the country.

Weekends over the fifties, sixties, seventies and even the eighties were often spent as a family with a picnic lunch down at Anzac Oval, watching the football. Football was one of the things that continued to bring people in from their work out bush. You would have football training out bush after work during the week. Then if you were picked for the game it was a quick drive into town on Saturday. Even after I stopped playing I would turn up with the kids to watch Pioneers play. Football days were very social affairs with lots of family and kids running around. There were Pioneers, Federals, Westies, Souths, Amoonguna and Rovers in the local competition during this time. But for most of us Gappies there was only one side we supported. The Pioneers were our club. We had built it up and made it the best club in the competition.

Pioneers Football Team 1977 From left: Alec Kruger, Curly Tuttleby, Dougie Turner, Joe Rawson, Jeff Myers, Eddie Kitching, Timmy Schwartz, Barry Freeman, Lance White Snr, Chippy Miller, Alan 'Ginger' Smith, Rod Magyar, Russell Bray, Jeff Eames, Lloyd Bray, Harold Furber, Bruce Tilmouth, Albert Pianta, Ray Satour, Athol Mitchell, Frankie Smith, Richard Kopp, Lionel Turner, Budgie Preece, Geoff Miller Snr, Cal Dean photo courtesy Kruger family

I had stopped playing football by the late 1950s. An old cartilage injury was playing up enough to finally end my career. The injury was from a broken leg, badly set after I had come off a horse as a kid at Loves Creek. It had healed crooked and got worse over the years from jumping and falling off too many horses. Finally it gave up on me and I could only hobble around on it like a tired old bushie. In the late 1960s I had an operation to reset my leg and could walk okay again at last.

Much later on Nita stopped her hockey. She was a marvellous player and a photo of her playing in the Territory team is still up on the Pioneer clubhouse walls. Playing hockey wasn't as popular with the men as the footie was. But a lot of the women and girls took it up. The games were played at the same time or a bit after the football. So there was rarely a crowd at the hockey games. But it was still very competitive. The sports tended to be family affairs with no drunks and hardly any fighting. The kids loved it.

Lynette and Melly played hockey for Pioneers following their mother's tradition. Lynette played soccer as well. Later on Anita played hockey and a bit of soccer. They were all quick and graceful like their mother. They didn't like losing much, and played in some really good sides. Wayne played rugby league and Aussie rules with Pioneers. I was working out bush and didn't have much to do with coaching or that sort of thing, and my injuries didn't help. Wayne showed a lot of talent and even ended up going up to Darwin to play rugby. Larry broke a family tradition and played football for Federals. He was a bit independent like that. Noel played football and rugby.

Throughout the 1950s and 1960s I worked hard to create a good life for my family. I wasn't a big drinker but enjoyed a social life that included a few beers. The rent was nearly always paid and Nita had enough money for the household. Things were on the up and up. Having a car helped make other things possible. There was often a group of men from the Gap Cottages that would go out on hunting trips or to collect firewood. It was in the evenings that hunting trips occurred, usually to the north of town, at Sixteen Mile Camp or at Harry Creek. There were Palmers living up that way. Other times we would head south, out past the Gap. We would all contribute to petrol and stuff. Sometimes a few beers would be taken as well.

Kangaroos were plentiful then. In the cool of the evenings they would stir from their daytime hideouts in the scrub. Some men might have had the time, energy and skills to hunt in the traditional way, but we always had someone in the group with a rifle and the kill would be shared across our families.

Church and the Missions

Occasionally Mr Long, the preacher man, brought out his slide projector and held a slide night. He was the same fellow that had so impressed my Mum. He had left the Top End and set up in Alice. His screen was just a bed sheet up against the wall down in his church at the Gap. The subject matter was often Mr Long's trips to other missions and places. He also took and showed a lot of pictures of local families. It must seem very daggy these days, but we were starved of entertainment. It was before TV ruined things for us all. In the fifties and sixties people loved seeing themselves on the screen. Even the films from faraway missions seemed magical. We were interested in that sort of stuff.

Mr Long's church played a role in our life at this time. We took to attending his services. Mr Long and his wife were attached to the Methodist Aborigines Inland Mission. They had no government funding, but raised their own money from within the church community. Not that we had much to give. But we all chucked in a bit.

This church had always been pretty good to us. Mr Long's ministry and his commitment to helping out families with food and clothes impressed me a lot. The Anglicans weren't much help in this way. And their missions, and the Catholic's Santa Teresa, were a bit of a disaster. The Longs always organised a big meal for us families at Christmas time. Even on normal Sundays they made an effort to pick families up and would later head to the town camps to preach under the trees. My kids liked the singing and activities, they even liked attending the Sunday school classes. But as the were a lot more things to do. We were getting ahead a bit too, as wages improved and we had more money left over at the end of the week. I was out bush a lot and had less interest in church matters.

In the sixties Mr Long's ministry moved from the Gap down to near Palmer's Camp. They started to work more with the Aboriginal families moving in from remote communities and camping there. It became more difficult for the Gap families to attend. The kids stopped being picked up and they drifted away from the Church. Now we only go to church for funerals and a few special occasions. Most of the Palmers drifted towards the Catholic faith. This was especially true of those that had moved to the Catholic mission at Santa Teresa.

Santa Teresa was started in 1953 when the government gave land to the Catholics eighty kilometres south-east of Alice Springs. It was marginal cattle country so no one else had a lot of use for it. Everyone had moved back into town in those days and was stopping around the traditional Central Arrernte camp called Middle Park. But the white folk didn't want a big mob living there. So the Catholic Church had support for its idea to isolate people away from town. Whole families disappeared to Santa Teresa. But the Catholics didn't get any financial support. The Church and the Aboriginal residents were given the job of building the place from the ground up.

The families who went out to Santa Teresa didn't have to worry for their kids. They got taken away pretty much straight off. The Church didn't believe it was a good idea for Aboriginal parents to bring up their own kids. So the kids were fenced off and fed in a communal kitchen. There were no rations as such for the adults. The big kitchen fed everybody in return for the jobs they did. This was supposed to teach them something about a Christian work ethic.

There were separate rough dormitories for the women and men. You had to build your own humpy if you didn't want to live in them. If you wanted to get married properly in the church, you had to collect enough rocks to build your own house on the bit of land they allocated to you. You didn't own the house, mind you, even though you had built it. It was all communal property. Which meant in real life that the priests owned everything. If you got on the wrong side of the whites out on the mission you were in big trouble.

What happened to the children was a great experiment. It was like going back to the old children's institutions, except that the kids also got to watch their parents' humiliation just over the fence. The kids lived in dormitories not much different to the ones I knew as a child. They were scrubbed, fed, schooled and sent off to church as one big mob. The priests recruited suitable older girls to be the dormitory bosses. They were the 'best girls'. The older boys got to escape the children's dormitories at puberty for the stock camps. The 'best girls' became the new religious 'true believers' in a white god and their own place in the Kingdom of Heaven. They didn't respect their parents' culture much.

The Church liked to keep people busy. Idle hands might cause mischief. So the bell rang for breakfast, dinner and tea. In between times you had your jobs. It might be in the garden or doing station work. The Church set up its own cattle station and over time Santa Teresa became close to self-sufficient in terms of meat and vegetables.

After a while the stockmen got an exciting new deal. The church decided it would contract them out to the local stations during the muster season. I can just imagine people's delight when they were told. Six weeks out at Old Andato, Loves Creek or New Crown. You didn't have to worry about transport. You got to travel on the back of a truck, the same way you'd gone out to Santa Teresa in the first place. You didn't have to worry about money. You weren't going to get any. The Church would look after all those irritating details. All you had to do was wave goodbye to your wife, if you could find her in the women's section, call out to your kids over the fence, if they even knew you existed any more, then head off for the season.

They even started contracting men for the fruit harvests down south. And it wasn't flying down in planes, staying at flash hotels. They protected people from that. Guess what? They drove everyone down on the back of a truck. You got to camp in some really flash humpies or in a camping ground. Again, you didn't have to worry about being paid. The Church took care of everything. An all-expenses paid holiday really, that other people paid large sums of money for!

Despite all the really great things the church offered, many 'ungrateful' families took themselves out of the place at the first opportunity. Better to live poor in town, picking up bits and pieces of work and surviving on bush tucker where you could. Missions like Santa Teresa were repeated all over the Northern Territory and the Government missions like Amoonguna were not much better.

Amoonguna started in 1960. It was the white folk who drove the move. Again they wanted to do something about the build-up of Aboriginal people stopping in town. Even after Native Affairs moved a lot of the Arrernte families out to Santa Teresa, there were lots of workers staying in the Aboriginal Compound at the Telegraph Station.

The Bungalow continued as a place of starvation and terror. There was no meat provided. No rations were given to residents who weren't supposed to be there or who were unemployed. It was overcrowded and rundown. The government finally decided to set up the place at Amoonguna, ten miles south-east of town.

As usual the government said there wasn't much money so people had to make do with what they had. The Bungalow dormitories were torn down and the place was handed over to National Parks. What was salvageable as building material was recycled out to the new reserve. The plans for Amoonguna didn't include family houses. Old-fashioned dormitories were the basic accommodation. Amoonguna was going to be the transient camp as well as the residence of people shifted out of town. So right from the start, the place was bursting at the seams and had a lot of different tribal and language groups living together in one place.

Like at Santa Teresa, it was mostly communal living. The government decided Aboriginal people were going to be graded depending on what the white bosses saw as their ability to live like white fellows. On the bottom rung you didn't have to worry about money or rations. They were going to give you a job and allow you to eat in the communal kitchen. The jobs were centrally organised. Employers in town had to apply for Aboriginal labourers. The families didn't have to worry about houses either. Dormitories would be all they could look forward to after a hard day. You didn't even need to worry about family. Women and men were separated and the kids largely taken care of.

The next rung up saw families with a shack of their own, if you were in regular employment and had satisfied some behavioural and hygiene standards. The shacks didn't have kitchens. But you got rent money deducted at a higher rate and had to pay to eat in the communal kitchen. The shacks didn't have bathrooms or toilets either. You shared the communal facilities. But your kids could at least share the space with you.

Stage three was when you got a place with its own kitchen and bathroom. Unfortunately there weren't a lot of these and you could be on a waiting list for years.

Amoonguna grew up a new leadership in town. Wenten Rubuntja, who headed up the Central Land Council in the mid-seventies, was one of these fellows. They developed their skills in a hotbed of angry political youth out there. By the late sixties and early seventies there was an accepted group of

Aboriginal people representing a lot of families and tribal groups that was agitating for big change. A lot of the residents of today's town camps grew up, went to school, and lived in Amoonguna. They demanded their own separate living spaces and the right to live their own lives in town.

Holidays

Christmas was always busy. I got my big holidays then and we spent time together. In the early days there was not much money for presents or trips away. We didn't even have a car. So we stayed around town. The build-up of presents under the Christmas tree always had the kids in a high pitch of excitement. You might finally get them to sleep late on Christmas Eve. Christmas presents were a lot simpler and more appreciated by the kids in those days. Parents saved up or made something special. Families were poorer and children often only got presents at Christmas, not whenever they felt like it, as happens today. Early on Christmas morning the kids would be out playing with their new gifts.

Christmas Day was a family event that usually involved some time at the Palmer's Camp. Nita's Mum, Mary, and the daughters organised everything. Us blokes just had to do what we were told. The whole lot of us would go down to the church. There'd be the biggest mob of people there. Lots of the men and their families only turned up at Christmas. After the service, someone from the church would play Santa and give out small presents to all the kids. We would stay for a bit of a picnic. The kids would run around playing games in the sun. Adults would sit in whatever shade was available. It was often forty degrees. You'd catch up with people you hadn't seen for ages. Then slowly families would start gathering up their kids to head off for their own Christmas teas. It was a big gathering of the clans.

Christmas dinner was usually held at our place or one of the other Palmer daughter's places. It was a huge meal complete with a traditional plum pudding filled with threepences and sixpences. Often there were twenty or thirty people. Nita's sister Annie Price was always around. Lots of families would drop in, and groups of us would head over to see other people. There were kids everywhere, spending their daytime hours floating between the houses. Some visitors without family were invited to stay for the evening meal. If you got a chance, you might even have a bit of an afternoon snooze to sleep off the overeating and drinking.

At that time there were very few drunks about the place. People were respectful and had a good time without too much alcohol. There might be a few beers away from the dinner table but nobody had too much. People were a lot poorer and looked after each other.

After Christmas Day the Palmer families might all camp out, often near Ross River, for a few days or longer. Nearby, the old Bloomfield home at Loves Creek Station had been sold off as a tourist place. The Green brothers bought it and built up a tourist trade at what they called the Ross River Homestead. An old friend of mine, Maxie Bloomfield, was employed to throw boomerangs for the visitors. Later, Lynette's husband, Brian Willis, worked at the place. We were usually back in town for New Year. There would always be something happening in town that night. But it wasn't the big event it is today. Just a bit of music playing and another family get-together.

After we bought the car I persuaded the family to pack up one year and head up to George's house in Katherine. Nita wasn't one to want to leave the Alice and her family. She got scared easily. Floods and crocodiles terrified her. But I insisted that the kids needed to get to know my family a bit. We left not long after New Year. It was a long trip and the car wasn't the best. The old highway wasn't too flash either. Leaving town through the ranges and creeks to the north was an event in itself. But eventually we were cruising through the flat country. We stopped to camp with the Allums at Elliott. Lots of the old blokes I knew from my droving days were about, and we spent a fair bit of time catching up. Then it was back into the hot car and driving north again. Nita had never seen the country and it worried her. The kids were better, but were pretty glad to get out of the car when we finally arrived at Katherine.

We camped at George's big old tin shed of a place. George was not long back from the leprosarium. Lily had her own place by then. Their kids were older and had mostly left home. George had a few of his old mates stopping with him. It was a pretty open affair. Nita was a bit anxious about the whole thing. I tried to be relaxed, but it was all a bit of a struggle. It was hot and humid. Luckily Jack Gibbs and Nita's sister, Melba had settled around Katherine at this time too. So at least Nita had Melba to catch up with. But she wasn't keen to let the kids swim because of a fear of crocodiles.

The Katherine visit lasted a couple of weeks. The kids were good travellers. We had taken our own swags. I had always liked George and we had an easygoing friendship. He liked sitting around talking about the days of droving and what was happening at the various stations. I had a few stories from catching up with people on the trip up. But he also had his old swaggie mates stopping. They too were good for a gossip about who was where and what people were up to. I liked that sort of stuff. The kids would wince once we got started. With Nita, they would drift off outside or around to Melba's or Lily's place to find their cousins, or to go into town. Us brothers in the saddle would often still be at it when they came back, a few bottles of rum circulating slowly.

George got on well with all his brothers and sisters, but he hadn't seen much of them for a long while. They were mostly based in Darwin and only occasionally would one or two of them come down. Gladys's and Ada's kids especially sometimes ended up around his place, working or travelling through. I didn't manage to get up to Darwin during this trip. Nita and the kids were tired of driving. We had planned to do it, but it never happened. Nita just wouldn't be in it and the money was running low enough. I ended up catching up with those kids myself, when I was stopping in Katherine during the seventies.

The Sixties

It was after the Katherine trip and with the babies getting older that Nita went to work in the hospital laundry. Mrs Baddock was in charge. She was blond and English but had a good heart. Nita was working alongside Lloydie Bray and his Auntie Elsie. Eva looked after the little ones and kept an eye on all the kids after school. The money was really handy. It gave us a lot more to play with. Playing around, though, was exactly what happened to a fair bit of it. We were perhaps a little bored with each other after all the kids and years together. So it was a big change in the way the relationship worked.

The 1960s was a time of many changes for us and all Aboriginal people in Alice Springs. A lot who had been living and working on cattle stations were forced back into town. This was because of the equal pay decision of 1964. We had to be paid the same as whites. But paying equal wages was not a tradition of the cattle industry, so instead of sorting it out, the station bosses took the opportunity to evict the local Aboriginal families. Most had never lived anywhere else and were caretakers for their country. But there was nothing they could do. Trucks came and loaded up their stuff, bulldozed their homes and drove them to the edges of the nearest town.

As a result, huge numbers of Aboriginal people who had rarely come to town, moved into the fringe camps. The Hermannsburg mission grew. The government missions at Papunya and Yuendumu expanded. People had a lot of time and energy on their hands. Drinking became a way of filling in the hours.

Aboriginal politics changed. Some of the young local men went off to the Vietnam War, like some of their fathers had gone to World War II. But these young fellows had a much more equal experience of it. They didn't have Aboriginal labour units. Everyone was mixed in together. The American army had lots of black soldiers and leaders. When the young men came back they talked up changes. Society stopped seeing us as some poor dying race needing to be protected. The community started demanding equality.

Charlie Perkins, a local man who had been in the Bungalow with me, became the voice of an angrier Aboriginal community. He led the Freedom Rides into rural towns in New South Wales to highlight the racism there. There was a lot of support for an end to racism by students and activists in Australia's cities. This was increasingly linked to demands for Aboriginal land rights in Alice Springs. The Institute for Aboriginal Development was formed and people like me were drawn into the struggle. I had been working with the unions and the Labor Party over the years. But there were other local blokes like Geoff Shaw, Neville Perkins and the Briscoes, who were more in the thick of it. I tended to be more behind the scenes. I've become a lot more chatty over the years. In the late sixties and early seventies, the Aboriginal community felt itself much more of a big family, one mob looking after each other. It has split a lot between various families since. There have been a lot of power struggles as land rights, mining royalties and access to big money have changed the way people get on. It has become really competitive and often corrupted by greed. I have kept somewhat out of these fights.

A whole new world

In 1962 the Commonwealth Government finally changed the rules so that all Aboriginal people could vote in some local and Territory elections. But there were still plenty of other restrictions about where you could live and what you could do. There were still drunkenness, loitering and vagrancy laws that let the police harass, move on and even arrest

Aboriginal people if they were so inclined. And there was more police in town than ever before.

The pubs could exclude people too, under dress codes or for antisocial behaviour. Being black in a white pub was considered antisocial all by itself. The bullyboys were happy to help out the bosses at any time. You risked getting bashed. Your things could be smashed up. If you were Aboriginal and camping out around town, the police, or even just gangs of white men, could wake you up in the middle of the night, trash your camp and move you on. The women risked being raped and everyone risked being violently assaulted. So the Aboriginal families mostly stayed out of town, until they were pushed off the cattle stations.

A lot of what was seen as an increase in problem drinking in town was caused by people leaving the stations, reserves and missions. There wasn't much happening out bush – no money, no housing, no jobs and a lot of troublesome white people giving you a hard time. A lot of the ones coming to town were young Aboriginal men. They were fit, looking for something different, and got angry when there was nowhere to live, not much work and still lots of white people telling them what to do.

The blokes from the more remote tribes were initiated men. They might have been shy in the white world but they were proud of, and respected for, their cultural knowledge. Even though they mostly kept to themselves, they still scared a lot of people. The white town people didn't like their power. They didn't like it that these black strangers had a secret world of their own with a different language and culture. The cattle stations kept sending them in, and the towns kept on trying to push them back. The Aboriginal mob caught in the middle had a miserable time of it.

Even us of mixed descent were hungry for the new things. We felt caught a bit in the middle of the power struggle. We wanted to keep what we already had. And we didn't want our kids to miss out. We feared everything would get spread even thinner. But we were also happy to see more money and power flowing through the town and into the Aboriginal community. Those of us that had already got an education and who might have seen a bit of the world became the leaders in the local push for greater Aboriginal services and rights.

White students, the unions and even the churches came onside in the battle for social justice. Over ninety per cent of Australians, a majority in all states, agreed to the 1967 Referendum that made all Aboriginal people citizens in our own country. But that ninety per cent wasn't evenly spread. The white bosses in the Northern Territory and other parts of rural Australia didn't agree.

In America there was a huge black power movement growing up, talking about an end to racism. We saw demonstrations on television. Cassius Clay, or Muhammad Ali as he later called himself, was a great favourite around Alice Springs. Big black American singers like Charlie Pride had cult followings too, in Aboriginal Australia. Some of the new black leaders were coming up to work with the Aboriginal community in Alice Springs. For Charlie Perkins, Joe Croft and others it was a homecoming. They brought with them a stream of mostly young educated white supporters. They made new demands for better housing, health services and education. Aboriginal land rights became the policy of the Whitlam Labor Party. It had strong Aboriginal support behind it across Central Australia.

I had got involved with the Labor Party in the late sixties. Union officials and politicians used to find me when they wanted to roll through and have meetings, especially out in the eastern country. I got to catch up with old stock camp mates from Elliott across to Mt Isa, up the Sandover Highway all the way to Lake Nash, across the Plenty Highway out to Indiana Downs and beyond, out to Santa Teresa and south. We signed people up for the unions and got people on the electoral rolls. I became a true believer in the Labor Party and social justice campaigns. Even though I was still a lone wolf and scared of pushing myself forward at meetings, I had become an activist.

By the start of the seventies the whole world seemed to be searching for something more in their lives. It found me ready to hear the message. There was a part of me that was thirsting still to be a player in a more defiant way. I wanted to see more of the world, meet new people and do new and exciting things. I didn't want to be some abused black victim, living in the area set aside for me in Alice Springs. I was restless. I was also feeling a bit older and a bit more desperate. There was a lot of company for me. I was 45-years-old in 1970 and I needed to make a few things happen.

I got a bit ahead of Nita in some of this. Instead of hanging around with the family, I was out with my new friends, drinking a lot more and generally not at home as much. She agreed with the politics but wasn't very fond of how it was changing me. By the early 1970s my marriage was in trouble.

We started seeing less of each other, and often we were fighting. I got it into my head that I needed to go up and see family in Katherine. She was even less interested in coming than she had been before. Nita had her job in the hospital. Her family and friends were in Alice. We decided to live apart. I planned to go back and live with my family in Katherine. I ended up hitting the road with Larry. He was the only one of the kids who wanted to come. He was a real loyal one. I love him a lot for what he did. I gave up my job, packed the car and took off. The older ones were busy with school and their own circle of friends. The younger ones needed their mum. So me and Larry hit the road. Two days later we were camped at George's place. A whole new world seemed to be opening up. Mind you, we were both homesick and a bit scared.

What had seemed like a good idea when you are tired and emotional seems more unlikely as you get further away from your loved ones and family. I was leaving my home and most of my kids. There is no doubt in my mind these days that your home is where you get married and grow up your kids. Alice Springs will always be my home and where I feel safest.

The Katherine years

Homesickness

It had been really hard to leave Alice Springs. But I was determined and eventually I got the kids to come with me. We packed up and headed north. But at Aileron I had second thoughts and turned around. Back we went over the roller-coaster highway into the Alice. I soon enough turned around again, but this time only Larry came. We kept on going all the way through Tennant Creek up to Elliott. I think Nita was expecting me back again pretty quickly. She knew my weaknesses and fears. But after camping the night me and Larry ended up pulling into Katherine and George's place.

It was great to see the old bloke. His kids were stopping with him. They all had a new-found enthusiasm for political action. Many of George's friends were around. The party was rolling on. The place could get pretty chaotic. I could see I needed somewhere else to base myself. I would have become a drunk or a pothead if I'd stayed. I had a puff of the green stuff myself. But it was too nice for someone as mixed up as I was at the time. And Nita would be on my back about Larry if I stayed at George's. Having the other kids up for holidays would become a real problem.

So after a bit we ended up stopping at Nanna Peckham's place down on the river. She had a big old house and room for extras. Her grandkids were stopping with her as well. I organised Larry into school with these kids. It was a walk across the old railway bridge. I went hunting for a job.

With the help of George's contacts I got work with the Australian Institute of Biology (AIB) Experimental Farm. They were testing new cattle breeding programs in partnership with the CSIRO. Santa Gertrudis and Brahmin cattle were being introduced into northern Australia. We were part of looking at production costs, meat ratios and suitability to the climate. They also wanted to work out about building immunity to cattle ticks and tropical diseases. Not that I did the science side of the work. They wanted a stockman who knew cattle and the country around the place. I reverted to what I had done as a youngster. Except that most of the time I had nice government vehicles instead of a horse. I worked with a vet and some scientific people. I shifted the cattle around according to instructions and generally kept the animals on good grass and in well-watered spots.

The job was Katherine-based, except when I had to take or bring back a bull from the Farm's property out west near Victoria River Downs. Larry came with me on some of these trips. If he had something else on, then I had to rely on family to look after him while I was away.

One of Ada's granddaughters, Marie, was living and working in town. She had married Jock McLeod and had a few kids. They lived in a place not far behind George's house. The kids were good company for Larry and I would often have him playing there when I was off working. From time to time some of Gladys's kids would be down for work so I caught up with them too.

It was hard work as a single father. I was gone early in the morning and often not back till late. It was a bit of a struggle for Larry after always having brothers and sisters about. Now he had cousins, but it was different. Larry often got homesick for Alice Springs. Nana Peckham was great and used to a few extra kids. I became very close to her. This helped me out a lot, especially with Larry and us being so lonely. Larry ran around with all the other 'grandkids' she looked after. But he must have missed the attention he'd got at home. Still, he stuck it out. It was a difficult time starting up again in a new town. I had never really lived in Katherine since I was a child. Me and Larry would often be close to tears and wanted to just pack up and go home. It didn't get much easier over time.

The school holidays came and it had been arranged for Noel and Anita to fly up to stay with us. I took some time off work and we all stopped around at Marie McLeod's. We didn't cope all that well but had an okay time of it. It was hot and sticky. The kids were missing their Mum and the house. They were still only little. Then the school holidays ended and Larry wanted to go back with them. What could I do? They all flew out leaving me behind. It was tough.

I was often ringing up. I always tried to be there for them. But being at the end of a phone was never enough for any of us. If my kids got sick, I wanted to be home. If they got really sick, I travelled back to Alice.

Wave Hill

I was in Alice Springs when Vincent Lingiari led Aboriginal families off Wave Hill Station on 26 August 1966. They were angry because, even though Aboriginal pastoral workers were meant to get award wages, the bosses weren't making the right payments. Native Affairs just let them get away with it. And conditions for the workers were still really primitive.

Sick people were getting no medicine. The kids weren't getting any proper schooling. Houses weren't being built. Old people got robbed of their social security money at the station shops that charged exorbitant prices. Vincent and the others decided to move about twenty-miles west, and set up a bush camp along Wattie Creek.

Vincent was a Gurindji man from the deserts west of Wave Hill. When Wave Hill was first set up it had mainly Mudburra families there. But over time the bosses recruited the Gurindji from further west. The families involved in the walk-off were a mixture of Gurindji and Mudburra families. So a lot of the mob camping at Wattie Creek was family for me.

Alec and fellow supporter (left) at the 40th Freedom Day Festival at Wave Hill 2006 photo courtesy Kruger family

I also knew a lot of the Wave Hill mob from my time working out there with Cammy Cleary. Part of my going to Katherine was to see how the walk-off was changing things, and catch up with some old mates. There had been walk-offs before and usually the bosses managed to starve people back to work, or got Native Affairs to threaten them. But by 1966 things had moved on. Vincent had publicity through writers like Frank Hardy and Douglas Lockwood. The strikers also had the support of the unions and funds were set up down south to get supplies to them. Vincent and the other strike leaders like Sandy Moray were able to persuade people that they could win the fight this time if they held out.

The strike went on and on. Wave Hill management got in interstate strikebreakers. These white staff were paid above-award wages. They got proper houses and were looked after. Despite the threat to their jobs, the strikers continued. The Wattie Creek mob got support to build their own houses and a school. Wave Hill management tried to block the roads, but some supplies kept getting through. It was a stand-off. People went back to bush tucker, fishing and built their own gardens. Years and years dragged on and not working at Wave Hill became the norm.

There were similar strikes at other stations, first at Victoria River Downs and then Pigeon Hole. Victoria River Downs' management showed the same sort of sensitivity as the Wave Hill bosses, by bulldozing peoples' humpies and destroying their personal things. But at Pigeon Hole, the Mudburra stockmen and their families went back home after a couple of months, having made their point. They said they felt sorry for their country.

By this time it was 1972. Gough Whitlam and Labor swept to power in the federal elections. They had promised, if they won, to give Aboriginal communities back some of their traditional lands. By 1973 they had an agreement with Wave Hill management for the return of 2,500 square kilometres of the 15,869 kilometres of the Wave Hill Station to the Wattie Creek community. This was less than twenty per cent of Wave Hill, but it was a start. The relationship between the old station and the traditional Aboriginal families that owned the land was changed forever.

I was in Katherine before the 1972 election. The town had a deserved reputation as the most racist town in Australia. Its rednecks fought against all the changes to improve Aboriginal wages, housing and access to services. There was even a big Ku Klux Klan group in Katherine. This section of the community didn't welcome any Aboriginal politics. They argued that giving money to Aboriginal families led to alcoholism, unemployment and the loss of good old-fashioned family values. They didn't want to ever stop treating us like slaves.

The Kruger family was part of taking it up to the white community. George and his mob of kids were always inclined to be a bit fiery, talking and stirring the pot. We were handy enough with our fists too. And there were always a few guns, tyre levers and other weapons hanging around. The police knew it and so did a lot of the old-timers. We had a lot of allies in the old families. They knew us from a long-time back. We had to be given a bit of grudging respect. The old white and black stockmen and prospectors, who had been about George's place forever, were still coming in and staying. They acted as a buffer for some of the gung-ho brigade in the white community, who might have felt free to target us otherwise.

The racism around Katherine eventually unified the local Aboriginal family and tribal groups. The newly formed Kalano Aboriginal Community Association Inc. started the struggle to get housing and services for the fringe-camp communities. Like in Alice Springs, these were mostly families that had been pushed off the stations, or had left the missions. Everyone started to come along to be part of the new dream. We had in mind our children kicking out the old white racist bosses and running the whole of Central Australia for our people. But the battle continues today. It is taking a lot longer than we thought.

A champion brother

My brother, George, was a big fellow. His mother was from Renner Springs and he was born in sight of Lubra's Lookout where the Aboriginal community could keep an eye on people coming and going. George's mother had died when he was young. Our father had taken him under his wing and from then on, George travelled in the carts and donkeys seeing a lot of the Territory. Father and son were very close and my dad taught George how to read and write and ride. George grew up tall, proud and with a reputation as a champion stockman. I envied him his time with our father. But he was a good mate to me and lots of other people as well, and gained the respect of those he worked with.

He was also a bit of a ladies' man. He had more than a few children running around on stations where he had worked. He probably had in mind taking them under his wing when they got older. But by then these kids had been taken away into the new institutions. He acknowledged them by and large, but couldn't save them any more than my father could save me. George was the older brother that I needed and he filled in a lot of the gaps I had in the family story. But he was very private about a lot of things too. I didn't press him as much as I should have. I enjoyed catching up with him over a few beers in the balmy Katherine evenings. The younger kids would be tearing about the place, but we would sit quietly watching the world go by. George liked a slow story and a bit of company. He got a fair taste for the grog but always handled it okay. He sometimes got sad and even angry, but his fighting days were pretty much behind him by then.

I left Katherine to go back home after a couple of years. So George and I lost touch a bit. Neither of us were people to get on the telephone or keep up a correspondence. He stayed in his house a long time. He had become a happy-go-lucky old bloke living on his pension. He remained kind-hearted to his mates and always had a feed and a place to stay for someone down on their luck. These mates were often the worse for wear by the time they left George's house. Usually some old cattle station boss or a family member would turn up and the old codger would be off bush again to dry out a bit.

Eventually George was persuaded to sell his house. The new Woolies was built on part of his place. His kids talked him into buying another house in the new part of town. He ended up sharing the new place with his son, George, and his family. George Junior had worked with Fred Hollows on the Trachoma Program and became a government health worker. As my brother got older and a bit sicker, he was persuaded to move again into a retirement flat down near the hot springs on the river. But he was terribly lonely there, with hardly any visitors. Even family didn't get round to see him that much. He was well into his eighties when he died there in 1987.

Return to Donkey Camp

I revisited Donkey Camp with George. It had become a hobby farm called Kambechie. The new owners didn't farm peanuts but ran some horses and cattle. They had built a house by the waterhole. Today the front of the place operates as a tearoom for holidaymakers on their way to Katherine Gorge, five miles further along the river. This road passes the sacred sites and cave paintings of the local tribes. The waterhole that is associated with the serpent dreaming stories of the area has a huge government pump and is the water supply for the township of Katherine. It is hard looking at it now and imagining the life of the Kruger family at Donkey Camp back in the 1920s.

I learnt new stories and re-learnt some old stories of my childhood with George and others. I was able to listen to tales of my father and mother, and a lot of the other old drovers and stockmen as we drank tea or a few beers around the kitchen table. There was Russian Jack for instance, famous for riding at full gallop across the railway bridge. Katherine had no shortage of mad white refugees from some earlier troubled life. In the 1970s I was part of a long tradition of men going to Katherine in search of meaning and a new start. Except for me it was going back to my birthplace.

Other family, other jobs

Living in Katherine was a confusing time. As always I worked hard and mostly kept my head down. I had no desire to become a target of the bullyboys in town. I had also started a new relationship which made things very challenging. Especially as I wanted to keep being involved with Alice Springs and the lives of my children.

But there was not really a sense of belonging or being at home in Katherine. I missed Central Australia, Nita and my kids too much. Holidays saw me driving backwards and forwards. My new girlfriend was not impressed. My older kids were angry and confused about the changes. They blamed me and took it out on me when they could.

The Katherine years

After the CSIRO job, I was offered work with the new Yulungu outstation service. I was helping to set up housing maintenance and training programs for new outstations. Government money had finally come through for these places. My boss was a fellow called Billy King, who was married to one of George's kids, Sally. We built and maintained outstations all the way west to Kununurra in Western Australian, north to Pine Creek, east to Elsey Station and the Roper River communities of Beswick, Bulman and Barunga.

I also met and got to know a little more about my sister, Bobby. She had married a local fellow called Dick Brumby. They had a place on the west side of town, close to where the thermal springs are. They had a grown-up family. Bobby was my mother's child by her tribal Mudburra husband from the Willeroo area, and I hadn't really met her much before. Bobby and Dick were pretty close to the action for Aboriginal rights through the Kalano Aboriginal Community Association.

I didn't see much of Ada and Gladys. I got up to Darwin once or twice for quick trips, often to the football. Some of Gladys's kids were big stars in the local competition. But what with work and going down to Alice Springs there wasn't a lot of time. I met up with my sister, Alice Mills, for the first time when she called in to see George, and then again on one of the Darwin trips. I didn't even know her until then. We caught up a bit later when we were both living in Alice Springs. She was born Alice Binjumba at Mataranka Station. She got taken away to Kahlin, but my dad always recognised her, which was why she was known as Alice Kruger. She married Rupert Mills, a Larrakia man, when she was young and working as a domestic for none other than Dr Cook, the Aboriginal Protector himself. Rupert was a wharfie. She had two kids, David and Barbara. She too was evacuated with her kids during the war, going all the way to Mulgoa near Sydney.

My brother, Jack Gibbs, was stopping around Katherine then. I knew him a bit because Melba was Nita's sister. It was a bit tough having split up with Nita, but he would often call in at George's. He had worked at Bond Springs during and after the war. So we had lots of people in common. He was a great bloke. He was later to write his autobiography, *Son of Jimmy*.

After more than two years I left to go home to Alice Springs for good. I was too far from Nita and my kids. My new relationship had never really worked out, probably because I was still in one down in Alice Springs. Anyway, with a feeling of coming home I packed up the car, said goodbye to family and friends and hit the road south again, hardly stopping along the way.

The homecoming

I was really pleased to be back in the Alice. It felt strange being in the house again. Both me and Nita had been a bit aged by the separation. Trust and loyalty were different. We were a lot lighter with each other in some ways. But we got irritated with each other quicker as well. She didn't need me in the same way. She had grown apart from me. That was a jolt. But we made a go of it. Looking after the six growing kids made it busy and a lot easier just getting on with things. Soon family and friends started coming around again and got used to me being back under the old 'tree of knowledge'.

For the younger kids it was soon like I'd never been away. The older kids were a bit harder to turn around. But even they got used to the idea that I was back and going to stay. It is hard now to say what the effect of my being up in Katherine for a few years was on the family. Certainly some things had changed forever. Nita had her work and a greater independence. I had missed a fair bit and the kids didn't quite come to me in the same way they had in the old days. I had to find time to build things with them.

Alice Springs too had moved on a lot. A new suburb had been built out on the other side of the railway lines. There were a lot more Aboriginal people living around the fringes of town. Some local families had gone ahead. We got a new proper house built for us at about this time. The old fibro places had asbestos in the mix, so they were demolished. We got a place just behind where the other place had been. They built a lot of flats along Gap Road and called them the Harold Liddle flats. Our new house was much flasher, built with concrete blocks, proper floors and verandah areas. It felt like another beginning for me and Nita in the new place.

Some of the smaller churches, including the Evangelical Church that had run the Aboriginal Inland Mission, had joined together to form the Uniting Church. They had a social justice agenda to hand back control of their missions to the residents, particularly the Ernabella Mission in the north of South Australia. Under the Reverend Jim Downing they had set up a place called the Institute for Aboriginal Development (IAD), to provide training and a voice for the new Aboriginal leadership and people on the communities. Money was starting to flow like it was happening in Katherine. A lot of it was going out to the communities to start building houses and services. But some was also building up things in the town itself.

Aboriginal people meeting under what was called the Central Australian Aboriginal Congress (CAAC), with Neville Perkins as the first director, now had some say in what services were needed. In 1973, the new Federal Labor government gave Congress funding for the incorporated Central Australian Aboriginal Legal Aid Service (CAALAS). A lawyer was employed for Aboriginal people in trouble with the police. You can imagine how happy the police were to have to answer for some of their actions in court. Anti-discrimination laws were put in place that stopped some of the more obvious racism. The problems in Aboriginal housing and health were acknowledged. Drinking and even petrol-sniffing were getting to be big problems in town and on some remote communities. There were lots of ideas about what needed to happen. And for perhaps the first time, there was often money to start programs that might fix a few things.

It was exciting. The town was changing fast. The old bosses were getting shifted aside as Canberra found money for Aboriginal services, and a wave of young bureaucrats and businessmen from Canberra and the big cities started to make Alice Springs their home. The population grew quickly.

The welfare institutions for Aboriginal kids were finally being closed down. By 1980 they were all gone with Retta Dixon closing its doors to become Bagot Community. Under Gough Whitlam the old Native Affairs was turned into a new Department of Aboriginal Affairs. Later on its boss was an old Bungalow boy, Charlie Perkins. Didn't that set the cat amongst the pigeons! There were quite a few of the old guard looking for new jobs. Charlie was often in town talking up a new deal for Aboriginal people that would allow them to get ahead. Nugget Coombs, an ex-Governor of the Reserve Bank, and a lot of other clever proposal writers were helping Aboriginal communities apply for money. And they were getting their proposals accepted and funded.

But the biggest change was the start of Aboriginal land rights. Soon after the election of the Labor government, Mr Justice Woodward was appointed to head a Royal Commission into Aboriginal land rights in the Northern Territory. There were meetings in Alice Springs. Even the old wise lawmen from the remote areas got to meet with the Commissioner. It was a really thorough job they did. Justice Woodward recommended that regional land councils be set up, including the Central Land Council in Alice Springs. The Council would represent the tribal families and language groups from remote communities. The Commission also recommended that urban Aboriginal people, who couldn't claim traditional ownership of any land, should be able to seek land anyway on the basis of need. Unfortunately, in 1975 the Labor government was thrown out. Under the new coalition government, taken away kids like me didn't get to be included in land rights claims.

By 1974 the Tangatjira (later Tangentyere) Council was established within the Central Australian Aboriginal Congress. They were to be the main ones trying to get housing happening on the fringe camps. The Central Land Council (CLC) was established in 1975. The CLC helped Tangatjira Council develop its case for town camps and present it to the government. The same year the Alice Springs land claims for twelve town camps started to be heard. We all thought land would change everything. The Palmers were heavily involved with the Tangatjira Council. I was often at the Congress meetings. We had high hopes.

Working at IAD

After coming back from Katherine I was offered work with the Institute for Aboriginal Development (IAD). It was moving from being run by the church into being one of the first Aboriginal community-controlled incorporated bodies in Central Australia. A fellow called Stuart Philpot was developing training programs for Aboriginal stockmen. The idea was for them to learn the skills to take over and run their own cattle stations. In particular, IAD was working with the communities down Ernabella way.

Jim Downing, the boss of IAD, and Yami Lester, a leader from the Pitjantjatjara homelands, were keen for it to happen. People from across the border were a big part of the IAD board. The Uniting Church had run the Ernabella Mission and was now handing it back to the community. So it was a bit of a test case for IAD in terms of what it might be able to do out of Alice. Nothing much in the way of businesses had particularly worked out on the Pit Lands. The missions had tried sheep, goats and a few other things over the thirty-odd years they operated out of Ernabella. But rabbits were the only things surviving well. The dry years in the sixties and early seventies hadn't helped much. There was little employment and a lot of boredom.

In the early seventies, youth hopelessness in the Pit Lands was a growing problem and a wave of young Aboriginal kids was taking up petrol sniffing in a big way. Often their parents were in town on the grog. It was horrible seeing the kids' wasted little bodies with cans of petrol tied around their necks. Some were barely into their teens. A few had died shocking deaths. Teaching stockman skills and building up a cattle industry was seen as providing a future for these kids.

I was no Rhodes scholar, but they didn't need a trained teacher. They actually had a fair few university-educated staff and volunteers to do all that sort of stuff. What they wanted was someone who knew a thing or two about horses, and what you needed to be able to do if you wanted to work on a cattle station.

In a way it was always going to be a bit unlikely. There were thousands of really great stockmen who had just lost their jobs in the last decade. Why waste a whole lot of money training people into one of the most oversupplied and shrinking workforces in the country? But we were optimists.

Anyway, I was pleased with the job. It was better paid than most of the other things I had tried. So I jumped in with the bright-eyed Stuart Philpot and other clever young things and did a tour of the homelands communities. We went to Amata, Mimili, Fregon, Ernabella and Kenmore Park. I got to see the Rock again and catch up with a few in the community. A few people put up their hands for the training program. A lot of the petrol-sniffers were dragged into it. We had enough for a trial run of the program. IAD had big plans of teaching it everywhere if it could be a success in Ernabella.

Once we started the course it was mainly me teaching these young kids how to do a few things like ride a horse. I had brought in a few of my own quietened stockhorses for the first part. They had been resting out at Dick Palmer's place. So we started trying to teach these young kids how to saddle up, how to get up on a horse, stay on for a while, get it moving and hopefully stop the horse and get off again without falling off.

It was pretty hilarious stuff, but no one got hurt and the kids by and large kept on turning up. A few of the older community blokes who had worked on stations like Victory Downs, Mt Ebenezer or Kenmore Park sometimes turned up to help out. I learnt my first few lessons in the art of teaching. Don't get too ambitious, and always start from where the kids are at. It meant throwing away the teaching manual. We still had to fake how useful it was when the bosses were about. Otherwise we might all have had to look around for something else to do.

We really had to start from the basics, like getting the kids to do what they were told from time to time. It got better after a while and they seemed just as proud as I was when they finally got the hang of having a bit of control over a big live animal. From there we started on a few more useful things, like following up a cow and learning how to work as a team to move a mob along to a set of yards. Soon some of them could chase after a cow that was making a break and turn it back into the mob. They wouldn't have got a start on wages with Harry Bloomfield, but at least he might have started them on rations. The real success was that the petrol sniffing kids had stopped sniffing and were hanging in on the course. The old blokes kept turning up. I was feeling pretty good about the whole thing.

We were also teaching the kids how to butcher a cow, skin it and cut up greenhide leather for ropes and whips. They liked the leatherwork because they could make themselves and their families, wallets and stuff. They were taught the basics of building a yard and fences. It was like going back to my teenage years at Loves Creek, except the hours and the money were much better.

I wanted the yards to teach them the art of breaking in some horses of their own. There were a few pretty feral horses around the place that hadn't been ridden much, if at all. I talked some of the old blokes into joining in more and giving us a hand. If I had a crew I was promised a bit of work on neighbouring Kenmore Park, mustering cattle and droving them to the railhead. A lot of the kids were just passengers really on the horse muster. But they learnt how not to get in the way and practised their riding. We were able to round up a number of good-looking horses, and get them into the solid yards that we had built. Now was the hardest part. It was just as well the bosses weren't about or I expect they wouldn't have let it go ahead.

It had been a while even for me, but we broke in those horses to the saddle eventually. It was a bit of a mixture of the brutal way of breaking in I had learnt in the old days, and the horse-whispering techniques that I had picked up over the years. Probably more of the former if the truth was told. I would be the one that got a rope around them, then later got the bridle on and finally introduced the horse to having the bit in its mouth. The kids got a go later on. Eventually me and the old blokes tied bags around the horses' midriffs to get them used to having things around their flanks. We would tighten them up slowly. Finally it was a blanket and a saddle on. I would ride the horse first. But once I had got up and ridden the horse out, they were pretty much turned over to the old blokes and kids to finish off. It was a bit of a circus some days. No one got killed, though it was often a pretty close thing. A fair few of the young fellows got tossed off more than once. But they were young and bounced a little more than I did at that time. I was always there if things got too out of control. Eventually we had enough rideable horses and were able to offer ourselves to Kenmore Park.

Kenmore Park management were a bit sceptical, but they knew me and some of the older blokes. So they were talked into giving us a go. We did their cattle muster in the old-fashioned way, with packhorses and swags. But I also managed to get a vehicle to come in every now and again with supplies and to keep an eye on things. Kenmore Park staff were often about for a bit of a chat and a laugh. We had a nice enough time of it.

I had been head stockman a few times at Dunmarra Station and other places so knew what was required. We mustered up some of the back country using some old bullocks as coaches. Eventually we had enough and travelled them a bit. Then the station organised for some trucks to come in and do the pick up in a paddock. We were a bit behind schedule. But they paid us up, so I could give some money to the old blokes and even the young kids. A lot of them were still passengers. But it had taken us a while to get the hang of stockwork when we were starting out too. They were doing okay. We were getting on pretty well and IAD were happy with me. Stuart Philpot was even able to write it up as hugely successful, and was busy getting on with instalment two, or three, or six for all I cared, of the curriculum.

Alec at Stapleton Station with Malley Brown, Dave Murray, Michael Schaffer and Barry Freeman with young men from McLaren Creek
photo courtesy Kruger family

I was less sure about where it was all going to lead to. There just wasn't a lot of stockwork happening. This was even though cattle prices were good and the seasons had been pretty wet. But then the Northern Territory Tuberculosis and Brucellosis campaign started. All of a sudden we had good prospects of work happening for a while. A lot of Top End cattle had been found to be carrying TB. When the scientists had a look they found that they had probably always had it. They had a lot of other diseases too. The scientists reckoned the TB had come in with the water buffaloes from South-East Asia where it was rife.

The homecoming

The fear was that if TB and brucellosis had spread out of Asia, then foot-and-mouth disease might spread too through the national sheep flock, via the feral animal population. It would cost huge amounts of money slaughtering animals to fight an outbreak. The other fear was that some countries, particularly America, wouldn't buy our beef if TB and brucellosis were seen as widespread in the herd.

The Northern Territory Cattlemen's Association saw it as a big chance to get rid of all the old scrubby Herefords that had been running feral in the Top End stations for a century, and to improve the herd by changing over to the new Brahmin breeds. The Commonwealth government set aside a lot of money to shoot out the feral water buffaloes and wild cattle of the Top End. Any mob of cattle that tested positive to TB or brucellosis was also to be shot out.

So we got work mustering up the cattle around Central Australia and down into South Australia. I was working with two great fellows called Garry Page and Timmy Jocelyn. Garry was the most deadly shot I'd ever seen. We were working for a mob called the Central Australian Aboriginal Pastoralists Association (CAAPA). It was the management body for a lot of the Aboriginal-owned cattle stations that were now starting up. They might have been stations handed back to Aboriginal communities by the churches. They might have been old government reserves. Or they might have been previously privately owned stations bought by the federal government as part of the Indigenous Land Trusts. We shot out the infected stock and the feral animals, like camels and donkeys. We also got contract work on privately owned stations that were paid so much per infected beast by the government to slaughter them. It was long-term work for the trainees and some of them did well.

The TB and Brucellosis campaign eventually came to an end and Northern Territory stations were declared free of the diseases. Surprise, surprise, there wasn't much of a market for Aboriginal stockmen after that. A few went on to get seasonal work. Some even moved on to longer term jobs. But cattle stations were rare in the Pit Lands. Limited access to feed, too many rabbits, not enough of a spread of permanent water, the cost of getting cattle to markets and a whole lot of community management problems saw the end of that dream. Eventually, after a fair few years, mostly working out of Ernabella, I packed it in and got a new job in town. I was sick of the travel as much as anything else.

Cyclone Tracy and its aftermath

I turned fifty on Christmas Day, 1974. Noel, our little baby, turned five. I was safely in bed when Cyclone Tracy ripped through Darwin, then turned around and took out the northern suburbs as well. Like all us old stockmen, I was up early, had stoked up the stove and was drinking my morning cup of tea when I heard the news. We tried to ring up and find out about our daughter, Lynette. She had just moved up to Fanny Bay in Darwin, with her husband, Brian Willis, and their two kids, Fabian and Adrian. We tried to ring Gladys, Ada and their families, but no one could get through. Later we found out that they were all safe. They had been taken down south in the planes that flew in to evacuate everyone. They had all survived and soon enough were desperately trying to find a way to get back home.

The news of the cyclone changed the day. I woke Nita and we spent a fair bit of the day nervously watching the TV and listening to the radio. But Christmas and Noel's birthday couldn't be denied. So we had the usual present giving, church, Christmas lunch with the Palmer family and a late tea. It was an exhausting day. We were just so happy Lynette and the family were okay.

Lynette had left school at sixteen in 1972. She soon after started a relationship with a young local fellow, Brian Willis. He was working out at the tourist place at the old Loves Creek homestead. She got pregnant and when she was seventeen, Fabian was born. In 1974 she had another boy, Adrian. She was eighteen when they all moved to Darwin. Brian had work up there. Adrian was just five months old when Cyclone Tracy hit.

Melly was sixteen then. She had started work at IAD. Wayne was approaching fourteen. Larry had turned eleven. Polly was already six-and-a-half. Soon there would be no kids at home during the day with Noel about to start school. They were all healthy and getting an education. Not bad for an old institutions kid who had often thought he would be lucky to see the day out.

Cyclone Tracy changed the Northern Territory in a big way. Inside a day the first car drove down from Darwin. Within a couple of days there were streams of cars pouring through Alice. Nita and I were doing our bit, helping out with people needing something to eat and a place to camp. I met up with a lot of Darwin people I hadn't seen in a while, and even recognised a few that I thought hadn't been in Darwin for a long time. People were getting free petrol, food, clothes, Christmas presents for the kids and even money to keep on going further south. Once there, they were being looked after with Church and government money. It was the best and most affordable holiday some people along the track had ever been on. Who was to deny a few bushies and their families joining the exodus south?

Commonwealth government money, even overseas money, came pouring in to rebuild Darwin. There were a lot of local Alice Springs tradesmen who headed up there for the big wages once the rebuilding work started. It created a lot of job opportunities. Inside a couple of years Darwin was rebuilt, bigger, flasher and with whole new suburbs of cyclone-proof government houses. The Darwin mob did alright out of the whole deal. Especially the old families that were still running what passed for a government. They had the focus of the whole nation and more money and support services started than people knew what to do with. Even Alice Springs got some of the extra Commonwealth money being chucked about.

But the big winners were the Country Liberal Party (CLP). They had a strong alliance with the carpetbaggers doing well in Darwin and the old white bosses running the cattle industry. The station owners were cashed up, because the drought had broken at home as well as across the eastern states. Cattle prices were high and the demand for Territory beef was strong. The CLP had a big fighting fund to contest every Aboriginal advancement campaign. By the end of 1975 they also had a sympathetic Coalition government in Canberra. The fight for self-government in the Territory started.

Paul Everingham was the CLP leader. He was the blokey sort of lawyer that the CLP seemed to specialise in. The Fraser government in Canberra agreed to a lot of self-government arrangements that would see services provided out of Darwin through our own Territory administration. In July 1978 Paul Everingham became the first Territory Chief Minister, with responsibility for health, education, police, the courts and planning. It was a circus.

Money for Aboriginal education ended up being diverted through Darwin and spent on building up white schools in Darwin's growing northern suburbs. It was the same with health and housing. Every claim under land rights was contested, delaying decisions sometimes for years. The

CLP government never won any of their cases but it didn't stop them. Every time Labor even looked like winning a Northern Territory election, the CLP would start talking about people's backyards, schools and services being taken away by Aboriginal people. They won election after election.

The place became a one-party state. Even with a Labor government in Canberra after 1983, no one could stop Aboriginal funding being syphoned off into the white communities.

The CLP incompetence was extraordinary. One story shows what a joke it was. At one stage the CLP decided to build a new school for the suburb of Tiwi on the edge of Darwin. But someone got the pronunciation wrong and Tiwi became Ti Tree. Ti Tree is two hundred kilometres along the highway north of Alice Springs. It has a population of perhaps fifty people at the pub on a Saturday night. Next thing you know Ti Tree has a primary school for about three hundred students built for them. The locals stood around bemused. Even if all the camp dogs were enrolled you couldn't have got that number of students. But it didn't seem to matter much. Business as usual, really, as far as the CLP was concerned, part of their commitment to Aboriginal education.

After running through a number of leaders after Everingham retired, the CLP chose Dennis Burke, an ex-major in the army, to lead them. He wasn't such a racist and didn't really push a big anti-black campaign. His reward in 2002 was to be the first CLP opposition leader. Territory Labor came from nowhere to win government with the support of some independents, after twenty-four years of CLP rule. Labor was as shocked as the rest of the Territory. It has taken them a good few years to recover and do anything much different from the old CLP.

During the eighties and nineties it got so that anybody who wanted to get anything up in the Northern Territory had to join the CLP. There was no other way of doing business here or getting ahead. More than a few important Aboriginal politicians ended up trying to suck up to the CLP. Not that it ever did them much good. There was a colour bar.

Despite the conservative government the Territory still went ahead. White people flocked here for the wages. They bought houses and often stayed. The Aboriginal population outbred everyone else, but still couldn't make much of a dint in the overall population mix. Alice Springs grew but not anything near like Darwin did. Darwin soon had more than half the total adult population of the whole of the Northern Territory. It dominates all the politics.

Congress Farm

After leaving IAD, I ended up working at Congress farm south of town on Ragonesi Road. Some start-up money to buy the property had come from the Commonwealth government to establish a sobering up place for the heavy drinkers in town who wanted to give it away for a while, perhaps forever. The property had been Mr Heenan's. It had a lovely home on it and well established gardens. Congress's idea was to keep the farm and orchard aspect of the place going as well.

Initially Bill Turner was in charge. There were some active detox treatments provided by Congress clinic. The work on the farm and other activities were seen as part of people changing their lives in the longer term. They had a number of successes but more often than not people took it as an opportunity for a rest and feed between paydays and binges.

By this stage the Central Australian Aboriginal Congress had developed into more than just a political forum for talking up land rights. It had money for a health clinic. Later it became a social services provider, running a tent program for homeless families at Charles Creek. It also helped set up health services in Papunya, Tennant Creek and out Utopia way. I had been a part of Congress at various levels since arriving back from Katherine.

The early days of Congress were pretty full-on with a young Neville Perkins as the first director. Dr Trevor Cutter was the first doctor, working at an incredible pace. They recruited the first of a long line of Aboriginal health workers. They also had a big welfare section that helped with food, blankets and transport. Congress supported people getting on to social security payments when they first became entitled, under the changes brought in by the Whitlam government. You needed a lot of support to get past the Department of Social Security staff employed in the Central Australian offices.

Dr Greg Wheeler was another of the early doctors at Congress. Brian Ede became the second director when Neville Perkins ran for the seat of

Macdonnell in the Northern Territory Legislative Assembly. Then came Tim Shaw's son, Geoffrey Shaw. Geoff had been in the army over in Vietnam and, after struggling a bit, was persuaded to take the job. He ended up running an independent Tangentyere Council for nearly twenty years. Congress next had Johnny Liddle who stayed on for a long time. He finally stepped down in 2001 and the first woman director, Stephanie Bell, was given the job. There were a few doctors that hung around for a long time fighting for an Aboriginal health service. Ben Bartlett, Peter Tait, Alex Hope, Lone Anderson and more recently John Boffa were amongst them.

I remember when Neville Perkins ran for parliament in 1976. He recruited me to travel around with him, talking up with the old ringers out in the communities. It was a busy time driving around catching up with old mates. The seat of Macdonnell took in most of the Aboriginal communities north of Alice. Neville was the first Aboriginal person elected into the Northern Territory parliament. I was very proud to have been there with him. We had a big party the night that he got in. Unfortunately getting one Aboriginal voice in parliament didn't change that much. The CLP won government and didn't lose it for another twenty-six years.

After leaving IAD, I got a job as a bus driver at Congress. Later when the money came for the dry-out centre at Congress Farm, my old mate Bill Turner approached me and I took the job as the driver there. When I wasn't driving I got busy keeping the huge gardens happening. We worked hard to involve the residents. With a few of the regulars we started a weekend shop for our vegetables. We even got a hawker's van to sell fresh fruit and vegetables in the town camps and door-to-door.

The farm side of the place went well but it was never enough to fund the costs of the alcohol programs and all our wages. There were times when we had to wait for the next bit of funding to get paid properly again. It was always a battle.

One of the things I started up at Congress Farm was taking residents out for a week or so to Mud-tank Camp in the gem fields, north-east of town. It was a rough sort of camping, but there was plenty for people to do. Or they could sit around under the trees. Occasionally you might even get lucky and find a bit of rock worth a second look. We would come in with a few bags of crystals with a bit of colour, and sell them at the gem store.

The homecoming

I knew the Gem Tree area from my travels in the sixties when I was trying to make my fortune as a prospector. I would take out some tinned food, but mainly the group from Congress Farm relied on bush tucker and hunting. We caught rabbits, goanna, kangaroos and anything else that moved. We often ended up bringing food back to the farm, or dropping stuff off to families in town.

But the residents often took off on paydays. Once they were on their feet a bit and the shakes had died down, they would want to be back in the drinking circle. There was not a lot of real work that was going to happen for them unless they really started to make some long-term decisions about what they wanted to do. Mostly they were sad and feeling lost. They felt they were too far-gone with the grog to be able to make it back into some other world they might have dreamed about. Many only came back when they were grog sick again, or someone was threatening them. It wasn't working much as a program to turn people around.

Rory O'Connor, a mad Irishman, became involved with the farm for a while. Rosie Maher was the cook out there then. Barry Cook, who went on to start up the Injartnama outstation near Hermannsburg with his wife, Elva, worked first at Congress Farm. Rory and I got a number of things happening. One involved taking a group over to Perth. This was a great holiday and adventure. I know it was a bit of an eye-opener for me. The idea was that if people saw how the other half lived, they would be inspired to make things happen in their own lives.

One of the problems with Congress Farm was that it was still close enough to town for family and other drinkers to pester our residents. The ones that copped it hardest were the old blokes on pensions. People would jump the fence on payday to harass them for grog money. They needed a resident caretaker to stop some of the intimidation that went on. Unfortunately there wasn't money for a caretaker. I got a bit frustrated after a while and started looking around for other work.

Congress Farm fell over as a going concern for a while in the 1980s. It wasn't that the alcohol problems in town had ended but that money wasn't coming in to pay salaries. Government cutbacks saw just a few old blokes living out there. The farm and gardens were abandoned.

In the early nineties there was new government interest in tackling the Aboriginal grog problem. The women from Hermannsburg and Papunya had made a big protest about the effect of chronic drinking on their communities. Governments wanted something that would work. In the end a new group including Doug Abbott and Doug Walker formed out of Congress and the local organisations. Many of their board members were survivors of teenage and adult drinking circles who had since become sober. They pushed hard to get people interested in developing a residential program at the old Congress Farm site again.

They even brought over some Native American Indians to talk about building up Indigenous culture as a way of turning people away from the grog. It was an Alcoholics Anonymous approach where no drinking was seen as the solution. In the early 1990s the Congress Farm property was taken over to start a residential program under the name of the Central Australian Aboriginal Alcohol Program Unit (CAAAPU). The service has struggled a lot. The same problems are happening, but it is hanging in there and at least has the ability to pay its workers properly.

The trip to Vanderlin Island

One of the things that happened while I was at Congress was that the Gap kids started running amok a bit. They had moved a lot of the old Gap families, and the old community spirit was breaking down. The kids were angrier and the adults didn't have the respect they used to. There were also a lot of kids with problems in the town camps. Their families were newer to town and sometimes struggled to avoid the drinking circles. The kids were on the streets a lot. You could live like that on the remote communities where everyone was family in some way. But in town the grog never really stopped, so the adult parties kept rolling on with nothing happening for the kids. There were a lot of people like Eli and Wenten Rubuntja, some of the Furbers, Margaret Heffernan, Carmel Ryan, Louise Raggatt and others that were working to get an Aboriginal school started.

Eventually some land on the other side of Lovegrove Drive was given to the group operating out of Tangentyere Council and a school started out of a few buildings cobbled together. Tangentyere buses picked kids up from town camps and they started getting a bit of an education. They formed their own incorporated body separate from Tangentyere and with representatives from most of the main language groups now living on town camps, Yipirinya School with a bilingual teaching staff, grew up in 1979. My kids were too old for it and the old Gap families were using Traeger

Park, Anzac Hill and later Alice Springs High. But it was a really big thing to get a school happening.

Rhonda Bird, Graham Ross, Amy Swan and other old Gap residents had been trying for a youth centre down the Gap. Our kids, when they weren't playing sport, were bored and getting into trouble. Some of the blokes, Graham in particular, would get a truck and take the kids on bush trips, shooting kangaroos and a lot of rabbits. Often as not the group would end up camping overnight. I sometimes went along with him when I had the time. It was all volunteer stuff at the beginning, but we got a bit of support from the churches. When we got an extra kangaroo or two, we would drop it off with one of the families that might have been struggling a bit.

On a balmy summer's evening Graham would hunt up some kids. He would have squeezed the local shops. There might be a dozen loaves of bread from the bakery, a few kilos of sausages and some bits of meat from the butcher, tomato sauce and a mob of swags that he had got from somewhere. The kids loved the trips. We would often just go up the Ross River Road to Patrick Hayes's place under Mt Undoolya. Over time, with scavenged building materials, a few adults and the kids, we built a bough shelter and some pit toilets and a fairly reasonable campground happened out there.

At one time there was a bit of money found. Perhaps it was from Congress. Anyway Graham had family connections at Vanderlin Island in the Gulf of Carpentaria. He decided to organise a trip to the Gulf with the help of some of the church mob. The Johnson family up at Vanderlin were happy to have us stopping at their place. We only had to get there.

Peter Lorraine was one of the party. He was a keen young white fellow working with the Catholic Church. He established a drop-in centre for Aboriginal kids next to the Catholic Church in Hartley Street. Perhaps it was him who helped find the money. He was good like that. I put up my hand to go along with a few others. I was one of the drivers. We had a whole bunch of kids lined up.

Amy Swan and Eva Harvey were cooks. My daughter, Lynette, came along to help out. One of the Congress doctors, a guy nicknamed Catweazle, joined us. We hit the road, going up through Tennant Creek to Elliott and across the old Barkly Stock Route to Borroloola. It had been a while since I'd seen much of this country. I caught up with a few old mates along the way. From Borroloola we went down to a place near Bing Bong Station on the coast called Maningara Station, where a boat was to take us over to the island.

The boat was delayed but finally turned up. All us desert mob got a bit seasick. Vanderlin is a big island not that far off the coast, but too far for us. We were very glad to be on land again.

We stopped with a fellow called Steve Johnson. He was a great host and had set up a camp for us. Vanderlin Island has some of the best fishing in the world. That was why the Indonesians had brought their boats down into the Gulf for centuries before white people settled the Top End. For our desert-raised kids it was a new world. A lot had never seen the sea before. The stories of big saltwater crocs and wild pigs had them pretty spooked even before we got there. They were hardly sleeping with the thrill of seeing so many new things and being so far from home.

Us adults were having a great time of it too. The croc stories always got me looking around a bit every time I ventured near the sea. I was playing the hard, experienced bushman, but I think I jumped higher than the kids when, after nightfall, there was a noise in the undergrowth and someone yelled out. The locals enjoyed having a few laughs. We had no trouble keeping the kids close. They almost slept on top of each other. No one wanted the edge of the circle around the campfires. The kids tried hanging on to their wee all night rather than go to the toilets. It was okay in the daytime. We all felt braver being able to see.

The Vanderlin Island mud crabs were sensational. Plentiful and easy to get if you knew what you were doing. Low tide left huge areas of mangroves and mud exposed. This was where the mud crabs could be found. You took big poles with nets attached to one end. These were usually a coat hanger with some nylon gauze sewn on to it. You had to walk steadily in the water and try not to stir up the mud too much. It was usually only up to your knees. The crabs would be just going about their own business at the bottom. If you were lucky you would see the mud crab before it saw you. Then it was a matter of having the net where the crab would rush to when it took off. You could use a second pole to try and wheel it if it headed another way.

They were pretty fast and didn't mind muddying the waters a bit themselves. We lost a lot more than we caught. Some of the boys tried operating together. That often got a bit hilarious. If a crab took off between someone's legs, or someone just felt it brush past them, you had kids screaming and scrambling all over the place. If you surprised another crab when hunting one that you had tracked, it could get a bit messy too, particularly if you had a few kids helping out, or someone following the other crab. The crabs certainly had their chances with a bunch of very nervous and excited kids on their tail.

Once safely in the net we dumped them in a bucket. We let go some of the small ones or females that had eggs. The crabs were pretty hard on each other in the buckets and there was often a claw bitten off when a few got stuck in. We took the buckets into the beach from time to time, because you might be worried you'd fall over and drop the whole lot. Dropping a bucket didn't make you too popular with the boys having contests about who caught the most.

These were big crabs with big claws. The claws would spring up at you when the crabs sensed you were about. They would move around to face you as you came towards them. That was often the first you knew of them being there. That or when they suddenly took off. They gave you a nasty bite if they got hold of you. It was easy enough to walk on one if they had buried themselves a bit. We used the poles to prod the ground in front. If you stepped on one it gave you a huge scare and you jumped a mile. The kids loved the thrill of the hunt. I think they even liked the bites. They were badges of honour. You could wear sandshoes if you had any, but no one really bothered.

You had to be careful when the tide was on the turn. It was easy enough to forget about it in the excitement of the chase. Once the water was muddied, some of the bigger kids would head further and further out in their quest for clear water and new crab grounds. The tide came up as quickly as it went out and you could be stuck with a bunch of kids a fair way from the shore. None of us were great swimmers, having been brought up where opportunities to swim were a bit thin on the ground. You had to find a way of floating and scrambling in. If you had any imagination you worried for a croc nosing out from somewhere or even a shark. The movie *Jaws* had been a big hit in Alice Springs. You could hear the 'doont-doont, doont-doont' of the theme music playing in your head. We didn't lose any kids, but it was a bit scary sometimes. They could be pretty fearless in the daytime.

The local families were really great to us. We spent the whole time living off the mud crabs and big saltwater fish like barramundi or gemfish. It got so we were so spoilt we didn't bother with the smaller feelers or claws, the stuff you fought for when you might have one at home. Some of us even started looking forward to a big slab of steak after eating fish for a week. It was paradise. I felt like staying forever. But soon enough it was time to pack up and go home. We caught the boat and drove the bus back. The kids were dropped off, often to pretty ordinary overcrowded town camps with everyone on the grog. It could get a bit disheartening like that, unless you kept in mind what a fabulous time we'd all had.

Like a lot of things that are really good, it took a while for it to happen again. Graham and Peter talked it up and went back with the kids lots of times over the next fifteen years or so. Lynette went on a few trips. But Congress ended up losing a good doctor. Catweazle liked the place so much that he ended up marrying up there. He shifted to Tennant Creek then Borroloola. It would still be a lovely thing to organise on a regular basis. A group in town called 'Bushmob' took some town camp kids up during the Christmas holidays in 2005.

The Johnson place where we stayed now has lots of school groups visiting and is run as a business by the family. Perhaps we could do an exchange with the kids from up that way staying out at Hamilton Downs or Mt Undoolya. We could take them kangaroo shooting and rabbiting. They could learn to ride horses or go on camel rides. Maybe sometime it will happen. Graham Ross is still talking it up.

The Gap got its youth centre eventually. It grew into something pretty flash with a basketball court and a hall. They had discos and parties there with families turning up to support the place. Amy Swan was a great operator with the kids. They expanded to school holiday programs, after-school homework centres, and a gym and an internet café are now operating out of it. There is even a school for young girls with babies so they can complete their education while having someone help out. Joey Hayes was the chairperson last time I heard and Graham Ross is still involved.

Later, when the land claim for Harry Creek was on and I had set up a big camp out there, Graham used to bring boys out for shooting weekends. There were plenty of kangaroos on McGrath's Plain, up at Snake Well and over near Top Bore. I had my horses out there too, so we taught a few kids to ride. It was good to keep involved. I knew a lot of the families. They were mostly the old Gap families. Later, lots of other people started stopping in.

The ongoing party

The kids were growing up while I was working for IAD and at Congress Farm. It was a lot better for us as a family, me being in town most of the time. For my children the 1970s and 1980s was the time they grew into their own person. They were becoming adults in a very different world to the one experienced by Nita and me when we were young.

The racism my kids experienced was less in your face. There were still a lot of bigots around. But people were much more careful. They were less patronising, but sometimes just as brutal and exploitative. It was from comparative or complete strangers too, not the same old mob that you had tried and true ways of avoiding.

Alice Springs itself was really taking off. The eighties saw a lot of new shopping centres and building. The number of people in town grew rapidly. You no longer knew just about everyone. New subdivisions sprang up. Lots of Aboriginal families moved out of the Gap into the new suburbs. Alice lost a lot of its country town feel with the knocking down of a lot of the old buildings. The general shops and family businesses closed down. Restaurants opened up. New schools, new faces and a changed world.

The town camps under Tangentyere started to build houses and get services going. There were heaps of Aboriginal families from remoter communities coming to town. They were nice people but sometimes struggling with the transition and being that close to the pubs. The trouble was often that people had lots of visitors, usually other family from out bush, who would come in and expect to stay and bring grog. People couldn't really say no because of cultural responsibilities and family obligations. In some cases the visitors didn't really go home much, or were stuck in town because of sickness or court business. It was the kids living in the town camps that mostly missed out because of the overcrowded and grog-soaked houses getting trashed by visitors.

There was a serious developing problem of Aboriginal drinking, especially public drinking. The police became fairly antagonistic. The old vagrancy laws changed but the police were still much the same. You would see them pull up to a group drinking, talking down to them, finding stashes of grog and pouring it on to the ground. Any trouble and people were locked up. Family values within the community changed. Kids were often more at risk. They didn't have the close family protection of earlier times. Whole families had problems with the grog.

With the ongoing party happening, Aboriginal men seemed to stop getting work. The jobs went to white people coming to town. Then unemployment benefits saw many Aboriginal men lose the motivation to work. The types of jobs that men had traditionally done seemed to disappear too. Women and children often packed up and left their unemployed men to their drinking and their mates. The single mother's pension made this financially a good idea anyway. It was all a bit sad with men seeming to spiral out of playing much of a useful role in lots of families. The Aboriginal community lost its work culture. It got a 'drinking and having a good time' culture instead. But of course you pay for the good times eventually. If not you, then certainly your kids. That was what happened in Alice Springs.

Alec and Nita attend one of the NAIDOC balls photo courtesy Kruger family

With Aboriginal fathers and their women not getting much work their kids didn't learn about working either. They couldn't get a start where their parents were working. They had no role models in their families.

Unemployment was what the kids expected. They lost any real idea that working was what people usually did unless they were disabled.

On the plus side, the seventies and eighties was also a time when big National Aboriginal and Islander Day of Celebration (NAIDOC) events started. They were big parties for an Aboriginal community not used to many large gatherings. Often there were two or three hundred people at the celebration dances. They would hire a hall and band. It was not so much a political event as in having to listen to speeches and such, more an opportunity for people to get together for a good time.

The Centre for Appropriate Technology

After I left Congress Farm I worked with the new Centre for Appropriate Technology (CAT) in Priest Street. I had a flat at the back of CAT as part of the job. CAT under its first boss, Bruce Walker, was looking at how to develop equipment and training for remote Aboriginal communities. It had a high profile but not enough money to do what it said it could. So the place was forever putting up its hand for other bits of funding when they came along.

One of my roles was to drive people around and talk things up. CAT had a lot of visitors and I was part of impressing them. I developed a few stories and a tour route to keep people interested. We worked closely with Centralian College's Gillen House, the government-funded tourism and hospitality school in Alice Springs. I would pick up tourists, give them a guided tour of the sacred sites and tourist centres of Alice Springs, and then drop them off at the casino or some other motel. The government was paying CAT to provide this service. We needed the money, and tourism was seen as a possible new Aboriginal training opportunity, especially for remote communities. But then in the late 1980s there was the pilots' strike and a lot of tourism places went broke. CAT didn't get a lot of business after that.

At CAT I had a lot of duties. Mostly I was the driver and caretaker. It was pretty flexible. They would ask me to do whatever came up. I was getting close to retirement age by this time, but liked being busy. The caretaker job was busy enough when a mob of people came in to stay for two weeks of training. We also had a group of regular students living there. So I had a bit of company but was always able to get home when I needed to.

I was doing a bit of cross-cultural work for CAT with some of the other organisations too. Sometimes Congress would want me to talk to the new staff. Sometimes it might be the government mob. I kept my hand in with a bit of private stockwork as well. It was a busy time with land claims being started out at Harry Creek and later Loves Creek. A breakaway Aboriginal group in town started talking up being able to have more of a say in what was happening. They felt that the Central Land Council was leaving them out of most land claims in favour of full descent Aboriginal groups and the newcomers to town. The Amoonguna land claim was a bit of a contest. It ended up with a lot of unhappy town people saying they were ripped off by the CLC.

Then in 1988 it was Australia's celebration of 200 years since Captain Arthur Phillip landed to set up a convict colony in Sydney. It was a series of big events. The Northern Territory Cattlemen's Association supported an application to set up a memorial to drovers at Newcastle Waters where the old droving teams used to kick off on the Barkly stock route into Queensland. As part of this they decided to do a re-enactment of a droving trip from Newcastle Waters to Queensland. They got approval and the federal government gave them a lot of money. I got invited to be part of the opening. Being a bloke that found it difficult to turn down a free feed and a piss-up, I made the trip up.

The Newcastle Waters Drover's Memorial

Newcastle Waters had really died a long time ago when Max Schaber opened up his new pub in Elliott. It was a sad little place after that, with only a small Mudburra community stopping in from time to time. Even most of them had long since moved into Elliott. The Memorial organising committee had a lot of renovations to do to get the old pub and a few buildings around it, like Jock Jones' bakery, looking okay.

Luckily they had Kerry Packer, one of the richest men in Australia, as a neighbour. He had bought Newcastle Waters Station, Beetaloo and a fair bit of the rest of the Territory as well. Kerry was using Newcastle Waters to breed up some of his polo ponies. He also liked to use it as an occasional holiday destination for friends looking for the 'real' Australia. His friends often sent their wayward teenage sons in danger of ending up in jail, off to Newcastle Waters too, to be given some time to straighten up. They were trained as high-class jackeroos. The real work of the place as a cattle station was carried on by the usual badly paid local stockmen. They also got the job of looking after the wealthy young fellows doing their stint in the bush.

So Max Schaber's original Junction Hotel got the cobwebs cleaned out and was tarted up for the occasion. Plaques with the names of old drovers were put in place. A bit of a white history was written up and displayed and the who's who of the Northern Territory Cattlemen's Association and the CLP rocked up. They were joined by Kerry Packer and his mates, the four-wheel-drive brigade and a few old-timers like me looking for a free feed. They even had a real drover and a motley mob of cattle for the re-enactment.

They managed to capture a bit of the old days well enough. There were no black faces anywhere near the bosses' tables. Nor did the Honour Roll Board have many black names on it. And there were some names of white blokes whom I suspect had never even been on a horse in their lives. Certainly I don't remember them in the stock camps let alone crossing the Murranji or along the Barkly stock routes as part of a droving team. Perhaps they had driven the route in a four-wheel drive, probably in convoy. Maybe it was enough to have flown over the place in their pretty little planes that were all parked at the local airstrip. That and having the money to pay their way into the CLP-organised event. They got their photo opportunity and the TV cameras rolled and recorded their speeches. They were competing with the Australian Stockman's Hall of Fame in Longreach. I could agree with that. As an old cattleman I shared the ringer's contempt for sheep. As if pushing a few sheep along fenced paddocks was much of a test of a drover. Why should Longreach celebrate that sort of rubbish?

Anyway, the rum and beer flowed at the back tables set up for the likes of me. It was great to catch up with some old mates. We had a good old laugh going through the Roll as to who got on and who had missed out. The organising committee even got shamed enough to say they would put up an addition when we gave them the real names. Then there was music and dancing into the early morning. Herbie Laughton and his father, Mick, were there and their names were on the board. Not that they had been Queensland-bound drovers, but at least they had been across the Murranji and taken cattle down the south road. The next morning a lot of us had shocking hangovers and struggled to participate in any further events. Like a lot of the old-timers I was feeling every one of my sixty-three years. It was a great night.

The organising committee had got a real live drover to do the re-enactment. He was a fellow named Pic Willetts. He certainly looked the part. He had always been a flash dresser. And he really had been about droving after the war. The name Pic was short for Piccaninny. He had been just a kid and a few years younger than me when I had first seen him and he was starting out in the droving game. He was a cranky bastard even when I knew him as a snotty-nosed teenager. He also had a terrible chip on his shoulder. A bad drunk, who could turn on people if he thought they weren't giving him enough respect. I had always steered clear of the fellow myself but I'd known a few people who had fought him. He had been a fine horseman though, and a drover who was good to his animals. Now he was probably in his mid-fifties and still doing a bit of droving over in Queensland.

I think the organising committee had been hoping for someone with a bit more class and diplomacy than Pic had ever displayed. Anyway, in the tradition of droving bosses, Pic refused to bend much to the government men or station owners. They wanted him to bring the cattle and droving plant into the town itself for the photo opportunity and for TV. There wasn't much feed about and Pic decided to camp close to the jump-off point and refused to go any further. Pic told them they could all 'go and get fucked, as far as he was concerned'. They could get themselves another drover if they liked. He was happy to get paid for coming over and would be on his way again. Nor was he up to doing any pretty speeches or reciting *Clancy of the Overflow*. Pic was one hell of a stubborn, non-communicative man. If you took the expletives away he hardly talked at all. I'm sure the organising committee had a quick hunt around but they were stuck with Pic.

He also made it pretty clear what he thought of the mob of cattle they had managed to muster up. Even I could see that they were a mangy bunch that needed to be taken out and shot rather than walked 800 kilometres across a pretty dry and disused stock route. Pic was consoled a little when they said they would have a convoy of four-wheel drives about, plenty of water from the stations along the way and they would even arrange feed to be brought in if necessary.

Having had a few victories Pic was on a roll. His next fight was when he got to have a look at some of the passengers he would have for the trip. The dismissive sneer was beautiful to see. Anyway, it was agreed that there would be the droving team run by him and the blokes who knew how to work cattle. Then there would be the others who could do pretty much what they wanted as long as they didn't get in the way. I would have liked to go on the trip. I'm sure it would have had some lovely moments. But I had to head back to Alice and the real world. The ragtag last droving expedition eventually rolled into Camooweal a few months later and was judged a huge success by some. I'm sure Pic was happy to have just survived it without murdering anyone and ending up in jail.

Anyway, with the cattle moving off to the east we packed up and headed back along the south road. I still had work to turn up for and my own plans. The Palmers had been part of putting in a claim for some land that had been the old stock route into Alice Springs. It was my wife's family's land. Her tribe had always lived on it up until the arrival of the cattle. Now that trucks had killed off the drovers the stock routes were unused. We had a chance under land rights to get some of Harry Creek back for our kids.

Harry Creek

Harry Creek was part of the old stock route coming up from Alice Springs towards Tennant Creek. It is about sixty kilometres north of town after McGrath's Dam and before you get to Burt Creek. It is lovely scrubby grasslands country. When the creeks are running it looks like you could run a lot of cattle. In the dry times, like everything else in the Territory, it is a different story.

The Palmer family ancestors used to live across this part of the Northern Arrernte tribal lands. They would have seen the fires announcing John McDouall Stuart's various expeditions in the 1850s and 1860s. The 1870s saw the land taken up as part of Yambah and Bond Springs Stations and other pastoral leases handed out by the South Australian government. These leases saw a lot of people pushed towards rations and the town of Stuart. Harry Creek became part of the old camel route north. The telegraph line ran through the land. It had been a long and hard transition for the families through station life, ration times and the institutions and missions of the nineteenth century.

The Harry Creek part of the stock route is bordered on three sides by Yambah Station. By the 1980s Aaron Gorey and his family owned Yambah. They are good, respectful people and mostly tried to help people out where they could. I had done some work with them over the years and we got on pretty well. On the south side, the Harry Creek area starts to get into Bond Springs Station. The Heaslip family owned Bond Springs and they could be a bit more hardline and disappointing. You often needed something pretty concrete that was going to benefit them to get a working relationship going.

Anyway, the stock routes were obviously not getting used any more. The big trucks with animal transport trailers had long since replaced all us old-time drovers. So the stock routes were informally being used as part of the properties themselves. But they came under the Land Rights Act. They were still Crown land and could be claimed. In the 1980s the Central Land Council laid claims for traditional owners to all the old gazetted stock routes. The Northern Territory government responded by trying to sell them off to the neighbouring cattle stations. In fact they offered to convert the whole of the cattle stations from what had been 99-year leased land into freehold title for their mates in the Northern Territory Cattlemen's Association.

The land claim in the mid-1980s was that the stock routes could, and should be used, to create Aboriginal community excisions that allowed homelands for families who had worked on the bordering stations, and had been pushed off when their labour was not required. It was a clever strategy because the stock routes went everywhere. In the old days, you couldn't have a property if it didn't have a stock route to get animals in and out. It was like owning a house but not having a road into it. Getting stock route excisions was very important to the old people. The Land Council could always find a place on the stock routes that was close by peoples' traditional country where they had cultural obligations.

When the general claim for the stock routes was tested in the courts, they found in favour of the Land Council. It was a happy day. But you were still required to go through the process of identifying traditional owners, establishing that these ties hadn't been extinguished by other land use, working through how the community continued to have ties to the land that was being claimed and all the rest of the procedures to get up each individual claim. The Northern Territory Government then fought every one of them.

My wife's family, the Palmers, was one of the claimants for the stock route north of town. All of Dick and Mary Palmer's children and grandchildren were included. There was not much difficulty in establishing their connections. Bond Springs and north was their traditional land. The kids had mostly been born at Bond Springs when Dick was the head stockman there. They had continued to hunt kangaroos and visit the area when they were living at Palmer's camp on the north side of town. Our own children had gone out to Harry Creek when they were kids, on weekends and school holidays, hunting with other members of the extended families.

The claim ran from Sixteen Mile, just out of town, all the way up a hundred kilometres north, past Burt Creek, through Yambah and on towards Tennant Creek. So there were lots of other families involved in the claim. They included the Stevens, the Lynchs, the Rices, the Turners, the Brauns, the McMillans, and the Furbers. Harry Creek was one of the bigger places in the claim.

The Kruger family camp at McGrath's Dam photo courtesy the Kruger family

I was still working at CAT when the claim was going ahead. I thought it important enough for Nita and my kids' sake to get heavily involved. I still had the old stockman's yearning for my own little station in my sunset years. Somewhere to potter around, establish a garden and watch the sunsets. We decided to set up a bit of a camp at McGrath's Dam. This was in the heart of Nita's family country. So in the late eighties some of us spent a fair bit of time out there. We kept our government house at Parke Crescent, of course. You needed a town base. I set about scavenging any building materials and station stuff that might be useful. There was a lot of land to plonk something on that might come in handy later. We got given a big old marquee tent that I repaired bush style and set up.

Water was the big problem. There was no drinking water on the place. I scavenged some old water tanks and collected as many old petrol and chemical 44-gallon drums that I could find lying around in town. Many of the drums were not galvanised and had some rust. Some were cleaner than others. At the time I was grabbing whatever I could. I linked the drums together out at the camp and brought out water from Alice Springs to keep them topped up.

So in my last years at CAT I was really busy. I would be often dropping things off to our camp after work. I used to camp on the place nearly every weekend putting up this and fixing that. After I retired I moved there practically fulltime, and started building a big shed. Me and Larry put in a tender to remove an old Department of Works shed for $100. We got the job and then slowly dismantled it, moving the tin and timber out to a new Harry Creek site, a bit further away from McGrath's Dam. I also picked up stuff that had been thrown away. Later we got the leftovers from the set for *Quigley Down Under* that had been filmed locally. We had a bit of a work gang helping out. Ian Woods, David Blair, Kevin Davis who was going out with my daughter Polly, Raymond Harvey, David Swan and Noel were all living there and giving us a hand.

Lynette and Melly were working in town at the time. But usually Melly, and sometimes Lynette, would come out for the weekends to help out. Wayne was away in the Top End at the time so I didn't see much of him. But Polly came out and stayed with us when she could. Later on Polly and Melly often had their young babies, Aaron and Neil, with them. Nita camped with us when she wasn't holding things together in town. It was a family adventure that we really got involved in. It brought us all together again.

While the men were building, the women and kids would be off hunting bush tucker and cooking the meals.

Several of the Palmer families camped at the place. Nita's brother, Xavier, and Melba's grandson, Earl, and of course Eva Kopp, were all there with their families. There was Norman Wiltshire, James Gorey and others. On the south side of the dam was another camp with Silas Turner and family. Donny 'Popsie' Lynch, with Margie and their kids, camped at the place too. The big protest camp set up near the front gate. It was a show of support for being given back our country.

I had bought a new Holden Rodeo ute with a Japanese motor with the money I got paid when I retired from CAT. We called it the 'Blue Mule'. It was the best car I'd ever had. I needed it to take the drums of water out to the block. As well as having no water, Harry Creek had no electricity or services at the time. There were no houses. It started out as just an old bush camp that I set up. But all that training around Newcastle Waters and Elliott came into practice. Then years of scavenging around town helped out. I had a few favours owing to me too.

It was my retirement dream. We had no superannuation or savings after decades of work. A big mob of kids, low paying jobs and the high cost of running cars and having a bit of a life meant I was always going to retire on the pension. So I was determined to make a go of it. I got a mob of chickens from home and a bit of a garden going. It was hard to keep it alive because of the water. I also planted a lot of trees, some still surviving today.

My growing mob of horses that I was always looking for a place for also came out. I had dreams of running a ranch for tourists or continuing to train up young kids in stockwork. Larry had been using them and looking after most of them for me and some had been at Palmer's Camp. I had built them up from a few quiet ones that I was able to get and had bred them in locally. But after a while the horses ended up eating out the area set aside for the camp when they couldn't get enough feed. They started getting into Yambah Station and causing a nuisance. I was an old mate of Aaron Gorey at Yambah, but they were stretching the friendship. I was even able to get Aaron to donate the odd killer for Harry Creek in exchange for a bit of free labour in season. But he didn't really need my mob of horses, and I didn't have the money to hand feed them. We ended up rounding them up and sending them out to the Petricks' Mt Skinner

Station at Harts Range. It was a shame because there were some good horses amongst them.

The beef we exchanged from Yambah was added to supplies from town and whatever bush tucker we could get. It was a bit of a struggle as the claim went on and on with the Northern Territory Government lawyers challenging and delaying everything. The situation at Harry Creek became such a scandal that it was one of the matters investigated as part of a major inquiry into Aboriginal living standards by Justice Marcus Einfeld in the late 1980s. I remember these meetings. Gerry Hand, the Minister for Aboriginal Affairs and Territories at the time, came out and we ended up having a long chat about nothing much. I was hanging around at the front gate avoiding the more formal meeting. He was looking tired and lost. He seemed a bit preoccupied. He left parliament not long after this. Eventually the Northern Territory Government was shamed into building a bore for the place and life became a lot easier.

At long last, in the late 1980s an agreement was reached between us and the Northern Territory government. This was around the time they had settled a few things locally to try to push through a big recreational dam at Bond Springs. They called it a flood mitigation dam and it was upstream from Alice Springs. All the families at Harry Creek had strong claims for this area too. It was all Northern Arrernte country. So they settled the Harry Creek dispute to try and split families about the bigger issue of the dam. We were advised to take the deal. So we did.

The Harry Creek agreement recognised the rights of the Palmers and others to build a community and live on an excision of the old stock route. Under the Land Rights Act, the CLC was to list the traditional owners and distribute land to them. The Ingkerreke Outstation Resource Services was set up to do the day-to-day management of all the different living places under the agreement.

All of the Palmers got a place in the Harry Creek excision agreement. The Kopps and the Palmers got money under the Aboriginal housing program to build a house. They are some of the concrete-block houses now at the place. Harry Creek became a bit of another Palmer settlement. It was like an extension of Dick Palmer's old camp in town.

It was great having the land out at Harry's. It became a bit of a refuge for animals as well as us. There was Doris, the pig. Lambsie, one of Lynette's foster children, caught her at the greasy pig contest at the rodeo. My idea was to breed our own pork. We even got a father pig, Horace, to keep the enterprise going. But of course the kids wouldn't hear of Doris being eaten, and piglets proved elusive. We also had a ram, some turkeys and a goose called Albert, that chased all the visitors. Albert would even have a go at us living there. One time he managed to latch onto Larry's kid and had him bailed up. It got so you had to be real game to go outside at all. You would be racing Albert across the yard to get through the gate and shut it before he caught you. We also had chickens everywhere and a spirited little bantam rooster. Nita used to complain that the rooster attacked her every time she went to hang up the washing.

It was a bit like our place in town on a bigger scale. I remember one dog that we ended up having to lock up every time anyone went shopping. Otherwise it tagged along with you. It got into the habit of rushing into the shop to help itself to meat. It even used to grab a can of Pal. The shopkeepers banned the dog. We also had two noisy white cockies that the kids trained up and set going whenever they felt like it. We had ringneck lorikeets around. The kids would feed them cereal every morning. Larry caught the hatchlings out at the block and Nita looked after them. We also kept one old horse that Uncle Clarence Palmer had brought him in from Santa Teresa. He had a white coat and we named him 'Loco Blue Range' because he would change colour when he got into a bit of a sweat. We taught the grandkids how to ride on him.

We tried the tourist stuff a bit. There were lots of visitors some times. Having anything set up that you could make money from was the problem. We needed stables, riding tracks and all the rest. One day we had a big busload of Japanese students. Someone must have invited them out or else they were lost. We had a great time showing off the shed and bushland. I'm not sure whether they understood much of what we said, but they were keen photographers and took pictures of everything. Lynette invited Bob Hawke's daughter and her boyfriend to the place one time. They knew each other from when Lynette's husband, Brian, was studying in Melbourne.

Nowadays our Kruger area has a house, my big old shed and some smaller tin sheds. There are seven houses in Harry Creek, as well as some sheds. The McMillan family is living at Snake Well. Sixteen Mile has the Stevens family. There is also Black Tank where Popsie Lynch and his family live. The Turners are at Sandy Bore; the Brauns at Gillen Bore and the Furbers and Rice families are at Burt Creek. All the different settlements receive support from the Ingkerreke Outstation Resource Services. At Harry Creek there is still a major problem with water. The bore water is barely fit for human consumption. The pipes out of the main tank run to the various houses. Each family is expected to contribute to the cost of running the pump.

But the tanks are rarely full. People can steal your water. There are lots of disputes over water. Power and other services happen a bit better. There is funding for a diesel system and a solar-generating system. But there is always something going wrong. There is a need for a trained diesel mechanic to fix problems across the different places. If things got sorted out straightaway it would stop the disputes developing.

My dream was for a homestead for my family. For that to work there would have had to be a school, shop and work happening. At the moment families have to put their kids on a bus to travel for an hour on dirt tracks to Yipirinya School. The bus gets around to all the little communities. But it means kids getting up at six-thirty and not getting home until four-thirty or later. It's really dark and cold in winter, often with frost on the ground. You just can't do that to kids. So families have moved back into town. There is no real work so people have to take jobs in Alice. Ingkerreke is ineffective some of the time, with no tools or materials to actually get anything happening.

The Pension

I turned sixty-five on Christmas Day 1989. The Centre for Appropriate Technology was a government-funded place and this was the official retirement age. There were no exceptions, even if they knew I needed the money. So they thanked me, I got paid out and was without a job for the first time in as long as I could remember. I had to turn up at the Department of Social Security for the first time and apply for a pension. They put me on special benefits while the claim was sorted. Then I was told by one of the old army crowd that I might get a Veterans' Affairs pension. Some of my old army gang had had their veterans' pensions put through.

I ended up going around to see a Veterans' Affairs bloke who operated from the RSL. Sure enough they had a pensions advisor there and he helped me apply. He was great. A volunteer ex-soldier helping out his mates. It was one of the few times I was glad they had the RSL. The government had made a few changes that I didn't know about. To get a veterans' pension you used to have to have seen service overseas, but some time after Bob Hawke got in they declared that the Top End had been an active war zone. They also pushed through a ruling that the Indigenous Works Unit was the same as serving in any other part of the army, so I met the eligibility criteria. The money was set to start rolling in. They also told me that, with me accepted, Nita would get a wives' pension, so she could retire as well if she wanted to. The catch was that they wouldn't pay me without a birth certificate. I had a date of birth on my army record but I had fudged that, and the Commonwealth knew about that from when they hadn't let me join up for Korea.

Getting myself a birth certificate wasn't the easiest thing in the world. The Northern Territory Department of Births, Deaths and Marriages couldn't even find me, except as someone who had married Nita and fathered a lot of kids. They couldn't even identify my mother and it seemed that my birth hadn't been recorded anywhere. In December 1924, with Christmas and the Wet season settled in, my father must have skipped over notifying them about me. Perhaps by the mid-twenties it was a lot trickier, legally, for him to be fathering children with my mother. Perhaps they would have been straight out to steal us away.

No hospital records registered my entry into the world either. I was born at Donkey Camp before there was even a nursing station at Katherine. No school records were available. Everything was a bit of a guess really. They weren't prepared to give me a birth certificate unless I could come up with some information.

I contacted my sister, Gladys, who tried to help. She put in a statement but it wasn't enough. She had been only three years old at the time I was born. So she wasn't considered a suitable witness.

Of the other kids, Ada was alive, but she was already at Kahlin when I was born. I couldn't even be found on any admission forms for being taken into Kahlin Institution myself. One for Gladys was there, but not one in my name. I must have been too young or something. I was a mystery child until I hit Pine Creek. Finally when they checked their files, they found a school record that said I had been to Pine Creek School and had finished in May 1933 when we were all sent down to the Bungalow. There were pictures of me at the Bungalow, but not a lot of paper records. I wasn't registered in employment at Loves Creek. I even started having doubts myself.

Gladys Ahmat photo courtesy Kruger family

In the end it just got too hard. We were able to put enough pressure on Veterans Affairs to just take my word for how old I was. Also a few old blokes at the RSL said I must have been such and such an age when they first knew me. They stated that they knew me from the army days and I had been enlisted in 1942. Plus the Aboriginal organisations in town accepted that I was an old tjilpi or grandfather and they had my birth listed as 25/12/1924. It finally got me my pension. I'm still waiting for a birth certificate.

The whole thing of finding an official identity was humiliating. To think all those years as a child in the government institutions and nobody had records of anything about me. They said some files might have been lost after the cyclone. There was this and that excuse. It made me angry. No wonder so many of us taken-away kids didn't ever go legitimate, or try to get a few things we might have been entitled to. I think if I didn't have a pension officer helping me at the RSL and going in to bat for me, I would have just withdrawn. The guy at the RSL was unpaid. A volunteer ex-soldier helping his mates out. Thank god for the volunteers. Anyway it took a long time, then they ended up back paying me. It was more money than I can ever remember having. So for a little while I was cashed up. Pity it hadn't happened when I was younger.

It makes me angry still. I think about all the times I've been ripped off. I could have cried thinking of all the knock-backs, when I had tried so hard to be a good boy. All the times me and all the rest of us Aboriginal people were left sitting around in camps with nothing, even after the government changed the laws in the sixties that entitled people to social security. The smug white clerks in government offices looking down on you, humiliating you and making things so difficult that you ended up walking out with nothing. The ones that made you so angry that you felt like waiting for them to leave at the end of the day and giving them a good kicking. Public servants they might have called themselves, but we obviously weren't the public they had any intention of serving.

I remembered the old Aboriginal ringers crippled up from too much rough riding and falls off horses. Old drovers I knew that had died on the stations working for white bosses. They didn't get any workers' compensation or disability pensions. You had to be dying to have a social security worker, or social worker, take an interest in you.

After that first useful thing the RSL did for me, they got me checked out for a disability claim. Some of the things I had just put up with as part of getting older, the department accepted as being injuries that were war-related. I got a whole lot of health care and hospital services I didn't know about before. It was not a bad little pension after years of slogging, not getting paid much. Nita retired too and spared herself the pain of getting up every morning to do the hospital laundry.

Between Nita and me we could live pretty well on just a pension. I picked up the odd bit of work. Later I got a bit of a steady earner talking to the new staff at Congress. Then the Parks and Wildlife people started using me occasionally as a guide out at the Telegraph Station. On top of this there were still people who needed a hand with some stockwork, or this and that out at the stations. So we had as much money as we really needed. Life was pretty sweet in lots of ways.

Grandparents

The kids were all growing up into teenagers, workers and parents in their own right. You spend so much time and energy being a parent. It becomes what you are, part of your identity. You are exhausted and feel underappreciated a lot of the time. Especially when they get bigger. Your kids don't remember the sacrifices. They don't want to know about when you got out of bed to hold them when they were upset as babies. All the treats you bought them or pets you looked after, games you played and things you did. The years and years of getting up tired and going to work so that they had food hitting the table. They are not interested in all the worries you had being there for them. They still think you should be there to help out in a crisis, but they don't really want to know how much hard work it was being their parents. That is the way of the world.

It was the same for me and Nita. The kids got older often without us particularly noticing. People started saying "You must be Lynette's father" or something like that. You had a new identity as an older person. The kids were able to become pretty independent and leave us before we really were ready. Not much we said mattered that much. Kids get smart earlier and earlier these days. But we loved them and they always came back. They were good to their mother, respectful enough of me. Then all of a sudden we were grandparents. Being a grandfather was okay. You did get to give the babies back eventually. And I got a chance to work alongside and do a few things with my grown-up kids.

Lynette had left school, formed a long-term relationship with a nice bloke and had a couple of kids by the mid-seventies. They had survived Cyclone Tracy in Christmas 1974. After that her partner, Brian Willis, got himself accepted into a Melbourne university to study law. That was big stuff. A professional man in the family, who would have thought it possible. Then the reality of them heading off, perhaps never to come back the same, hit us all.

Brian was a Kaytetye man from country north of Alice Springs around Barrow Creek. His mother was Ruby Willis who mostly lived in Darwin. When he was a kid, Brian had been put into foster care with a Darwin couple, Bluey Battersby and Betty Fisher. Brian, Lynette and the two kids had come back to Alice after being caught in Cyclone Tracy. It was the Central Australian Aboriginal Legal Aid Service (CAALAS) that got Brian into the course to study law.

Family photo 1988 Back row: Anita, Lynette, Fabian, Melly (holding Neil), Wayne (holding Kyle), Noel. Second row: Larry, Nita, Alec, Laura. Front row: Darren, Alec Junior, Noel Moseley photo courtesy Kruger family

Seeing Lynette and her family jump on the Melbourne plane made both me and Nita a bit sad. Them being in Darwin was different. I knew Darwin and we had family there. We had a few extended family connections to Melbourne, but it seemed like another country. To make it okay we all got busy planning a trip down to see them. It took a fair bit of time to get the money and organise it. But then we flew down during one of the holiday times. It was the first time for me in such a big city. Nita was even more in shock at the size of everything. The holiday was pretty exciting for us all.

One of Brian's teacher/mentors was Gareth Evans, who went on to be the federal Attorney-General, and later the Foreign Minister, in Bob Hawke's government. He took the time to help Brian, Lynette and the kids get settled. They were often visiting Gareth's house. Finally, after three years, the family came back to town. The grandkids had all grown up a lot and started school. They had been back for holidays, but it was great to have them come home for good. Brian started working at CAALAS. We were really proud of him and Lynette for getting through all the study. It was a really big thing.

Brian followed the Kruger family tradition of playing football with the Pioneer Eagles. Alongside him were some of the early CAALAS lawyers, Geoff Eames and Dave Parsons. They were known as the 'legal eagles'. Brian was a lovely fellow and a bit of a football star. They had a house set up and things looked really good for them.

Over the next few years more grandkids came along and Nita would often be looking after them all at our place. Lynette had three children: Fabian, Adrian and Laura. She was also a foster carer with lots of kids staying at her place as well. It was a bit like our old family home in the Gap. Lynette had the full-time care of a young fellow, Noel Moseley. He grew up as one of her kids. After she had settled back into town Lynette went to work at Tangentyere Council with their new Homemakers Service. They would teach the new mothers from the town camps how to survive in town when they were used to living out in remote communities.

Melly, only a couple of years younger than Lynette, had also left school young and started work at IAD. Melly worked in various jobs, making her way up in the Institute for Aboriginal Development offices. She was at different times the driving instructor, bus driver and general administrative person. She ended up taking a lot of the students on excursions. She even went on a trip to New Zealand, helping out with the Arrernte elders that were attending the Three Nations Conference. They had Aboriginal, American Indian and Maori representatives. It was the start of a new political push to get colonised people recognised as victims of colonisation. They started funding international indigenous meetings looking at everyone's shared history of oppression.

Melly still played hockey after finishing school. She continued to star and played on until the late 1980s. Her and her partner, Ben Bailey, have three children – Neil, Cody and Kiara. She was much more settled than Lynette in some ways. Didn't move around the countryside.

Wayne was a bit more of a wild one. At a young age he had a daughter, Maria. He headed north at one stage, even staying for a while on Melville Island with Denise McLean from Garden Point in the early eighties. When his first son was born, he called him Alec after me. They had four kids. After Alec came Kyle, Kiawani and Cora. They eventually separated with him having custody of the two boys. Kiawani went to live with Lynette. Cora stayed in Darwin with her Mum. His most recent additions are two little girls named Wendelle and Carson.

Larry is, and was, the quiet one in the family. He is pretty handy at most things mechanical. He is a champion welder. He is great at planning out his work and getting things going according to the plan. He would sit down and work out what might make something happen in his head before starting it. Once he had it nutted out he would be able to carry it out perfectly. He likes things to have an elegant solution.

Larry's first job was with the Alice Springs Town Council. He then worked as a stockman for the Central Australian Aboriginal Pastoralists Association (CAAPA) out at Woolla Downs. I had taught all my kids to ride, especially the boys. We would go out to Dick Palmer's place where a few of my horses were. The kids had often helped out over the years when I was doing bits and pieces of work out on one of the stations. Larry's job saw him travelling about as part of a work crew. One week he might be picking up cattle from Yuendumu. The next week he might be working out at Santa Teresa.

Larry formed a relationship with Shelley Williams during the early 1980s. They had one child, Darren, born in 1984, when Larry was twenty.

I remember going out on a few jobs with Larry. One time he was mustering up a mob of cattle out in the Western MacDonnells. I was helping out when this bull charged me. I was on foot and it was bearing down. There was nowhere really to hide. Luckily Larry was in the Toyota at the time and had his gun. I was dodging about with the bull after me. He just managed to shoot it before I got so tired it would have caught up with me. I was very relieved, though we just laughed it off the way you do. Larry was pleased as punch to have saved me. It was a great shot under pressure.

Larry took a construction job in town after a while. He was involved in building the Yeperenye butcher's shop for Dave Murray. A lot of us got a bit of work with Dave. He had set up the abattoir out the back of Amoonguna. Dave was a pretty casual sort of bookkeeper and manager. Everything was written down on the back of an envelope and might or might not go into the proper books later. I worked rounding up and pushing the cattle into the slaughter room. Larry was working the shooting of them with an old bolt-action mercy killer. Noel was working there too at one stage doing the slaughterman work. It was a family operation. Dave used to kill maybe fifty beasts a day.

A lot of the meat went through Dave Murray's Alice Springs Quality Meats in the Eastside shops. It used to be next door to the bike shop. Dave was a good mate. A white fellow originally from Victoria. He had three girls and was a good family man. He had started out working in a butcher's shop and as a slaughterman but he had built himself up to owning his own business. He treated Larry really well. Eventually the abattoir licensing people closed him down. Dave then got a contract for killing old horses for pet food. It was Dave's plan to get the place fixed up,so that he could get his permit for cattle slaughtering back later on. But it didn't happen. Amoonguna went downhill and he couldn't make it work.

Larry went on to work for five or six years with John and Tim Lander. They had a Northern Territory government contract to maintain and repair old stock bores. The Lander muster crew worked from an old converted double-decker bus. They spent a lot of time mustering up, yarding cattle and relocating them between bores to better pastures.

I visited old Limbla outstation down the Hale River a few times when Larry was there. The place had been done up. They had put up a proper house and had lots of smaller rooms for the stockmen to camp in. It was a station on its own by that time. Harry Bloomfield had sold out and bought the old Andato Station further west. Limbla was an Aboriginal-owned station by then and part of CAAPA.

After Limbla, Larry moved back to our camp on the land claim at Harry Creek. He helped build the shed and later the house that us Krugers now have out there.

Polly's first job was at Kentucky Fried Chicken. She was still at school and went on to complete Year 11. She started a traineeship as a secretary with IAD. Then she got a job as a trainee with a new group that was setting up an Aboriginal Cultural Awareness Program. It trained Northern Territory government employees to work better with Aboriginal families. It was a good program and she was working with James Bray and Lynette Duncan.

Polly was a real go-getter and managed to get ahead. After leaving that job she worked as a Tenancy officer with Tangentyere Council. She had to go around and get families to say who was living in the houses and get some rent shared. Otherwise it was just the old people paying for everything. The younger people often had no money and just ate up other people's stuff. She got them on social security. It was hard work.

Polly was living with her first partner, Kevin Davis, by this time and they had their first baby, Aaron. A few years after that, her daughter, Jordan, was born. Polly was able to get a bit of work in the Northern Territory public service after the babies grew up. She ended up in a new relationship with Wayne Clarke. More recently she worked at the Office for Aboriginal Development. She was helping link-up interpreter and cultural programs with other Northern Territory government departments. Then she got an important new job with the Department of Employment, Education and Training as the Student Attendance Officer, trying to retain Aboriginal kids in school.

Polly went back to being Anita some of the time. I suspect it worked better for her. Later in life she had her third child, Joshua, with her second partner Wayne Clarke. They're buying their own place in Sadadeen. This is where I'm living at the moment. Much of this book has been written out on their back verandah.

Our younger child, Noel, left school early and hung around the Gap Youth Centre. The Centre, with help from Graham Ross and Peter Lorraine (Catweazle), Amy Swan and Eva Harvey would take the kids out hunting on weekends on Yambah Station. The station owner, John Gorey, gave the Youth Centre some Welsh mountain ponies to break in and teach the kids how to ride. And a horse breaker by the name of Des Kirk taught some of the older lads how to break horses in. I was out there a few times myself helping out. I was always interested in how different horsemen worked. I was a bit old by this stage to jump on a horse myself.

This is where Noel first learned how to ride. From there he completed a six-week course with Bill Meacham, learning livestock and station skills on Mt Ebenezer Station, owned by the Kunoths. It wasn't that much different from what I had done with IAD years before. But they had shortened the course.

Then about a year later Noel got a job with the Kunoths mustering cattle and trucking them to Kenmore Park Station for agistment. Mt Ebenezer was suffering from drought at the time. Sometimes he would travel to their other station, Lamboo, in Western Australia where Ted and his wife, Val Kunoth, were managers. When he had finished with the Kunoths, Noel worked with Bill Meacham, this time teaching the station skills course on various Aboriginal communities. Noel completed an Adult Education qualification so that he could teach.

Noel even worked for Ian Conway on Kings Creek Station where they had the contract for catching wild camels. It was a good experience for him, learning to ride a camel. One year he rode in the Camel Cup.

Noel left the camels to do some casual work with my other son, Larry, when he was working for Dave Murray, the manager of the small abattoir and butcher shop for CAAPA. They would go out to the communities to pick up cattle and bring them back for slaughter.

After that Noel worked at Tangentyere for a while, doing catering. Then he got a job at the mines working in the mill, processing gold.

All this time Noel had a long-term relationship with Jennifer Swan. Jennifer is Monty and Amy Swan's youngest daughter – a very lovely girl. Then on 12 October 1993 their first child Leela was born. On 3 June 1995, their second child Noel was born.

When Leela was born, Noel was working for the Cavanaghs at Ambalindum Station with his friends Eddie May, Ian Woods and Roger Harvey. He decided to come to town and worked for IAD as a Lecturer in Adult Education in Community Development and Leadership. His cousin, Debra Maidment, was the Coordinator for the course.

Then tragically his wife Jennifer died. It was a terrible shock because she was still young and a beautiful mother to her children. Noel left work to look after the kids fulltime.

Noel has also met his older son Patrick Perkins that he found out about not that long ago. He was from an earlier relationship. Patrick now calls around and we have all got to know him. He is becoming part of the family.

Celebrations

As our kids grew up, birthdays became big events. When Polly had her twenty-first birthday in 1989 it was held at the Old Buffaloes Club Hall on Gap Road. It was the first big family event to be held outside of our family houses. Polly's night was a gathering of the old Gap Cottage families. Earlier events had tended to be a lot quieter. For example, when Melly turned twenty-one a surprise party was organised by her aunty, Eva Kopp. This was ten years before, in 1979. Eva had her own place by this time, bought after Nugget died. So we all hid ourselves at 31 Nicker Crescent and waited for Melly to arrive. She took a bit of persuading but eventually turned up, having been told her aunt needed to see her. Eva was like a second mother to those kids so Melly had to come. Then we all came out. She was so shocked and happy. It was a lovely night and a great thing for Melly.

That night at Eva's place we had George Kruger Junior down from Katherine as the guitar man. He was a great fan of country music. It was Charlie Pride songs like *Me and Bobby McGee* and all the old favourites that got a hearing. Eva's oldest boy, Peter, was assisting. Georgie even played and sang the old Darwin Buffs football song for me. I loved those family parties. No one got too out of hand and everyone had a great night of it.

But ten years later and parties had become a much more public event. Polly had decided to have everyone there and we hired the Old Buffs Hall. The invitations went out. It was a dress-up occasion, me with a suit and tie for once, Nita and the girls with their hair done up and flash new dresses on. There were perhaps fifty or more people, and a record player. Mostly it was still family and friends, but lots of outsiders too. We made a real night of it. It was funny being the old ones there and the first to leave. All the young ones wanted to get down to serious partying without us. Just like we had at the Cloncurry claypan dances. I got a taste of how the old people had felt.

Noel's twenty-first was at the Harry Creek block. Like always it was Christmas and my birthday too. Sixty-six and a pensioner by this time. Not that it was slowing me down much. I had put up our big shed by then, and there was always stuff to do.

Everybody was there and it was the first party out at Harry's. It was like the old Gap Cottage home parties with heaps more grog and ganja. Plus we didn't have to worry about the police or even Welfare shutting the place down like at the Gap. We had organised a bus service with Lynette and others driving people from town and back again. There was a lot of singing and dancing that night. All in good fun and no real fights. It was like some of those good nights on the rum at the old Junction Hotel.

There were a few funny incidents. One bloke, I think it was Bunker Campbell, who was determined to get a lift into town, decided to sleep on top of one of the cars. But he was so out of it that he passed out. Early the next day when he woke up he found himself lying on top of one of our old wrecks, sitting on blocks. At one stage some of the old ladies got real scared. The kids had told them that they had seen a Kaditja man. They were back in the bus and into town in a flash. The party rolled on. If there were any Kaditja men out there, they were probably just enjoying seeing a bit of music and dance happening again on their country.

The dam

Like most parts of the inland, Alice Springs can get some big storms and even floods. In 1988 there was a reasonable-sized flood that saw parts of town get a fair bit of rain damage as water flowed out of the usually dry riverbed and into the shopping centre. In a couple of days the water receded and after a bit of a clean-up, life went on as usual. But the damage bill was huge. It seemed to have been a surprise that low-lying areas of town flooded, and that it wasn't such a great idea to be putting shops and houses in swamp areas. If you did build there, you should have some plans about what you might do if it rained and the river came up.

Anyway, the Northern Territory government decided to look at ways of stopping flooding in Alice Springs. Some of their engineers came up with an idea that if you built a big dam back before town, the water could be collected there instead of rushing through the streets and businesses. They decided Junction Waterhole on Bond Springs Station, with its natural canyon, was the best spot. They also decided that it would be good to set the place up as a water recreation centre. So they wanted the dam to have a fair bit of water in it all the time. This would allow people to go boating, skiing, swimming and even fishing all year round.

But there were a few problems. One was that filling the dam with water seemed to defeat the purpose of having a dam when the floods came. Some were concerned that dams can burst, and that Alice would really be washed away if they didn't get the dam wall strong enough. But the main objection was that they wanted to flood an area with a lot of Aboriginal sacred sites, particularly a women's dreaming site. This was a big problem for the Aboriginal custodians involved.

What with being traditional owners of the area, the Palmer family was heavily involved in this dispute. The CLP used the issue to say Aboriginal people were selfishly ruining it for the rest of the community. It became a real election winner for them. The Aboriginal organisations rallied together to protest against the plans. Environmental groups came onside, saying the proposed dam was unnecessary. What was needed was to increase the flow capacity of the river through town, by dredging it of the sand build up caused by introduced grasses.

They also pointed out that there were three rivers that carried water through town. Damming the Todd upstream wasn't going to affect the water that flowed through from the Charles River or along Chinamen's Creek. The cost of weed reduction and dredging the river was small change compared to the dam option. It was also pointed out that a dam loses a lot of water in evaporation. Town water would have to be used to top up the dam if it was to be a recreational lake. They also suggested that the government stop giving approval to buildings in known flood areas, and that a levee bank or a river wall could be built instead.

Next to bashing the black organisations, the CLP liked most having a go at greenies. So instead of working something out, the CLP opted to go ahead with the dam. The CLP had a lot of members that liked recreational fishing. They liked big monumental projects. To a lot of people it sounded great. The fact that blacks and greenies opposed the plan wasn't going to make these people think again. The CLP were not going to lose any votes. They organised a contractor and sent out bulldozers to start ripping into the countryside. As far as the CLP were concerned, negotiations had stopped. They just went ahead even though some of their own engineers were starting to have doubts.

An Aboriginal women's camp was set up at the site to disrupt the work going ahead. They led appeals to the Commonwealth government to step in. Meanwhile, the CLP had some meetings with other Aboriginal family groups not directly involved in the dispute. Offers to settle long-running land claims around the town were made. They even said they would build houses and services on the new blocks. It split the local Aboriginal community. Some people, who had been waiting a long time for their land, signed up for the deal.

In the end, the Commonwealth Minister for Aboriginal Affairs, Robert Tickner, stepped in. The Commonwealth Aboriginal Heritage legislation was used to block building the dam for twenty years. Amazingly it was a political triumph for the CLP. They didn't have to find the money for the dam. They had the Labor government in Canberra to blame. And it reinforced the idea that Aboriginal organisations had too much power to block things that were good for the rest of the community. They won easily at the next election on the dam issue.

The effect on a lot of Aboriginal people of seeing other families sell them out was hard felt. It became easier for the CLP to recruit some Aboriginal families to their side. The fight spilled into the Aboriginal organisational politics. A shared common purpose across the Central Australian Aboriginal organisations was not recovered for a decade or more.

Nita's illness and death

Nita was heavily involved in the campaign to stop the dam, but she was struggling with her health. She had diabetes. This proved harder to control as she got older. They blame a lot of things for diabetes. Some say it is the white flour, black tea and sugar diet everyone had as kids. Some say it is the childhood infections, scabies and bad housing that the Aboriginal community had. Others say it is genetic, or that it happens because people eat too much junk food, don't drink enough water and don't exercise. I always thought the bad water out at Harry Creek was part of the problem. Nobody seems to be able to say for sure.

Nita's sister, Eva, had similar problems with diabetes. She also had heart trouble. It required an operation in Adelaide. It was successful, but complications set in and she died a month later. It was a shocking time for her kids and for all of us. She had been such a big person in our lives. Then Nita got unwell and ended up going on to kidney treatment.

It became harder for Nita to come out to the Harry Creek block, so we moved back to town. She lost weight and was tired. Then she suddenly died. It seemed she had nothing much left. It was a big funeral and, like for Eva, another gathering of the clan. So much sadness for us all.

I hadn't really prepared myself. I had always thought that Nita would outlive me. That was what happened to all the blokes. Now I was alone, trying to keep it together for the kids. Feeling guilty about all the bad things I had done over the years. I felt guilty especially about the chemical and petrol drums I had collected and used for water out at Harry's. Nita had always thought the water was bad there, but I had pushed ahead anyway. It took a long time to come to terms with being on my own so much. I went into panics a lot, looking around for her. You never really get over a death. You just get better at getting up and keeping going. That is what I had always done. Shut down on hard emotions and kept walking. It helped me get through the funeral and everything else. Thankfully I had the kids there, lots of things to keep me busy and a lot of anger just under the surface. Otherwise it would have taken a long time to just get out of bed again.

A broken dream

Life moved on, as it always does. The Loves Creek land claim came up. I was spoiling for a fight. It was one of the more humiliating things that ever happened to me, getting involved in that claim. I had been back and forth out there to the old station over the years. In the sixties, I had walked the whole country as part of my mining dreams that had come to nothing. My kids had worked out there in the eighties and nineties. People knew my story, so I was invited to come along when the land claim was going ahead.

It was after the Harry Creek claim had been settled. There were groups still upset at what had happened out there. Land rights had distorted some of the easygoing friendships across family groups, as people jostled to tell their stories and position themselves to get more recognition and payouts than perhaps they were entitled to. Anyway, I was not really expecting much. I knew that the legislation had made it difficult for people like me, adopted and initiated into different tribes. It wasn't our fault but we were left out of a lot of things because of being taken away. But another part of me thought I should be looked after.

The Central Land Council was running the show. There were the anthropologists, Jenny Green and a fellow called John Hercott. There were the usual crowd of lawyers. There were meetings held and evidence gathered. I was left out of a lot of the early meetings, but talked to the anthropologists and went out to one of the big meetings held at Loves Creek itself.

The story for the families that I had known had become difficult during the war. Most of them had been taken out to the Arltunga Mission. From there they had drifted into the town camp of Middle Park and ended up at

Santa Teresa when it started up in 1953. Afterwards some had come back into town. I had kept up with a lot of them, particularly those that spent any time in town. The ones that stayed at Santa Teresa I had caught up with on our trips out there. But lots of people I hardly knew. I was an older bloke to a lot of them. I knew their parents, grandparents, and even great-grandparents more than I knew the younger ones. Everyone had married across language and tribal groups.

People in the claim included members of the Wallace, Doolan and Bloomfield families. Agnes Abbott, Baden's daughter, was an important player. I spent a bit of time sitting down with Agnes. It was at this time that she spoke of including me as someone who would look after the place. But it is hard for people to speak up for me. Agnes's statement was lost. Other claimants were greedy and dropped me out. They were supported in doing this by the CLC.

I was hoping that I could build a place out near Atnarpa, with Larry and his son. It would give me continuity with the area, even more than at Harry Creek. I could see how you could run a small shop or business for tourists and prospectors. Protect the sacred sites from neglect and other abuses. We could pass on the stories to the families and even do shows for tourists.

The Loves Creek people were the Alchilpa tribe that moved between Little Wells through Loves Creek and up towards Harry Creek way. Kamara and Parultja country. Peter Ulyerre and his wife, Maggie, were from there, but had no children. It was Peter and Maggie that had looked after me at Atnarpa and took me in for much of the seven years I was there. I grew up and became a man there. I know the dreaming stories, sacred sites and was taught the dances.

No other families were really at Atnarpa. It was the starting-off point for the musters through Loves Creek and Limbla. But not the home base for the Aboriginal families other than Peter and Maggie. Jack Cavanagh grew up at Claraville with John and Alec Cavanagh, but their story belongs out Ambalindum way. His family had been connected to Old Engwardi Fred Cavanagh, who had a caretaker role for the sacred site back from Bitter Springs Gorge. The Laughtons and others have stories connected to White Range and Paddy's Plain near Arltunga. South of Atnarpa has stories connected to the Bloomfields. It was always going to be difficult connecting people up because, even before my time, there had been mining and cattle stations moving the Aboriginal families around since the 1880s.

Some money might be made from a few cattle and mining claims in the area. The yam dreaming and sacred rocks stories around Loves Creek that used to be cared for by Fred Alchilpa, Harry 'Mouth' Arigida and Indera Aripulra may well be lost. New families that perhaps only visited the place as part of being employed out of Arltunga Mission or to work on the Bloomfield stock camps during the war will see another ending of Aboriginal people living there who know the old stories and traditions.

At the meeting it was only the old people that knew me and wanted to do the right thing. There were just not enough of them. Nor did they get to say much. It seemed some deals had been done well before the meeting. I suppose I should have just walked away. But I had my kids to think about and for some reason, it just seemed too sad to listen to a lot of the bullshit that was being told as the right story. Anyway I decided to speak up. It was probably tied up in my shame for neglecting the old people's claims when I didn't come back after the war, as someone who knew the ceremonies and of the spear in the cave drawing me out. I decided to speak up. I saw myself as having a caretaker responsibility. Plus I was feeling shamed and sick of being silenced by all the so-called white experts.

There was a lot of talking. I started correcting what I knew to be wrong in some of the stories they were telling. Some of the young people there didn't like it. They thought I was being a know-all. The old people who could have stood with me were silenced by these younger ones. The young ones even accused me of being an uninitiated man. That really got me going. None of the young ones had been through an initiation like mine. None of them had walked the country or knew any of the old stories very much. They couldn't sing the songs or dance the corroborees. I even offered to show them my initiation scars. I lost it a bit. I said things that I probably shouldn't have. When I think back on it, I was more of a sad and tired old man than I had been letting on.

At the meeting I spoke of the rain stones being given to Strehlow and that this is why the area doesn't get the floods and the good rains of earlier years. I knew of the white powder area, the most sacred of places where the old men gathered dust to confound their enemies. They used to chuck it into the air to blind invaders. But it was a different time. I had no white powder any more to baffle my own enemies. Just words.

The meeting was all over for me then. I took a few people out to the cave. I had told that story. The spear was still there. I sang some of the songs and even danced again for my country. But it was too late for all of us. The claim went through without me. Some people got what they wanted. I was entirely left out. No dreams left for me and my kids of having a house out there looking after the country. Some people, like Norman Wiltshire and others, came and apologised to me later. That helped heal me a bit. But they couldn't stand up for me at the meeting.

Today there are some new houses built out on Loves Creek, at Atnarpa and Limbla and around the place. But there is nobody living there. Like Harry Creek, it is hard for families without schools, shops and work. Henry Bloomfield was in charge of Atnarpa. He gets out there from time to time. But the generator for his rebuilt house has gone and the whole place has become rundown. The cattle are left pretty much to their own devices.

There are still some beautiful horses running free. From time to time, someone might muster them up a bit. A cow might get killed and the meat taken back to town. The place gets mustered properly every so often and the cattle sold. But there is no one singing the songs or owning the place. Like across many other parts of Aboriginal Australia, the intense caretaking done by the old people in my youth is perhaps entirely gone. Now it is just a part of Aboriginal history. It dies with us old ones.

More disappointments

I had been back to Katherine a few times since leaving in the 1970s. With the discovery of uranium at Coronation Hill the place had become a political hot potato. Mining companies lined up to win the contract to open up the site and make lots of money. The Aboriginal groups in Katherine had to make decisions about whether to mine on a sacred site, and what to do with the royalty payments if mining did go ahead.

Environmental and anti-nuclear organisations threw their weight behind a boycott of the site. Protesters turned up prepared to lie in front of trucks and bulldozers. The CLP started its usual ranting about Aboriginal people stopping progress in the Territory. The mining industry was happy to contribute money to the CLP and also run a big pro-mining advertising campaign. It was a very busy time for the local Aboriginal leadership.

The Jawoyn Association was formed to manage the tensions. The Jawoyn people are the traditional language and tribal group for the Katherine area. As well as worrying about mining, they had ownership of the Katherine

Gorge tourism developments and other tourist plans in Kakadu. There was a lot of pressure. Membership of the association was a big issue. Coronation Hill, for example, was perhaps beyond the old Jawoyn tribal boundaries. But lots of people from further north towards Pine Creek had lived in Katherine for a long time, generations even. Were they to be given membership? There were big decisions to be made about who could join.

Jack Ah Kit was the man in the hot seat for a lot of the time. My grand-niece, Lisa Mumbin, one of my sister Bobby's grandkids, was also heavily involved. I was travelling a bit as part of talking up compensation for institutionalised kids. So I got to Katherine every now and then. I joined up with some of the local Krugers to press our claims to be in the Jawoyn Association.

This too ended up as an exercise in frustration. Not many had their own family stories sorted out. Institutions, government policy and moving around for work to survive, meant that people were often a long way from ancient homes. People had lost whatever might have been their original language and had married across different groups. Aboriginal people who had been born and lived all their lives in or around Katherine were expecting to be automatically included. But it wasn't always like that. You had to prove Jawoyn descent. The way records had been kept, proving anything was never going to be easy.

It was during the Jawoyn process that we established that my mother Polly was a Mudburra woman. Even with being in Katherine since the early years of the century, having had kids in Katherine and dying there, wasn't going to be enough for her descendents. Even her having married Lightning, a traditional Jawoyn elder, after my father died, didn't help. Bobby's descendents got in because of the Brumby family heritage. But my side, the Krugers, got told not to bother.

Despite being born almost under the rainbow serpent at Donkey Camp, I was ruled out of contention. Having been sent to Kahlin and the other institutions from three-and-a-half years of age, I had been away too long. Even having been in and out of Katherine since World War II, and having come back to live there in the seventies, I was told that I could even choose to live and die in Katherine, without getting accepted. I was in good company. Nearly all the Krugers were excluded. The Ahmats didn't make it either. Money, greed and power certainly changed the inclusive nature of traditional Aboriginal culture.

These days my family has grown in status within the Jawoyn Association, and I am recognised as a traditional owner by some in the community. The money that originally came from having Jawoyn status has all been handed out. So no one is worried these days that I might take something away from them. In the same way, Mudburra claims were not for me. Mudburra people accept my story and connection through my mother. But it was a long time ago that she lived there, and I was not born there or lived there much. I don't really know their tribal songs, ceremonies and stories. It would be a nice thing to do except I'm old now. It looks like I will not have the comfort of being able to call some bit of land my own. I will have to settle for my kids' claim around Harry Creek. Anyway I want my family around me. My brothers and sisters are all passed on now. My kids and my home are Alice Springs.

Opening Australia's eyes

Two hundred years of colonisation was celebrated by white Australia in 1988. The Prime Minister, Bob Hawke, at the Barunga Sports Festival, promised Aboriginal people a treaty that would recognise them as the First Australians. It would help make up for the abuses of the past. It didn't happen. The lawyers said it was too hard. The next Prime Minister, Paul Keating, even listed a lot of the crimes and acknowledged the racism and theft of land from Aboriginal communities. But it was only words. A treaty still hasn't happened. Poverty, homelessness and hopelessness are still everywhere in Aboriginal communities.

In a tremendous correction of the law, the High Court of Australia ruled in the Mabo case in 1992, that Australia hadn't been terra nullius or empty land when the British arrived in 1788. Aboriginal people had title to their land at the time of colonisation. This title continued unless land usage had changed since. This worked out well for isolated island communities and some Aboriginal groups in inland Australia. It also meant there might be compensation paid to Aboriginal people whose land had been taken away.

I can remember even earlier some black activists going over to England, planting the Aboriginal flag and declaring England to be a colony of the Aboriginal state. These were interesting times. Michael Mansell, an activist from Tasmania, and other national Aboriginal leaders had been agitating for recognition that Aboriginal kids had been taken away from their families by various governments. Michael Mansell started legal action in the World Court charging the Commonwealth government with genocide against Aboriginal people.

In the 1990s, Archie Roach, with his wife, Ruby Hunter, wrote and sang a song called *They Took the Children Away*. It struck a huge chord across Australia. Archie had been taken away and brought up in foster care, so he wrote from the heart. It was difficult for people not to hear the message of Aboriginal mothers left crying as police and governments took kids away from them and put them into institutions. Children's fathers having to be held back as the police and welfare moved in. We became good friends and he often calls in to catch up when he is in town.

Alec and Archie photo courtesy Kruger family

Another song by a local Aboriginal man, Bobby Randall, called *Brown Skin Baby* also got attention. Australians learnt that it wasn't just a few kids involved. It had been government policy for hundreds of years that had seen Aboriginal children taken away from their families. It continued until quite recently. Still today too many Aboriginal kids are in foster care and juvenile centres.

This was the backdrop to getting something happening for us survivors of the institutions. I was a part of a group locally that was looking at legal action for being taken away from our parents. I had been in Katherine when they started talking about it there. The Katherine Regional Aboriginal Legal Aid Service (KRALAS) and a lawyer called David Dalrymple did a lot of the work at the beginning to get a case going. From there Darwin and Alice Springs got involved. The Northern Australia Aboriginal Legal Aid Service (NAALAS) started documenting people's stories.

Later there were lawyers from Melbourne that came to talk to a few of us in Central Australia. They talked of possible compensation for being locked up, and for not being paid wages. Then an Aboriginal project officer, Jacqui Katona, was appointed in Darwin through NAALAS. This must have been in the mid-1990s.

The Stolen Generations

In 1994, a service to help taken-away children get in contact with their families and community, Link-up, and members of the Arrernte Council, organised for people who had been at the Bungalow to come together for a weekend. Herbie Laughton, Kevin Buzzacott, Charlie Perkins and others were involved. Funding was found to bring many of the old Bungalow kids back from interstate. The event happened over a weekend in September. There were songs, ceremonies and a good time. There were speeches but mostly it was more a social event. It was to be the first of many such gatherings.

Herbie Laughton sang his song *I Remember the Old Mission so Clearly*. This brought tears to a lot of old eyes. There were people there who hadn't seen each other, or been back to Central Australia, for a long, long time. People got to talk of what had happened and got some recognition from the town about the black history of the place. It was a very healing couple of days with lots of plans coming out of it.

The Telegraph Station didn't look anything like in the old days of the Bungalow. The dormitories and sheds were long gone. The place had lawns and gardens where there had been dustbowls. Even the old waterhole that had been the reason for setting the place up at that particular spot, and where we had spent so much time in summer as kids, swimming and playing, was sanded up and without much water. But the weekend was a great 'coming home' gathering. The Bungalow might be a different place, but it was still a chance for people to get together, tell and listen to the old stories. For some of our kids and grandkids it was the first time they knew what had happened to us, and the first time they met people who knew us from those days. There was a lot of crying.

From this event the Central Australian Stolen Generations group gathered momentum. It was never an easy job keeping the group together. Even if you just counted the people living in town, everyone had a different story and a need for it to be acknowledged within the group. And some people's stories overlapped but were very different. People can be very touchy and can get upset easily. The Bungalows stretched over a lot of different places and times. You had the Town Bungalow, the Jay Creek Bungalow, the Telegraph Station Bungalow before the war and the Telegraph Station Bungalow after the war. It can be quite a contest sometimes as to who had the worst time of it, who should get the most acknowledgement and who should make the decisions.

But despite the challenges the group keeps going. After the Bungalow weekend there was a national stolen generations conference in Darwin. I was one of the people who travelled up for what was called the Long Way Home Conference in October 1994.

There were really two meetings. The first was a workshop held in late September 1994 at the St Mary's Football Club where Ross Howie from KRALAS outlined the legal issues and the possibilities for action for people taken away from their family.

After a lot of discussion we went on to the big conference determined to start something happening. It made the Long Way Home Conference a really influential event. The newspapers were there and people got a voice in the national media.

I was there with my sister, Gladys, and her friends, and was able to get much more involved in the discussions. We had a common purpose. The conference decided to go ahead with legal challenges as soon as possible. We also pushed the Federal government to hold an inquiry into Aboriginal kids being taken away. Words like 'genocide' were spoken loudly. A challenge through the United Nations was talked up. For people like me, used to being told to shut up, it was a real thrill to be at the centre of a national debate. You got a real sense that big things could happen for us.

So many people sharing the pain of having been taken away was a powerful healing moment. Like in Alice Springs, many had not been back home before. Many spoke of a deep sense of personal rejection by the Aboriginal organisations and community, because of land claims problems. It was good for me and others to speak up about our anger at being humiliated by our own mob. These things needed to be said. We made some big statements and got a lot of press. I got to see my photo in the newspaper and to see all of us on television. It was a big step forward.

The conference decided to put me forward as one of the test cases to be run. I was tickled pink - imagine being taken that seriously. The aim was to get recognition of our history, and our pain. Also, compensation was to be sought from government agencies and possibly missionary groups. I was hoping I might get some money as well as the glory. But wiser heads said I might have to wait a long while.

We also wanted changes to our land rights' status, to get us acknowledged. It was a big thing. If it had happened I would have loved to have gone back to those CLC lawyers in Alice Springs and made them apologise. Maybe I will get a bit of revenge yet.

Moving on

The Commonwealth government agreed to our demand for a Royal Commission into kids being taken away. Justice Ronald Wilson was given the job of heading it up. He had been a High Court judge so we knew we had got somewhere.

Justice Wilson held hearings around Australia to capture as many stories as he could. Mine was told at sessions held in Alice Springs. After more than two years the Commission's findings were published and became known as the *Bringing them home* Report. It was released in 1997 and caused an explosion of emotion. Our personal stories were read out in Parliament and people cried. For the first time there was a push to acknowledge and make amends for some of the terrible things that had been done to us. The Report recommended an apology and compensation.

Unfortunately for all of us, there was a change of federal government in 1996 with the Coalition parties under John Howard coming to power. John Howard was already trying to water down native title. He wasn't interested in reconciliation with taken-away Aboriginal people. A few steps were taken to provide counselling and support services, but John Howard was never going to apologise or pay compensation. We were left in limbo. But we still had the court cases to go through.

The claimants before the High Court in 1997 were me, Hilda Muir, Connie Cole, Peter Hansen, Kim Hilm and Rosie McClary. The court case became known as *Kruger & Ors v The Commonwealth of Australia*. For me it was an enormous recognition of my life story. A second test case involved George Bray, Marjorie Foster and Zita Wallace (*Bray & Ors v The Commonwealth of Australia*).

I got a lot of photo opportunities from being the face of a test case. I needed it. There was so much of me that was still sad about Loves Creek, Nita's death and just the whole retelling of old stories. It gave me a lot of things to get busy with. I got used to talking up and having a say. But the whole thing was not very exciting. We never really got our day in court. The lawyers fought it out on technicalities. The researchers chased through dusty old files. We were mostly just there to look suitably sad and dejected. I got good at that. Sometimes I felt like the old tjilpi standing on one leg, holding a spear for the tourists to photograph.

In the end the High Court rejected our cases. I couldn't follow why exactly. There were issues about consent. Then they declined to find that the government had intended us harm. As to whether we were neglected, they seemed to say we were treated badly, but not badly enough to allow our claim. The lawyers talked about going to the International Court of Justice. But in the end not much happened. The years went by. The lawyers tested a few new angles but couldn't find a way through. They occasionally say that they will start some new test case. We get excited for a week or so but it never amounts to anything.

The test case didn't make a huge difference for me in Alice Springs. People didn't notice much or care. The family did when they could follow what was happening. But the town as a whole is much more interested in football than politics. I would have been better recognised if I had been in front of the local magistrates than having made it to the High Court. I might have had more of a sense of being heard down at the local court too. Such is life. I have put aside my plans of setting myself up on some huge compensation payout. They didn't even manage to get my wages paid from working out at Loves Creek.

On the plus side I got to see a lot of Australia. I went to Canberra and met some important people. A lot of young students made a fuss of me. I liked that. They thought I was cute. There were lots of nice meals and meetings with people who wouldn't have even noticed me thirty years before. I got to play a bit of politics. There were lots of healing rituals, festivals and events. It was like being a movie star. We even had the cameras waiting for us at the end of the court case. I think they wanted a few tears or defiant gestures. We were all a bit old for that. It's a funny world.

The one big plus was our very own funding for a Stolen Generations Association in Alice Springs. It became a bit of a meeting place. We had regular get-togethers and there were staff to help us with lots of different things. It was great. I was on the management committee. That was the first time I can remember sitting down at the big table where the decisions were being made. A lot of us old blokes enjoyed the attention. There were events organised, people who wanted to meet us, and always a few things to look forward to. Even my kids started to be impressed. The car would roll up to pick me up. I might be off to Canberra, or to talk at a meeting up the track in Tennant Creek, Katherine or Darwin. We had celebrities turning up, and were treated a bit like celebrities ourselves.

High Court claimants. Left to right: Emily Liddle, Daisy Ruddick, Hilda Muir, Herbie Laughton, George Bray and Alec Kruger photo courtesy Kruger family

We didn't manage to get our own counselling service as the *Bringing them home* Report recommended. But we did get special treatment from the counsellors at the Central Australian Aboriginal Congress. I even got the start of this book written through the counsellors.

We helped organise and had our own healing ceremonies. At the big Indigenous Yipirinya Festival held in Alice and televised across Australia, we had a starring role. It really did start to feel like we had come in from the outside to warm ourselves at the fire. People took me seriously. I got invited to schools to do talks. My grandkids got to hear my stories and see them retold in the newspaper.

I'm not sure where the stolen generations movement will finish up. I'm getting to be a tired old man. I had a big eightieth-birthday party at the Pioneers Football Club just before Christmas 2004. It was the biggest party ever held in my honour, the first and perhaps the last until my book comes out. Hopefully this book will do okay. Perhaps I can make a little money to leave to my kids finally, after all the disappointments of not striking it rich before. I still live and hope. Money doesn't heal much. But when you have always been poor, it seems an okay place to start things from.

I probably won't need money or the support of the movement for much longer. But for the younger ones still caught up in sorting out the chaos of being taken away from family and not knowing who they are, the support of the association and of friends and loved ones will continue to make a big difference.

There is still a long way to go for justice, recognition and social equality for Aboriginal people in our own country. Hopefully my story will help with getting things talked up. I would like to sit back now and watch what unfolds. It has been a long, long way home for me.

Family History

Franz F Kruger
d 1931

Margaret Pearce
b 21 January 1861
d 1934

Franz 'Frank' Kruger
b 1880 Mt Eba Station, lived in Katherine
d 2 April 1938 Darwin

Prior relationships

Polly Yrambul Nungarai
b 1895 Mudburra from Wave Hill
d 17 May 1950 Katherine
married 'Lightning'
after Frank's death in 1938

George Kruger
b circa 1903 Renner Springs
d 6 August 1987
married Lily Carter born near Booraloola

Alice Kruger
b circa 1910 Elsie Station
married Rupert Mills, later
George Cummings

Leslie Kruger
drowned as a teenager at Knott's Crossing,

John Kruger
drowned as a teenager at Knott's Crossing

Gladys Kruger
b 1 August 1921 lived in Darwin
married Johnny Ahmat

Alec 'Bumbolili' Kruger
b 25 December 1924 Donkey Camp,
Katherine
married Nita Palmer 10 October 1955

Daisy Hull

Edna Perkins

Jimmy Gibbs
owner of St Vidgeon Station from 1918

Nellie
Mara tribe

A Mudburra tribal man
from around Willeroo, Pidgeon Hole /
Wave Hill area
married Polly Yrambul Nungarai

Ada Gibbs
b circa 1910 lived in Darwin
married William 'Putt' Ahmat

Jack Gibbs
b 1918 St Vidgeon
married Melba Palmer, then Nancy

Bobby Nungala
b circa 1915 lived in Katherine
married Dick Brumby

Dick Palmer
d 20 July 1979

Mary Palmer

Nita Maureen Palmer
b 16 February 1937 Bond Springs Station
d 15 November 1994
tenth child of thirteen: Ben, Tilly, Howard,
Anne, Henry, Melba, Rupert, Victor, Eva,
Nita, Fitz Xavier, Barbara and Marie
married Alec Kruger 10 October 1955

336

Marilyn Stuart
b 1950s

Patrick Perkins
b 1950s

Lynette Willis
b 11 January 1956

Brian Willis

Fabian
b 20 February 1973

Adrian
b 9 July 1974

Laura
b 27 June 1979

Troy Bettles

Isaiah
b 13 January 1999

Shania
b 26 January 2001

Ezekiel
b 27 August 2004

Noel Moseley
b 23 June 1983 (foster child)

Tiarna
b 1 September 2002

Simone Hayden

Vanessa 'Melly' Anne Kruger
b 9 February 1958

Ben Bailey

Neil
b 20 June 1988

Cody
b 24 March 1991

Kiara
b 22 May 1992

remaining children continued overleaf

337

Family History

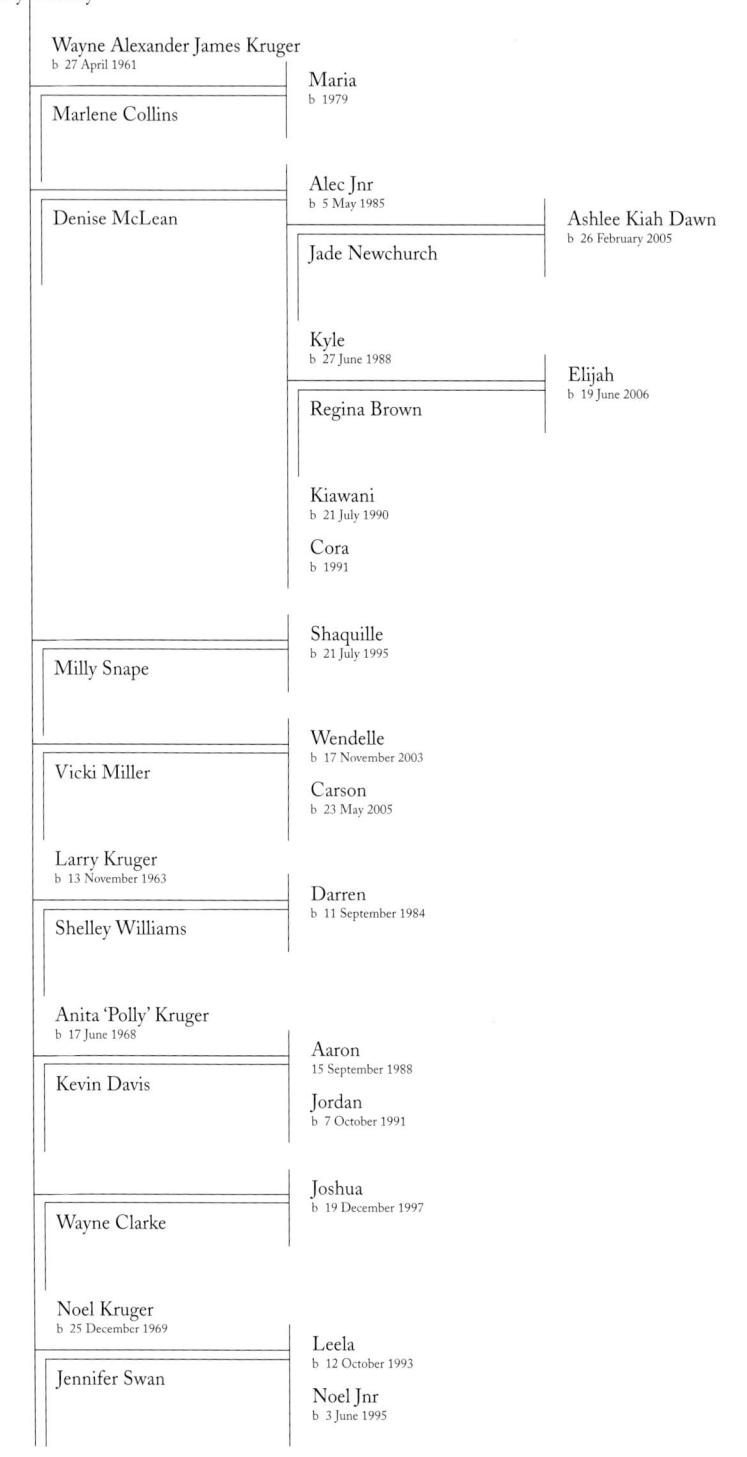

- **Wayne Alexander James Kruger**
  b 27 April 1961
  - Marlene Collins
    - Maria
      b 1979
  - Denise McLean
    - Alec Jnr
      b 5 May 1985
      - Ashlee Kiah Dawn
        b 26 February 2005
    - Jade Newchurch
    - Kyle
      b 27 June 1988
      - Elijah
        b 19 June 2006
    - Regina Brown
    - Kiawani
      b 21 July 1990
    - Cora
      b 1991
  - Milly Snape
    - Shaquille
      b 21 July 1995
  - Vicki Miller
    - Wendelle
      b 17 November 2003
    - Carson
      b 23 May 2005

- **Larry Kruger**
  b 13 November 1963
  - Shelley Williams
    - Darren
      b 11 September 1984

- **Anita 'Polly' Kruger**
  b 17 June 1968
  - Kevin Davis
    - Aaron
      15 September 1988
    - Jordan
      b 7 October 1991
  - Wayne Clarke
    - Joshua
      b 19 December 1997

- **Noel Kruger**
  b 25 December 1969
  - Jennifer Swan
    - Leela
      b 12 October 1993
    - Noel Jnr
      b 3 June 1995

References

Tony Austin *I Can Picture the Old Home So Clearly: The Commonwealth and 'Half-caste' Youth in the Northern Territory 1911–1939*, Aboriginal Studies Press, Canberra 1993

Max Cartwright *Missions, Aborigines and Welfare Settlement Days in the Northern Territory*, Max Cartwright, Alice Springs 1995

Barbara Cummings *Take This Child… from Kahlin Compound to the Retta Dixon Children's Home*, Aboriginal Studies Press, Canberra 1990

Peter F Donovan *Alice Springs: Its History and the People Who Made It*, Alice Springs Town Council, Alice Springs 1988

Peter F Donovan *At the Other End of Australia: The Commonwealth and the Northern Territory*, University of Queensland Press, St Lucia 1984

Peter F Donovan *A Land Full of Possibilities: A History of South Australia's Northern Territory*, University of Queensland Press, St Lucia 1981

Peter Forrest *Springvale's Stories and the Early Years of Katherine*, Murranji Press, Darwin 1985

Jack Gibbs *Son of Jimmy*, Historical Society of NT, Darwin 1995

Nathalie Gorey *The Alice: A Story of the Town and District of Alice Springs, Northern Territory*, Alice Springs Branch Country Women's Association SA, 1960

Jenny Green, Jo Dutton, Margaret Conway, Petronella Wafer, Lesley Salmon, Teresa Ryder and Rod Moss (time line by Frances Coughlan) *Social History Of The Town Camps of Alice Springs*, Tangentyere Council, Alice Springs 1992

Mrs Aeneas Gunn *We of the Never-Never*, Hutchinson of Australia, Richmond 1908

Xavier Herbert *Capricornia*, Angus & Robertson, Sydney 1972

References

Ernestine Hill *The Territory*, Angus & Robertson, Sydney and London 1951

Human Rights and Equal Opportunity Commission *Bringing Them Home: Report of the National Inquiry into the Separation of Aboriginal and Torres Strait Islander Children from Their Families*, Human Rights and Equal Opportunity Commission, Sydney 1997

Rowena MacDonald, Australian Archives *Between Two Worlds: The Commonwealth Government and the Removal of Aboriginal Children of Part Descent in the Northern Territory*, IAD Press, Alice Springs 1995

Roy McFadyen *At a Cost*, R McFadyen, Golden Beach 2005

Glenville Pike *Frontier Territory: The Colourful History of Northern Australia*, Corey Books, Darwin 1980

Deborah Bird Rose *Hidden Histories: Black Stories from Victoria River Downs, Humbert River and Wave Hill*, Aboriginal Studies Press, Canberra 1991

Tim Rowse *White Flour, White Power: From Rations to Citizenship in Central Australia*, Cambridge University Press, Melbourne 1998

Tim Rowse *A Social History of Alice Springs*, IAD Press, Alice Springs 1990

Wenten Rubuntja with Jenny Green *The Town Grew up Dancing: The Life and Art of Wenten Rubuntja*, IAD Press, Alice Springs 2002

Archival resources and newspapers

Alice Springs Collection of the Alice Springs Library
http://www.alicesprings.nt.gov.au/library/

Births Deaths and Marriages Office, Northern Territory
http://www.bdm.nt.gov.au/

National Archives of Australia
http://www.naa.gov.au/

Northern Standard

Northern Territory Archives Service
http://www.nt.gov.au/dcis/nta/

Northern Territory News

Strehlow Research Centre
http://www.nt.gov.au/nreta/museums/strehlow/index.html